Turkish Region

Turkish Region

State, Market & Social Identities
on the East Black Sea Coast

Ildikó Bellér-Hann
Chris Hann

James Currey
OXFORD

School of American Research Press
SANTA FE

James Currey
73 Botley Road
Oxford OX2 0BS

School of American Research Press
Post Office Box 2188
Santa Fe, New Mexico 87504-2188

British Library Cataloguing in Publication Data
Turkish region : state, market & social identities on the
   East Black Sea coast. - (World anthropology)
   1. Anthropology - Turkey   2. Turkey - Civilization 3. Turkey -
   Social life and customs
      I. Title   II. Bellér-Hann, Ildikó and Hann, Chris
301'.09561
                                       ISBN 0-85255-279-3 (paper)
                                       ISBN 0-85255-274-2 (cloth)

Library of Congress Cataloging-in-Publication Data
Bellér-Hann, Ildikó
   Turkish region: state, market & social identities on the east Black Sea coast / Ildikó
   Bellér-Hann, Chris Hann.
      p.cm. -- (World anthropology series)
   Includes bibliographical references (p.) and index.
      ISBN 0-933452-70-5 -- ISBN 0-933452-71-3 (pbk.)
   1. Black Sea Coast (Turkey)--Economic conditions--20th century. 2. Black Sea Coast
   (Turkey)--Social conditions--20th century. I. Hann, C.M., 1953– II. Title. III. Series.

HC492.B455 2000
956.6'2038--dc21   00-066148

Typeset in 10/11 pt Monotype Photina
by Long House Publishing Services, Cumbria, UK
Printed and bound in Great Britain
by Woolnough, Irthlingborough

Contents

Illustrations

MAPS

PHOTOGRAPHS

Acknowledgements

In carrying out the research on which this book is based we have been grateful for advice and support from many individuals and institutions in Turkey, Britain and elsewhere. We especially wish to thank Ali Ihsan Aksamaz, Neal Ascherson, Anthony Bryer, Ayşe De Barros, Wolfgang Feurstein, the late Fikret Görmen, the late Fahri Kahraman, Gabriele Rasuly Paleczek, Geoffrey Roper, Alihan Telatar, Alexander Toumarkine and Aziz Vanlı. Kitty and Murat Çızakça, George Hewitt, Riva Kastorianu, Michael Meeker, David Shankland and Martin Stokes all provided helpful comments on an earlier draft.

Our work has been much influenced by two giants of British social anthropology. Alas, neither Ernest Gellner nor Paul Stirling is alive to see this publication. Its title is intended to echo Stirling's own *Turkish Village*.

Our greatest debt is to the people of Lazistan, especially many people, including officials, in the counties of Fındıklı and Pazar who welcomed us into their homes. We have taken the precaution of changing personal names and some village names, to protect their privacy.

We are also indebted to the authorities in Ankara for issuing research permits and to many state officials in Rize province for facilitating the main stints of fieldwork in 1982–3 and 1992; we acknowledge a scholarship awarded by the Ministry of Education in 1982–3 and the friendly support of staff at the Ziraat Fakültesi of Ankara University (Tarım Ekonomisi Bölümü – especially Taner Kıral, Hasan Erdem and Erkan Rehber). Corpus Christi College, Cambridge, supported this period of the work by permitting the extension of a Research Fellowship. The main source of financial support has been a series of grants from Britain's Social Science Research Council (currently known as the Economic and Social Research Council, after renaming in the heyday of Margaret Thatcher's control of the British state). We are required to provide details of these grants in all publications. They are as follows:

1982–4 HR 8790/1 Social and Organisational Aspects of New Agricultural Specialisation in Turkey;

1988 R221022 Follow-up Study of HR 8790/1;

1991–3 R23320801 Culture and Economy among the Laz.

Further short fieldtrips were made in 1997 and 1999.

We have benefited greatly from collegial environments in England at the Universities of Cambridge and Kent. The writing up was completed in equally excellent scholarly environments in Germany: at the Wissenschaftskolleg zu

Berlin, and at the Orientwissenschaftliches Zentrum of the Martin Luther University and the Max Planck Institute for Social Anthropology, both new foundations in Halle.

This book is dedicated to our families. In particular, our children have shared most of the research experiences with us. These have included five arduous overland journeys to North Eastern Turkey in a variety of vehicles, none of them fast or comfortable, and living conditions that were sometimes very different from those to which they were accustomed. But like us they keep wanting to go back.

IB-H, CH
Halle

Note on Transcriptions & Rates of Exchange

We have followed modern dictionary spelling for Turkish terms even when local pronunciation deviates from this norm, except where an older form is established in English. In order not to confuse the English reader we have used 's' to indicate plurals: hence *aghas*, instead of *ağalar*, *kaymakams* instead of *kaymakamlar* etc.

Due to high inflation rates we have sometimes given prices in dollars. The rate of exchange was 183 Turkish Lira to the dollar when we arrived in Turkey in Autumn 1982. Seventeen years later it was approaching half a million.

Glossary

açık	open, uncovered	*il*	province
alım yeri	tea collection point	*ilçe*	county
atmaca	falcon/hawk	*imam*	imam, mosque prayer leader
aydın	enlightened, secular	*Imam-hatip*	schools founded during the republic to train Islamic religious personnel
ayıp	shameful, disgraceful		
		imece	mutual aid, cooperation
bağlama	binding		
baklava	sweet pastry	*jandarma*	gendarme, rural police
başlık	bridewealth		
başörtü	headscarf	*kadrolu*	enrolled, on the official payroll
		kapalı	closed, covered
çarşaf	female over-garment (part of full Islamic veiling)	*kaymakam*	county governor (cf. sous-préfet)
		kemençe	small violin with three strings
çay	tea	*kına gecesi*	henna party
cenabet	impure, unclean	*kız kaçırma*	the kidnapping of a girl, elopement
cin	genie, demon, djinn	*komşuluk*	neighbourliness
		kültür	culture
dernek	association	*kuma*	second wife (married without divorcing the first, usually with religious marriage only)
devlet	state		
dua	prayer, blessing		
düğün	wedding		
düğün salonu	municipal wedding hall	*Kurban Bayramı*	the Muslim Festival of Sacrifices
evliya	saint		
		lise	secondary (grammar) school
farz	religious precept, binding duty, obligation	*mahalle*	neighbourhood, village quarter, urban district
gazino	restaurant (with alcohol and music)	*mangalcılık*	humorous banter between the relatives of the bride and the bridegroom at the traditional wedding party
geçimsizlik	incompatibility		
günah	sin		
		meci	mutual aid, cooperation
halk	people	*medeniyet*	civilisation
Halk Eğitim Müdürlüğü	Adult Education Department	*mekruh*	abominable
		memleket	country, (home) region
haram	forbidden by religion, sinful	*Mevlut*	1. the birthday of the Prophet Mohammad 2. poem depicting his birth
hemşeri	fellow countryman, compatriot		
hoca	hodja, teacher		
horon	a circular dance	*mezra*	summer camp or simple building in the high pastures
iftar	the breaking of the fast, meal taken at sunset	*millet*	nation, people (united by a common faith)

müftü	mufti (nowadays the head of Religious Affairs at county level)	*Rus pazarı*	'Russian market'
muhtar	village headman	*salon*	see *düğün salonu*
		sevap	good deed, meritorious deed
namahrem	a relationship with any person of the opposite sex whose kinship does not form an impediment to sexual relations/marriage	*sihir*	magic, sorcery, witchcraft
		sosyete	the local elite
		söz kesme	the conclusion of a marriage agreement
namaz	ritual worship, prayer	*sünnet*	ritual circumcision
namus	honour	*Şeker Bayramı*	celebration marking the end of Ramadan
nikah, imam nikahı	religious wedding ceremony		
		şeref	honour
Nüfus Müdürlüğü	Population Office		
		talak	Islamic divorce
nuska	charm	*tarikat*	religious order, mysticism
		tarikatçı	member of a religious order
oruç tutmak	to fast	*torpil*	'connections'
		tulum	bagpipe
pazar	market		
peri	fairy	*vakıf*	pious foundation
rakı	raki, arrack	*yayla*	summer pasture
rekabet	competition	*yenge*	sister-in-law, aunt
rekat	complete act of worship with the prescribed postures/prostrations	*yöresel*	local
		zekat	alms
Ramazan	Ramadan, the ninth month of the Muslim calendar during which Muslims fast between dawn and sunset	*zina*	adultery

1
Introduction

The unit of study

Since the term *Lazistan* is rarely found on maps and will be unfamiliar to many readers, let us begin by explaining why we have adapted this name for the region which forms the subject of this book. It is emphatically not our purpose to argue for new maps. Let it be clear that this is our term and it is *not* used by the inhabitants of this corner of Turkey themselves, or by other Turkish citizens. They identify territory by naming major cities and provinces, and at a higher level many recognise the east Black Sea (Doğu Karadeniz) regional identity. The region that concerns us falls between these levels and does not correspond to current administrative boundaries. Lazistan is simply a convenient term to fill this gap. Its use is not meant to imply that this name or the coastal territory to which we are applying it have ever been a focus of group identifications.

Lazistan was the name of an Ottoman sub-province (*sancak*) which extended from the eastern boundary of Trabzon (Trebizond), the ancient centre of the Black Sea's Pontic Greek communities, to lands that now lie deep inside the Georgian Republic. When the frontiers of the Ottoman empire were redrawn at the Congress of Berlin (1878), large areas of Lazistan, including the town of Batumi, passed to the Russian Czar. The capital of the new sub-province then created was Rize, previously attached to Trabzon[1] (see Map 1.1). Borders were again redefined after the collapse of these empires and the old name was soon dropped in the new Turkish republic.[2] Historic Lazistan was divided between the new provinces (*vilayet*, later *il*) of Rize and Artvin, units which have survived into the twenty-first century. The state border with Georgia has also remained stable throughout this period. In this book the term Lazistan refers to the entire province of Rize and three adjoining counties (*ilçe*) of Artvin (see Map 1.2). Other parts of Artvin are excluded because the human settlement and natural environments south of the Kaçkar Mountain range have more in common with the rest of Anatolia than with the coastal zone. Lazistan does not have a clear political or geographical boundary in the west. Somewhat arbitrarily, we have

---

[1] Birken 1976: 152.

[2] Toumarkine 1995: 64–5. The designation Lazistan was officially banned in 1926, together with the use of personal names such as Laz Mehmet. According to Toumarkine the name was considered by Kemalists to be an 'unpatriotic' invention of the *ancien régime*. At no point does any effort seem to have been made to draw the political frontier in this region in accordance with linguistic or religious boundaries.

1

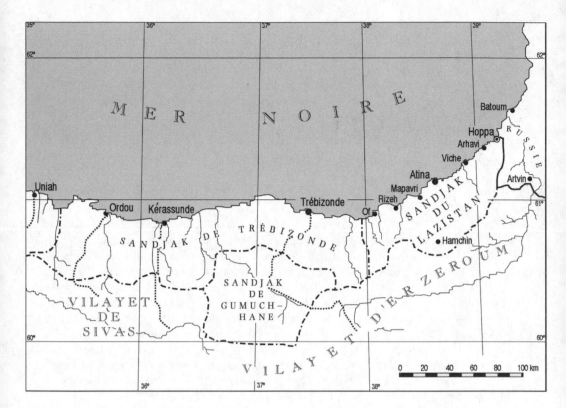

Map 1.1 Late Ottoman Lazistan, 1878–1921.
(From a map of the Vilayet de Trébizonde in Vital Cuinet, *La Turquie d'Asie Géographie administrative, descriptive et raisonnée de chaque province d'Asie Mineure*, t. 1, Paris, E. Leroux, 1890)

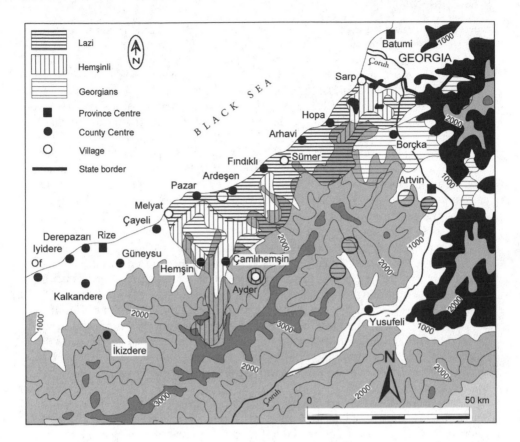

Map 1.2 Contemporary Northeast Turkey: main settlements and minority groups.
(Drawn by Fr Edda Schröter, Department of Geography, Martin Luther University, Halle)

selected the present provincial boundary between Rize and Trabzon for this purpose.[3] Thus defined, Lazistan has a coastline of about one hundred and twenty kilometres between the county of Of and the Georgian border at Sarp. Within this region, as we shall explain below, most of our research has been concentrated in the central counties of Pazar and Fındıklı.

The region can be divided into three geographical zones. First, there is the sea and land immediately adjacent to it, where most of the towns are located. Second, there is an intermediate belt of gardens and woodland, with a dense network of hamlets and villages. Third, there are the pastures (*yaylas*) and snowy peaks of the Kaçkars, where summer camps (*mezras*) are a continuing reminder of patterns of transhumance that in recent decades have lost much of their economic significance. The population is concentrated in the coastal zone and densities are substantially higher in the western counties. Lazistan has approximately 400,000 permanent inhabitants. This figure rises significantly during the summer months when, in addition to many natives who return to their towns and villages to spend their holidays, there is also an influx of temporary labourers lacking roots in the region. The largest city is Rize, which grew from a fishing port with a population below 15,000 in 1945 into a city of 30,000 by 1970, rising to about 75,000 by the end of the century. The urban population is nowadays larger than the rural, which began to decline in absolute terms in the 1970s. The total population peaked in the late 1980s. In the last decade even the urban total has been declining; falling birth rates and out-migration, mainly to Turkey's large western cities, have exceeded the effects of continuing rural–urban migration within the region.[4]

By any standards this is a coastline of great beauty – perhaps less dramatic than the cliffs and emerald harbours further west in the vicinities of Amasra, Sinop or Perşembe, but stunning nonetheless. The differences creep up on you gradually as you move east from Trabzon. After Rize, the Kaçkar foothills come ever closer to the sea. The changes in topography would have been more salient in the era of Ottoman Lazistan, when the principal means of transportation was by sea. In those days more of these hills would have retained their rich natural vegetation, though a mariner's telescope would also have picked out orchards of hazelnuts and fruit trees, and maize plots.[5] The climate here is too damp for the wheat that is staple throughout the rest of Anatolia. High rainfall has also

---

[3] The Ottoman boundary lay further west at Sürmene. Drawing the boundary at Of allows us to exclude from consideration the significant category of Greek-speaking Muslims, very few of whom are found within the boundaries of Rize province.

[4] The 'rate of net migration' for Rize province between 1985 and 1990, the last period for which official national statistics are available, was −9.1 per cent, compared with −5.4 per cent for the Black Sea region as a whole. The total approximation of 400,000 is based on published figures for October 1997, when the figure for Rize province was 325,581 (of whom 172,662 were officially recorded as urban). To this we have added the combined figure of 74,115 (36,032 urban) for Arhavi, Hopa and Borçka counties of Artvin. For more detailed analysis of the Rize patterns see *Cumhuriyetimizin 75 Yılında Rize* 1998.

[5] Bryer (1980 VII: 398) has described post-medieval changes in production and consumption. According to Bryer and Winfield American maize became available to the people of Lazistan in the eighteenth century (1985: 5,n.22). Koeler found that it was the staple in Batumi in 1842 (Ritter 1843: 225–7). Marr in the early twentieth century remarked that locally produced maize provided enough food only for eight months of the year so that additional supplies had to be imported from Russia (1910: 616). See also Bryer and Winfield 1985: 6.

Plate 1.1 Small-scale fishing near Pazar.

Plate 1.2 Hemşinli houses and farm buildings south of Çamlıhemşin.

helped to save this region from the kind of tourist development that has afflicted so much of Turkey's coastline.[6] Apart from a few backpackers who head up into the Kaçkars, there is virtually no western tourism east of Trabzon.[7]

The sea has always been of immense importance to the people of this region. Yet its harbours are for the most part small and unsuited to modern maritime commerce. The best of them was Batumi, lost when the Ottoman empire contracted in 1878. The modern Turkish state has invested heavily in breakwaters and small jetties all along the coast. Hopa, the last town before the border, has acquired deep-water facilities. It serves the transit route across the mountains towards Iran, but the traffic remains light. Small fishing boats still ply from many smaller ports, and a few still follow the traditional long distance routes around the Black Sea. But over-fishing and serious pollution in recent years have decimated the anchovy stocks.[8] Men still fish from small boats in shallow waters close to their villages, but some do so as much for subsistence or recreation purposes as for commerce. The peace of the cormorants that perch on countless crags and rocks is rarely disturbed.

Most rural houses are scattered over the hills and ridges, forming small clusters or hamlets rather than the nucleated villages more common in most of Anatolia. The old *konaks*, the mansions built of stone and timber for the local *aghas*, the effective rulers of their districts in Ottoman times, have mostly disintegrated. The new house types follow the architectural styles and use the same mixture of brick and concrete found in most other parts of the country.[9] There is nothing resembling the traditional high mud walls found elsewhere in Anatolia and in many other parts of the Islamic world. Still conspicuous on the rural landscape are the *serenders*, timber maize stores elevated to afford maximum protection from the damp vegetation. Many families now maintain two homes and use their rural dwelling only during the spring and summer.

The major change in the rural topography in the second half of the twentieth century was the replacement of hazelnut trees and maize gardens by tea bushes. Tea has brought wealth and land prices are among the highest anywhere in the country, though there are few sellers. The population is not just richer but better educated and better nourished than in the past. The high mortality rates have fallen sharply and average family size is closer to European levels than to those found in most other parts of Eastern Anatolia.[10]

---

[6] In most parts of the region average annual rainfall exceeds 2000 mls. Compared to most of Anatolia, summers are significantly cooler and winters are relatively mild, with no more than a few nights of frost in the coastal zone, where any snow melts within a few days. Conditions are more severe even a few miles inland, a factor that has contributed to the large-scale movement of population into the market towns on the coast.

[7] For general descriptions of the terrain see Meeker 1971: 319–20; Feurstein 1983: 6–11; Bryer and Winfield 1985: 1–16; Magnarella 1998: 171–2; *Rize İl Yıllığı* 1973: 7–11. Domestic tourism in Lazistan has increased in recent years but remains small in comparison with other coastal regions, and in comparison with the numbers who return in the summer for family and/or economic reasons.

[8] See Ascherson 1995: 145.

[9] On local settlement structure and architecture see Tandoğan 1977; Feurstein 1983; Karpuz, 1993, 1997.

[10] Statistics for Lazistan as we have defined it are not readily available. Statistics for Rize province, which constitutes some four-fifths of the region, show that in 1990 a total population of just under 348,776 was divided into 64,327 households (average household size: 5.4 persons). At 42 per thousand, infant mortality is well below that of the country as a whole (67) and the Black Sea region (73).

It has become easier than ever before to travel to and within this region. It is possible to finish work in Ankara, or even in Istanbul, on Friday afternoon, and by taking an overnight bus, to spend the weekend in the family home more than a thousand kilometres away. The main road that now runs all along the coast was completed in the 1960s and is currently in the process of being upgraded to a motorway. It has been supplemented by countless minor arteries that have made the great majority of houses accessible to motorised transport. Most people value this improved access to the outside world. We ourselves would hardly have been able to see as much of Lazistan as we did without this road network. But there are still plenty of places where it is possible to see the more traditional routes of communication: steep winding paths between the gardens and hundreds of intricately dug steps. Plank bridges have limited life-spans, as almost every year brings fresh flooding. The streams they cross used to provide the power to grind maize flour, but few mills are still in use. Some of the many stormy rivers can still be crossed by elegant Ottoman stone bridges.

History

Lazistan has a complicated history of human settlement which is almost entirely unknown to present inhabitants and which it is not our purpose to reconstruct.[11] The best-known stories belong to the Greeks, who formed trading communities all around the Black Sea and in some parts, though not in Lazistan itself, settled and farmed well into the interior. In one of their myths Jason travels with the Argonauts to Colchis in search of the Golden Fleece: he would have enjoyed the coastal scenery of Lazistan on the last leg of his outward journey. Colchis may have been the early Georgian polity of Kolkheti. It incorporated the entity known as Lazica, a vassal state of the Romans when they were disputing the Armenian interior with the Parthian Kingdom. The Greeks survived this and many later vicissitudes. Trabzon remained the centre of a vibrant Pontic Greek culture even after the Ottomans, following their seizure of Constantinople, put an end to the Trapezuntine Empire in 1461. The foundation for group distinctiveness in the centuries that followed was not the ethnic group or the nation as we know it today, but the religious community. The Ottoman Sultan ruled over diverse religiously defined communities, within which the Muslim *millet* enjoyed a privileged position. Each *millet* contained a great deal of linguistic and cultural complexity, but this had no significance for the practice of government.[12]

Nineteenth-century travellers to Lazistan remarked upon significant commerce, both long-distance and local.[13] Away from the coast, however, a subsistence

---

[10] (cont.) The total fertility rate of 2.33 for Rize compares with 2.65 for the country and 2.59 for the region. As in the rest of the country, women's life expectancy is significantly higher than that of men.

[11] The best general source is the magnificent tapestry woven by Bryer and Winfield 1985. See also Feurstein 1983.

[12] For the concept of *millet* see Lewis 1961: 329–30; Braude and Lewis 1982.

[13] See Koch 1855: 96. At the bazaar of Batumi Koeler noted 'a poor supply of the usual import articles', including Russian iron, German steel, zinc, English wool, coffee, sugar and pepper, Crimean wool, salt, Turkish manufactured articles, and local agricultural products. Export articles included wood maize, rice, wax, honey, fish. Commerce was largely limited to the winter months, 'because from

economy predominated, based on simple, labour-intensive technology. Many families kept only a few animals, often only a single cow, since pasture land was extremely scarce. Further inland, higher up the slopes of the mountains, people kept more animals and ate a diet rich in red meat and dairy products – at any rate, that is what their descendants typically say. Some coastal folk used to take their animals up to higher pasture grounds in the summer months, where they sometimes came into conflict with the people from interior villages.

People speak of pre-republican times as an era of poverty in this peripheral region. Many men sought work elsewhere: in Ottoman armies, in the cities of the Russian Empire, and in ports such as Istanbul and Izmir, to which they enjoyed relatively easy maritime access. As with later patterns of labour migration, the men who moved in search of work often had to leave their families behind. Much of the farm work was therefore devolved to women. This made the roles and responsibilities of women in Lazistan rather different from those of women elsewhere in Anatolia. This became the foundation for one of the stereotypical features of this region, namely the exceptionally heavy physical burden carried by women; we shall question this stereotype and investigate gender relations more carefully in later chapters. People also recall that many families with only small landholdings were dependent on wealthy *aghas* for the cash and the corn they needed to survive.

The end of the long Ottoman experience of social plurality came, following Mustafa Kemal's defeat of the Greeks, with the massive 'exchange of populations' dictated by the Treaty of Lausanne in 1923. Most remaining Pontics were despatched to an unknown 'homeland', the modern Greek state.[14] For most of the twentieth century, in sharp contrast to the past, movement across the Black Sea and eastwards into the Caucasus was drastically curtailed; instead of plurality, in the Kemalist republic every effort was made to integrate this region into a new and homogenised Turkish nation. Kemal himself later adopted the name Atatürk, 'Father of the Turks'.

Labour migration did not cease but continued in new forms in the republican period. Some men still managed to go to Russia in the 1920s and 1930s, but the poor, hierarchically structured society of Lazistan was transformed above all by the introduction of tea as a cash crop in the years after 1950. This story is outlined in Chapters 2 and 3. The former maize gardens were almost completely replanted with tea bushes. Fruit production largely ceased, and many hazelnut trees were dug up to give way to the more profitable crop. Contemporary visitors to Lazistan need a lot of imagination to conceive of the hillsides as they might have looked before the arrival of the new monoculture. This material transformation is a fundamental element of what we term the experience of modernity in this region.

[13] (cont.) the beginning of June until the end of September not only do merchants and craftsmen depart for home but also the inhabitants of Batumi leave the city for the mountains, on account of the unhealthy climate. Only a few people stay behind, partly to watch the locked houses and partly because they are lured by the great profit to be earned from selling salt to inland settlements. During this time the houses are left in the undisturbed possession of numerous swallows, and millions of mosquitoes float over the swamps...' (in Ritter 1845: 25–6).

[14] On the scale and nature of this exchange see Lewis 1961: 348–9. On the Pontic Greeks see Bryer 1980, Bryer and Winfield 1985; Mackridge 1987. It has been estimated that around 2000 Greeks and Armenians left Rize as a result of the exchanges: see *Rize Il Yıllığı* 1973: 13. Some Greek-speaking Muslims were classified as Turks and on this basis avoided deportation to Greece.

People

Although the Greeks were by no means the only traders to arrive from the Mediterranean, historic Lazistan seems to have been influenced more by small peoples from the Caucasus than by the west.[15] At any rate, Caucasian languages have been spoken in this territory for a good deal longer than Turkish. Lazistan, which had been only loosely integrated into previous imperial systems, was more effectively incorporated into the Ottoman empire in the closing decades of the sixteenth century. Islamisation proceeded rapidly in the same period.[16] Four centuries later Islam has a secure monopoly in the sphere of religion, yet although Turkish has long been dominant, some linguistic diversity has persisted. According to their self-classifications, the contemporary population of Lazistan can be divided into four categories. It must be stressed that this classification has no decisive social significance for local people themselves. Not everyone in the region acknowledges these four categories, and perhaps only a few see them as forming essentially equivalent groups. Nonetheless, if pressed nowadays to declare to which *millet* they belong, most will understand this as a question not about religion, as in Ottoman days, but about some form of secular belonging, nation or 'ethnic group'.[17] They will place themselves in one or more of the following categories.

First, Turks are the defining group of the modern Turkish state and much the largest in contemporary Lazistan as we have defined it. Although Turkish speakers originally entered Anatolia from the east, they spread into this region from the south and west in the period both before and after the demise of the Trapezuntine polity.[18] We should not think primarily in terms of Turkish nomads dramatically displacing earlier inhabitants, though this may have happened in certain places, but rather of long-term processes in the course of which existing populations adopted the characteristics of the new power, notably their religion and their language.

Second, the Lazi (in Turkish Laz) are the people who gave their name to this region in Ottoman times and they constitute the second largest category today.[19] They form the majority within the zone, which extends from the Turkish–Georgian border westwards as far as the village of Melyat, near Pazar (see Map 1.2).[20] Their principal marker of distinctiveness is knowledge of Lazuri, a South

[15] The rocky ruins of a fort off the promontory where we lived in the town of Pazar (old name: Atina) are thought to date back to Genoese traders. Bryer and Winfield note that the historical memory of the Lazi tends to attribute most old ruins and buildings to the Genoese and to Christians generally: 1985: 18; see also 339. Cf. Feurstein 1983: 24.

[16] Bryer 1980 XI: 42. For indigenous accounts of conversion processes among neighbouring groups see Poutouridou 1999.

[17] The adjective *etnik* seems to have entered Turkish during the period of our research, but we rarely heard it in Lazistan. We return to these points at the end of the study.

[18] Bryer argues that the main component of the early Turkic settlers were the Çepni Turkomans: 1966: 192; 1980 XI: 41–2.

[19] In this usage we follow Meeker (1971: 321) who proposes a distinction between the Lazi, speakers of a non-Turkic language, and the wider category of 'Laz' used in a regional sense. On the Lazi see also Marr 1910; Bryer 1966–7; Feurstein 1983, 1992a; Feurstein and Berdsena 1987; Paleczek 1987; Benninghaus 1989a; Vanilişi and Tandilava 1992; Toumarkine 1995; Özgün 1996; Zhordaniya 1996; Aksamaz 1997.

[20] Linguistic evidence indicates that Lazi influence may have extended into more western districts in

Caucasian language related to Mingrelian and, more distantly, to Georgian. It is unrelated to Turkish. Neither this language nor any other basis for Lazi distinctiveness have been recognised by the modern Turkish state.

The third category brings out further complexities. The people who call themselves Hemşinli are found in two separate pockets, sometimes distinguished as the Eastern Hemşinli and the Western Hemşinli. The Hemşinli appear to have been 'attracted to Islam from since the fifteenth century'.[21] They converted to Islam from Christianity 'before it was politic to do so'.[22] They are thought to have lost their language, related to Armenian, at about the same time, though it survives among small numbers of the eastern community. Western Hemşinli do not stress language as the basis of their identity, but are aware of having possessed a different language in the past. Most are reluctant to acknowledge any affinity to Armenians. This persists among them as an uncomfortable private secret. Many see themselves as a kind of Turk – not simply in the sense of being Turkish citizens, which obviously applies to all inhabitants, but in the sense that the Hemşinli are a sort of sub-species of Turk in an ethnic or racial sense.[23]

Fourth, there is a Georgian category in this region, concentrated mostly in Borçka, a county of Artvin province; only small enclaves exist elsewhere. They too are Muslim. In the absence of any state policy to promote cultural differences, knowledge of the Georgian language seems to be weakening among the younger generation.[24] No traces of Georgian Christianity are visible in Lazistan, though some people are aware of the existence of ruined Christian churches in the interior south of the Kaçkars.

In Ottoman Lazistan these four categories of people, together with smaller numbers of Greeks and others, lived alongside and intermingled with each other. The picture was rather less complex than in other parts of the empire, since all had converted to Islam. The significance of these distinctions at the local level is hard to ascertain.[25] For example, it is difficult to know if there might have been circumstances in which Muslim Georgians were more willing to act in solidarity with other Christian speakers of the Georgian language than with speakers of the Turkish language who belonged to their own *millet*. No doubt such alternatives rarely presented themselves in practice. In general it seems that religion was the single most important principle for the regulation of social life. Linguistic and cultural diversity were the characteristic condition of preindustrial empires and the late emergence of the idea of an 'Ottoman citizenry' did little to eradicate these forms of diversity in this region.[26]

[20] (cont.) the past, up to and even beyond Trabzon. See Brendemoen 1990b: 56, 58. Estimates of the current numbers of Lazuri speakers vary. Feurstein (1992a) gives a figure of 250,000, but there are probably not more than 100,000 Lazuri speakers within the region itself. The diaspora in Istanbul and elsewhere is large, but the number of speakers is probably smaller than the number in the homeland.

[21] Bryer 1980 XI: 42.

[22] Bryer and Winfield 1985: 337.

[23] 'Race' is here an imperfect translation of the Turkish *soy*. For more on the Hemşinli see Benninghaus 1989b, Bryer and Winfield 1985: 336–7; Magnarella 1998: 183–92.

[24] For discussion of assimilation processes in a Georgian community in western Anatolia see Magnarella 1979.

[25] On the basis of surviving consular documents and other sources Meeker (1996: 58, n.1) concludes that the criterion of language played no role in determining how groups and alliances were formed in the neighbouring district of Of in the early nineteenth century.

[26] For a recent analysis of late Ottoman developments see Deringil 1998.

The four categories of contemporary Lazistan can be reduced to three if we exclude the small numbers of Georgians. They are not randomly distributed, Turks predominate in the districts to the west of the Melyat boundary. To the east of this line, those who call themselves Turks without further qualifications are mostly recent immigrants. The boundary between Lazi and Hemşinli is more complicated, as can be seen on Map 1.2.

In general the Hemşinli are associated with the more upland regions and with pastoral forms of economy. Following relatively recent migrations, however, numerous enclaves of Hemşinli can nowadays be found in coastal districts that are predominantly Lazi. The ethnic boundary has probably never coincided with an economic boundary, since there have also existed over a long period upland communities of Lazi with economic profiles virtually identical to those of the Hemşinli. This book pays more attention to the Lazi, since they form the most numerous group in the counties where most of our fieldwork was undertaken. They are a closely guarded secret – not well known to the world, or even to the majority of modern Turkish citizens. They are described by a nineteenth-century German traveller as follows:

> The *Lasisch* inhabitants of this stretch of land betray their connections to the Caucasian races not so much through their bodily and facial features, which in general are not very attractive, as through their language (a Georgian dialect) and customs. As far as these latter are concerned, one should mention their most typical characteristic, the stubbornness with which they continue to practise blood feuds, which only too often lead to casualties. For example, within the five weeks preceding my arrival in Batumi it caused eight murders. It is natural that out of the caution warranted by these conditions, no one leaves his house unarmed. So whenever one sees a *Lase*, no matter whether he is on his way to his fields, going up to the forests or rowing out to sea, he is always carrying his arms, a rifle on his shoulder, a *jatagan* in his belt and, whenever possible, also a couple of pistols... They are used to taking the law in their own hands from childhood and are always equipped for both attack and defence. They have such a wild and rapacious character that, not undeservingly, among the Turks and the Georgians they have a bad reputation. They would have long been disarmed by the Pashas, but for the fact that they are needed for border defences.[27]

Given the locations he mentions, it is probable that this author is describing ancestors of the people who declare themselves today to be Lazi, but this is not necessarily so. The term is an almost endless source of confusion. Most Turks are familiar with the people they know as 'Laz' through a range of stereotypes that they associate with a region much larger than Lazistan, embracing the entire Black Sea coast east of Sinop or Samsun. Qualities of 'Lazness' are thought to intensify as one moves further east. In popular perceptions Trabzon is often seen as a quintessentially Laz city, though some reserve this distinction for Rize. Some inhabitants of these cities accept the label, whether or not they know of the existence of the Lazi a short distance further east.

What are the typical Laz qualities? The Laz male character in the traditional shadow play known as *Karagöz* is impetuous and emotional, ambitious and restless in comparison with the sedate inhabitants of the interior. The Laz are *different*, even if they do not look it. Not only do they have difficulty in pronouncing standard Turkish, but even their minds work differently: Turks tell

[27] Ritter 1843: 222–4, italics added.

Laz jokes in rather the same way that English people tell jokes about the Irish (or used to tell them). Other elements in the stereotypical representations include an association with the sea, a penchant for violence, strong concerns with honour and religious loyalties, and an industriousness that has helped Laz to enter lucrative economic niches in the big cities of the west, including real estate, construction, and the patisserie sector. The stereotype of the Laz female is less well developed. Its main element seems to be an extreme degree of subordination: in particular, Laz women are expected to shoulder physical burdens even greater than those women must put up with elsewhere in Anatolia.[28]

A full evaluation of these stereotypes is beyond the scope of this study. No doubt some of these elements can be linked to Lazistan's economic base, the unusual diet, etc. We know that Lazi men learned the skills of the pastry cook, alongside Hemşinli, who were probably the first in this field, in the cities of southern Russia in the late Ottoman period.[29] The image of the overworked Laz woman may also have a basis in reality, due to the consequences of male out-migration. However, the point we wish to stress is that these stereotypes are applied in modern Turkey to the East Black Sea region as a whole, and not specifically to the Lazuri speakers who live between Melyat and the state frontier. The existence of this distinct language is not known to most Turks. The Lazi themselves are, of course, aware of the existence of these stereotypes; most do not take them very seriously, and no one could explain to us how and why their ethnonym had been adapted to refer so loosely to the population of a much larger territory which had never possessed any knowledge of Lazuri.[30]

Anthropology without Argonauts

Although we hope that this book will be accessible to wider audiences, it is based on research that we have carried out using the methods and perspectives of modern social anthropology. This section is intended to provide both initiates and non-initiates with enough background to recognise the main issues that interest us in this Lazistan case. We do this by outlining some key developments in the history of the discipline and by noting some of the important studies previously undertaken in Turkey. We then proceed to discuss methods and the conditions in which we worked in the region between 1983 and 1999. The final section of this introduction provides an overview of subsequent chapters.

Anthropologists often find it difficult enough to explain their professional identity to other scholars and scientists in their home countries, let alone to the people who are the objects of their enquiries. It is often easier to assume other

---

[28] For discussion of these stereotypes see Meeker 1971: 323–6; Toumarkine 1995: 73–7; Magnarella 1998: 183–92.

[29] Marr 1910: 618.

[30] Meeker suggests that the extended usage of Laz began in the Byzantine period: 'the later Byzantine term "Laz" was probably somewhat analogous to the present day term used by the Turks. The transition in the meaning of the term was probably coincident with the transition of non-Greek Pontic peoples from consisting of numerous distinctive and autonomous tribes to being a more homogeneous Byzantized group, integrated into the empire and in various stages of assimilation with the Greeks.' (1970: 25–6)

identities. Our official purpose in the ten months we spent in Turkey in 1982–3, a time when Turkey was emerging slowly from a period of martial law, was to carry out a study of the social consequences of the introduction of tea as a cash crop in the east Black Sea region. Our formal affiliation was to the Economics Department of the Agricultural Faculty of the University of Ankara. During the months we spent in the east Black Sea region we maintained close links with the state's Tea Corporation (*Çay Kurumu*) at its Rize headquarters. Officials here and elsewhere soon realised that our interests extended beyond the impact of the tea industry. We did not seek to justify ourselves using the label social anthropology, because the discipline is not known in this part of Turkey. Only to a few closer acquaintances did we try to explain the academic background in any depth. With most people, including officials, we colluded in the understanding that our real purpose was to find out more about the 'traditional customs' (*örf-adetler*) of the region.

Yet this book is not about traditional Lazistan. It is about a region of Turkey as it was during the last decades of the twentieth century when we lived there, and it emphasises this region's *modernity*, i.e. the very considerable extent to which the goals of Kemalist republicans have been realised. So what do anthropologists really study, and are they prone to schizophrenia, duplicity, or worse?

One answer begins by defining the discipline in terms of encounters with 'other cultures'. An appropriate antecedent in this context is the encounter between the Greeks and the Scythians, as documented by Herodotus. The Scythians differed from the Greeks, and yet Herodotus does not represent them in a crudely negative light, in order to heighten by contrast the virtues of the Greeks. On the contrary, their otherness had its attractive, noble qualities, as befitting a people who, like the Greeks, had defeated a common enemy, the Persians. Herodotus is often acclaimed as the first historian, but he also has a claim to be viewed as the first anthropologist. Indeed, some modern anthropologists have come to see their subject as a branch of history. But Herodotus, though arguably free of what we nowadays call ethnic prejudice or racism, did not offer the kind of detailed empirical account of either his own or Scythian society that one would expect of a modern anthropologist. His stories are perhaps better seen as foundation myths, whose historical reality was doubtful and in any case irrelevant to their social role.

Others, unlike Herodotus, applied emphatically negative stereotypes to the peoples they encountered in this region. Apollonius of Rhodes denigrated the otherness of the Mossynoekoi in the following terms: 'Whatever is right to do openly in the market place, all this they do in their homes, but whatever acts we perform at home, these they perform out of doors in the midst of the streets without blame.'[31] Strabo reported wild natives who ambushed travellers from their tree huts, while Agathias and Procopius concluded that in Lazica 'neither corn nor wine nor any other good thing is produced.'[32] Byzantine accounts described the Laz as slave traders, and considered them untrustworthy allies.[33]

Whatever else they may do, anthropologists strive to offer more balanced and

[31] Cited in Bryer 1966: 175.
[32] *Ibid.*: 175, 176.
[33] *Ibid.*: 176–7.

sophisticated understandings than these. The modern discipline traces its origins to gentlemen scholars in mid-nineteenth-century Europe. It took a little longer before 'the study of man' found a place in the universities. The British tended to recognise three branches of the new science: archaeology was the study of material remains, physical anthropology was the study of human biological diversity, and social anthropologists concentrated upon social and cultural characteristics. Elsewhere, notably in America, the study of language was included as a fourth branch. The nineteenth-century context was one of European colonial expansion on a global scale, in which officials, traders, travellers and missionaries all partici- pated in novel encounters with native peoples. Intellectually, the climate was still set by the rationalist universalism of the Enlightenment. This was embodied in the famous opening sentence of Edward Tylor's *Primitive Culture*, in which he uses the terms culture and civilisation interchangeably:

> Culture or Civilization, taken in its wide ethnographic sense, is that complex whole which includes knowledge, belief, art, morals, law, custom, and any other capabilities and habits acquired by man as a member of society.[34]

The scientific aspirations of the early anthropologists were increasingly framed by Darwinian evolutionism. The American lawyer Lewis Henry Morgan investigated the social organisation of North American Indians and drew comparisons with the societies he knew from histories of the Ancient Mediterranean. His emphasis upon property relations as the basis of evolution was taken over by Engels to become the orthodox Marxist philosophy of history, a straitjacket which restricted the scope of Soviet anthropology for most of the twentieth century. In Britain the Scotsman James Frazer epitomised both the modern spirit of scientific rationalism and the style later characterised dismissively as 'armchair anthropology'. He carried out most of his research from his study and library in Trinity College Cambridge, and was never himself tempted to collect primary data from 'savage' peoples.

All this changed shortly after the First World War when Bronislaw Malinowski began to publish the results of his investigations among the Trobriand Islanders. Malinowski, a Pole who later became Professor at the London School of Economics, lived among these people over several years, learned their language well and presented accounts of their customs and beliefs that amounted to a revolutionary break with Victorian evolutionism. His manifesto was laid out in the Introduction to the first of his Trobriand monographs, *Argonauts of the Western Pacific*. The anthropologist who learned to understand, through observation and participa- tion, the native's view of his own world, was almost bound to be dissatisfied with diagnoses of superstition and speculation about evolutionary ranking. The 'savages' were found to be basically no different from the 'higher peoples'. Malinowski's ethnographic investigations represented the Trobrianders as being, within their unique *culture*, highly rational, calculating individuals, people like us (perhaps too much like us, according to some of his later critics). He replaced the old evolutionist approaches with a new, more sociologically oriented approach that he called functionalism. The anthropologist should no longer approach curious customs as 'survivals' from some distant past, but as components in a

[34] Tylor 1871: 1.

functioning contemporary society. It followed that, for Malinowski, the social anthropologist had nothing to say about the past. Foundation myths were a good illustration; they merited attention not as a basis for speculative historical reconstructions, but as social charters for the contemporary community. The main task of anthropology was synchronic: the study of how communities organised their social lives at the time the fieldworker lived among them.[35]

This is a simplified but not grossly distorted account of a decisive shift in the history of anthropology. The Malinowskian revolution 'continues to define the status quo in the discipline'.[36] Many have pointed to the difficulties in obtaining accurate and value-free accounts of other cultures through fieldwork, but few have been tempted to revert to Frazer's confident Victorian evolutionism. The work of Evans-Pritchard on the Azande, for example, showed that the patterns of thought of an African tribal society were as logical and rational as our own.[37] The goal of understanding the other culture in its own terms did not necessarily commit the anthropologist to a fully-fledged cultural relativism. At the end of his exhaustive analysis Evans-Pritchard could still assert that, by the measure of western science, the African system was deficient. To this extent he was still loyal to Frazer. Nevertheless, the main thrust of much twentieth-century social anthropology was a reaction against the scientific aspirations of the nineteenth century founding fathers and an extension of a relativism that was left largely implicit by Malinowski himself. Anthropologists no longer studied *culture*, a singular term synonymous with civilisation, but *cultures* in the plural, conceived basically as closed and integrated wholes.[38]

The relativising of 'other cultures' is closely associated with the tendency to romanticise them, to exaggerate their distance from our own social worlds, leading to claims for incommensurability, and even for differing cognitive capacities. This is foreign to Malinowski, who was only rarely guilty of 'exoticising' the natives. Contemporary researchers in the Trobriands are unlikely to hail their subjects as 'Argonauts'. Yet, while the world has in some senses been getting smaller and people in most places have become mobile, many anthropologists have continued to choose marginal groups for their investigations and to emphasise the 'otherness' of their subjects. This remains true even when they work closer to home, as many now do. For example, anthropologists working in Britain have characteristically concentrated on the specific identities of ethnic groups in the inner cities and the Celtic fringe. Euro-American work on the Mediterranean has paid disproportionate attention to villagers' ideas about honour and shame, which are held to distinguish the people of this region from their northern European neighbours.[39]

---

[35] Malinowski acknowledged the need to pay more attention to precise historical contexts only in the very last of his Trobriand monographs (1935: 479–81).

[36] Gellner 1995: ix–x. It should be pointed out that others made major contributions (e.g. Franz Boas and W. H. Rivers) and that Malinowski himself had a penchant for personal myth-making. See Stocking 1993, Kuper 1996.

[37] Evans-Pritchard 1937.

[38] The origins of this usage are commonly traced back to German reaction to the universalist aspirations of the Enlightenment: where the *philosophes* spoke of individual human rights, Herder invoked a cosmopolitan world composed of many different cultures, each with its own standards of morality and happiness. This seems to have been the first time that the term culture was used in the plural. For a recent critical account see Kuper 1999.

[39] See Gilmore 1987.

Some of the work done on Turkey, we shall argue, also betrays exaggerated distancing and exoticising tendencies.

One key problem concerns temporality. Malinowski presented the 'essential Trobriander' as standing outside real historical time. The convention that the time-less essence of a culture could be grasped through a single 'snapshot' period in the field has now been abandoned by most anthropologists, who are careful to explain the precise temporal constraints that influenced their work. Instead of cramming a discussion of social change into a token final chapter, they try to integrate processes of change into their analyses. However, even the ethnographer who writes about social change may create the impression that a more coherent and intact traditional culture had persisted until the recent past. The field study that presents itself as a 'threshold' or 'transition' study implies a normal condition of stability at the beginning of this transition, possibly with the implication that another will follow at the end of the process. But this normality or 'equilibrium' is an illusion.

Underlying the failure of anthropologists to work out adequate theories of social change, to find ways of depicting, understanding and explaining different beliefs, habits and practices, without rendering them as exotic and radically 'other', is the central concept of culture. What exactly is culture? Is it possible to speak of 'a culture' without implying a bounded and patterned whole? How can this be squared with the older European usage, which links culture to ideals of cultivated society and civilisation? Malinowski, in contrast to Tylor's definition, quoted above, suggested reserving the term civilisation for 'a special aspect of more advanced cultures'. In a wide-ranging article for the *International Encyclopedia of the Social Sciences* he went on to sum up culture as comprising 'inherited artifacts, goods, technical processes, ideas, habits and moral values'. For him, culture, rather than civilisation or society, provided anthropology's master concept, for 'social organisation cannot be really understood except as a part of culture'.[40] Although the range of this definition remained as broad as Tylor's, the term culture was later used more restrictively to refer primarily to ideas, representations and a cast of mind conceived as specific to a given population; often this population itself was then termed 'a culture'.

Curiously, the British school established by Malinowski did not follow the founder in prioritising the concept of culture. Under the influence of the socio-logical theory of Emile Durkheim, mediated in part by Alfred Radcliffe-Brown, they preferred to emphasise society. More precisely, they emphasised social structure, social organisation, or simply social relationships. Edmund Leach led the way in challenging notions previously taken for granted concerning the appropriate unit of study. He reluctantly followed Radcliffe-Brown's advice to interpret 'a society' as meaning 'any convenient locality'.[41] The region he researched in Burma lacked the clear boundaries and equilibrium tendencies that functionalists had reported elsewhere. It had a measure of cultural unity but for Leach, at least in this early work, culture was merely a superficial 'dress'. The social anthropologist was concerned not with costume but with deeper questions of social order and political structure.

[40] Malinowski 1937: 621.
[41] Leach 1954: 5.

British-trained social anthropologists of this generation were among the pioneers of the concept of ethnicity, which acquired widespread currency inside and outside the academy in the last quarter of the twentieth century.[42] The new characterisations of ethnic group were an improvement upon the notion of a tribal 'culture' outside of historical time, as outlined by Malinowski for the Trobrianders. Clyde Mitchell and other members of the Manchester School pointed out that African tribal identities were often radically altered in colonial conditions, especially in industrial settings such as the Copperbelt. Abner Cohen developed the idea of 'retribalisation' to explain how Nigerian Hausa living far away from this group's main territorial base in the north systematically cultivated and modified this identity to preserve the political and economic advantages that it conferred. Cohen did not neglect what he termed the 'symbolic dimension'. He recognised the importance of a common language and common rituals for maintaining group solidarity, but he did not expand this into an encompassing concept of culture. In the more extreme formulation of his position, an ethnic group is perceived exclusively as an interest group that promotes its members' utilitarian objectives, typically through informal networking.[43]

Others highlighted different aspects of ethnic identity. Bill Epstein paid particular attention to the subjective and emotional attachments that so many members seem to feel towards these groups. Fredrik Barth, too, in his introduction to an extremely influential volume, argued that ethnicity provided a person with their 'basic, most general identity'.[44] Some authors were interested in the patterned contents of a group's identity, and not merely in sociological function. The elements selected to establish identity might remain constant even in circumstances when, as Barth's own material showed, individuals made rational choices on the basis of their political and economic advantage and these determined migration and 'osmosis' across group boundaries.

The scope of these debates has continued to widen in recent years, reflecting the increased salience of ethnicity and nationalism in world affairs. Both ethnic and national identities have been 'deconstructed' to reveal the many layers of myth, of 'invention' and 'imagining' that support them.[45] It does not, however, follow that social identities can be manipulated at will by activists. John Peel has criticised excessive 'presentism' and called for recognition of the 'weight of the past' in setting limits to the identities that can develop among a given population at a given time.[46]

It is nowadays difficult to identify a specifically British school in anthropology. In the much larger American tradition the concept of culture never lost its central place, but its idealist bias intensified. For Malinowski, culture was 'essentially an instrumental reality' that transformed individuals into organised groups in order to satisfy biological needs.[47] For scholars such as Clifford Geertz

[42] For useful summaries see Eriksen 1993, Banks 1996.
[43] Cohen 1974.
[44] Barth 1969: 15.
[45] See Anderson 1983, Hobsbawm and Ranger 1983, Tonkin, Chapman and Macdonald 1989.
[46] Peel 1989. For this reason it seems preferable to use the term 'construction' in preference to 'invention': identities are creatively shaped and reshaped from existing materials, they are never in the strict sense invented.
[47] Malinowski 1937: 645.

and Marshall Sahlins, two of the most influential American anthropologists of the second half of the century, culture is concerned with 'webs of meaning', with the 'symbolic ordering' of social interaction. Material motivations and constraints on human behaviour are overlooked or neglected. This concept of culture implies a more or less coherent patterned totality, with a tendency to closure and the exaggeration of 'otherness'. The anthropologist's concept of culture hardly differs from that of ethnic and nationalist activists, who typically insist on a shared culture as the basis of their group's distinctiveness. Culturalist approaches emphasise symbols and rituals, and offer elaborate analyses of the associated discourses and ideologies, while neglecting the social factors shaping the identity and the variable extent to which individuals internalise it and use it. Some scholars have dispensed with the term ethnicity in favour of even vaguer terms such as 'public identity', 'collective selfhood' and 'the production of national cultures'.[48]

Outside the academy, the concept of culture is ever more entrenched, pervading the models even of those who explicitly reject nationalist assumptions. Thus debates about multiculturalism have been largely predicated on the highly misleading assumptions that most members of a society can be classified in one named bounded group, whose individual members share a bundle of characteristics that distinguish them from the members of other like units. In the characteristic reversal of Enlightenment universalism, culture is increasingly invoked to defend differentiated notions of justice and citizenship.[49] Under the impact of new bodies of theory, including those associated with 'globalisation' and with 'cultural studies', the master concept of Tylor and Malinowski may be collapsing into confusion.[50]

How might the culture concept be applied to Lazistan, past and present? Can this region be viewed as comprising a plurality of cultures linked to the various languages and other differences that distinguished Lazi, Turks, Hemşinli and Georgians? If so, then our next move might be to contrast Ottoman multiculturalism with Lazistan as it is today, after three quarters of a century of republican efforts to construct an entirely new form of society. The modern society is a nation-state, whose citizens allegedly share a single national culture. At least, that is the official view, the Kemalist view. We can also term this the Gellnerian view, after the leading social science theoretician of nationalism. Ernest Gellner defined nationalism as the principle that the political unit should be perfectly congruent with the national unit, premised in turn on a common culture.[51]

Yet such a contrast between traditional and modern cannot possibly be the whole story, for it excludes too many threads of continuity in Lazistan that also have a claim on our attention. The Kemalist elites who came to power in the

---

[48] Fox 1990.

[49] For recent influential discussions see Taylor 1992, Kymlicka 1995.

[50] For a recent assessment of the anthropological field, including contributions by Geertz, Sahlins and other influential modern theorists of culture see Borofsky 1994. Eric Wolf often made the basic point we are making in this section, namely that our concept of culture has been intertwined since its inception with the European model of the 'nation-state'. See Wolf 1998 for his attempt to specify a 'serviceable' concept of culture. See also Kuper 1999. On globalisation, see Featherstone 1990, 1995; Robertson 1987; Friedman 1994. On cultural studies see Nugent and Shore 1997.

[51] Gellner 1983: 1–7.

1920s stressed not so much a transformation of culture as a civilisational divide between east and west. Following many late Ottoman predecessors, they were convinced that the closest possible imitation of western institutions and practices was the only way to overcome centuries of stagnation. However, as with other modernising elites, closer inspection of the outcomes of their social engineering project shows a much more complex picture – transformation has been partial, there has also been continuity, friction, and an abundance of paradoxical hybrid forms. Our principal aim in this book is to illuminate the complexities of the Kemalist society by describing how the modernity it has brought has been experienced by 'ordinary people'. At the end of the day we do not find the concept of culture very helpful in this undertaking, though it is important to see how it has been used by elites and to investigate whether the idea is gaining strength in 'local models', i.e. in people's own representations of the social conditions in which they live.

Culture is one of two basic terms that we problematise in this study. The second is modernity. In this case the proprietary claims of the anthropologist are markedly less strong. With a few notable exceptions, including again Ernest Gellner, anthropologists have not been prominent in theorising this term. How could anthropology, given the way it developed as the study of those traditional, integrated, patterned cultures, have anything of significance to say about a world in which those patterns have been destroyed? It is not surprising that most theorising about modernity, together with related terms like modernisation, has come from other disciplines.[52]

If the old concept of culture can have only antiquarian value in dealing with the modern world, what would an anthropological approach to modernity look like? In one sense, the sense in which all these terms derive from a Latin root referring to the present as distinct from the past, Malinowskian ethnographers have been the unwitting witnesses of modernity all along, wherever the particular places they have worked. This contribution should not be underestimated. A modest amount of fieldwork often suffices to puncture the grander constructions of sociological theory, particularly of the Eurocentric sort. But we have a further goal. Through this study of a region of Turkey we also wish to show that the 'grassroots' perspective of the ethnographer can shed useful light on sweeping changes wrought by the state and other external forces. Our assessment of Turkish modernity is critical, but it is at the same time nuanced and not grounded in any romantic notion of traditional patterns of culture.

The social organisation and institutions of Kemalist Turkey certainly fit well enough into most definitions of modernity. The fit is also close if one follows the more 'cultural' definition favoured by the comparative macrosociologist Goran Therborn, for whom modernity is '*an epoch turned to the future*, conceived as likely to be different from and possibly better than the present and the past.'[53] The modern Turkish experience also fits well into the model outlined recently by James Scott, who takes a predominantly jaundiced view of the record of twentieth-

---

[52] For examples of what is already a vast literature see Lash and Friedman (1992), Featherstone, Lash and Robertson (1995).
[53] Therborn 1995: 4. Italics in original.

century ideologies of 'high modernity'.[54] He argues that greater respect for local knowledge and local practices (*métis*) could have spared millions of people from the disasters provoked by state interventions such as Stalinist collectivisation. Though Scott makes little use of the concept of culture, many anthropologists find his perspective congenial. We shall suggest, however, that in the Turkish case his assumptions do not open up a helpful anthropological approach.

We are by no means the first to broach such questions in the Turkish case. The first and most significant steps toward a de-exoticised anthropology of Anatolia were taken by Paul Stirling, who after preparations in Oxford under Evans-Pritchard began his fieldwork in the vicinity of Kayseri in 1949.[55] In the monograph *Turkish Village* and in a number of seminal articles, Stirling has charted the slow processes by which top-down reforms came to transform ordinary lives. His work was Malinowskian inasmuch as it was rigorously grounded in fieldwork and paid little attention to the long-term historical context, but Stirling never took the community of Sakaltutan to be a self-contained unit. On the contrary, as his work progressed he paid increasing attention to the developing mechanisms of integration into the national society, and those that reached further afield into Europe. He was also fascinated by the expansion of social knowledge among villagers and migrants, by what he called their changing 'cognition'.[56]

Many themes in Stirling's work have been pursued by later fieldworkers, who have also filled out some topics that he neglected. Villages have remained attractive bases for some, while others have preferred small town and even city studies.[57] Most relevant to this study is the work of Michael Meeker just outside the western boundary of Lazistan as we have defined it. Meeker has combined interests in political and economic changes with a sensitivity to the persistence of practices and values that were deeply engrained in local communities. In recent papers he has emphasised the latter. Unusually among anthropologists, he has sought to uncover continuities by working in the Ottoman archives. For example one recent paper was concerned 'not with the full texture of everyday life, but only of one aspect of it, what has been called a philosophy of citizenship, a philosophy that is thoroughly patriarchal in character.'[58] This approach brings new insights, but documents can reveal little about the implementation of such philosophies. It is impossible to do fieldwork in the past. Most fieldworkers have addressed the tension between the modernising thrust from above (or at least from outside the community) and the persistence, or revival, of alternative forces. Some have followed the model of the 'threshold' study, while others, including Meeker, have argued that a single integrating cultural system persists behind the dissonances of modernity. An idealist bias in some recent ethnographies makes

---

[54] Scott 1998: see especially Ch. 3.
[55] Stirling has discussed the circumstances of his first fieldwork (along with many other matters) in a posthumously published interview. See Shankland 1999b.
[56] See Stirling 1965, 1974, 1993b.
[57] For village studies see Schiffauer 1987, Paleczek 1987, Sirman 1990, Delaney 1991, Strasser 1995. The pioneer of urban work was Mübeccel Kıray: see Kıray 1964. Later small town studies include Benedict 1974a; Magnarella 1974; Fallers 1974; Tapper and Tapper 1987a. For city work see White 1994.
[58] Meeker 1996: 55. See also Meeker 1970, 1972, and forthcoming.

the people of rural Anatolia seem more different, more 'other', than in Stirling's representations from an earlier generation.[59]

The time frame and regional context of this study make it different from these earlier contributions. The lifestyles and identities of all the people who live around the Black Sea have been changing continuously for thousands of years. We share the view that an accelerated process of change was initiated in the republican period.[60] We approach this as Turkey's version of the 'great transformation'.[61] The best abstract model of this transformation and the basic principles of modernity remains that developed by Ernest Gellner.[62] Gellner's work takes industrialisation as the root cause of accelerated social change but concentrates more on the features of its main organisational form, the nation-state. The typical polity of the pre-industrial era ('Agraria') was a culturally plural and hierarchically structured empire such as that of the Ottomans. In modernity the political unit becomes congruent with the cultural unit, so that a single 'high culture' is generalised throughout the society by means of a national language and a standardised and well disseminated education system. The labour force is 'generalist' and highly mobile, and the entire society is pervaded by an ethic of egalitarianism.

We find Gellner's model a useful starting point for an exploration of Kemalist Turkish modernity, even though hardly any single detail of his ideal type corresponds closely to the Turkish realities. His emphasis on industrialisation needs to be scaled down and more attention paid to the role of the state and ideology. Standardised education does not necessarily generate better access to labour markets and egalitarianism seems questionable not only at the level of sociological outcomes but also at the level of general principle or ethic. We are particularly interested in transformations of social identities. Gellner's view of modern cultures as unifying blocks is over-simplified. The nation does not transcend all earlier sources of difference and identification. We see identities as emerging from the continuous flow of social interaction. It is therefore important to investigate how national identity combines with identities of a more traditional sort, such as those linked to language, gender, family and religion, and with newer identities that people create in increasingly globalised marketplaces. Kemalism implied a sharp division, in line with classical liberal conceptions of modernity, between public and private spheres. But social identities depend on both and the distinction may prove untenable or at any rate unhelpful ethnographically.

---

[59] Delaney (1991) is the author who relies most heavily on an encompassing concept of culture, based on a patriarchal Islamic cosmology exemplified in procreation beliefs. Strasser (1995) and Schiffauer (1987) have a similar idealist bias, though Schiffauer explicitly allows for conflict between the model deriving from honour and that supplied by Islam; the latter gains in strength over the life course. He is also a good example of an author who uses a 'threshold' model to explain other sorts of conflict: it is argued that migration and other material changes are weakening the hold of these two models by the time the fieldworker appears on the scene.

[60] Michael Meeker argues, in a forthcoming publication that will break new ground in historical anthropology, that an earlier modernisation process took place in the Ottoman period. This work was not yet available to us in the preparation of the present text, but we are grateful for personal communications.

[61] Polanyi 1944.

[62] The fullest version of the model is given in Gellner 1988. Gellner's approach is more abstract than the large literature associated with 'modernisation theory'. For examples of the latter as applied to Turkey see Lerner 1958, Ward and Rustow 1964, Weiker 1981.

The region we are calling Lazistan is a convenient location to explore all these questions.

The seeming rupture that brought the Kemalists to power in the early 1920s makes it hard to avoid drawing a dichotomy between the forces of modernisation and the forces of tradition; sometimes local people themselves speak and act in terms of this polarisation. This way of thinking reinforces the tendency to think of cultures in a holistic way, adding discontinuities in time to boundaries in space. We argue, however, that the recent history of Lazistan cannot be explained in terms of a shift from one stable integrated totality to another one. Many commentators on Turkey have highlighted a clash between the rival cultures of Kemalism and Islam. We argue that social life cannot be reduced to two conflicting ideologies or cultures, let alone to one single encompassing system. The content of Kemalism has been frequently modified and so has the content of Islam in Turkey. There is no archetypal 'traditional culture' that modernist projects have rudely disturbed. We know that many people in Lazistan were well integrated into the Ottoman polity; that trading networks and intermarriage following long-distance migration were common in this period.

It follows from all this that a social anthropological study of modern Lazistan is bound to diverge significantly from the Malinowskian prototype. The assumption of an integrating holism, which he summed up as the 'native culture', is an implausible starting point here. We follow Malinowski in basing our analysis primarily on fieldwork and in being concerned primarily with contemporary realities. Like him, we want to show that what particular groups and individuals do may diverge from what they say and from the values they assert. Unlike him, we do not assume that people hold a unifying world view, constituting the essence of their culture. Both modern Turkish national identity and Islam are potentially encompassing ideas of this sort, but neither of these, nor any synthetic combination of the two, can bear the weight that some anthropologists load onto them.

What do we offer in place of this notion of culture? We identify the main forces that shape values, ideas and social behaviour, and we explore these ethnographically. People combine elements from different clusters, both in their beliefs and in their practices. They may say they are firmly committed to one or other variant of a modernist cluster, yet fail to live up to this in their behaviour. If politicians and market-oriented entrepreneurs heed the employment needs of their kin, this should not lead us to conclude that they are in thrall to 'tradition', any more than the actual behaviour of politicians and businessmen in our own countries are easily reducible to idealised models. In short, we emphasise variation and identity *combinations*, both new elements and older elements which have persisted in modern conditions. One particular element, or cluster of elements, is ethnicity, which we view not as the receptacle for, or expression of, an encompassing concept of culture, but rather as an emerging and specifically modern form of social identity.[63]

---

[63] Ethnicity in contemporary Anatolia has not been intensively researched, but see Andrews 1989, and forthcoming. The Kurdish question is so different in scale that comparisons with the groups of Lazistan are not especially fruitful. Paleczek 1987 and Magnarella 1979 are both concerned with the integration of minorities that originate in, or at any rate close to, Lazistan; but these investigations were made in the communities' new locations in the west, where the forces promoting integration are very different.

Methods

Modern Lazistan, the region as it has developed within the borders of Atatürk's republic, especially from 1950 onwards, has lost much of its earlier diversity as a result of accelerating social change. How does one conduct an anthropological study of these processes?

The chapters that follow are based primarily on our fieldwork in the region between 1983 and 1999. Unlike Malinowski among the Trobrianders, we are dealing here with a population that has been at least partially literate for centuries. But we did not work in the Ottoman archives and shall have very little more to say about the past: the task of assembling a more detailed factual history of this land and its people must await further research. In this fundamental sense our project is a Malinowskian one. In other respects, however, it is very different. We have relied heavily on a wealth of secondary materials, for Lazistan is part of a large state, with flourishing media and communications industries, generating with every single day masses of information of potential interest and significance to social science researchers. There is a large academic literature on Turkey, and on aspects of Turkish society that can also be explored in other parts of the Middle East and even further afield. All of this has influenced our selection of themes and the way in which we have addressed them.[64]

Altogether we made six research trips, spread out over almost seventeen years. This means that we have been able to do a little better than the classical Malinowskian 'snapshot' portrayal. We have been able to trace detailed demographic changes in families that we have known over the whole period, and compare actual outcomes to earlier plans and aspirations. We have been able to assess the impact of exogenous changes. New state policies towards the tea industry in the mid-1980s had major consequences for all those who worked in it. The decision to open the state border crossing into Georgia in 1988 had far-reaching repercussions a few years later, following the dissolution of the Soviet Union. We followed these trends in successive fieldtrips, thereby bringing a diachronic element into the study, however limited. Where we have used the present tense, this refers to patterns of behaviour that we found in essentially the same form throughout our fieldwork. We have used past tense forms in describing more specific events and tracing changes that occurred during our research period.

We did not initially plan to focus on the regional unit. It was always clear to us that, due to the long history of out-migration, no village in this region could be approached as a surviving microcosm, as a relatively closed community, in the way that others had tackled village research elsewhere in Anatolia. Among the options we considered was that of extending the social field from one village to include its various diaspora groups, but this task too had been admirably undertaken by others.[65] In the end, contingencies and serendipity led us to choose an

---

[64] Of course we cannot claim to have read more than a fraction of the materials potentially of relevance to this study. In particular, we have not done justice to a large body of work by Turkish social scientists and folklorists. We have tried to read all the published materials directly concerning this region, but some items have no doubt escaped our attention. Our sampling of the literature in other languages has also necessarily been limited.

[65] Notably by Schiffauer 1991.

Plate 1.3 The coastal highway at Pazar; the Kaçkar Mountains mark the horizon.

Plate 1.4 The central neighbourhood of Sümer.

option for which we found no clear precedent in the literature. After six months of preparations in Ankara and one month in the provincial capital of Rize, we spent about three and a half months in the summer of 1983 in the village of Sümer, district of Fındıklı. This is a large village with a total of around 1300 inhabitants, located close to the coast in the geographical centre of the Lazuri-speaking districts.[66] We were fortunate in being warmly received by many local families, and were able to achieve a great deal more than was specifically required that year for the project on the tea industry.[67] In 1988 we returned to Sümer for a further six weeks and renewed these contacts. However, by the time we embarked upon our later fieldtrips in 1992 (seven months) and 1993 (one month) we were aware of other research in adjacent areas.[68] We decided at this point to broaden the focus and to base ourselves in the small town of Pazar (population then about 12,000), at the western end of the Lazuri-speaking zone. Though it has been overtaken in size by its neighbours Çayeli and Ardeşen, and also by Hopa, Pazar was more important than any of these in late Ottoman times, when it was the second town of Lazistan after Rize.[69] From this base we were able to build up a picture of social life in an old market and administrative centre, and also to visit all but a few of the forty-one villages in the present Pazar county.

Inevitably many of these visits were brief, but some were followed up on numerous occasions. In addition we continued to visit our friends elsewhere in the region, and especially of course in Sümer. Thus this study is not a conventional micro-level investigation, nor does it pretend to deal evenly with the entire zone between the Of valley and the state border. Rather, based on detailed study of a few hamlets in Sümer, relatively systematic surveying of urban and rural landscapes in Pazar and more sporadic visits to other parts, including a month in the main city of Rize, we have built up an understanding of Lazistan as a whole that pays due attention to its internal differentiation.

In a regrettable departure from usual anthropological practice, we have violated the convention that requires anthropologists to become fluent in the native languages of the people they study. All our fieldwork was conducted in Turkish, the dominant language of the region. We never learned more than a few words of Lazuri, though this is still the first language of a significant proportion of the region's population. We have numerous excuses: there were no practical grammars or dictionaries to help us, time was limited, and – most decisively – it would have been difficult politically to be seen to be committed to mastering a language that, in the eyes of the authorities, does not exist.[70] Fortunately, with

---

[66] Sümer is an old village, though its modern inhabitants are unaware of this fact. With 62 households in the late fifteenth century, it was considerably larger than Viçe (Fındıklı), the contemporary county centre.

[67] See Hann 1985, 1990a.

[68] Feurstein 1983. Correspondence and discussion with Wolfgang Feurstein helped to confirm our view that it would be preferable to work further away from the region on which he himself had concentrated since the 1960s.

[69] It was formally recognised as a county in 1864. For brief descriptions of Atina (as Pazar was then known) in Ottoman times see Ak 1999a, 1999b.

[70] We were aware of the existence of some older, largely descriptive grammars (e.g. Rosen 1845, Adjarian 1898, Kluge 1913). The availability of publications on Lazuri, including simple texts to assist new learners, has significantly improved in the 1990s: see Feurstein 1991, Holisky 1991, Kutscher et al. 1995, Zitasi 1994 (1935). When we attempted to draw up Lazuri–Turkish word lists

the exception of a single elderly lady in Sümer in 1983, everyone we talked to was fluent in modern Turkish. This, we were told, has been the case for the great majority of the population since at least Ottoman times, and possibly for a lot longer. Many Lazi, certainly most under forty, say that their Turkish is better than their Lazuri. Some state Turkish to be their mother tongue. Nonetheless, this is certainly a weakness in our research, and in particular for our analysis of ethnic identity. In particular, in some inland communities children learn Lazuri before they learn Turkish. Even among urban dwellers on the coast whose grasp of Lazuri is weakening fast, there are doubtless some aspects of their lives and cultures that would have had a different complexion if communicated to us in Lazuri. There may be, for at least some people, an intimate world of communication that provides a further commentary on the dominant Turkish-speaking world. If so, others will have to report on this through further research. We heard only those commentaries that were uttered in Turkish.

Our research methods deviated somewhat from those most commonly employed by anthropologists. In particular, we attempted to make more use of questionnaires. To some extent this was dictated by the expectations of officials in Turkey. In 1983 it was taken for granted that we would want to investigate the social consequences of the tea industry by taking a lengthy questionnaire around to as many households as possible. We did our best to oblige, completing one hundred lengthy forms with the help of garden owners in Sümer. We also completed forms with a sample of the population of temporary sharecroppers, and engaged an assistant to collect similar data from garden owners in the county of Pazar. This use of the questionnaire was fairly readily understood by most villagers as well as by officials, but from our point of view it was often a tedious constraint. Fortunately we were able to include some rather general questions concerning gender relations, and these often elicited the most interesting responses. The shorter visits of 1988, 1993, 1997 and 1999 were all made without official research visas, so methods were necessarily more informal. In 1992, however, we used official administrative channels to distribute questionnaires concerning changes in marriage customs to village headmen throughout the region. The results were not terribly useful, as will be explained in Chapter 6. Perhaps the main benefit of this exercise was that it helped to convince some of the officials that our concerns were relatively innocent, and that the informal, even nebulous anthropological methods of 'participant observation', which we tried to explain to them, really did produce better understanding than reliance upon the questionnaire instrument.

The officials of foreign governments are not alone in their suspicion of anthropologists and their methods. 'Participant observation' is a phrase that has occasionally troubled the Social Science Research Council in England. Other academics see social anthropology as a 'soft' discipline, in comparison with their own scientific rigour. Some have doubted the credentials of a discipline which seems to define itself largely or primarily in terms of its research methods. Anthropologists themselves have frequently been forced onto the defensive in the

---

[70] (cont.) and grammatical paradigms in Sümer in 1983, young people offered enthusiastic help. But we often ran into difficulties when trying to write words down: they declared this to be impossible! By 1992–3 we were able to show them Feurstein's transcription system.

generation that has followed the demise of the overseas colonial empires. However, despite much doubting and soul-searching in recent years, most anthropologists still consider it essential to rely on the so-called soft, qualitative methods for the kind of understanding they are trying to achieve. Even in fields such as economic anthropology, more susceptible than most to quantitative approaches, significant dimensions of behaviour will be overlooked or misunderstood if the investigators are not prepared to spend time sitting down with the shopkeepers, traders and consumers, probing and exploring through unstructured conversations, and simply listening and observing. So this is what we did, fully aware that our presence often affected the nature of the interaction. For example, it is likely that our status as foreign researchers caused some local people to make more protestations of their Turkish patriotism and to foreground issues of identity.

Despite these limitations, participant observation enables the investigators to build up an understanding that goes beyond the anecdotal. To achieve this it was essential that we lived among local people and visited them frequently in their homes. During the main stints of fieldwork in 1983 and 1992 we rented our own accommodation, in Sümer and Pazar respectively, but were constantly dependent on others for maintaining our household.[71] Given the significance of gender divisions in this society, a single investigator would necessarily miss out on a great deal. We have aimed at a balanced coverage in this respect. Finally we should note that being accompanied by our children virtually throughout the research helped to open up many networks that we would probably not have explored otherwise.

Anthropological fieldwork often evolves in unforeseen ways. Our work in Lazistan was easier to explain in the first phase in the 1980s, when we had a project with a reasonably specific focus, the consequences of the tea industry, and an elaborate questionnaire as a prop. The work in the 1990s was quite different, because the themes and the unit of study had become much broader. In 1992, alongside a general focus on the Lazi, we also aimed to investigate a specific facet of economic change, namely changes in the accounting principles used by small businessmen and shopkeepers. Repeated attempts to collect data on this subject, even among close acquaintances, bore little fruit. On the other hand, the sudden proliferation of new markets throughout the region in the early 1990s, in the wake of the collapse of the neighbouring socialist empire, provided us with a much more fertile research field. Although we had not mentioned this at all in our project application, these markets eventually became an important focus of the research – necessarily so, as they were much frequented and discussed by virtually all local people.[72]

In addition to lasting friendships, most projects in social anthropology generate ethical dilemmas, misunderstandings and tension. The friendships can themselves be problematic. The moment you ask someone whom you know well to provide full details of all the payments made in a recent family wedding, you are establishing a gulf between you; the very act of gathering information in this way implies distancing. It is pointless to pretend that we ever felt completely 'at home' in this region. We were generally perceived as being from Britain, a richer and

[71] During the shorter fieldtrips, accommodation ranged from local *otels* to a tent.
[72] See Hann and Bellér-Hann 1992, Hann and Bellér-Hann 1998.

more powerful country than Turkey.[73] We are not Muslims. We look a little different and dress differently from most local people. We were working in Turkey in times of considerable political tension and instability, which created problems in broaching certain kinds of group distinction in modern Lazistan.

But we would like to emphasise that almost everyone, officials as well as ordinary people, was well disposed towards us. They were enthusiastic about the idea that foreigners wished to write about their traditional customs. Since many of these traditions continue to affect contemporary behaviour, we saw no contradiction between declaring an interest in the habits and customs of the past and our intention to write a book about the present. Most of the people we came to know seemed in any case comfortable about revealing to us many facets of their contemporary lives: this was the basis for their invitations to visit their homes, factories, mosques, women's groups and so on. So, in terms of the ground they cover, the analyses that we present are unlikely to be a surprise to our informants. The study might surprise a few officials, who may have thought that our interests were closer to the folkloric, or to social anthropology's nineteenth-century origins. If so we must ask for their pardon. We should also thank everyone in Lazistan and elsewhere in Turkey who gave of their time to help us in so many ways. We can never repay them. Social anthropology is in this sense an exploitative subject. We feel guilt over the many letters we have exchanged, knowing that the cost of posting a letter for our correspondents in Lazistan is in real terms much higher than it is for us. All we can say to all those who have helped us is that we have tried, to the best of our ability, to present an account that does justice to some of their experiences. The framework of this book is one that we have imposed, but we have designed it with the goal of shedding maximum light on their society, including their own understandings of it. Where we have put forward analyses and predictions that have not come from local people, we have made it clear that these are ours alone. If these pages are ever read in Lazistan or elsewhere in Turkey, we hope that people do not find our main arguments either entirely obvious, or trivial, or naive.

Plan of the book

We begin with the state. This might seem an odd choice to those who suppose that anthropologists study social life at the grass roots and movements that emerge 'from below', while the state is something to be investigated by political scientists and others. But developments initiated 'from above' have been decisive in the emergence of modern Lazistan, and so it seems sensible to open in this way. The Turkish state-nation has a pervasive presence in social life for all Turkish citizens and, inevitably, it also looms large in the experiences of foreign researchers. From the moment you start to seek your authorisation and visa from the Embassy in London, you realise that the Turkish state is a little different from

---

[73] This aspect of our self-presentation was actually more complicated. Those who came to know us soon discovered that only CH is British (a very few learned that his *millet* is better described as Welsh). IBH's Hungarian identity generated quite different reactions, since Turks perceive Hungarians both as close relatives and as members of the old socialist bloc.

your own. When you settle in a small town you must present yourself at the office of the *kaymakam*, a post that corresponds to that of *sous-préfet* in the French administrative system that Turkey decided to adopt in the 1920s. He is the appointed representative of the central government. Above him, every province is governed by a prefect known as the *vali*. The town also has a *jandarma* and a military garrison, not to mention various economic and educational institutions also under the aegis of the state. Since every town has as its symbolic centre a statue of Atatürk, the urban landscape is an ever-present reminder of the force of the state in modern Lazistan.

After outlining the broad contours of republican political history, we discuss the system of administration and some of the less direct ways in which state authority is asserted, through the dissemination of new conceptions of space and time. Educational practices play a central role in producing citizens who take pride in their national identity. We also show how the state has transformed the economy of Lazistan through the introduction of tea. Although most state interventions have been externally directed and implemented by officials from outside the region, we note the ways in which the state has been woven into the fabric of social life in this region, including fabric usually considered as part of the private sphere. People do have a tendency to reify the state, to cast it as a remote and alien power. Yet it is also described with intimate kinship metaphors, and distinctions are drawn between different groups of functionaries who are recognised as wielding different forms of state power. Even those least in sympathy with secular republican ideals have difficulty in envisaging a world in which the state were to give up the major social and economic responsibilities it has assumed.

Yet significant forces in the modern history of Lazistan have pushed for a contraction in state roles. In Chapter 3 we focus upon the principle of market economy: not the traditional 'voice of the bazaar', but the principal modern countercurrent to top-down state power. The main political parties have long been differentiated in their stance toward this principle; those emphasising in their rhetoric greater reliance upon free enterprise have consistently fared better at the polls in Lazistan. We relate these preferences to the social structure of the region, and show how the small towns serve as market centres that integrate town and countryside. We look at how market values were applied in limited ways to the tea industry itself from the mid-1980s, and at the consequences of this partial liberalisation. The recent expansion of the market principle has also had mixed consequences in another context. The proliferation of 'Russian markets' following the opening of the state border and the influx of 'trader-tourists' from many parts of the former Soviet Union brought both new economic opportunities and new moral tensions. The people of Lazistan welcomed these markets, not simply for the novelty of the experience but also because of the range of cheap goods they offered. At the same time they deplored the poor quality of many goods, and the lack of public control over trade, including more intimate forms of commerce in which some of the foreigners engaged away from the market places.

Also in Chapter 3 we consider the consumption-oriented national society of which Lazistan is now a part. Some of the patterns that can be observed today are the consequences of radical changes in communications that far outstrip the state-nation. But increasing globalisation in production and consumption is still significantly filtered at the national level. Where economists tend to stress impersonal forces of supply and demand and have little or nothing to say about what determines consumer preferences, anthropologists examine the contexts from which judgements about taste emerge, and the social relationships which motivate consumer choices. The market principle, like the state, is an abstraction that needs ethnographic investigation.

Too much market can easily lead to too little community. Even when the social factors that underpin markets are fully recognised, there remains a sense in which capitalist economies are predominantly individualist, even atomising in their impact. They stimulate competition and selfish acquisition. Even when they facilitate the efflorescence of gifts, these are given in a context dominated by considerations of profit and economising. In contrast, we look in Chapter 4 at realms of voluntary association, at patterns of sociability which are not regulated by the rules of either market or state, though they may be rich in economic and political implications. We begin the chapter with a discussion of political parties: the intimate way in which they have been built into the structures of the state points to the difficulty of separating out these spheres. Parties and other formal associations are dominated by men, but women too get together regularly outside their households. Among both men and women, informal networks of friendship and trust seem more important than formally constituted groups. For these reasons, we are critical of the way the concept of 'civil society' has been used in recent academic work. It has too often been employed as a blanket term in opposition to the state. Such a stark binary opposition is unhelpful in understanding social life in modern Lazistan, even though such perceptions are sometimes articulated by local people themselves. We prefer a tripartite schema, in which state and market are mediated by a realm in which social behaviour is driven neither by the top-down pressures of the state, nor by the atomising consumerism of capitalist markets. Perhaps the best designation for this realm is simply community. Like state and market, this realm has both public and private aspects.

The tripartite schema is expanded to reach further into the private sphere in Chapter 5, where we consider how far an ideology of patriarchy, well developed in stereotypes and symbols, continues to characterise kinship relations in modern Lazistan. The state has intervened here too, but ineffectually. Traditional gender roles have been modified but not radically altered, though there is considerable variety within the region. The position of women varies according to social class, geographical location, education and other variables. The socialisation that takes place within the family in many respects pulls against the values indicated by the state. Families provide the bedrock of personal identity; the long-distance physical separation caused by migration does not necessarily weaken family ties, at least not in the short term.

These generalities are explored further in Chapter 6 with reference to marriage, the central institution of family life. A high proportion of contemporary marriages are the product of choices made by parents, often with the help of a 'go-between'. Many people still marry first cousins, in spite of campaigns by the state to discourage this practice. In this respect the people of Lazistan seem to be conservative, refusing the blandishments of western models of modernity. Traditional patterns of marriage payment, however, have been abandoned, and the rituals of most modern weddings are quite different from those of earlier periods. The incidence of divorce remains low, but an examination of the factors involved in divorce cases brings out some of the tensions of contemporary family life in this region.

State, market, civil institutions and family life all contribute to the constitution of persons and social relations in modern Lazistan, but none can serve as the base for an all-encompassing account, as the ultimate source of a world view. Each is better seen as offering a cluster of values and guidance for action: different groups will draw on them in different ways, and individuals will vary their practice in different situations and over the course of the life cycle. There is, however, one further candidate in this region for the position of ultimate source, the basis of a holistic cultural system. Islam, broached frequently in the earlier chapters, becomes the main focus of Chapter 7. Although its characteristics and overall strength vary considerably within the region, very few inhabitants of this region deny their Muslim identity. On all important occasions in family life, such as a bereavement, even those apparently at the secular end of the spectrum, working for the state, have recourse to their traditional religion. There are strong pressures to observe the fast during the month of Ramadan. Many parents send their children to religious education classes at their local mosque, and the state itself has introduced an avenue for secondary education based on Islamic principles. In some districts a significant slice of the private wealth created by the tea industry has gone into the construction of imposing new mosques.

In theory the state has control over all religious affairs and faith is a matter for the individual in the private sphere. The reality is much more complex. There is a popular stream of Islam that includes a range of practices of which better educated *imams* themselves thoroughly disapprove, but which they have difficulty in eradicating. The state has not been able to prevent the establishment in the region of a fundamentalist outpost, despite repeated harassment and obstruction; this too is discussed in Chapter 7. Extremist sentiments in the field of religion would seem to have been gaining ground in recent years, partly for reasons to do with the recent developments on marketplaces. These trends, evident in high levels of support for the religious parties in general elections, seem to be more than a short-term reaction to economic adversity, more than a 'moral panic' fomented by the media, though this is certainly a part of the picture. The unifying influence of religion is a continuing reminder of flaws in the republican programme of modernity and the *hubris* of its social engineers. Yet Islam is no monolith and some aspects of religion do not unify; the dominant religion has itself changed with the times, developing as an active and creative agent in social life, and not simply a brake or a resister.

This completes our attempt to outline the major factors that shape personal and social identities in modern Lazistan. Each one of them contains an amalgam of complex, sometimes contradictory meanings. They intersect in a multitude of ways, with patterning determined not only by age and gender, but also by geographical location within the region and by social class. In Chapter 8 we ask if attitudinal and behavioural variation are additionally influenced by ethnic differentiation. The Turkish modernist state has consistently downplayed and even denied the linguistic and cultural diversity of this region. We seek to understand the importance people themselves attach to their group allegiances, and find that this is not an aspect of state policy that has encountered significant resistance or even passive resentment. Language apart, and even this criterion has weakened substantially, there is virtually nothing to distinguish the various ethnic categories from each other. Outside Lazistan, however, in Istanbul and in Germany, some people are now asserting the rights of the Lazi to some form of recognition as a cultural minority. The issues involved here are tricky ones for anthropologists, whose general inclination to respect the views of the people who live in the communities they study may come into conflict with their wish to avert the destruction of linguistic diversity and the infringement of 'human rights'. There are signs that some new kind of ethnic consciousness could spread in the Lazuri-speaking parts of Lazistan. In this chapter, and again in the short Conclusion that follows, we feel obliged to take a further step and make it plain exactly where we stand on these sensitive matters. Our position is unlikely to satisfy either those Turkish officials who deny the existence of ethnic minorities, or those activists who see the Lazuri-speaking district as the homeland of a group with a culture quite different from that of the rest of the country.

The Conclusion presents a balance sheet for modernity in this region and recapitulates our problems with the concept of culture. The significance of the national institutions of Atatürk's republic can hardly be exaggerated. Virtually everybody feels at home in this country and identifies with it. Most of the social divisions of this region duplicate divisions of the national society. Most of the consumption trends of the national society find an echo here. At the same time local ties, *hemşerilik*, remain very important: people identify strongly with the specific hamlets and market centres where they and their forefathers were brought up, and they form groups on this basis in the diasporas. Alongside all these sources of social identity there may also be room, if the state allows, for the consolidation of a new and more explicit consciousness of ethnic identity. This can have little justification in terms of an anthropological argument based on contemporary *cultural* difference. A better case can be made by recalling the original *civilisational* goals of the Kemalists. However, the final word on whether Lazi and others achieve any form of recognition as distinct ethnic groups should be left to the people of Lazistan themselves.

2
State

Kemalism and nationalism

All human communities are undergoing social change all the time, but some experience change in more gradual, cumulative ways than others. For example, English society has undoubtedly been transformed in the last two centuries. Yet there is room to disagree about the decisive dates, the turning points. The continuities have been strong, at the level of political institutions as well as social practices.

In contrast, Turkey exemplifies the 'big bang' model of change. The creation of a secular republic in 1923 established new forms of government and society, based on principles entirely different from those of the Ottoman empire. The new state emerged after centuries of Ottoman decline. The more proximate antecedents were military defeat in the First World War, followed by a military victory over the Greeks by Mustafa Kemal, in what the Turks have ever since referred to as their War of National Independence. Mustafa Kemal became President of the new republic and quickly instigated breathtaking changes. He abolished the Caliphate, the centuries-old institution that had invested the Ottoman Sultan with the powers of God on earth. Religious courts were abolished. Kemal introduced a minimally modified version of the Swiss civil code in place of the accumulated traditions of Islamic law and transformed the state's administration to ensure better penetration into the grass roots of society, areas that had been effectively outside the reach of previous regimes. He had the capital moved from Istanbul to Ankara, where European town planners were called in to design a rational modern city around the ancient Anatolian nucleus.[1]

In the real history of large human communities, revolutions are seldom all that their proponents or opponents make them out to be. The need for reform of the Ottoman empire had been widely recognised long before its final collapse. Many of the policies implemented by Mustafa Kemal in the 1920s can be seen as a continuation of the programmes of the Young Turks between 1908 and 1918. Some had their roots in the intellectual movements of the Young Ottomans two

---

[1] The classical analysis of the emergence of modern Turkey is Lewis 1961, but see also Zürcher 1998. On Atatürk himself see the biography by Lord Kinross 1965; see also Özbudun and Kazancigil 1981. The main principles of the new system, as formulated by Atatürk himself in 1931, were republicanism, (*cumhuriyetçilik*), nationalism (*milliyetçilik*), populism (*halkçılık*), etatism (*devletçilik*), secularism (*laiklik*) and revolutionism (*devrimcilik*).

or three generations before. Their most basic characteristic, the look westwards for more viable models of government and society, can be traced back at least to the *Tanzimat* reform period, which opened in 1839.[2]

The 'big bang' proposition can also be questioned from the opposite angle: how effectively did the Kemalist programme break with traditions and how consistently was it implemented? The new state was highly centralised, focused on the person of Kemal (until his death in 1938), just as the previous empire had been focused on the person of the Sultan. Tentative experiments with political pluralism in the early 1930s were abandoned in favour of a one-party model that had some affinities to the communist model simultaneously emerging under Stalin. Just as some continuities in social life at the local level survived even the massive dislocation caused by Stalin's collectivisation, so the historians of modern Turkey, where no such dramatic interventions were ever attempted, can trace continuities in the social organisation and the mentalities of the inhabitants of the villages and small towns of Anatolia. After all, in a country that still had very little industry, this was where the vast majority of the thirteen million population lived.

Mustafa Kemal, known after 1934 as Atatürk, a surname that no one else was allowed to use, seems to have understood that to transform a society it was not enough to enact legislation and transform institutions at the national level. It was also necessary to transform the ways of everyday life, the 'world view' of the mass of the citizens. No area of social life was excluded from the Kemalists' ambitious plans. The weekly holiday was moved from Friday to Sunday and the Muslim lunar calendar definitively replaced by the Gregorian. The official method of oath taking dispensed with the Koran and invoked only the honour of the individual. The fez was abolished and although the headscarf was not generally proscribed, it was forbidden to state employees. The Kemalists tried hard to promote gender equality, not simply by legislating but by public campaigns against the patriarchal bias of the traditional society. In the words of a recent analyst, 'the position of women in society was the touchstone of Kemalist civilisation'.[3]

Atatürk recognised the importance of literacy and communication. The Arabic script was replaced in 1928 with an alphabet based on Roman letters which quickly became the medium of instruction in a new system of nationwide secular primary education.[4] The language itself, and not only the script in which it was written, was subject to radical changes from above, designed to purify it of a heritage of Arabic and Persian loanwords and constructions. The work of the Turkish Linguistic Society (*Türk Dil Kurumu*, founded 1932) was matched by the work of the Turkish Historical Society (*Türk Tarih Kurumu*, 1935), which promoted a version of Turkish national history that emphasised glorious origins in Central Asia and downplayed the many centuries of Islamic influence.[5] The new history was propagated not only to children through the new school system, but also to adults

---

[2] See in addition to Lewis 1961 and Zürcher 1998 the analyses of Berkes 1964 and Davison 1990.
[3] Göle 1996: 65. For a discussion of the early phase of Kemalist state feminism see Küper-Başgöl 1992.
[4] The classical study of the language and script reforms is Heyd 1954. For an extensive bibliography of this field see Brendemoen 1990a.
[5] See Landau 1995.

through the network of 'People's Houses' (*halk evleri*) that was established throughout the country.[6]

These policies encountered opposition, most seriously in 1925 among Kurdish
tribesmen in south-east Anatolia. In the case of Lazistan, it is reported that when
Mustafa Kemal visited Rize in 1924, he was told by local religious leaders of their
dissatisfaction with his reforms.[7] Apparently he countered with a robust defence
of his programme. Opposition would no doubt have been much greater had not
the poor infrastructure and communications of Anatolia impeded the full
implementation of the Kemalist agenda in the first decades of the Republic.[8]
Kemal had to be rowed ashore at Rize because Lazistan had no jetty at which his
boat could dock. The state that he created did not yet have the resources to
secure the full inculcation of the new national model.

Fuller implementation had to await the years following the Second World
War, which also saw significant modifications made to Atatürk's state. The most
obvious new departure was the acceptance of political pluralism. The opposition
Democratic Party triumphed in the General Election of 1950, and the Republican
People's Party founded by Atatürk struggled at the polls thereafter. From one
point of view, this political system was highly unstable. Elected governments were
displaced three times in twenty years by military coups. Levels of violence escalated,
especially in the late 1970s. Yet on each occasion the generals returned to
barracks and organised a relatively smooth transfer back to civilian rule.[9] The
names of political parties changed regularly, but there was a lot of continuity in
both the leaders themselves and the underlying forces they represented. Electoral
majorities were usually commanded by political parties that most European
commentators would classify as 'centre-right'. They emphasised the principles of
free enterprise and offered concessions to demands for greater recognition of
Islam in daily life. The Republican People's Party was more emphatically
committed to the Kemalist secular state. Under the leadership of Bülent Ecevit it
acquired in the 1970s a left-of-centre profile resembling in some respects that of
a western Social Democratic party. Other major parties were explicitly committed
to expanding the role of Islam and to Turkish nationalism.[10]

The party system underwent a partial overhaul in 1983, at the end of the
country's most recent period of military rule. The programme of the newly
established Motherland Party (*Anavatan Partisi*) led by Turgut Özal included a
more radical liberalisation of the economy than had been attempted by previous
governments. It also came to include a greater rapprochement with Islam. This
combination proved attractive in Lazistan. A young Member of Parliament for
Rize, Mesut Yılmaz, succeeded Özal as party leader and Prime Minister for much
of the 1990s.

Despite the instability of the party system, the Turkish economy has undergone continuous rapid transformation over the last half century. Rates of growth
have been consistently high, but so have rates of inflation (usually in excess of 70

[6] See Karpat 1963.
[7] This visit is commemorated in a small Atatürk Museum in Rize. See *Rize Il Yıllığı* 1973: 4–5; cf.
Yazıcı 1984: 41.
[8] This point was made repeatedly by Paul Stirling: see e.g. 1974, 1981.
[9] Cf. Gellner 1994b.
[10] For introductions to Turkey's party system see Dodd 1983, Hale 1981.

per cent) and population growth (from around thirteen million when the republic was founded it increased fivefold by the end of the century). In spite of (but perhaps in part also due to) efforts to distribute economic opportunities more equally, there has also been massive and unprecedented movement of population – mainly from the villages of Anatolia into the cities of the west, and above all into the mega-city of Istanbul. In contrast to socialist counterparts, the modern Turkish state never attempted seriously to regulate these processes of internal migration. It did make efforts to control the labour migration abroad that began in the direction of Germany in the 1960s and continued towards Middle Eastern countries in later decades, but even these efforts enjoyed only limited success. The state's modernisation of transport networks (with significant assistance, especially in the 1950s, from the United States) facilitated these migration processes.

The modern state depends upon easy mobility, geographical as well as social, to weld its citizens into a national community. The development of political pluralism and the spread of schools, roads, electricity, radios and television all played a part in realising this goal in Turkey after 1950. Schematically we can summarise by suggesting that the first quarter of a century of Kemalism was taken up largely with institutional reform at the centre, while the second quarter saw the changes disseminated throughout the country in the framework of a classical modernisation drive. The third quarter has witnessed the continuation of these policies, but also increasing signs of tension and conflict.

One central strand of continuity running throughout these three periods has been nationalism (milliyetçilik), perhaps the most vital ingredient in the modern package introduced by Atatürk. Other ingredients, notably secularism (laiklik), were always going to be difficult for most of the population to consume, but by building up pride in Turkish national identity the Kemalists could inject a new element into the social edifice, a new sense of social identity. It is encapsulated in the most famous of all Atatürk's sayings, inscribed in many public places and often quoted in speeches: Ne mutlu Türküm diyene ('How proud/happy/fortunate I am to be a Turk'). Atatürk himself has remained at the epicentre of nationalist rituals. His statue can be found in every town, his image on every important official's wall, in miniature on postage stamps and massively enlarged as a legendary figure cut into limestone hillsides. Everyone knows of his concrete historical achievements, yet there is also a sense in which he exists 'outside time', a symbol assuming mythological qualities.[11]

With certain obvious exceptions, notably among sections of the Kurdish population, the Kemalist national ideology has been very successfully disseminated. Some people in Lazistan, perhaps especially for the benefit of foreign anthropologists, occasionally made unfavourable comparisons with other parts of the world, notably Europe and America. Yet at the same time, even though many are aware that Greek and other languages were widely spoken along the Black Sea coast until quite recently, and many can trace their family origins back to territories that lie outside the present boundaries of the modern Turkish state, virtually all the residents of Lazistan consider themselves to be Turks and evaluate this identity positively. They take this identity to a large extent for granted. It is axiomatic that there always existed a Turkish nation, and that it

[11] Tapper and Tapper 1987a: 63, 70.

has been settled and consolidated in its present territory for many centuries. This, as Ernest Gellner often pointed out, is the basic conjuring trick of the nationalist – successfully to persuade the members of the nation that they have *always* been exactly that, even when the latent essence of the identity was not manifested in its present political form.[12]

Gellner defines nationalism as 'a political principle which maintains that similarity of culture is the basic social bond. Whatever principles of authority may exist between people depend for their legitimacy on the fact that the members of the group concerned are of the same culture (or, in nationalist idiom, of the same "nation").'[13] According to Gellner, all human beings have always lived in more or less clearly bounded cultures, but cultural unity throughout a territory has been historically exceptional in preindustrial empires such as that of the Ottomans. The modern alignment of culture and politics implied radical change. It was relatively easy to achieve in Germany and Italy, which had a significant measure of cultural unity before they achieved political unification in the late nineteenth century. However, when Massimo D'Azeglio declared 'We have made Italy, now we have to make Italians', he was drawing attention to the obvious fact that a great deal more work had to be done before the citizens of the new state would acquire the consciousness of belonging to a single national community.

The Turkish case is somewhat different and particularly striking because of the way the new nationalism emerged from the ruins of the Ottoman empire. We noted the main organisational principles of this empire in the Introduction. It was not based on any recognition of nationality in the modern sense. Between the emergence of the Greek state in 1828 and the final demise of the empire the Ottomans fought rearguard actions against numerous other nationalisms. The forging of the Turkish nation, which finally emerged from the ashes of the Ottoman empire, was complicated by the fact that the Ottoman elites had minimised the Turkish origins of their culture. 'Turk' was often used by elites in a pejorative sense, to refer to uncultivated rural folk. Yet it was on the basis of a primitive peasantry which still lacked any conception of a national identity that Atatürk decided to build the new nation-state. We prefer to speak of a 'state-nation', inverting the usual formulation in order to emphasise that this nation was called into existence by its state.[14]

Apart from the linguistic purification and the new histories already noted, the new nationalism was propagated by a new, secular ritual calendar, centred around themes of national liberation.[15] The spread of new communications technologies ensured that, during the second republican generation, those unable to witness the power of the new state in the big cities on the major holidays would have the spectacle and commentary broadcast into their homes, thanks to the state's control of radio and television. State cultural policies also promoted nation-

[12] See Gellner 1965, 1983, 1997. For a recent critical assessment of Gellner's writings on nationalism see Hall 1997.

[13] Gellner 1983: 1.

[14] For an innovative analysis of the Turkish state from a political science perspective see Heper 1985. Limitations of the rational bureaucratic state, and in particular its inability to replace the older sources of emotional identity that it swept aside, are brilliantly explored by Mardin 1989.

[15] For a rich account of this early period by a foreign observer see Webster 1939.

building in less obvious ways, for example through the support given to styles of classical music and folk dancing that were considered to be 'authentic', while other styles were rejected.[16]

The state was never the only actor in these processes. The gradual emergence of a privately controlled mass circulation press also did much to foster the new sense of common identity. National and international sports competitions played a role. Labour emigration to Europe and later to various parts of the Middle East gave millions the experience of radically different cultures, and of being classified as Turkish by the natives of those other countries. The growth of the tourist industry had similar effects in many parts of Turkey itself.

The precise contents of this evolving national identity are elusive and ultimately unimportant for this study. When pressed to define their 'national character' many Turks do not find it easy to articulate answers, apart from a few generalities about being hospitable, caring, decent people. The *Türk milleti* is usually imagined as a community of descent, and markers are found in the realms of food, clothing and religion, as well as in language and history. The qualities associated with Turkishness often include ideas such as honour and respect for the integrity of family life, which they may explicitly contrast with degenerate values in western and in communist societies. Some people acknowledge the tension in taking pride in Turkish values, such as the purity of their women, which are at the same time 'backward' (*geri kalmış*) in comparison with more 'enlightened' (*aydın*) attitudes in western countries. One common idea, much cited by both politicians and ordinary people, is that Turkey's key role is to serve as a bridge between East and West, or between Christian Europe and the Islamic world.

In a comparative framework, Turkish nationalism can be viewed as a mixture of 'French' ideals of unitary state-building and 'German' traditions that emphasise the cultural unity of the nation as a common descent-group.[17] The development of the latter, more 'ethnic' variant of nationalism led to grand claims about the continuity of the Turks on Anatolian soil from the times of ancient civilisations. Yet simultaneously it was claimed that the Turks originated as heroic nomadic warriors on the steppes of Central Asia. This contradiction was gradually resolved by distancing Turkish nationalism from extreme theories of the blood line and racism. Most Kemalists seem nowadays to accept that people of other backgrounds have mixed with and been absorbed into Turkish stock over the centuries. However, the ideology has not recognised the persistence of other, non-Turkish traditions within the boundaries of the Turkish state (apart from the small groups of non-Muslims who remained, mostly in the major western cities, as a memorial to Ottoman religious diversity after the Lausanne Treaty of 1923). The state for many years classified some twelve million Kurds as 'mountain Turks'. The vast bulk of the population is officially considered to be not just citizens of the Turkish republic, forming a single *halk* ('people' in the sense of the French *peuple*), but also a single *millet*, no longer understood in the old Ottoman sense of a religious affiliation, but as an ethnic group ('people' in the sense of the German *Volk*). For

[16] See Stokes 1992.

[17] The major figure in the early promulgation of Kemalist national ideology was Ziya Gökalp, who was primarily influenced by the French tradition of *civilisation* rather than the German tradition of *Kultur*. See Gökalp 1959.

Plate 2.1 Equestrian Atatürk next to the central mosque, Arhavi.

Plate 2.2 Children's Day parade (23 April) in Pazar, 1992. Below the state officials on the tribune stand young women members of the radical Islamic group.

many citizens, this ideology is much too far from the reality to be understood in a literal sense.[18] However the effects of three generations of ideological fictions have been significant. There are nowadays many millions of Turks who have grown up with little or no awareness of ethnic diversity in their country, present or past; many of those who do have such an awareness tend to amnesia, to suppression or elision of differences that cannot be expressed in public social interaction.

How has Turkish nationalism been developed and deployed in the context of Lazistan? The basic patterns have been the same as everywhere else. Each town has its own liberation day ceremonies, marking the retreat of occupying Russian forces in the spring of 1918. Historians have argued that, like the Kurds, both Lazi and Hemşinli are really people of 'pure' Turkish stock.[19] They may acknowledge linguistic differences but treat these as accidental and insignificant acquisitions by Turkish tribes in the course of their migrations. This distortion of the past may not be very significant in practice, since although the leading proponent of these views has lectured in Lazistan, and copies of his articles are available in the library in Rize, very few inhabitants know anything at all about him or his ideas. Regional history is not taught in schools and there have been no attempts to popularise extreme nationalist views. Nevertheless, the dissemination of nationalist ideology has been effective. Lazi who are uncertain or indifferent as to the origins of their group tend to be vociferous in condemning those who undertake action thought to be prejudicial to the indivisible unity of Atatürk's state. This criticism is regularly prompted by the continuing tragic violence in South-Eastern regions of Anatolia. Hardly anyone we encountered in Lazistan expressed any sympathy for the cause of the Kurdish 'terrorists'. Instead people support their government. Young men killed during their military service are treated as national heroes and martyrs, and their graves are decorated with the national flag and other symbols. It is not only state officials who vigorously condemn separatism (*bölücülük*) at every available opportunity; other, ordinary people sometimes misinterpreted our efforts to document ways in which Lazi might differ from Hemşinli and other neighbours. Discussion was then brusquely terminated with the assertion that Lazi, Hemşinli and Turks were all one and the same people.

We shall return to the issue of ethnicity in Chapter 8, but remind the reader at this point of the problems we faced in this field as foreign researchers. Turkish nationalism was by no means the main focus of our research. However, since we wished to consider categories of group difference in Lazistan that, according to nationalist ideology, did not exist, we could not avoid its effects. In one awkward incident when we were living in Pazar in 1992, an acquaintance greeted us in his shop one morning with the news that a man (he would not name him, but used the term *vatandaş*, 'a compatriot') from a village we had visited the previous day had alleged that, in the course of a conversation, we had compared the cause of the Lazi to that of the Kurds. This was nonsense, but we were unsure how to handle the situation. For a moment we were suddenly afraid of the power of the Turkish state – to put an end to our research, and perhaps worse. We decided to

[18] See Andrews 1989 and forthcoming for comprehensive surveys.
[19] See Kırzıoğlu 1946, 1972, 1976, 1986, 1990. For a critical discussion see Bellér-Hann 1995a.

go directly to our chief patron, the *kaymakam*. It was the eve of the holiday to mark the end of the holy month of Ramadan, and so the chief of police and other local dignitaries were guests of the *kaymakam* when he received us in his spacious office. We blurted out the whole story, protesting our innocence of the allegation. There were murmurs of surprise from the audience at the seriousness of the accusation, and perhaps also at the fact that we had chosen to bring it to their attention ourselves in this very direct way. After only the briefest of pauses the *kaymakam* assured us that we had done the right thing in coming to him. We finally relaxed, and heard nothing further about the matter.

Administration and control

The *kaymakam* is the key local official in a system of state administration that has not changed fundamentally since Kemal's adoption of the French prefect model in 1924.[20] In this section we describe its structures and take a look at the personnel who represent the central authority and at their interaction with the local environment.

The *kaymakam* is usually to be found behind a large desk in the largest room in the Government Building (*Hükümet Konağı*) that is generally located in the centre of the county town. On the wall behind him, gazing down over the *kaymakam*'s every action, is a large portrait of Atatürk. We experienced this gaze on very many occasions, because the support of the *kaymakam* is essential if foreigners wish to stay for extended periods and enquire into local social conditions. Both inside the office, which is large enough for several visitors to be received simultaneously, and in the anterooms, we had some opportunity to observe how the *kaymakam* works. His (there were no females in this role in Lazistan at the time of our research) main role seemed to be that of the 'fixer', the broker whose telephone word is necessary and sufficient to unblock bottlenecks wherever they occur in his county, in private as well as public sectors. The *kaymakam* needs above all to have the social skills to maintain a network of connections with other people of influence in his realm. It helps if he has a wife of similar temperament who, whether or not she takes a job locally, is willing to socialise with these people away from their offices, often providing hospitality in the *kaymakam*'s official residence.

Most of the *kaymakam*s we knew were young men, aged between twenty-five and forty. They had a vigorous, 'can-do' approach to their work. None had family roots in the region, for this is prohibited. At the end of a three-year posting they would be moved on, perhaps to the other end of the country. This short term of duty clearly limited the ability of a *kaymakam* to get to know his county well. Nevertheless some of them plunged themselves into local causes with impressive dedication, taking up advocacy roles both at the level of the province and also with central government. For example, one *kaymakam* took the initiative in publishing an information booklet about his county (including biographies of current state officials, in hierarchical order). He also campaigned successfully,

[20] See Lewis 1961: 356–94. The Ottoman state relied heavily on local *agha* families, some of whom were able to retain their influential positions in the early republican period. Cf. Meeker 1972.

both inside and outside his county, to raise the funds needed to provide more ecologically sound methods of rubbish disposal for the county town; educational schemes were also close to his heart. His methods of fundraising were various. For example, before authorising the opening of a new cafe, of which he thought his town had more than enough already, he would 'invite' the applicant to make a donation worth some 25 dollars. Not everyone approves, but such efforts can earn a *kaymakam* the respect and cooperation of local people.

These officials are the formal embodiments of Kemalism. As representative of the state the *kaymakam* presides over a number of public ceremonies, usually held either in the centre of town close to the Atatürk statue, or at the sports stadium (if the town has one), or at the largest school playground in the town. Other state officials join the *kaymakam* on the podium as national flags are paraded by school children, who sing patriotic songs, recite poems and perform folk dances. An exhortatory speech by the *kaymakam* is the climax. The *kaymakams* we knew carried out these ceremonial tasks punctiliously. They undergo years of training at university level, including exposure to very different conceptions of local government and administration. Whereas Atatürk looked mainly to France and Germany for his models, later generations have looked more to the English-speaking countries. The late Turgut Özal himself was partly trained in the United States, and his governments sent large numbers of mid-career administrators, including some of the *kaymakams* we knew in Lazistan, on intensive courses of English language study, sometimes with a leavening of 'management studies' or 'administrative science'. During the period of up to one year that the official spent abroad he was also expected to note how local organisations functioned and how services were provided. The assumption seemed to be that he would imbibe an alternative approach, which would then feed into his mode of operation when he returned to Turkey to resume his regular career.[21]

The *kaymakam* stands at the apex of county level officialdom. Only the *vali* at the level of the province stands between him and central government. Each county centre has many other officials working for the state and ancillary organisations. The top level includes judges and prosecutors, the directors of tax offices, tea factories, schools, hospitals, agricultural and forestry units, banks, police, *jandarma* and military garrisons. Many of these officials, particularly the more senior, will serve relatively short terms of duty in Lazistan before being posted elsewhere. The majority of those on these public sector payrolls live in state-owned apartments (*lojman*) in the county town. To some extent they form a distinct social group, a colony of officials separated from the local people among whom they work. However, for most officials and employees the demarcation lines are by no means sharp. Many of them are local people, who (though they

---

[21] The cases that we came across left us with some doubts about the efficacy of this strategy. Some officials did not thrive in provincial English towns, separated from their families, particularly if they had not studied English before and found themselves in classrooms together with younger, more agile minds. Some made few contacts outside those with fellow-Turks, and they learned little about British or American life during their time in those countries. In some cases, perhaps especially where the official's own family and upbringing in Turkey had already exposed him to western values and behaviour, the experience was enjoyable as well as career-enhancing. But many officials nowadays come from modest backgrounds in the smaller towns of Anatolia, and this enforced acquaintance with the west through educational secondments could have distinctly negative effects, the very opposite of those intended.

may still choose to live in subsidised state accommodation) also own private houses and tea gardens. Some, though not of local origin, have married here and have come to feel fully at home. It is true that some representatives of the state build high walls that serve to exclude the local society. The headquarters of the Tea Corporation in Rize had a luxurious restaurant facility for its senior staff. It was open to visiting researchers, but not to the ordinary public. The small town of Pazar had a NATO early-warning radar station nearby. Its officers could enjoy an exclusive *gazino* in the very centre of town. The facilities were just visible across high fences from the public park nearby, but in this case not even foreign researchers could gain access. Some officials were criticised or ridiculed for their inability to manage a hundred-yard walk to their nearest grocery store without calling up their official chauffeur. These, however, were the exceptions. Most state officials interacted with a wide range of people. Age, gender and class factors seemed to matter more than the fact of being in public sector employment.

The wives of short-stay government officials, especially if they do not work themselves, are sometimes accused of bringing 'bad customs' and moral decay into the local community. Although part of the local elite for the duration of their stay, officers' wives are often singled out as more immoral than the others by more conservative, religious families. According to this stereotype, most army officers are from very poor families or they are orphans raised by the state.[22] This is a popular explanation for their dedication to the state and to Kemalist principles. Yet even those who hold this view also admire and respect the military and the role that it has played under Kemalism.[23]

At lower levels, state presence in the countryside differs slightly from its high profile in the town. The smallest urban unit is the neighbourhood (*mahalle*). Its residents elect councillors, generally persons of repute who are nominated through party lists. The municipality (*belediye*) is headed by a mayor, normally a leading figure in the party that fares best in the elections. He (again, we were not aware of any women holding this position in Lazistan at the time of our work) has responsibility for the permanent officials of the municipality, including planning and infrastructural development.

The basic unit of administration in the countryside is the village (*köy*). Each village has a headman (*muhtar*) who receives a small income from the state and is expected to act on its behalf in certain matters, notably confirming the names of young men liable for military service. He is assisted by village elders, and sometimes by a deputy and by a watchman (*bekçi*) whom he himself can appoint. Political considerations may play a role in the election of the *muhtar*, but personal qualities are usually of greater significance. The office does not itself carry much prestige and is not much sought after. A *muhtar* prepared to serve further terms of office is often unopposed, unless he has done something to upset a significant section of his constituency.[24] The presence of a mobile rural security force, the *jandarma*, in each county ensures that any outbreak of violence, however remote

---

[22] Sometimes they are even called *piç*, 'bastard'.

[23] Military service is generally viewed as a desirable part of male education and conscription is marked with extensive sending-off parties, in effect a life-cycle ritual, both at home and on a larger scale the next day in the county town.

[24] For an ethnographic account of the status and activities of the *muhtar* see Schiffauer 1987: 75–81.

the location, is now speedily dealt with. Law and order has not been seriously disturbed in most parts of Lazistan at any point in the republican period. Patterns of feuding that were widespread in the past have died out almost completely in the last generation.

Recognition of the village as a unit was part of the state's strategy for imposing its order on a complex settlement structure in which most of the non-urban populations lived in small hamlets scattered across the mountains and valleys. Sometimes one strategically positioned hamlet was designated as the village centre, lending its name to the whole administrative entity. In Sümer, the village we know best, a cluster close to the coast on the main track through the valley was selected for this role. The state decided to open a post-office here and to build a large new school. This encouraged others to build new houses and open shops here, and not in the more distant hamlets.

Like any modern state, the Turkish state attempts to keep track of its population. Most people have occasional need to visit the Population Office (*Nüfus Müdürlüğü*) of the Government Building, where records of births, marriages and deaths are meticulously maintained (*muhtars* play a limited role in this domain, but all data are ultimately controlled from this office). Identity cards record one's place of permanent residence and other personal data. However, effective surveillance is difficult to achieve. The records maintained in the Population Office often misrepresented the identities people declared for themselves and acknowledged in others. It was difficult for us to trace genealogical links in cases where close kin had opted for different names when first required to adopt surnames in 1935; sometimes these names were changed back again later, with or without official registration. Birth dates are often filed late and it is easy to substitute a later date. Officials, too, are quite candid about manipulating their birth dates in order to facilitate such matters as university entrance or conscription.

The limits of effective control and the confusions that can result when the state's norms diverge from those observed by the community are abundantly illustrated in the records of the county courts. These too are generally located on the premises of the Government Building. Judges, attorneys and clerks all have their offices here. During a session the corridors are typically filled with the family and relatives of plaintiffs and accused. From this local court, serious cases are referred upwards to provincial level. Kemalist legal officers have a clear picture of the state laws they are meant to uphold, but they are again and again obliged to come to terms with local custom. For example, the state recognises only marriages registered in the civil office. If a man takes a second or even a third wife according to Muslim law, such religious marriages have no force and no property claims arising from them will be recognised by the courts. This law is intended, at least in part, to improve women's position. However, given that the practice continues on a modest scale, as we shall see in Chapter 6, the effect may be a more radical disempowerment of the second wife, whose children are registered as the offspring of the first, legal wife.[25] The danger that her position under the new civil code could be worse than in the framework of custom and tradition is in practice circumvented by special property transfers. This is one of several fields in which,

[25] Also noted by Lewis 1961: 267. The practice persisted in Lazistan into the 1990s.

three quarters of a century after the introduction of the Swiss code, the *pays réel* and the *pays légal* remain far apart.[26]

Regional development

From the discussion so far it might be concluded that the modern Turkish state is little more than a powerful bureaucratic apparatus concerned with control and surveillance. However, it was also the prime agent in republican development strategy. The construction of new administrative buildings, schools, clinics and hospitals, banks and forestry headquarters all had an impact on the regional economy. Fishermen were assisted by the construction of new harbours. Road construction had far-reaching effects on these previously isolated valleys.[27] The main road over the Kaçkar Mountains to Ispir and Erzurum, designed by a European contractor in the Ottoman period, was finally completed by 'volunteer' Rize labourers in the 1930s.[28] Completion of the asphalt road along the coast in 1967 (most sections were ready well before the opening of the Arhavi tunnel in this year) both transformed the speed of communications within the region and prised it open to the wider world. In some districts this road required the draining of substantial areas of previously unusable land that could now be effectively exploited. The construction of roads up the major valleys gave most interior villages ready access to the coast and their market centres.

The rural economy in the early republican period was still primarily directed toward subsistence and the staple was still maize. A wooden plough was pulled by an ox (seldom a horse) and on some of the steepest slopes all of the field preparation was done by hand.[29] Women took surplus vegetables to the local marketplace, if it was close enough. Occasionally they would sell a calf or a cow. Transhumance was important, especially for inland communities. Most households were largely self-sufficient but some remained dependent on the patronage of their local *agha*. Levels of trade were probably little changed from the previous century. Hazelnuts and a little fruit were exported, but most of the income accrued to a handful of merchant families, including a German concern which exported apples from Pazar.

The major contribution of the state to the development of Lazistan's economy was to transform this backward 'peasant' economy into one in which the majority of households became prosperous through planting their land with tea bushes and selling the fresh leaves for cash, three or four times in each summer

[26] For cases from other parts of Turkey see Starr 1992, Schiffauer 1987, Yalçın-Heckmann 1991, Magnarella 1998. The gap between *pays réel* and *pays légal* is regularly commented on from a different perspective by organisations such as Amnesty International. However, issues of human rights infringements, whether concerning so-called political prisoners or more generally, are not discussed in this region. Among those aware of Turkey's negative image in this field, most blame an unwarranted campaign by foreign enemies to discredit and weaken their country.

[27] Topography rendered Lazistan impenetrable by that other great symbol of modernisation, the railway, which could come no closer than Samsun. On the main communication routes of pre-modern times see Bryer and Winfield 1985: 17–65.

[28] Karpuz: 1993: 14.

[29] According to Feurstein this plough (*karasapan*) was never used by the Lazi. He sees this as an ethnic characteristic, the reluctance being justified in terms of disdain for such a method of working the soil (Feurstein 1983: 36). However, in the coastal counties many elderly people confirmed widespread use of the *karasapan* in their childhood, i.e. in the period before tea was introduced.

season, to the state. This new tea economy, made possible by the distinctive climate of Lazistan, is a striking example of 'top-down' development.[30] Its origins are obscure. It seems that tea production was unknown in Ottoman Lazistan, though by the end of the nineteenth century it was already well established in neighbouring regions of the Caucasus. The initiator of experiments undertaken in the Rize area in the 1920s was Zihni Derin, not a local man but one of the first cohort of Kemalist teachers posted to this region by the new state. Trials using seed imported from Georgia yielded promising results and by the end of the 1930s several small-scale factories had been established. In 1940 the Ankara parliament passed a law to promote and regulate the growth of the infant industry. However, it was only after the Democratic Party assumed power in 1950 that the new product made inroads into the subsistence production of small-scale farmers and spread rapidly throughout the region. This party was ideologically committed to the support of the rural population and family enterprise. Moreover, by this period the state was in a good position to provide the investments necessary for a viable tea industry. In addition to the infrastructure improvements already noted, allowing transportation of the final product all over the country, the state built the factories needed to process the leaves produced by smallholders, and it trained the workforce needed to operate them.

The structure of the agro-industry that resulted was unusual in the international context. Elsewhere, for example in South Asia, tea has more commonly been grown on large-scale plantations. In the Soviet Union, following collectivisation, it was grown on large-scale farms owned by the state. Where tea is grown on small parcels of land, as in parts of East Africa, the factories which process the product are usually privately owned (nowadays they are likely to be components of multinational corporations). The Turkish combination of a smallholder base, giving households incentives for efficiency and private accumulation, with a state monopoly over leaf purchase and processing, seemed for a long time to be an unqualified success story. It could be taken to exemplify the Turkish model of modernity, based upon strong direction from the state coupled with (this is the contrast to collectivisation in the socialist bloc) the harnessing of family energies at the grass roots.

This development depended on state action to protect its infant industry from foreign competition. Supplies of tea were potentially available from other parts of the world. According to the arbiters of taste and quality at the epicentre of the trade in London, the Turkish product has never compared favourably in terms of quality with rival products. In terms of cost, it is plain that a country in which plucking is confined to the summer season (May–October) is unlikely to be able to compete effectively with countries in the tropics where plucking is possible all the year round (and where, moreover, the costs of labour tend to be far lower). It was therefore necessary for the Turkish state to exclude these rivals from its home market. This was effectively managed over many decades, during which the Turkish consumers became accustomed to the Lazistan product. The state did not need to define, let alone enforce, quality standards.

[30] For further detail on tea development see Hann 1990a. The state's role in the promotion of economic development is well discussed by Keyder 1987.

How was the new crop disseminated in Lazistan? It seems to have spread by example outwards from Rize, as new factories were built and technical advice was made available by the state's agricultural experts. Many people rushed to convert their former maize fields to tea without seeking any inputs from experts. They simply planted whatever cuttings they could get hold of, on any land they had available. The dominant incentive was financial, for the prices offered by the state in the 1950s and 1960s for the green leaves compared extremely favourably with the profitability of other crops (not only those that could be grown in this region but also nationwide). Looking back a generation later, people often reckon in terms of the amount of sugar they could obtain for each kilo of tea that they sold. The ratio was so favourable in the early phase that people became increasingly content to meet their subsistence needs through the purchase on the market of produce imported into the region, in order to maximise the production of tea leaves on their own plots. Maize bread, previously the staple, was rapidly displaced by the standard wheat varieties found throughout the country.

Tea was adopted with enthusiasm, but not all parts of the region were equally suitable for it. More remote upland areas were disadvantaged. They campaigned as vigorously as they could for the roads and the factories that would give them a share in the new wealth. The production area was gradually extended to the limits of ecological viability. By 1980, the state's Tea Corporation (*Çay Kurumu*) had 45 factories, which altogether processed 476,084 tons of green leaves, supplied by 178,805 registered growers. The official statistics for the area under cultivation and the total output of processed tea are shown in Table 2.1.

Table 2.1 Garden area and output of processed tea, 1940–1999.[31]

Year	Area of tea gardens (hk)	Production (tons)
1940	990	0
1950	2992	207
1960	13488	5815
1970	27888	33431
1980	53811	91778
1990	90500	177219
1999	76700	153000

Apart from producing a new income stream for the growers of tea leaves, the consolidation of this industry brought many spin-off benefits to the people of Lazistan. The factories required labour, though only during the plucking season, which was prescribed to last 120 days, spread between early May and October. These factory jobs offered a degree of security and carried a range of fringe entitlements, from supplies of processed tea to rights to medical care and a pension. Almost all of these jobs went to men. For the first time, large numbers of

---

[31] We thank Aziz Vanlı for helping us to compile this table. The decline in both garden area and production in the 1990s is due in part to a large-scale programme of pruning the bushes; additional factors are discussed in the following chapter.

Lazistan men had a source of stable waged employment within their native region, an alternative to labour migration. The industry also brought benefits to local businesses, for the state did not attempt to manage every aspect of the industry itself. In particular, transportation of the leaves from rural collection points to the factories was generally contracted out to local hauliers. Other small businessmen, though not directly involved in the industry at all, benefited from the money generated by tea, which was spent on new housing, furniture, sanitation equipment, clothing and a burgeoning range of consumer durables.

For all this to happen, Lazistan tea had to be a success with consumers nation-wide. The earlier coffee culture did not disappear entirely, but coffee cannot be produced inside Turkey and the tariffs were kept high. In periods of economic stringency it disappeared altogether from the market. Tea was much cheaper, and it was rapidly adopted throughout the country. It was distributed by the state in the same way as tobacco and other monopoly products. The tea house (*çayhane*) became the main form of sociability for men in the public sphere. Tea also became the main beverage at home, both for ordinary everyday consumption and for entertaining. Compared to coffee, its impact was egalitarian. It is not too far-fetched to see in this humble product a symbol of the modern democratic ideals of Kemalism, designed to replace an older social order in which consumption patterns were heavily differentiated according to rank by a new society of funda-mentally equal citizens. Certainly the social impact of the new industry seemed to be egalitarian in the region where it was produced, at least in the short term. Thanks to the new cash crop, many households were able to escape from poverty, long-term dependencies and ties of political patronage to former *agha* families. Indeed, this term became rapidly obsolete in most districts. In short, the general adoption of tea enabled rural Lazistan to approximate the goal of the Democratic Party, the establishment of a society of independent small-scale producers.

In other respects, however, the impact of the industry was less egalitarian. First, it created new spatial inequalities within Lazistan by conferring advantages upon localities close to the coast, where communications were better and leaf yields higher. Yields declined significantly at higher altitudes, and for some people (including disproportionate numbers of the Hemşinli) tea was not an economic proposition at all. This was a reversal of the previous pattern, in which the pastorally oriented settlements of the interior had held an economic advantage over more densely populated areas closer to the coast.

Second, the tea industry introduced a new class of managers into the social structure of the region: the white-collar officials, many of them strangers to Lazistan, who ran the factories and staffed the Tea Corporation headquarters in Rize.

Third, by giving the jobs in the new factories to men, the introduction of tea entrenched an older division of labour whereby the majority of field tasks continued to fall on women. This division of labour was sometimes rationalised in terms of nimble female fingers being better suited to the delicate task of plucking the leaves. Men were generally responsible for the initial establishment of tea gardens and for constructing collection points. They often took charge of the final delivery to the Tea Corporation at this collection point. But women have always been more prominent in routine plucking and in getting the leaves to these points. We shall discuss this division of labour further in Chapter 5.

Fourth, the socially egalitarian effects of the new crop proved in some areas to be short-lived as the owners of larger tracts of land, often former *aghas*, built up tea gardens in excess of what they could cultivate using family labour alone. The need for additional labour was mostly met by temporary migrants who flocked to the more productive areas from adjacent regions of the coast, from the less well endowed parts of Lazistan itself, from the Anatolian interior, and finally, in the 1990s, from the successor countries of the former Soviet Union. Some worked as pluckers for a fixed daily sum in cash, but sharecropping soon became the main mechanism for incorporating outside labour, particularly in the less densely populated eastern districts. Some sharecroppers (*yarıcı*) came, like the day labourers (*işçi*), for the plucking season only. But increasing numbers of them settled permanently in accommodation provided by tea garden owners (often the old family house, while the owners moved into a new modern dwelling close by). A few were able to buy land, build their own houses and become effectively integrated into their new places of residence. For the great majority, the high price of land and its general lack of availability on the market meant that this was never a feasible option. These people came in a short time to form a new rural proletariat.[32] They made their living not through the ownership of gardens but solely through the expenditure of their labour in plucking. Their remuneration was usually 50 per cent of the sale value of the leaves, supplemented by free accommodation and access to a small subsistence plot for vegetable production. The owners of large gardens, some of them absent for much or even all of the year, formed a *rentier* or leisure class, assured of a steady income stream once their bushes were established, without any significant further financial outlay. This was one of the main unintended consequences of the state's development of the tea industry of Lazistan. It was the predictable outcome of strategies followed by the traditionally dominant *agha* stratum to re-establish its superiority. It did so, as in the past, by exploiting the labour power of others, the difference being that this was now the labour of immigrant sharecroppers rather than that of local villagers.[33]

By the 1970s a number of other trends were giving the state controllers of the tea industry more immediate cause for concern. The price paid for green leaves was fixed by the state at the beginning of each season. Owing to high inflation it was raised every year, but relative to the prices of other products, the remuneration to the growers of tea leaves became gradually less attractive. By the 1970s a certain disillusionment seems to have set in. Expectations of further economic improvements were not being fulfilled. Work for one hundred and twenty days was not enough to generate the incomes to which people now aspired, and new opportunities for labour migration, notably to Germany, came to be seen as the more attractive option. In these circumstances the people of Lazistan began to

---

[32] This proletariat was then available to meet the needs of other rural families which did not have large holdings, but which lacked labour for one reason or another, usually migration. In the past, temporary shortages of labour were usually resolved informally within the kin group or neighbourhood, but there has been increasing readiness in all categories of garden owner to hire labour from members of this new underclass.

[33] These inequalities are further explored in Hann 1990b.

Plate 2.3 Women queuing to sell tea to the state.

Plate 2.4 The headquarters of the Tea Corporation in Rize, decked in flags to mark a national holiday.

subvert state control over their main crop. They could do this with relative ease by flouting the stipulated rules for the sale of green leaves, a subversion that became widespread when local ironmongers perfected a new tool to replace nimble female fingers. Gathering leaves with a pair of small shears (*makas*) instead of by hand made it possible to harvest large quantities of leaves with much less effort. In theory, only the top two leaves and a bud should have been accepted by the Tea Corporation's controllers, the officials whose job it was to check the quality of the leaves delivered at the collection points. But these experts (*ekisper*), the lowest level of employee in the Corporation, were themselves local people, usually with gardens of their own. They had little sympathy with their bosses and were inclined to turn a blind eye, as growers sought to increase their incomes by delivering greatly increased quantities of inferior leaf. This led to a crisis in the industry, since the factories were unable to cope with the quantities of leaf purchased. Large quantities had to be dumped into the Black Sea, and the quality of the final product declined significantly.

This process of subversion was accentuated by the worsening political instability of the 1970s. The parties that alternated in government vied with each other in offering higher prices for the leaf product. The result of this rivalry was only to increase the spiral of inflation. No government was strong enough to avert the irrational processes set in motion by the growers' evasion (perfectly rational from their own selfish point of view) of the quality controls. Only the military intervention of 1980 brought a reassertion of the power of the state. Its leader, General Kenan Evren, made a speech in Rize in which he attacked the tea growers for serving the rest of the country with an inferior product. His rhetoric was backed up by action from the Tea Corporation, which lowered the prices paid to growers, forbade the use of shears and introduced a quota system (*kontenjan*) to ensure that the supplies it received from its producers would not in future exceed the processing capacity of its factories.[34] The result of these measures was a massive decline in production and incomes for growers in 1981. In 1983, the year of our first fieldwork in the region, the rules introduced by the military rulers were still in place. There was still a good deal of anger and frustration among growers, who were continuing to undermine central policies by any means possible (e.g. giving fraudulent figures for their tea acreage, in order to circumvent the effects of the quota restrictions).

Under the Motherland Party government that took office late in 1983, state control of the tea industry was modified by an opening to market forces. We shall outline the most recent twists in the story of the tea industry in the following chapter. But the state Tea Corporation has remained the dominant power in the tea industry and in the economy of Lazistan. It has not added in recent decades to its total of 45 factories, but it remains by far the major employer. The price paid to growers, the most important economic indicator for the people of Lazistan, is still determined by political fiat at the beginning of each plucking season. When people are dissatisfied with this price, or with other developments

---

[34] The price per kilo of leaves in the second half of the 1970s averaged over $0.56. In the first half of the 1980s it fell to $0.33, before declining even further to $0.26 in the latter part of this decade. It rose slightly in the 1990s (average $0.31). (Figures supplied by the Tea Corporation. Unfortunately no data were available for the years prior to 1971.)

in the tea industry, or with virtually anything else in their environment, it is normal to blame the state. Some complain in the idiom of kinship: why, they ask, is the 'father state' (*devlet baba*) not living up to his responsibilities to provide conscientiously for his children?[35] Why has the level of support been allowed to weaken since the golden age of the 1950s and 1960s?

Education

The state's most important weapon in its ongoing struggle to influence ways of life and ways of thinking is its control over the education system. Before the republic, provision in this region was patchy and almost entirely tied to religion. Atatürk gave high priority to secular education and primary schools (*ilk okul*) were built to enable the implementation of a five-year programme in every village. The primary objective was 'the elimination of illiteracy through the introduction and organisation of a unified and general primary school education, to provide knowledge of a scientific nature, and to replace a morality based on religious principles with a morality based on ideas of order and freedom.'[36] All forms of institutionalised religious education were abolished between 1927 and 1948, though informal transmission certainly continued. It was partially reintroduced in primary schools after the Democratic Party's victory in 1950, and again became a bone of political contention in the 1990s.[37]

In Lazistan few families have sought to evade these new educational norms. The great majority, rural as well as urban, express enthusiasm for educating their children. No one ever suggested to us that the extension of formal school knowledge might impact negatively on informal ways of transmitting other types of knowledge, within families and communities. By the time our research began a high proportion of pupils were continuing for a further three years at 'middle school' (*orta okul*). Following a long period of prevarication, in the late 1990s the separate *ilk* and *orta* schools were formally merged to constitute a general programme lasting eight years.[38]

In the counties where we worked over half of all children (among whom the numbers of girls and boys were roughly equal) completed a further four years of high school (*lise*) education or equivalent vocational secondary schools (*meslek lisesi*). Since the mid-1980s Rize has had an *Anadolu lisesi*, the main distinguishing feature of which is that most instruction takes place in English. (Foreign language teaching is otherwise poorly developed or non-existent.) In 1996 a second *Anadolu lisesi* opened in the town of Pazar. This type of school is not fee-paying but entrance is through competitive examination and the substantial cost of materials (and of transport if you live away from where the school is located) make it fairly exclusive in practice.[39] It is seen by some as a symbol of westernisation. However, Kemalist critics alleged in 1992 that a picture of Kemal

[35] For further discussion of the use of kinship imagery in political rhetoric see Seufert 1997a: 32.
[36] Kurt 1989: 216. For further accounts of the development of the Turkish educational system see Başgöz and Wilson 1968, Kazamias 1966, Akkaya 1994.
[37] See Kurt 1989: 231, 296; cf. Seufert 1997a: 65–71.
[38] See Kurt 1989: 356–7; Cordan 1998; Özyılmaz 1998.
[39] See Kurt 1989: 374–9.

Atatürk in the school had been defaced, without the boy responsible being punished in any way. They also complained that, throughout the region, strongly religious men were being singled out for promotion as headmasters and county Directors of Education. These critics were particularly concerned over the deployment of state funds to expand the number of secondary schools for training religious functionaries (*Imam – Hatip Lisesi*).[40] We shall return to this point in Chapter 7. Here we simply note that education is another sector where state policies have shifted over time.

Many *lise* graduates sit the examinations for entry into higher education, but these are fiercely competitive. Although levels of success in Lazistan seem to compare well with most other parts of the country, many students are disappointed at this juncture. Rize has a number of private crammer schools (*dershane*) which provide preparatory courses for university entrance exams. These are patronised by those parents who want and who can afford to pay to give their children the best possible chance of university entrance.[41] Success is sometimes the occasion for an entire family to move to a new home in one of the big cities.

There are significant variations within the region. Provision is weak in some of the remoter villages, where depopulation has made it difficult to justify a building and a teacher. The recent rationalisation of primary education (it is known as 'centralisation', *merkezleştirme*) has induced a spate of closures. The desire to ensure better schooling for one's children has been one of the motives prompting permanent migration to the towns and cities and dual residence. Some urban families host the children of their rural relatives to enable them to attend the larger school.

The supply and the quality of the educators has become an increasing cause of concern. Low salaries have made the teaching profession less attractive and prestigious than it was in earlier decades. One Director of Education (*Milli Eğitim Müdürü*), the official responsible for all aspects of the provision of services throughout a county, conceded that he had regularly been forced to use unqualified teachers, some of them not even *lise* graduates, to work in the more remote villages within his jurisdiction. Men seemed to predominate over women in the schools that we knew, and the general *esprit de corps* was good. Some young village teachers were strangers to the region, undertaking a compulsory stint of service outside their home province following qualification (the state normally requires five years in return for material support while the prospective teacher obtains his or her qualification). After this period they can ask to be appointed (*tayin olmak*) in their home area. In the towns of Lazistan the great majority of teachers are local people, with family roots in their communities. The proportion with left-wing political loyalties seems to be greater than it is in the general population, perhaps in part as a consequence of the patterns of training established

---

[40] For the background to these schools see Akşit 1991; Shankland 1999: 26–8.

[41] Young *lise* graduates who are not successful in passing the university entrance exams may follow a correspondence course at the Turkish Open University (*Açık Öğretim*); economics seems to have been the most popular subject in recent years. Rize also has a branch of the Black Sea Technical University (*Karadeniz Teknik Üniversitesi*), a large institution based at Trabzon. At the end of the 1990s provision was still limited to a few specific courses, but the establishment of a fully autonomous university is expected soon.

in the early decades of Kemalism.[42] But teachers are not a uniform social group. Since all government employees retire after what appears to be a relatively short service, men after 25 and women after 20 years, some teachers move on to new careers, e.g. as small businessmen. Perhaps due to the way in which teachers were recruited in earlier decades, there seems to be no strong tendency for their children to follow them in the profession; in Pazar it was noted that the teachers' own children were by no means very successful in the competition for university entrance.

Whatever their personal views, all teachers must work within the constraints of a strictly defined national curriculum that leaves them with little scope for independence and innovation in the classroom. Some teachers perceive this limitation and are critical of it; some disapprove of the physical punishments meted out to pupils by their colleagues; some criticise the examinations system and the emphasis it places on memorising and repetition; but most seem to accept all of these things as natural and inevitable. No one ever mentioned possible continuities with the teaching styles of religious establishments in the past.

Apart from vocational secondary establishments, all schools are coeducational. The general (*düz*) *lise* is typically mixed and is thought to give better preparation for university entrance exams, yet no special examination is required for enrolment (poor performance will soon lead to withdrawal). On the other hand, an examination is necessary for acceptance by the vocational schools and this is one of many arenas in which people often allege manipulation and use of 'connections' (*torpil*). In Pazar there were three such institutions in the early 1990s. The girls' health high school (*Sağlık Lisesi*) trained nurses and midwives, while a second vocational school for girls (*Kız Meslek Lisesi*) focused on embroidery and other handicrafts and was said to be more popular with conservative and religious families. The solitary boys' vocational school specialised in electricians (*Elektrik Meslek Lisesi*). One issue that often came up in conversation, with pupils as well as staff, concerned the teaching of evolutionary theory in *lise* biology classes: this was rejected outright by strict Muslim families. Some families gave as a reason for not sending their daughters to secondary school their worries about the unsupervised contacts they would have with the opposite sex.

This was the only prominent concern expressed to us by local people. They did not express concern about the absence of local or regional history from the curriculum, or about the atrophy of traditional knowledge as a result of so much emphasis on modern science. Taken for granted and therefore not commented upon by them, but striking to us, was the prominence of nationalist elements in the curriculum. That the history syllabus should present the transition from Ottoman empire to modern republic in the terms enunciated by Atatürk and reiterated with minimal variation by all his successors was no surprise at all. But we had not been aware that all primary school children still start each school day with a rendering of the national anthem and the ceremonial raising of the

---

[42] Those trained in newly established 'village institutes' in the 1940s and 1950s were widely regarded in Lazistan as atheists and even communists. The nearest institutes to Lazistan were located in Trabzon and Kars. Rather more local people went to the training college at Rize, which until the 1970s used to admit pupils at the point when they had completed *orta okul* and provided them in effect with the equivalent of a *lise* education.

Turkish flag. Symbols and slogans decorate most classrooms and corridors, and each school has a kind of shrine to Atatürk and the heroes of the war of independence.

Mention should also be made of the Adult Education Department (*Halk Eğitim Müdürlüğü*) which exists in every county. Its role in raising adult literacy rates is nowadays much reduced, since these rates (at least among natives of this region, as distinct from recent immigrants) are very high. But this body continues to provide a range of courses that are widely taken up in both towns and villages. Some of these may be seen as purely recreational, such as folk dancing or singing classes. Others have a vocational slant, such as courses in accounting. Some have elements of both, such as foreign language classes. By the late 1990s computer courses were on offer in several urban centres. Sewing and embroidery courses remain extremely popular among village women of all ages. It is not hard to understand the attraction of a class which provides women with a regular venue to leave their homes to meet neighbours and friends, while at the same time acquiring skills that may be of considerable material and social value to them (e.g. in the assembly of their own trousseau). However, the arm of the state, even in this apparently benevolent form, is not universally welcome. Such courses are resisted in a few of the most conservative villages. In 1992 the director of the Adult Education Department took particular pride in inviting us to the presentation ceremony which followed the end of a course in the primary school of the village generally reputed to be the most conservative in Pazar county.

Time, places, patriotisms

The Kemalist revolution, consolidated over three quarters of a century of rapid social and economic change within stable borders, has impacted on how people understand their place in the world and even their perceptions of time. The Kemalist orientation is resolutely futurist, a characteristic shared with communist modernisers, whatever their differences. The good society is one that is to be built here on this earth, within the present boundaries of the state. In Turkey, as in the Soviet Union, the ritual calendar was reinvented, while language and script reform achieved an even more radical break with the society's past. How far, though, has the state succeeded in breaking or interrupting social processes of memory and knowledge transmission, in changing people's most basic 'mental maps'?

Fully satisfactory answers are impossible, since we have few means of gaining access to the historical consciousness and subjective identifications of the people of Lazistan three generations ago. When we asked people about the origins of their village and of their family and of the ethnic category to which they assigned themselves, answers were usually thin and vague. The new town names introduced by the state in the very first decade of the republic (Pazar rather than Atina, Fındıklı rather than Vitse, etc.) seem to have achieved general acceptance. However, the names used for the smaller places with which people identify strongly are often quite different from the new names shown on official maps.[43]

[43] These place names have a complex provenance. For further examples see Hann 1997. A scholarly analysis of Lazuri toponymia is given by Feurstein 1986a.

Even among younger people there are many who used the older hamlet names in preference to those of the 'experts' who invented the new ones.[44] In these cases the maps in people's minds, their own conceptions of their landscape and their group loyalties, have resisted the new grids of the state. Our neighbours would usually speak of *Sermeni* rather than Sümer. Many villages in Pazar and Fındıklı, especially those located away from the coast, have retained a rich vocabulary of names, often non-Turkish, for neighbourhoods and for specific tracts of land within them.

Similar themes were prominent in investigations carried out in 1987–8 in Arhavi, using questionnaires that were filled in by *Halk Eğitim Müdürlüğü* course teachers.[45] The questions reveal how 'folklore' was understood by the officials of a low-level Kemalist institution. Information was sought on the dates, names and origin of the first settlers of each village. Further historical questions concerned martyrs of the War of Independence, the existence of historical monuments in the village and the age of its oldest building. Local costume, food, musical instruments, festivals and life-cycle rituals were all addressed, though no mention was made of death and circumcision, rituals perhaps perceived as more intimately intertwined with the Islamic tradition. Some questions sought to elicit traditions of oral poetry. Education and traditions of cooperation among the villagers were also investigated. Despite their imperfections as sources, we can see in these documents both evidence of the Kemalist world view and fragments of historical memory and self-perception, as these seep through in the villagers' answers.

The Arhavi documentation supplies both new and old village names, together with (in most cases) a folk etymology for one or both. The etymology is characteristically based on Turkish, even when this is completely unfounded in the case of old names.[46] Thus the village of Yukarı Şahinler ('Upper Falcons') used to be called Napşit, which is glossed as 'famous village' from the Turkish noun *nam* (= name) and verb *işit* (= to hear), i.e. everybody should hear [i.e. know] its name. *Gidreve*, the old name of Dereüstü, is explained as follows: 'In the old days camels (*deve*) were widely used in local transport. The camels, unable to climb up

---

[44] Like Pereira (1971: 239), Toumarkine (1995: 67) dates the Turkification of Lazuri village names around the 1930s. However, we were frequently told of Turkish names that were bestowed on villages only in the 1960s.

[45] This material has been made available to us by the Arhavi *Halk Eğitim Müdürlüğü*. The teachers responsible for assembling it were usually women running sewing and embroidery courses. Unfortunately we do not know who answered the questions. It may have been the village headmen; it may have been females taking part in the courses. The questions were as follows: 1. name of the village; 2. population; number of men and number of women; 3. number of houses; 4. date of the first settlement in the territory of the village, and names of the first tribes/families; 5. oldest house in the village; 6. old remains/monuments in the village; 7. educational level of the villagers (number of university graduates/students); 8. number and names of villagers aged 75 and above; 9. heroes who took part in the War of Independence; 10. names of those heroes who are still alive; 11. names and addresses of people who can recall the War of Independence; 12. martyrs of the War of Independence; 13. village events that have generated songs or poems; 14. names of musical instruments played in the village, with names and addresses of people who play them; 15. traditional male and female costumes; 16. engagement and wedding customs; 17. knowledge of seven types of local dishes (with recipes); 18. traditional activities on the seventh day after a baby's birth; 19. traditional New Year's celebrations; 20. traditional religious holidays; 22. housebuilding traditions, including the rhymes or songs composed for the occasion; 23. mutual aid (*imece*) in the village.

[46] See Feurstein 1986a.

steep slopes, were urged to carry on with the words *git deve* (= go, camel), hence the name Gidreve.[47] Kemerköprü received its new name from the historical bridge over its stream (*kemerköprü* = arched bridge), but in this, as in several other cases, the older name is not elucidated. In other cases it is conceded that the older name is Lazuri or Georgian. Yıldızlı or Starry Village (*yıldız* = star) used to be called Nobogleni. The explanation given is that Başköy and Yıldızlı used to be one community, and the villagers of Başköy used to have their summer houses where Yıldızlı is situated today. These houses in Lazuri were called *nobogeni*, from which the old place name derived. The old name of Arılı ('Bee Village'), Papilat, is said to have been the proper name of the first Mingrelian settler of the village.

It is clear that the old place names are remembered and used. Sometimes the explanations given for new Turkish names are set in the distant past, perhaps a deliberate attempt to increase their legitimacy. However, in contrast to the town names, few new village names have passed into everyday usage. This is rare, even when the new name sounds rather close to the old (as in Sermeni and Sümer). Older people remember the name-giving procedures of government officials in the early 1960s. The repetitiveness and bland uniformity of the new names is obvious and unwelcome. People observe a double standard: births and deaths are registered according to the new system, and in all dealings with officialdom; otherwise they stick to the old. The old names are preferred not only among the bilingual Lazi of Arhavi but also among monolingual Hemşinli and Turks elsewhere in the region. They preserve a small slice of local history that new names obscure, especially in cases where boundaries have been radically altered by the state. Şendere ('Joyful Valley') was separated from Tektaş ('Single Stone') around 1968, but local Hemşinli usage continues to refer to both together as Bogena.[48]

Patriotism, a pride in the virtues of one's own people and land, begins at this local level. It is often accompanied by negative stereotypes of the neighbours. The category of 'neighbour' can mean very different things: the inhabitants of another hamlet within the same village, of an adjacent village, another valley, another county, another province or another ethnic group. Villagers typically claim to be more hospitable (*misafirperver*) toward strangers than their neighbours. Many point to incidents of violence in the neighbouring village in order to maintain that people there are 'wild' (*vahşi, gangster*), while their own people are more 'civilised' (*medeniyetli*), genteel (*efendi*) or 'clean' (*temiz*). High levels of

---

[47] It seems unlikely that camels were ever widely employed on the difficult terrain of historical Lazistan.

[48] This situation has some parallels in the domain of personal names. In official contexts the new Turkish surnames are used, but in colloquial speech people are often referred to by their nicknames. Like placenames, surnames were also introduced by the government, but they came earlier (1934–5) than the new toponyms, which they also resemble in their artificiality and repetitiveness. Close relatives have sometimes chosen different surnames, and many families have changed their name at later dates. This can cause confusion to officials (and also to anthropologists), but of course local people have no difficulty in retaining clear diagrams of relatedness, often with the help of an older name that appears nowhere in the Population Office. On the other hand, radical changes have entered the realm of first names, especially for boys, with the introduction of Kemalist names such as Cumhur (Republic), Egemen (Hegemony) and Savaş (Battle) . These have become widespread in all social groups, though some of the boys who receive such names are also known by a traditional Islamic name.

education (measured in the proportion of *lise* graduates, university graduates and civil servants) are often cited to justify local pride. Those who cannot cite such data may try to turn the tables by laying claim to strong religious commitment; one sometimes suspects that piety is deliberately cultivated in order to supply symbolic resources in the continuous battles over prestige with neighbours. A history of extreme poverty will be admitted, but only in order to claim that, following their large-scale emigration, the people of this village have overtaken their neighbours in terms of civilisation and education, as well as materially. In these ways, all over Lazistan villagers celebrate the qualities of their local community. When you ask a man who has spent his whole working life outside Lazistan and who owns a comfortable apartment in Istanbul why he spends as much time as possible in the old village home, he talks typically about the cleaner air, the quality of water, or the tranquillity of the rural environment. Some people (mostly men) talked about their 'love of the soil' *(toprak sevgisi)*. For some people this is enough to justify violence, if a piece of their soil, however small, is threatened by the construction of a new road. The norm of patrilocal residence tends to make this sort of attachment weaker among women; where they grew up is their father's home, it may no longer be their own home after marriage. Men return frequently, e.g. to tend graves. Women tend to make the journey only when it is warranted by economic tasks, notably the management of tea gardens in the summer months. They too express attachment to their region, but they often add that life in the big city is better and means less work for them.

Villages which in one context are rivals may unite as allies if confronted by a challenge from a more distant third party and such 'segmentary models' may have been important in the maintenance of order in the pre-republican period, before central power was more effectively consolidated. Hamlets and villages in turn belong to county towns, which are also the focus of patriotic commitment, nowadays reinforced through glossy publications and occasional festivals. All the residents of Arhavi and Fındıklı, rural as well as urban, take pride in the strong educational record of these counties. The residents of Pazar look at neighbouring Ardeşen with some distaste but speak more respectfully about Fındıklı, the next town along. Ardeşen used to be one of Pazar's villages. However, as more coastal land was drained, Ardeşen expanded rapidly, while Pazar was constrained by unfavourable topography. Today Ardeşen is significantly larger, but both the town and its rural hinterland are said by the people of Pazar to have all the typical shortcomings of *nouveaux riches* (e.g. a reluctance to pay taxes honestly, whereas almost every small business in *your* town is exemplary in this respect.) Ardeşen residents may counter by emphasising their energy and entrepreneurial qualities, in contrast to what they see as the sterility of Pazar. Further new counties have been carved out in recent decades, for reasons that everyone agrees are mainly to do with electoral bribery. Thus Hemşin and Çamlıhemşin have acquired some of the formal trappings of county towns, but in practice the residents of these towns and their surroundings continue to identify with Pazar and Ardeşen respectively.

The next level of state administration is that of the province *(il)*. Most of Lazistan falls within the province of Rize, but the counties of Hopa, Arhavi and Borçka are affiliated to Artvin (as was Fındıklı until 1955). The most likely reason for visiting the *il* centre is a bureaucratic or medical one and the provincial capital does not seem to be a significant focus of emotional identification. In spite of a spate of publications and the publicity that Rize receives as the undisputed capital of the tea industry, only those in the immediate vicinity of Rize seem to identify strongly as *Rizeli*.[49] In the Lazi areas where we spent most of our time, Artvin and Rize were spoken of as remote towns, nearer than Trabzon geographically, but hardly any closer in terms of providing a focus for their *memleket* or regional identity.[50]

If the people of Lazistan feel a wider regional identity, this is likely to be the Black Sea or east Black Sea region, of which they form the easternmost section. The western boundary of this region is usually given as Samsun, or occasionally Sinop. Perceptions of this region are cemented by children's school atlases, and also on a daily basis by the presentation of the weather forecast and by the media. In addition to regional newspapers, the national newspaper *Hürriyet* publishes a popular regional supplement. In the 1980s a short-lived local newspaper was called *Rize Kaçkar, Rizeliler'in ve Doğu Karadenizlilerin Gazetesi* (*Rize Kaçkur. The Newspaper of the People of Rize and the People of the Eastern Black Sea Region*). This juxtaposition seemed to raise the possibility that the people of Rize did not quite fit into the larger regional category, an uncertainty that was replicated in some of the articles published in this paper.

The officially sanctioned regional identity subsumes Rize in the east Black Sea region and includes a strong emphasis on the physical setting. Rize is not simply beautiful (*güzel*), it is 'like heaven' (*cennet gibi*). Tea is referred to as *yeşil altın* ('green gold'). The combination of this tea and sea (sometimes 'mother sea' (*deniz ana*), mountains, rivers, and fresh air give the *Karadenizli*, and above all the *Rizeli*, an almost perfect environment. This is usually coupled with highly positive characterisations of the people who live in this region: among the commonest traits cited are their bravery, and their speed and agility, both physical and mental.[51] In comparison with the sea, where problems of pollution have been well documented in recent years, the publications place greater emphasis on the beauties of the high pastures (*yaylas*) and the opportunities they present for relaxation and entertainment. A key concept in the proliferating local publications is the term 'local' itself. *Yöresel* is vague and neutral enough to be applicable at almost any level: the Black Sea as a whole, the east Black Sea, Rize province, or the various counties within it. The term is particularly associated with the realm of folklore, including dialects, foods, dances, handicrafts, wedding customs and falconry. Some contributors to the regional journals give strong endorsements to folkloristic features and lament any signs that the people of Rize might be giving up their

---

[49] Publications include the journals *Rizeliler, Rize'nin Sesi, Rize'nin Sesi Bülteni, Yeşil Cennet Rize'nin Sesi*. Expensive coffee table volumes have also appeared recently, e.g. *Rize* (published by the Rize Tourism Directorate and financed by the Office of the Prime Minister, 1997).

[50] Trabzon itself, with some 200,000 inhabitants, is the major city of the east Black Sea coast. Its principal rival is Samsun, which is often thought to mark the western frontier of the east Black Sea region. Samsun is substantially larger, thanks to its better communications; but some people in Trabzon still tend to view the people of Samsun as upstarts, much as the people of Pazar view their neighbours in Ardeşen.

[51] Kırzıoğlu contrasts the Lazi with the 'mean' Mingrelians, as part of his argument that these groups are unrelated in any way: 1972: 443–5.

distinctive costumes and their typical local dishes.[52] Continued diversity in these realms is consistent with and ultimately strengthens overarching Turkish unity.[53]

It seems likely that, despite all the image-making that has taken place in recent decades, much of it promoted by state authorities, the category *Rizeli*, together with the other regionally based categories such as *Karadenizli* and *Doğu Karadenizli*, acquires importance only away from the region itself, among long-term migrants. Those who settle permanently in Ankara or Istanbul, or even in Berlin or München, are more likely to develop loyalties at this level than those who remain within the region.[54] They may claim that the east Black Sea region has exceptional vitality, that it has more regard for family values than western parts of the country, while being more 'civilised' than eastern parts of Anatolia, characterised negatively as 'the East' (*Doğu*). The east Black Sea region is never confused with this Anatolian East.

The strong attachments that we find at the level of the hamlet, village and town reappear at the level of the state-nation, as we have already noted in this chapter. Pride in being Turkish is particularly strong among high school boys. The impact of the opening of the frontier was probably a contributory factor in the 1990s. Some boys emphasised past military encounters in which Turks had distinguished themselves, such as heroic tales about Gallipoli and the War of Independence. Others drew attention to those many branches of sport and the arts in which Turkey can be considered a world leader. Atatürk was almost universally revered; in one village it was proudly claimed that local men had been his first drivers. Some were familiar with reports that in other parts of the country the reputation of the founder of their republic was under attack from extreme Islamists and this was deplored. We do not wish to suggest that everyone in Lazistan is a Turkish nationalist and in fact national identity seldom comes to the fore in daily conversation. Rather, Turkishness is taken for granted, it does not need explicit formulation.

The Kurdish question provided the chief context in which people rehearsed their national identity for us. One young man invited us to agree, in the privacy of his office, that the Kurds were an *ulus*, a nation which had every right to withdraw from the Turkish state if they wished to do so. He was young and clearly wishing to be provocative; he would probably not have spoken in such terms if other locals had been present. The vast majority articulate a sense of outrage that small groups of terrorists should be inspiring others to acts of treason. This, the official government line over many years, receives periodic reinforcement whenever a young soldier dies in the conflict and is brought home

---

[52] See Karaca 1991: 36–7.

[53] Others are less comfortable with the persistence of local diversity. When Korkmaz (1991: 13) highlights the fact that a great many villagers in Rize use 'words of non-Turkish origin for objects of everyday usage, tools, plants and animals,' it is not clear if he means the use of non-Turkish 'dialect' words among monolingual Turkish villagers or if he is referring to the widespread use of Lazuri in the eastern part of the province. Use of the term *Rizeli* allows him to avoid explicit mention of Lazi bilingualism, while making it plain that he disapproves of all linguistic deviation. Such traditionalism, according to Korkmaz, must be corrected through education, reading and culture. Meanwhile Kırzıoğlu goes so far as to reduce the Lazuri language to a local folklore phenomenon (1972: 423).

[54] For examples of organised social events in Istanbul based on common regional *hemşerilik*, see *Rize'nin Sesi* 1993, No. 8, pp. 39–48; *Rize'nin Sesi Bülteni* 1990, Nos 1–2, p. 13.

to be buried with full military honours in his native soil. Some people hold Europe, and Germany in particular, responsible for the tragic prolongation of violence in the south-east. Without incitement from the west, they say, Kurdish opposition would never have developed to such strength. Some say that since many state leaders, including the late President Özal, have been either fully or partly of Kurdish descent (*Kürd kökenli*), it is absurd for any Kurds to want a separate state.

The Kurdish issue is not the only one that leads some people in Lazistan to define themselves in opposition to Europe. There is a deeply-rooted suspicion that Europe perceives Turks as 'other', as more fundamentally different than other close neighbours. Suspicions were amply confirmed in the early 1990s when a number of former communist countries in Eastern Europe were able to jump ahead of Turkey in the queue to become full members of the European Union. We were often asked, reproachfully, to explain the reasons why so many people in Europe hold negative views about Turks.

The escalating patriotisms stop at the level of the state-nation. The universal community of Islam, so important in the constitution of moral persons, does not offer a higher level of social identity. Rather, Islam provides an extremely important component of this national identity.[55] Even when Europe seems to be rebuffing them, few people in Lazistan draw the conclusion that their country should instead begin building closer partnerships with other Muslim countries. At this level the logic of forming alliances according to a segmentary model has little force.

None of these levels of identification has a strongly developed temporal elaboration. A Kemalist historian has argued that, like the Kurds, both Lazi and Hemşinli are really people of 'pure' Turkish stock.[56] He acknowledges linguistic difference but treats this as an accidental and insignificant acquisition by Turkish tribes in the course of their migrations. This distortion of the past may not be very significant in practice, since although the leading proponent of these views has lectured in Lazistan, and copies of his scholarly articles are available in the library in Rize, very few inhabitants know anything at all about him or his ideas. Regional history is not taught in schools and there have been no attempts to popularise extreme nationalist views.

At the local level the Arhavi questionnaires reveal only weak historical consciousness in the villages, with few inhabitants having any clear idea of when their settlement had been established. A few answers indicate the survival of oral traditions: for instance, that three Georgian brothers came from the east to found Dikyamaç, Ortacalar and Başköy. More commonly, however, specific families (*sulale, kabile*) are cited as the first settlers. The first settlers to Ortacalar are said to be 'Turks from the Caucasus'. In Dereüstü several old lineage names are mentioned and linked to new surnames. Some of the founding families of Yukarı Şahinler apparently came from Sinop. For hundreds of years this settlement seems to have consisted of five families only, who before embracing Islam were thought to have been 'under Greek influence'. In another case an individual mentions that a village was formerly an Armenian settlement, but this was all old history

---

[55] For an ideological elaboration of the 'Turkish-Islamic synthesis' see Kafesoğlu 1985. We examine religion in Chapter 7.
[56] See Kırzıoğlu 1946, 1972, 1976, 1986, 1990. For a critical discussion see Bellér-Hann 1995a.

from 'before Ottoman times'. Remote regions such as Syria or the Balkans are mentioned, but Russia, more specifically the Caucasus, turns up more frequently as a place of origin.[57] An informant in the village of Balıklı says that its first settlers came from Russia, but were of Mingrelian origin (*Rusyada Mengrellerden gelmiştir*). In this text the word *Mengrel* (Mingrelian) is marked as *yanlış* (incorrect) by a different hand – presumably that of a Kemalist official.

We found a similar picture in the villages of Pazar, where Central Asia was also occasionally cited as the homeland of the original settlers. Some people, usually those with a higher level of education, specified that the ancestors were Turks from these regions, but, even more than in Arhavi, many claimed Caucasian origins and blood or linguistic relationship with the Mingrelians (more seldom with Georgians). Mention of the pre-Islamic era is extremely rare. Large-scale group migration is buried in the mythical past, while the migration of specific individual families is connected to more recent times. No ruins or historical monuments in the region are attributed by the Lazi to their own ancestors. Some people cite dated carved tombs as evidence of the antiquity of their village, but the oldest of these is mid-eighteenth century.[58] Many claim Caucasian origins, but there is no powerful collective memory. In any case these origins are often reconciled with Turkishness: no one articulates an identity as non-Turk.[59]

What we do not know is whether the collective memory was substantially different before the interventions of the modern state. All we can say is that the Kemalist programme has been successfully consolidated over three quarters of a century and that it has brought 'rapid, irreversible and fundamental changes' at all levels of society.[60] It is Kemalism which, in the terms of James Scott, has 'discovered' that society, transformed its 'naming practices' and made it generally 'legible'.[61] It has promoted an orientation towards the future, towards progress and civilisation, generally understood to mean the west. There have, however, always been constraints on Kemalist 'futurism', and these became increasingly evident as democratic processes took root in the post-revolutionary generations after 1950. There can be little doubt that many people's most basic personal and social identities have changed, in particular through a newly disseminated national consciousness as Turks. This consciousness is gendered in a way that demonstrates fundamental social continuity. Both the *anavatan* (motherland) and the *devlet baba* (father state) are viewed positively by their citizen-children.[62] Yet there are also signs that local loyalties have remained strong. We shall turn in later chapters to other facets of identity that have resisted the transformations planned by the social engineers of Kemalism.

[57] Russia and the Soviet Union were often used interchangeably in the period when these questionnaires were completed.

[58] In any case tomb inscriptions, including the date, are an enigma to most villagers because few can read the Arabic script or understand the old calendar.

[59] The motivation for such claims may be complex. Those who say they are Turks often accommodate this Turkish identity alongside more local ones. Many people who consider themselves to be Lazi and to have special links with the peoples of the Caucasus do not think that this precludes the claiming of a Turkish identity: not just state citizenship, but some fuller sort of national identity. We return to these themes in Chapter 8.

[60] Stirling 1965: 88.

[61] Scott 1998.

[62] Cf. Delaney 1995.

3
Market

Market principle and marketplace

The prime connotation of the word market (*pazar*) for the people of Lazistan is the gathering held once or twice weekly in each county centre for economic exchange. The sellers are mostly small traders selling perishable goods and a wide range of household goods and clothing. They exist alongside extensive networks of permanent commercial premises in every coastal town. These too, though not described as *pazar*, fall within the sector of market-regulated activity. As we have noted, trade and markets have existed around the Black Sea coast since ancient times. Here, however, we argue that the market as a principle of social organisation has gained greatly in prominence in Turkey since 1950. This principle complements that of the state, but it may sometimes be antagonistic to it. If state denotes primarily 'top-down' philosophies of social change, market denotes a 'bottom-up' principle, allowing more scope to the strategies of individual actors. This is precisely the source of much of its appeal in contemporary Lazistan.

The market principle has a long history. In Scotland in the eighteenth century Adam Smith elucidated the advantages of economically rational divisions of labour, based on what he believed to be man's natural propensity to 'truck and barter'. But Smith and his contemporaries were also concerned with the moral bases of community life, a concern that is often forgotten or dismissed by the neo-liberals who invoke Smith's name in support of radical 'free market' policies in our own times. Closer to our own age, Karl Polanyi highlighted the negative social aspects of Victorian laissez-faire capitalism.[1] He saw it as the first in human history which had, in effect, allowed the economy to break free of its roots in society (in Polanyi's terms, to become 'disembedded'). Polanyi and the substantivist school that he established in economic anthropology insisted that the 'modes of integration' of pre-industrial societies did not depend upon price-forming markets. Even if various forms of trade and market were of considerable importance, the market principle was subordinated to the principles he termed reciprocity and redistribution.[2]

Polanyi's views were further developed with reference to markets by some of his students. Paul Bohannan and George Dalton drew out a distinction between

[1] Polanyi, 1944.
[2] For a summary of the substantivist position see Polanyi 1957.

the *marketplaces* that were characteristic of the traditional African societies they examined and the modern *market principle*, based on laws of supply and demand.[3] They noted the paradox that the spread of a market principle might lead to the decline of the marketplace; for example, as farmers became more specialised in their production and crops were produced for export rather than for local sale, so local and regional marketplaces would decline. In highly commercialised industrial societies the marketplace no longer plays important social, political and even religious roles in addition to its economic function. The high 'transaction costs' of the bazaar haves been replaced by more impersonal institutions, exemplified by the supermarket and the shopping mall.

The debates provoked by Polanyi have long since subsided. Most economic anthropologists would now agree that this substantivist school exaggerated the contrast between traditional and modern economies. The discontinuities brought about by the industrial revolution were not quite so radical, since 'market forces' were often very significant in the earlier epoch. Equally, modern market behaviour is by no means free of personal and social influences, nor do any markets ever completely escape from political controls. A careful reading of his work shows that Polanyi was aware of these complexities. Rather than seeing the two principles as mutually exclusive, his concept of 'mode of integration' allows more nuanced approaches to the balance and interaction of market and state. These abstract principles can be brought down to the level of tangible realities through ethnographic work. In this chapter we explore the modern market principle in Lazistan empirically, against the background of changes in the wider national society and also global changes. In some contexts local people do themselves use the rhetoric of 'expanding free market competition'. But what does this mean in practice for shopkeepers and tea growers, for market traders and consumers? We shall see that, in the case of Lazistan, increased ideological emphasis upon the market principle has led not to the extinction of marketplaces but to their efflorescence in a new and distinctive form.

The integration of town and countryside

For Polanyi, much as for Marx, modern market exchange was a mode of economic integration that threatened the life of the community. The view from modern economics, grounded in assumptions of scarcity and competition, also emphasises its atomising, individualising qualities. We begin this discussion, however, by insisting on the role played by markets both past and present as a force for social integration in this region.

In Ottoman and early republican Lazistan, rural producers (often women) took small quantities of surplus garden produce, and more rarely an animal, down to the nearest coastal 'spot' on a designated day. There were many such small-scale sellers in the market, and very few who sold on a larger scale. The purchasers were principally residents of the small urban centre who lacked their own garden

---

[3] The distinction between marketplaces and market principle is drawn in Bohannan and Dalton 1962. For a recent anthropological survey of this field see Dilley 1992. For classic anthropological studies of 'bazaars' see Geertz 1963, 1979.

supplies. Occasionally other villagers purchased an animal for a newly established household, or to fatten up prior to slaughter at the Kurban festival. Before the republican period, apart from sheep that could be brought in from the interior, there was little overland exchange of goods and information with other regions. Maritime trade, as we have noted, was more significant, but it brought in mainly industrial goods such as iron and luxuries such as coffee.

These periodic markets did not exist in an impersonal world of pure competition. After selling the produce that she brought to market in a basket on her back, the rural woman would often visit a shopkeeper to obtain goods she would consume later at home – sugar, cloth, or household items. She would probably turn to a shopkeeper she knew well from previous trips, perhaps a member of the ethnic group she herself belonged to, even a native of her village or a relative. She might well have an account at this shop, which she settled irregularly, for example after the sale of an animal. Personal links were undoubtedly important also in the more significant commercial exchanges of Lazistan, notably the export market in hazelnuts. Producers were concerned to ensure they had a trader in the town who would take up their harvest. They were much less bothered to ensure whether or not this man was paying the best prices in a particular year. In short, markets in Lazistan facilitated a rather limited range of exchanges but they provided an important mechanism for the social integration of town and countryside.[4]

In modern Lazistan, though the size of the towns and range of exchanges has increased enormously since the introduction of tea, this mechanism is not so radically different. The county units of administration correspond closely to the effective commercial catchment area of the towns along the coast and in addition to their economic exchanges, many people combine their visit to the market with some business at the hospital, or at the government or municipal offices.[5] Fresh produce is now imported from the rest of the country. Full-time market traders (among whom Hemşinli are particularly numerous) buy their supplies from wholesalers in Rize or Trabzon, and use the lorries they own to sell at each of the small towns in the course of the week. The availability of vans and shared taxis enables large numbers of rural residents as well as townspeople to purchase most of their food supply in the marketplace. The road network also allows some goods, notably bread, to be brought daily into villages for sale from small shops. The people of Lazistan therefore consume the same bread as their compatriots. Many families still make maize bread for special occasions, but it has been supplanted as the staple.

Away from the marketplaces, the networks of small shops have also been greatly extended. Grocery businesses stock the food brands available nationwide. Retail outlets for consumer durables such as refrigerators and washing machines squeeze their goods into cramped premises in the small central shopping streets. The demand for such goods, like that for modern factory-made furniture, has

---

[4] According to Koeler the market in Atina (Pazar) in the early nineteenth century consisted of 'thirty or forty shops which formed two small streets and enclosed a large area. A couple of bakeries, some blacksmiths' workshops and the big house of the *agha* family all stood nearby' (Ritter 1845: 52–3).
[5] The correspondence has been weakened with the recent creation of new counties (e.g. Hemşin) for party political reasons.

increased rapidly. There has been an expansion in the number of small restaurants, pastry shops and cafes, of photographers and of professionals, including lawyers, doctors and dentists. These last usually hold posts at state hospitals, but they supplement these with more lucrative work in the private sector. The great majority of businesses are family concerns and many are transmitted from father to son. Some are run jointly (*ortak*) by brothers, or by more distant relatives. In Pazar the largest such business is a bakery, which employs eighteen persons in total, which would count as large even in Rize, the province capital. At the other end of the spectrum, many small businesses are by no means the principal source of household income. Some seem to provide the owners or leaseholders with a central social base, in which the consumption of tea with a stream of regular visitors is as important as the occasional commercial transaction. In other words, a social dimension is still very prominent in the realm of exchange. For many purchases (e.g. clothing as well as food) people tend to turn to their regular supplier. Credit is routinely offered, even though there is often a large notice behind the counter proclaiming the contrary. It is offered in a way that people describe as traditional. The agreed price is higher than that charged if full payment were to be made at the time of purchase, and the debt is typically paid off when the purchaser receives the next instalment of tea income. People deny that they charge interest, and indeed, the extra amount paid does not seem to be systematically calculated in relation to the time which elapses or the precise rate at which the currency is devaluing (around 70 per cent annually for much of the field research). In these circumstances the extension of credit amounts to a generous subsidy to the consumer, who may end up paying substantially less in real terms than the shopkeeper himself paid for the goods originally.

Pricing policies are complicated by these high inflation rates. Many small businessmen operate a simple mark-up over the price they paid for their stock; this mark-up is sometimes as low as ten per cent. People do not take full account of transportation costs, nor the cost of their own time in finding and importing the goods (e.g. some clothiers travelled regularly to Istanbul for this purpose), or the cost of storing the goods on their premises. By the time the goods are sold the shopkeeper might, by any rational capitalist calculations, be making a substantial loss. However, any income that nominally exceeds the original outlay is perceived as 'clean' (*temiz*) gain. For some items, notably bread, prices are regulated. For most foodstuffs the grocer has some flexibility but not a great deal. But in, for example, the furniture stores, the position is more complex. Prices are seldom publicly displayed: a prospective purchaser has to say what s/he requires, and upon being shown the product will enquire about the price. Bargaining is expected, but it is usually brief, even perfunctory, and entirely decorous. The general position, emphasised by the shopkeepers themselves, is that they have no entitlement to excessive profits. They are of course justified in taking more than they originally paid to a wholesaler (or their expenses for materials and labour if the product has been self-produced, as some of the furniture still is) but it is sometimes said that a mark-up in excess of 20 per cent would infringe Islamic norms.[6]

---

[6] This compares with the figure of 10 per cent cited by Schiffauer 1987: 148. For a discussion of business practices and 'ethical considerations' in a western Anatolian town in the 1960s, much of which is still pertinent to contemporary Lazistan, see Benedict 1974.

Plate 3.1 The vegetables and spices corner of the market in Pazar.

Plate 3.2 Women at the marketplace, Pazar.

A good deal of price determination appears to be rather arbitrary. Traders do not keep precise records of what they pay, nor of how long they have stored an item before sale. Few local businessmen seem to be profit maximisers in the style of an ideal-type western entrepreneur.

Overall the continuities with traditional practices and the contrast with dominant modes of doing business on contemporary western European high streets are striking. The differences are most visible if one arrives around lunchtime on a Friday. Most premises do not close at a stipulated time for a lunch break, but commercial life comes to an almost complete halt in the smaller towns during Friday service at the mosque. This is considered acceptable by most people. It was one of many features considered unsatisfactory by the head of a nearby military installation, who became so frustrated at the poor service he thought he was receiving from local shopkeepers that he transferred all his business to the cities of Rize and Trabzon. Small businessmen themselves stress that there is no competition between them (*rekabet yok*). Even where it clearly does exist, it is heavily disguised behind a wall of intricate social relations. For example Pazar, with a total county population of forty thousand, had nine chemists after a new one opened in 1992. Only one of these, conveniently located close to the main bus-stops, was run in a highly brisk and businesslike way, employing additional non-family labour to cope with demand. The others were little frequented and made no attempt to compete. Most of their customers were well-known to them personally, and they chatted about other matters while making their purchase. Unlike most small businessmen, a chemist has to study and acquire formal qualifications. Pazar had obviously produced too many for the sector to be economically rewarding for most of them, but they seemed to accept this philosophically. Some had close ties to local doctors, who stopped by after their surgery hours to relax over a glass of tea.

The Motherland Party that governed Turkey from 1983 until 1991 took a number of steps to promote a more rational business environment. A value added tax was introduced in 1985, though small businesses with low turnovers were treated differently from other business taxpayers. Accountants play a key role in the preparation of most tax returns, but there is a widespread feeling that the new rules have done little to make taxation more fair. Some modestly successful family concerns are resentful that some of the richest businessmen in the country can exploit loopholes and avoid paying any tax at all. Some are scornful of the luxury modern villa, quite out of keeping with its surrounds, which a Hemşinli has built in his native village from the proceeds of a successful career in the banking sector. Few have confidence in the state's efforts to regulate and tax fairly.

Some businessmen (and businesswomen – a small number of stores were operated by women, notably those specialising in women's clothing) do now adjust their prices upwards with greater frequency. Like those with contacts abroad, these people are likely to hold bank accounts in German marks or American dollars. More and more have contractual agreements to sell the products of national chains, in which case their price lists are continuously updated for them; but this does not mean that there is no room left for bargaining. Those who have only short-term leases on their premises have to pay careful attention to their balance sheets. The payment of substantial 'goodwill money' (*hava parası*) when a very good location is sub-let is a further indication of the spread of a more commercial ethos, though this custom itself is by no means new.[7] Just as more attention is paid to profit-maximising on the supply side, and some people do go bankrupt, so consumers are nowadays more likely to shop around before making their purchase. There is more competition than in the past in most sectors. Some consumers said that they do not expect a merchant or craftsman from their village to offer them any favours; unless they have a specific link to him or his family, they may even fear that a shopkeeper from their village will seek a larger than normal profit margin at their expense.

Business expansion can take a variety of forms. A few grocery stores have begun the transition to operating as self-service supermarkets, and a few specialists in other sectors have opened additional stores outside their native town. This remains very unusual, and other wealth-creating strategies are more common. Some bakers have begun to diversify into other activities. The proprietor of the solitary businesslike pharmacy in Pazar was a man of great energy; his strategy was to move outside his sector, indeed, to leave the world of trade and commerce altogether in favour of property investments. The market in urban real estate has become lively in most towns. Families which owned land in central commercial areas have been able to reap huge sums by selling land to the state or for private development. About half of all small businesses in Pazar pay rent. Some of the property owners have invested in shopping arcades, in which most shops are sub-let to other businesses while one or two may be retained for a family initiative.[8] One local entrepreneur has erected a ten-storey block on cliffs at the edge of the town. Apparently it was at one stage intended to provide accommodation for tourists; it eventually served to provide three luxury apartments for family members and almost twenty other apartments which were let at commercial rates. This entrepreneur later embarked upon a second such block a short distance away, and upon timber contracts in Georgia. He was an activist in the Motherland Party and an articulate spokesman for its policies to promote 'free market economy' (*serbest pazar ekonomisi*).

Meanwhile, this individual's elder brother managed a very traditional clothes store in the centre of town and projected a very different image. The family had been in this line of business for several generations, but the shop had been built up in its present form by their father, now in his seventies but still the official registered proprietor and in the shop on most days to keep an eye on the business. He prayed in the main central mosque several times each day, though some townspeople said that his business practices had not always conformed to the highest standards of Islam. The old man insisted that commercial borrowing was a religious offence, and that he would never allow any members of his family to go down this path. Day to day control of the clothes store has for many years been in the hands of the eldest son, who travelled regularly to Istanbul to purchase goods. He and his more entrepreneurial brother were the joint owners (*ortakçı*) of

---

[7] Cf. Magnarella 1974: 79.

[8] In several towns the municipality (*belediye*) has built shopping arcades for this purpose, where rents are usually below those in the private sector. Rize has a purpose-built 'industrial zone' away from the town centre, which is almost entirely given over to the motor trade. Other towns are beginning to follow suit.

Plate 3.3 Traditional workshop selling agricultural implements, Pazar.

the multi-storey accommodation block, but all tenants paid their rent to the latter. The elder brother clearly had no wish to be directly involved with the financial details of residents' rents and he was not active in local politics. Instead he had followed in his father's footsteps as a pilgrim to Mecca. Lacking the entrepreneurial zeal of those who were the most conspicuous beneficiaries of the Özal decade, it was the elder brother who enjoyed the higher status in the community. Those who were critical of the more successful entrepreneur would often add that it was not the whole family they were criticising, for they saw the elder brother as a devout man of real integrity. The elder brother's elder son worked regularly in the clothing shop after dropping out of *lise*, so that grandfather, son and grandson were often in the store together. When it emerged that the grandson was temperamentally unsuited to the bargaining routines required in this sector, his father set him up, shortly before his marriage, in rented premises nearby as a goldsmith. Other sons were going through higher education in the fields of economics and business, but it was unclear if they would stay in Pazar in the longer term. In addition to the three shops they controlled, this family enjoyed significant rental income in town and owned substantial tea gardens in their nearby village. Although they grumbled about the frequency with which they were called upon to make donations to charitable causes, everyone knew that they could well afford to pay up.

Large-scale building investments have transformed the Lazistan landscape in recent decades and destroyed many older properties in the process. The new entrepreneurs have not attached much value to the preservation of the older houses of the region. Some magnificent buildings are falling into ruin; nor does the state seem to attach much priority to their preservation. Most marketplaces have central locations and some modern amenities. However, there is still a corner of the marketplace where middle-aged and elderly women predominate, selling eggs, dairy products and a little fresh salad. Close by there are still craftsmen who make wood-burning stoves, doors, beds and other furniture using traditional techniques; while others have adapted to changing conditions by making new products, notably shears for cutting tea and wheelbarrows and carts to transport it. Quite a few workshops still take in boys for apprenticeships that last for several years.[9] In short, the combination of marketplace and network of small-scale businesses in each market centre is still an extremely important one for the social integration of Lazistan. The increased volume of exchanges, after the wealth brought by tea had destroyed the old subsistence economy, has not 'disembedded' the economy from social contexts.

Limited marketisation in the tea sector

The tea industry that, more than any other factor, was responsible for the prosperity of modern Lazistan, was not itself exposed to any of the winds of the market until the mid-1980s. The platform of the Motherland Party included a commitment to opening up large state monopolies to private competition. Many of those

[9] In some cases youngsters are recruited from the new immigrant underclass on terms that seemed highly exploitative.

who campaigned for the party (such as the dynamic entrepreneur discussed above) hoped for a radical programme that would have included the full privatisation of the Tea Corporation. In the event the government proceeded more cautiously: in 1985 it abolished the state's monopoly over tea, thereby opening the door to private sector ventures to compete with the 45 factories of the Tea Corporation. In 1986 the reputation of the Tea Corporation was dented when it was alleged that tea leaves affected by the Chernobyl nuclear catastrophe had been processed and sold to unsuspecting consumers. This helped to create a favourable climate of public opinion towards the first private investors in this sector in the next few years. The honeymoon turned out, however, to be short.

Some of the consequences of this policy were already visible when we made our first revisit in 1988. The most dramatic was a vast hoarding by the main road at the western approach to Ardeşen advertising a new factory manufacturing Lipton's Yellow Label brand. This was as large as most of the Tea Corporation factories and as such, although it had not generated quite so many jobs as a state sector factory of equivalent size, it had been warmly welcomed both by new workers and by the growers of the district, who gained a new outlet for their leaves. Further enquiries revealed the involvement of the transnational Unilever, proprietor of the Lipton's brand name, to be rather limited. It was providing some initial technical advice to ensure that the best possible quality levels were achieved, but the capital investment came mainly from an Istanbul-based Turkish company. Its aim was to carve out a niche in the Turkish market for a superior quality tea. Even the best Lazistan product was considered incapable of competing on international markets; production costs were much lower and quality higher in most other tea-producing regions. Lipton's Yellow Label in Turkey was actually a quite different product from the same label produced in other parts of the world.[10]

Several other large-scale private factories had been established, or were in the pipeline, and quite a few local businessmen were establishing factories on a much smaller scale, with the aim of producing tea at the lowest possible cost, to undercut the Tea Corporation. One such venture was based in Sümer. After the frustrations of the early 1980s, when the Tea Corporation had tightened its quality controls and ceased building new factories, most people were initially enthusiastic about private sector development. Young men hoped that the jobs created in the construction of new factories would be converted into regular employment contracts once they were operational. Growers hoped that, with the breaking of the state's monopoly, they would never again be constrained by quota controls and by what they saw as the heavy-handed behaviour of the Tea Corporation.

By the time of our further fieldwork in 1992–3 most of the hopes and expectations invested in the private sector had been dashed. The Tea Corporation had retained its dominance. The price paid to growers was still fixed politically, with the private sector factories all matching this price. The main difference between public and private sectors was in the actual timing of the payments to growers for the green leaves delivered. Whereas the state-owned factories paid up reasonably promptly, usually within one or two months, many private factories (including the makers of Lipton's, by now entirely Turkish-owned) were taking a great deal

[10] For further discussion see Hann 1990: 37–8.

longer. Delays of six months and more were by no means exceptional. This was the most frequent complaint of the growers. The workers in private factories complained about similar delays in the payment of their wages. Even if cash payment was eventually made in full, high inflation meant that workers and growers suffered substantial losses. Payment was sometimes made in the form of processed tea. Many private firms, large as well as small, had gone out of business, leaving both growers and employees with no hope of recovering the money they were owed. The owners of some larger concerns came in for especially scathing criticism. It was alleged that they had taken advantage of cheap credits from banks and from the public sector when setting up their factories and secretly deployed some of these resources elsewhere. The bankruptcy of their tea enterprise had little impact on them personally, but a considerable impact on their workforce and suppliers. There was also a sense of betrayal and bitterness towards smaller operators. The Istanbul-based businessman who had been lauded in 1988 for his plans to invest in his native village was by 1992 apparently too embarrassed to show his face in Sümer. His debts were considerable and the factory he had built stood derelict.

Whenever they have a choice between the public sector and the private sector, it is hardly surprising that people choose the former. When set alongside the unscrupulous behaviour of private owners, the state's reliability in making payments commands respect. Only the owners of above-average gardens who need additional buyers for their tea at peak periods, when their local state factory enforces quotas, are thankful for the supplementary private outlets. Producers' trust towards the public sector is also manifest in consumption patterns: most locals prefer to consume tea processed by the Tea Corporation and claim that it is the only high quality tea produced in the region. Only in the 'up-market' tea-bag sector of the market does the private sector (notably Lipton's) have the competitive edge.

An economist might have more to say about this situation. It might fairly be pointed out by a neo-liberal that merely lifting the state's monopoly was never going to be sufficient to harness the advantages of the market. A full privatisation of the Tea Corporation would undoubtedly have had more radical consequences. On the other hand, if the logic of the marketplace had been fully carried through, then many Tea Corporation factories would probably have gone bankrupt. The quality of their product would almost certainly have plummeted. Whatever these 'might have beens', the views of the majority of the people on the ground were clear. The extension of the market principle into the region's dominant industry had provided no more than a short-term fillip to the economy. Within a few years people were again complaining that 'tea is finished' (*çay bitti*) and bemoaning the lack of attractive alternatives.[11] In the longer run it bred more resentment, and caused even committed supporters of the *serbest pazar ekonomisi* to recognise the need for effective public regulation to control the imports of cheap, 'unhealthy'

---

[11] The principal alternative encouraged by state officials in the 1990s was an initiative in kiwi fruit production. Some families in Sümer did indeed experiment with this new product, but most were deeply sceptical, just as they were towards a similar initiative in the early 1980s to promote silkworm production. The problem was that the state would not take on any responsibility for purchasing the product. Without this support villagers did not consider the switch of orientation to be a risk worth taking. Those who planted kiwi saplings did so in small quantities on additional or spare land, and not as a replacement for tea bushes.

foreign teas and to punish the abuses to which the private sector was obviously prone.[12]

Consumerism's national filter

In the tea sector most people in Lazistan expect their government to protect the market from foreign competition and most still prefer to consume the Turkish product. In this section we broaden the picture and consider some of the many other products that people nowadays acquire through markets. Our assumption is that changing patterns of consumption may reveal a lot about changing attitudes and identities.[13]

The mass media play a vital role in the creation of both new markets and new political communities. The importance of newspapers was understood by the early Kemalists, who maintained tight controls to ensure that the media served their cause of secular modernisation. However, controls over the press were gradually relaxed in later decades. The readership of the daily *Cumhuriyet* ('Republic'), which was closest to the Republican People's Party and the Kemalist tradition, fell away as more populist papers prospered. Using a language that was closer to that of ordinary people and abundant illustrations, often shocking readers with female flesh or with garish photos of the bloodstained victims of both terrorist attacks and bus accidents, this vibrant press (e.g. *Sabah, Hürriyet, Milliyet*) has nonetheless retained close links to the state. Editors and senior columnists are much courted by politicians.

Newspapers have remained relatively expensive. Although they reach Lazistan quickly, thanks to overnight delivery networks, they do not enter all households every day. There are some households which they do not enter at all. Television has been present in most households, rural as well as urban, since the 1970s, and radio for much longer still. These are the main channels through which people obtain information about what is going on in the rest of the country and the wider world. The state retained its monopoly here until the mid-1980s. Though the quality of some cultural output in fields such as music and drama was high, the entertainment potential of these media was not fully exploited. Television did what the state required, e.g. in transmitting many hours of coverage of military parades during annual Independence Day celebrations; but it is not so clear that such broadcasting held the attention of any viewers, or that the political messages regularly infused into news bulletins or current affairs programmes actually had the effects intended by programme controllers.

All of this changed when the Motherland Party opened up this sector to private competition in 1985. New private channels showing mostly popular entertainment, much of it imported from western countries, were particularly successful. Sports coverage was greatly extended. People began to spend more hours in front of the television. Women would drop whatever domestic tasks they were performing in order to keep up with the action in soap drama imported from

---

[12] For further recent discussion, including criticism of both public and private sectors, see Özyurt 1997.

[13] For a lament that the people of Lazistan are in the process of changing from a community of producers to one based primarily on consumption see Baran 1999: 7.

Mexico. Western films became an integral part of discussions whenever women got together. More and more owners of tea houses began to install televisions, realising that their customers might move elsewhere if it was not available. Villagers in areas which did not enjoy good reception began to complain about this disadvantage, which had not greatly concerned them previously. In short, viewing habits underwent a rapid change in a rather short period; and if a highly commercialised television industry is one of the litmus tests for modernity, Turkey crossed this particular threshold in the later 1980s.

But it was not only in television that the Turkish media changed rapidly during the decade of Turgut Özal's premiership and presidency. The popular music industry experienced an efflorescence, partly as a result of greater media exposure. Western style ballet and orchestral music continued to receive their public subsidies in the capital and the state continued to promote more popular forms of folk music (*halk müziği*) as part of its goal of forging the nation. However, in the towns of Lazistan young customers were increasingly likely to ask in their local music stores for the latest Arabesk cassettes from Istanbul. This music, above all a music of the big city, with its origins in Egyptian film music of the 1940s, was a medium that offered more outlets for emotion and self-expression than either the state-supported popular music or any western style.[14] The Arabesk styles could express the identities felt by young people. The personal lives of its top performers, like those of other celebrities, film stars, politicians and fashion models, were covered intensively by the press.

Elite sportsmen (seldom women in this field) became the object of similar attention. The Kemalists, like other national movements, emphasised the virtues of sport for discipline and vigour in the modernisation drive. However, although obligatory in the school curriculum, few people in Lazistan (and virtually no females) participate in sports on any regular basis. They have few opportunities to do so. Instead, people enjoy watching it on television and reading the sports pages of newspapers. Football (soccer) is the dominant sport and the three main professional football teams of Istanbul have long enjoyed large followings in Lazistan.[15] The commercial climate of the 1980s allowed the top teams to consolidate their position by clinching new sponsorship deals in the private sector. Many youngsters in Lazistan grow up wearing the colours of one or other of these teams, becoming lifelong supporters before they leave primary school. Even rural women and girls may be enthusiastic fans. These teams play regularly in European competitions and their players are recruited internationally. At the same time, the performance of these clubs is also viewed as a matter of national self-esteem. Even the fans of a rival team take pride in a good performance by a Turkish club in international competition. The national side's progress to the finals of the European Championships in 1996 and again in 2000 was followed by a tremendous wave of public support.

In a relatively affluent region such as Lazistan, many people can afford to

[14] See Stokes 1992, 1998; cf. Özbek 1997.
[15] These clubs are Beşiktaş, Galatasaray and Fenerbahçe. Although the Trabzon-based team Trabzon-spor has had an outstanding record since its establishment in 1967, almost on a par with these Istanbul teams, its proximity to Lazistan did not lead to very high levels of support in this region. Support for the Rize team was also weak and it weakened further in the 1990s when the team's performances deteriorated.

emulate the consumption patterns of the advanced urban communities of the west, as transmitted to them not only through the media but through a myriad of informal social channels. Most of these patterns have some distinctive Turkish inflection, even though many products of global capitalism are now readily available in most of Turkey. Young men and women in small towns pay close attention to Istanbul styles of dress, while older women keep up to date as best they can with changing tastes in jewellery. Many newspapers carry supplements with tips concerning the decoration and furnishings of houses, and the primary framework is national. What people take from Istanbul may have cosmopolitan origins, as the Arabesk style in popular music certainly does, but it is subjectively experienced as Turkish.[16] The best fiddlers and pipers of the Black Sea region also make their recordings in Istanbul. Their cassettes are available in most towns and also in the Gima Superstore that opened in Rize in 1999, selling everything from Korans to ladies' swimwear. The bread selection here includes maize bread, the local speciality. Even the most celebrated instance of globalisation, the McDonalds fast-food chain, undergoes a partial transformation. As of 1999 it was not yet represented in Lazistan proper, but there was a flourishing branch on Trabzon's principal square. It was decorated with large images of local architecture and folklore performances, and advertised itself by appealing to the values of the family.

Here we see how the market can be a powerful force for social integration at the national level. It complements the 'top-down' unifying activities of the state with a 'bottom-up' process rooted in social judgements about fashion and taste as shaped by advertising and the media. Through tea, Lazistan has itself made an important contribution to the daily rituals that reproduce a distinctively Turkish community of consumers. However, not all products have the same benign integrating effects. Marx, Polanyi and many others are right to note also the ways in which markets isolate citizens from one another, undermine the traditional foundations of community and generate new antagonisms. Status competition always carries an edge of tension, even when people enter the game with equal resources; but of course this is far from being the case. In some poor regions of South-Eastern Anatolia few people are admitted to this game at all. In Lazistan most of the population are players to some extent, but there is considerable variation. Social differentiation was markedly increased by the pro-market policies of the Özal decade, and this was widely commented upon within the region. At one extreme, poor rural families who depend entirely upon tea for their income have suffered from adverse economic trends in that sector. At the other is the stratum sometimes known as *sosyete*, which includes professionals and top state officials as well as businessmen. Some entrepreneurs who used to travel by coach on their business trips to the west can now afford to fly to Istanbul from the airport at Trabzon. Their incomes are rising exponentially as a result of successful property investments, or some new business linked to the open-border policy, to which we shall turn below. They change their cars regularly and tend to favour glamorous western imports. Some seek to legitimate their wealth by donating some of it to the building of new mosques, or by financing a Koran

---

[16] For anthropological studies of the interaction between global and local forces in contemporary capitalist consumerism see Friedman 1994.

course for youngsters. Some splash out on the pilgrimage to Mecca, from which, in addition to spiritual gratification and religious souvenirs, they return with an array of secular goods that they might well have purchased almost anywhere else in the world.

The Russian markets

One further expression of the Motherland Party's commitment to the market principle had far-reaching consequences for the people of Lazistan from the end of the 1980s. Under the banner of 'Black Sea Economic Cooperation', Prime Minister Turgut Özal sought to create closer links with Turkey's neighbours in the region, at that time still uniformly socialist.[17] In the summer of 1988 the coastal border crossing into the Adjarian Autonomous Oblast of the Georgian Autonomous Republic at the Lazi village of Sarp was ceremonially opened for the first time since the 1930s. Turkey and the Soviet Union of Mikhail Gorbachev were agreed on the desirability of expanding trade links. This crossing was not intended to have the full status of an international frontier crossing point; rather, it was to facilitate bilateral trade. The opening of the border had little initial impact on Lazistan, since for individual travellers the process of obtaining passports and visas was still a cumbersome one on both sides.

The open border policy had more significant effects for the people of Lazistan only after the disintegration of the Soviet Union at the end of 1990. For the new Georgian Republic the early 1990s were years of political turmoil and violence. A secession movement in Abkhazia was supported, directly and indirectly, by Russia. When Eduard Shevardnadze assumed power in Tbilisi in 1992 the country was in political chaos and the state was fundamentally incapable of enforcing law and order in much of its territory. The country experienced a severe variant of the economic dislocation that was general throughout the former Soviet Union in the wake of the collapse of the centralised socialist economy. In these dramatically altered conditions the border crossing at Sarp offered an economic lifeline. The post-communist authorities were ready to issue travel documents, and the Turkish authorities had already committed themselves to facilitating commerce at all levels. Petty traders with tourist visas therefore started to flow into Turkey in large numbers, not only from Georgia but from all parts of the old Union. At least initially, Lazistan was the main conduit for this trade, and many of the participants never travelled further into the country. The small towns of this region therefore bore the brunt of a novel phenomenon, which quickly acquired the name of the Russian market (*Rus pazarı*), even though few of the traders were in fact ethnic Russians. These markets became the focus of enormous fascination and controversy, especially during our fieldwork in 1992–3.[18]

In the first place, the new merchandise obviously had direct economic consequences. Most trader-tourists had the basic goal of returning home with as many dollars as possible. They therefore endeavoured to spend as little as possible

[17] See Hale 1995: 57–61.
[18] For further discussion of these points see Hann and Bellér-Hann 1998. For comparisons in the Bulgarian context see Konstantinov 1997.

Plate 3.4 A Lada from Georgia attracts a small crowd in Pazar, January 1992.

Plate 3.5 Market day in Pazar, April 1992, when the *Rus pazarı* was at its peak.

during their stay, bringing their own food and often sleeping in their cars or buses (a high proportion came in organised coach parties). Even so, particularly in the winter months they often needed accommodation and sustenance. They therefore provided custom for the proprietors of small hotels and, to a lesser extent, restaurants. Other shopkeepers benefited if they stocked goods that were cheaper in Turkey than across the border. Extreme shortages of most goods created many opportunities for Turkish entrepreneurs.

Many local shopkeepers, however, stood to lose from the arrival of the trader-tourists, who, in addition to perishables and consumables such as surplus fuel from their vehicle's tank, offered a wide range of cheap socialist manufactured goods. Many among the less prosperous families of Lazistan found these goods attractive. They were able to buy, for example, crockery or kitchen appliances they would not otherwise have been able to afford. Some local shopkeepers undoubtedly lost business and they were vociferous in condemning the poor quality of the imported merchandise. Others, for example in the clothing sector, themselves bought material from trader-tourists, for later resale from their shops. Some tailors did good business as people ordered clothes to be cut from ex-Soviet cloth and silk, instead of buying Turkish goods off the peg.

In some respects these new markets operated very much as any economist might predict. Some of the objects transacted were standard items that exchanged at 'equilibrium' prices: an expansion in supply would lead to a fall in the price, and vice versa. It was not possible for us to test this in any rigorous way, partly because the flow of goods was highly irregular. We did not find much variation in prices for such standard items in different parts of the region, though it was sometimes claimed that the best bargains were to be found in the markets closest to the border, while further along the coast traders attempted to charge more in order to compensate themselves for higher transportation costs. In general, good communications enabled both buyers and sellers to keep track of price levels through the informal sharing of information. Although we could not assess the overall macroeconomic impact of these markets, we were struck by the large numbers of people who visited the marketplaces to inspect the goods available, with no serious intention of buying anything. They sometimes popped by several times in a day, if word spread that some fresh coaches had arrived. The markets became a constant topic of conversation in all social circles. Neither the goods nor the people selling them had been seen in the region before, and their very novelty was a source of excitement, even though their initial impact on local taste and consumer preferences seemed very limited. There were a few exceptions to this, such as children's toys, where the trader-tourists filled a previously neglected niche. We noted some demand for paintings with unlikely religious imagery. Members of the local elites started collecting crystal ware (vases, ashtrays, bowls). Some women accumulated large stocks of materials, especially patterned silk and cotton. One affluent family with grown-up children built up an impressive collection of dolls. In general, however, people bought basic goods from utilitarian motives.

Local people were careful not to buy clothes or other items of personal adornment that would cause them to be mistaken for or even associated with the visitors. The trader-tourists were perceived as poor, enduring difficult, even humiliating conditions because of the complete failure of communism. Such people might be objects of pity, particularly perhaps if they happened to share your religion; but the most basic feeling of local consumers towards these traders was one of superiority. For most Turkish citizens such feelings are comparatively rare. The rhetoric of Kemalism has never concealed the fact that a significant gulf in living standards still separates them from most western European countries. Turks are quite used to comparing the products of Turkish industry unfavourably with the products of foreign competitors. Many people in Turkey, and not only those who supported left-wing parties at the polls, had taken it for granted that standards of production in the socialist world were similarly high. Hence it was a surprise, a gratifying surprise, to discover that many of the trader-tourists were visibly poor, and that some of the goods they marketed were shoddy in comparison with home-produced equivalents. Even people who bought these goods, because they were so much cheaper, often disparaged their quality. People who had previously viewed their own currency as highly unstable and preferred to hold their own savings in foreign currency accounts now saw it in a different light. The Turkish lira was a currency convertible into dollars, and for this reason alone a positive symbol of Turkey's successful capitalist economy.[19]

For these reasons we think that the proliferation of the Russian markets had a unifying rather than a divisive impact on the people of Lazistan. This was not readily predictable. It might have been expected that the opening of the border and the influx of traders, many of them from Georgia, including some who spoke a language (Mingrelian) closely related to Lazuri, would have led at least the members of this category to recognise that, historically, they had closer ties to the Caucasus than to the rest of Anatolia. We did not notice any such effect. Lazi sometimes found communication on the marketplace a little easier than other local residents, but even for them the traders were always emphatically foreign, Soviet, socialist and poor. Similarly, it was occasionally remarked that some of the traders deserved sympathy as fellow Muslims, but this was hardly sufficient for the establishment of any sentiments of solidarity.[20]

Popular sentiments towards these markets were not shaped solely by the disparities in economic conditions and political history. Many people in Lazistan

[19] The consequences of this opening of the border to the east can be compared with attitudes in an earlier period, for Russian influence in this region is not new. When Ottoman Lazistan had strong trading contacts with the Russian Empire, Russian money was extensively used and highly valued. (Marr 1910: 616–19) The sentiments that we found towards the eastern neighbours echo the feelings expressed by Lazi men to Marr in 1910. They considered Russia to be a poor and backward country, where most land was concentrated in the hands of a few. In contrast in Lazistan 'every worker had some property' (ibid.: 555). Everybody knew that Russia had no freedom (ibid.: 625). On the other hand, those with pro-Russian inclinations emphasised the superiority of Russian education (ibid.: 561). In spite of the fact that many migrants and traders could speak some Russian, Marr was amazed at the complete lack of knowledge of Russian culture among the Lazi: to judge from his accounts, they were far better integrated into the Ottoman-Turkish world (ibid.: 624–5).

[20] We did, however, hear rather more sympathy expressed for the economic plight of the traders in their native countries in the eastern parts of Lazistan, as compared with Rize and more western counties. The closer you were to the border, the more opportunity you had to see the poverty that was motivating most of the visitors; some of them were obliged to remain in the vicinity of Hopa and Arhavi, because they lacked the resources to venture further along the coast in search of customers and higher prices for their goods. For discussion of the impact of the border opening on the Georgian side see Pelkmans 1999.

condemned 'the Russians' as 'dirty' (*pis*). This was not primarily a reference to the personal appearance of trader-tourists who were living in their vehicles, nor to the often deplorable sanitary conditions on the sites they took over to sell their goods. The additional ingredient that prompted strong moral condemnation was sex. This is a dimension of human social behaviour which seldom fits easily into the logic of the market and is frequently the object of state laws. Republican Turkey did not attempt to eradicate prostitution altogether, but it did effectively regulate the sector by confining brothels to the major cities. Trabzon was said by people in Lazistan to have retained its 'red light district' until comparatively recently; but by the 1980s the nearest location for sex in commodity form was Ankara, more than 800 kilometres away. This has to be understood in a regional context (not just Lazistan but the entire east Black Sea) where emphasis on female chastity and honour codes is very strong, perhaps even stronger than it is elsewhere in Anatolia.[21] This is a key element in explaining attitudes to the expansion of the Russian markets in the early 1990s, when they became closely associated with new and unprecedented forms of prostitution. In Lazistan, where sexuality is not a topic easily broached in conversation with the other sex, including one's own spouse, the appearance of prostitutes from the ex-communist east was guaranteed to spark controversy. Many of those who entered at Sarp gravitated towards Trabzon, where their activities attracted extensive media coverage. But Rize and each of the smaller coastal towns of Lazistan also had its slice of the action.[22]

The close association that people made between the daily marketplaces and the prostitution business was not objectively warranted. Few prostitutes, popularly known as Natashas, frequented the marketplaces. The market traders were mainly men and older women. The prostitutes stayed in cheap hotels and, though some might carry a small assortment of goods as a pretext, it was obvious to all (certainly to other traders) that their business was elsewhere. Some met clients during the day, and sections of restaurants were sometimes partitioned off for them to make their contacts.[23] But most activity took place in the evenings, much of it lubricated by alcohol, on premises that were specially built or adapted to facilitate this trade. Most women came in pairs or small groups, but these often coalesced into one larger group in the *gazino* in the early evening. Linguistic understanding was often minimal, but gradually the women would be individually propositioned – to dance, to eat, and then elsewhere, back to her hotel or perhaps to a secluded spot on a nearby beach. Some of the women seemed to be in full control themselves of all their activities, while in some cases a higher level of organisation was in the hands of older women – male pimps were rarely in evidence.

[21] For discussion of other districts of the Black Sea region see Meeker 1970, 1976, 1996; Schiffauer 1987; Strasser 1995.

[22] One of the reasons why many people in the small towns of Lazistan found the experience particularly distasteful may have been the fact that more attractive, younger women moved directly to Trabzon, or further to the west, leaving only relatively old and unattractive women in the border region.

[23] Some restaurants adapted an already existing partition, designed to separate the area where only men consumed from the area where women were also served, known as the 'family room' (*aile salonu*). The local families for whom this space had been created then had to be seated in the male-only area.

We were not able to make any careful investigation of the motives and social background of the prostitutes. From talking to a few women on the marketplaces as well as from personal experiences we knew that some foreign women found the attentions of local men an unwelcome irritant. They spoke of frequent harassment by 'uncultured' people and some described local men, more strongly, as 'animals'.[24] In this respect the trader-tourists clearly felt that, despite their economic inferiority, their own level of 'culture' was superior. In other words, the moral condemnation was reciprocated, although neither party was fully aware of the impact of their interaction on the other. Traders at the marketplaces condemned the prostitution, but offered dire economic circumstances at home as providing at least some extenuating circumstances. Turkish media accounts highlighted financial motivation, and concentrated on the top end of the market: cases where well-qualified and attractive blonde Russian women from as far afield as Moscow were attracted by the big money they could earn in Trabzon or Istanbul.

The position of the local women in Lazistan was radically different. The new prostitution led both men and women here to evoke the traditional regional stereotypes of female exploitation. Both stressed the excessive physical burdens on local women in explaining why their men were attracted to the foreigners. Rural women themselves said 'we wither fast' (*çabuk yıpranıyoruz*).[25] These points were taken up by a group of self-styled 'feminists' in Trabzon, middle-class women who concluded that the main lesson to be drawn from foreign prostitution was that local women should spend more money on exercise, clothes, hairdressing and make-up, and learn from the prostitutes how to keep themselves attractive to their men folk. Some of the women who advocated these strategies had never set foot in a village and had no knowledge of the plight of rural women. They were forthright in condemning Turkish men and demonising the foreign women but the remedies they prescribed were hardly realistic.[26]

Women in Pazar also condemned the immorality of the business. They petitioned their *kaymakam* and *vali* to do something to stop it, because it was draining household finances and destroying family life. The religious party was prominent in the articulation of these sentiments, emphasising the region's loss of 'honour' (*namus*). This was frequently coupled with fantastic projections of an AIDS threat. Rumours circulated about how unscrupulous husbands had seized

[24] The regional press reported these sentiments of harassment, but typically in somewhat understated forms. such as 'Russian tourists consider people from the Black Sea region (i.e. local men) uncouth and tending to be inquisitive' (*çok görgüsüz ve tecessüse mayyal kişiler*). See *Ardeşen Sesi*, 4 December 1990.

[25] A similar view was stated by a Lazi man interviewed by a BBC World Service reporter in an Ardeşen *gazino*. The man acknowledged that local women were overworked. He went on to say that contacts with attractive foreign women had been an invigorating experience for him personally. The interview was broadcast on 3 July 1997.

[26] For further details see Bellér-Hann 1995b. The influx of Russian women is not entirely new among the Lazi. Marr was told that many long-term labour migrants, young and old, returned from Russia with Christian wives and as a result at that time about 800 Russian women were living in Atina (Pazar). But in the account of the Russian traveller, it was the foreign women who were deceived: Lazi bakers pretended that they were Christians and assured the women that they would be taken as wives to Christian communities. They only discovered the truth when they had already arrived in isolated mountainous villages, far away from the sea. Eventually they succumbed to the hard life of Lazi women, converted to Islam and learned to communicate in Lazuri. (Marr 1910: 619–20)

jewellery belonging to their wives in order to pay for sexual gratification, or how teenagers had looted their families or robbed strangers in order to pay for sweet pleasures unavailable to any previous generation.[27] These stories were not entirely without foundation. One young man in Sümer walked out on his wife and young family to return to Georgia with the 'friends' he made. He stayed until his money ran out before returning, deeply repentant, to be forgiven by his family. But the stories we could verify did not always carry the implications of female helplessness. Some women seized upon the notoriety of the prostitution business, typically at the time of some local *cause célèbre*, in order to insist that they exercise overall control over family finances, new business ventures, and the marriages of children. Women put pressure on brothers to give up spending on prostitutes by threatening to exercise their legal right to inherit their share of land, which they normally forego according to customary law. Others reported their husbands' immorality at his workplace. Some women argued that post-communist prostitution was going to bring them long-term benefits, by inducing rural women to assert themselves more, e.g. by opening their own bank accounts and insisting that the cash earned from tea plucking be channelled here. Whereas urban, middle-class housewives were gripped by moral panic but helpless to deal with it, some rural women were able to follow through practical strategies for coping with their situation. Such women were more likely to express sympathy with the prostitutes, whom they saw as having to cope with similarly difficult existential conditions.

The social consequences of the new sex trade were therefore complex. Some people made a clear distinction between this and normal market trade, condemning all manifestations of prostitution while forging ahead in new business partnerships with acquaintances in Georgia. State officials made similar points – it was important, they said, not to over-react to the prostitution, which was unimportant in comparison with the long-run benefits that would flow from the 'open border' policy. But most people seemed to see a very close association between the foreign bodies for sale and all the other paraphernalia being sold on the marketplaces. The emotions induced by the prostitution did affect attitudes to petty-marketing and, for some people at least, this led to a more general condemnation of the market principle. The Russian markets gave the people of Lazistan a common sense of sharing in Turkey's economic superiority, but this same phenomenon brought disorder into family lives and polluted the local environment, both literally and figuratively. Local shopkeepers objected to the almost total freedom enjoyed by the trader-tourists, who could spread out directly competing wares on the pavement in front of their own shops, while paying no local taxes. Many, perhaps most, citizens felt that something was seriously wrong if practices that so obviously needed to be brought under effective control were continuing undisturbed. Thus, like the experiments with competition in the tea sector, one of the main effects of the Russian markets in the early 1990s was to create sourness and disillusionment with the principle and the values of *serbest pazar ekonomisi*.

[27] A few pointed out that the phenomenon was not quite as new as some women claimed it to be. Men had taken and sold gold belonging to their wives in earlier years. The arrival of the Russians had merely provided them with new forms of entertainment on which to spend their money, whether illicitly obtained or not.

By the end of the decade the picture had changed again. State officials had insisted all along that complaints about dirt and impropriety and all the negative stereotypes were only short-term reactions, which would give way to more trust and mutual respect as more sophisticated forms of trade developed. In 1997 and 1999 we found these expectations partially confirmed. The earlier excitement had faded completely. Numerous entrepreneurs had built up working relationships with Georgian partners. Some traders sold alongside local Turks at municipality-built covered markets in the larger towns (Rize and Trabzon), where the goods include Dubai tablecloths, Indian skirts and Chinese bras. The traders had all but disappeared from smaller towns like Pazar and Fındıklı. The foreigners entering Turkey at Sarp no longer headed for small county towns, but aimed instead for the larger centres, notably Istanbul. Instead of selling bundles of disparate consumer goods, many were coming primarily as buyers. Local people assumed that the influx of cheap goods has stopped because 'these people have sold everything they had.' There was a certain nostalgia for the 'good times' in the early 1990s, when the traders had little idea of the real value of dollars and of their own merchandise. By the end of the decade they knew better and there were no bargains left. The marketplaces had become quieter and the centre of economic gravity had shifted decisively back to the permanent shops of the urban centres.

Prostitution, too, ceased to be a sensation. The business was largely confined to hotels and restaurants, which other people learned to avoid. Foreign women, though easily recognisable, were no longer harassed by strangers if they walked in the streets. In some local families where we had noted strife in 1992–3, peace had returned, however bitter the memories on the side of the woman. A few foreigners have settled in Lazistan more permanently, sometimes in contravention of the employment regulations. In 1997 in Pazar a clothes shop catering specifically for the taste of foreign shoppers employed two Russian women, both fluent in Turkish, to ensure better communication with customers and to advise the owner on the types of goods likely to be most popular with customers. Some foreign women became objects of pity, such as the long-haired girl with crutches who, everybody knew, had been regularly beaten up by her Turkish boyfriend. Some married local men and we were told of cases of women being duped into a religious wedding which had no force in the eyes of the state.[28]

Few people of Lazistan have much inclination to travel into Georgia, which many still think of as dangerous and politically unstable, even at the end of the century. Those who did manage to visit, including a few who did so with their families, usually reported that they had had to modify their previous stereotypes. In particular, people commented positively on the hospitality and high educational attainments of those they met. They were attracted by the more orderly urban planning, and by the cleanliness of streets in the cities. Meanwhile some of those who never crossed the eastern border began to see their visitors in a new and more positive light, and to deprecate behaviour on their own side. In Arhavi

---

[28] For many people, however, the religious wedding is sufficient for legitimacy. When a local woman pointed to a heavily pregnant 'Russian' woman in the street and said that she was 'one of those women', her companion, a woman with a reputation for piety, corrected her by pointing out that she had married with a proper religious wedding. The first woman then apologised for her error.

some Lazi men related that a Georgian male trader had died while visiting Turkey. He should, according to local norms, have been buried the same day, but local people had refused because he was an infidel. Eventually his body had to be taken back to Georgia by his relatives. Our informants were appalled at the behaviour of their fellow countrymen. Some government officials claimed that the availability of prostitutes had led to a decline not only in forced elopements (see Chapter 6) but also in child abuse. The concern with pollution and AIDS was still strong at the end of the decade, but some people told us that the 'Russians' practised 'safe' sex, and that if AIDS were to become a social problem in Lazistan, it would probably be the fault of their own people's misdemeanours in the west. Other commentators focused on 'culture' and urged that more should be done to encourage tourism from the east as it would raise the standard in Lazistan. In one town a highly respected figure made his pleasure in the company of foreign women very public, without attracting the general condemnation this would have brought him in earlier years. Press documentation of immoral actions committed by persons associated with the religious party undermined their ability to maintain a campaign of moral critique.

In summary, Prime Minister Özal's marketisation initiatives made a dent in the economic wall built by the Kemalists around the modern Turkish nation-state. In the first phase of the Russian markets the media lavished attention on the sex trade and contributed to heightened awareness of a cultural wall. However, by the end of the decade this encounter was generating more nuanced discourses. These markets had a significant economic impact and provided good entertainment over several years, but few have been able to develop significant long-term trading partnerships. The most significant effects have probably been those on gender relations at the familial level, to which we shall turn in more detail in the following chapters.

4
Civil Society

Party politics

The principles of state and market are to be found in all human communities and their relative strength is everywhere determined politically. Between, or at any rate distinct from these principles, Turkey has a public sphere that offers space for many kinds of social activity and forms of sociability. These include the non-governmental or voluntary associations that some analysts believe to constitute the kernel of 'civil society'.[1] Just as some actions by the state may promote inequality and division among its citizens, and just as the market may be a force for unity and integration as well as individualist competition, so, too, the space of civil society can be a zone of ambiguity and contradiction. It is tempting to link civil society closely to the market principle, since both emphasise the free choices of individual actors. Some theoreticians, especially those who worked on socialist countries of Eastern Europe, fused market and civil society in a dichotomous model that opposed them to the state.[2] Historians and political scientists have applied similar binary models to the Ottoman-Turkish case.[3] We avoid such models because they do not fit either with the ethnographic realities of contemporary Lazistan or with the perceptions of its population. In later chapters we shall show, as we explore social identities further, how the workings of state, market and civil society are all modified in practice by principles and values rooted in family life and religion.

Compared with the principles of state and market, an ethnographic account of civil society in Lazistan reveals still more substantial deviation from the ideal types of western theoreticians. Formal clubs, associations and non-governmental organisations are not of great importance in the lives of most inhabitants. Cooperatives play a major role in urban housing construction, but they have not developed wider social functions. Most tea growers are nominally members of a village-based cooperative, but most of these exist solely to distribute chemical

---

[1] For a wide-ranging discussion of this concept see Hall 1996. For further anthropological discussions see Hann and Dunn 1996.

[2] See various contributions to Hall 1996 and Hann and Dunn 1996. See also Hann 1990c, Gellner 1994a.

[3] Heper (1985) and Mardin (1969, 1973, 1995) have theorised dichotomous models in the context of the Ottoman state tradition. Keyder (1987) identifies civil society under Kemalism with the market principle. For further discussion of the Turkish case see Hann 1990a.

fertiliser and members do not otherwise cooperate at all.[4] Similarly, urban businessmen are nominally members of their local 'chamber of commerce' (*Sanayi ve Ticaret Odası*), but few play any active role and even fewer believe that this organisation is very effective in representing member interests. Most tea factory workers belong to a trade union, but they are rarely mobilised for action. In one small town in 1992 a number of teachers spoke out for the establishment of a trade union to represent their profession, in what might be seen as an exemplary 'civil society' initiative. However, many other teachers were as apathetic as the wider public. Protests against the new prostitution, discussed in the previous chapter, attracted greater attention, but then died away as quickly as they had arisen without ever establishing any formal organisation. Given this lack of purchase, the concept of civil society can only be applied here if it is interpreted rather loosely. If the 'third sector' in Lazistan looks quite different from that of, say, Scandinavia, we need to ask what other institutions and forms of sociability exist in its place. Such an extension, though diverging from most contemporary usages of civil society, may actually bring us closer to the sense in which it was deployed by scholars such as Adam Ferguson in the eighteenth century. For this great contemporary of Adam Smith, civil society was not a sphere to be contrasted to state or to market, but rather a way to explore the bases of *civility* and *civilisation*, social organisation in the widest sense, with only the military excluded.

The contrast with the currently fashionable ideal type (remote from reality in many western societies as well) is clear in the case of political parties. They are in this region intimately entangled with the structures of the state, with the development of the tea industry, and with the market positions and capacities of activists and supporters. The political complexion of Lazistan is not uniform. Parties which in western terms would be considered right-of-centre, including the religious parties, have traditionally been strong in and around the city of Rize, and they predominate in the region as a whole.[5] Left-of-centre parties have, however, fared better in a number of the smaller towns to the east, and even in some of the adjacent rural districts. People do not choose their party affiliations arbitrarily or without reflection. For many people, party allegiance is an important expression of their basic differences in values, of convictions about the good society and about human nature. People say that, whereas it was once common for families and even larger descent groups (*sülale*) all to vote the same way, nowadays it is common for brothers to support different parties and even for young men to vote differently from their fathers. (It is less common to hear that a husband and wife support different parties.)

During the period of our fieldwork the principal parties on the right, apart

---

[4] In some cases, notably if energetic leaders emerge, these cooperatives may diversify into other branches of commerce and rival village shopkeepers.

[5] 'The religious parties' refers to various parties which, since the 1950s, have been closely identified with Islam. Essentially the same single party has persisted throughout this period, but political vicissitudes have caused it to be suppressed and renamed on several occasions. For most of our research period the party was known as the Welfare Party (*Refah Partisi*). After briefly forming the main party of government, this party was accused of undermining the Kemalist Constitution and suppressed in 1995. It was reformed as the Virtue Party (*Fazilet Partisi*). For further discussion of political parties see Dodd 1969, 1983; Hale 1981.

from the religious party, were the True Path Party and the Motherland Party. The principal parties on the left were the Social Democratic and People's Party and the Democratic Left Party. These parties had at least a minimal organisational presence in each county of Lazistan. Other, smaller parties, including the strongest nationalist party and other parties on the left, were less widely represented, in some cases only in Rize itself. The differences that exist between the various parties are not manifested in their mode of organisation or in their actions when they hold power. Right across the political spectrum, those who engage actively in party politics are overwhelmingly male. The appointment in 1992 of Tansu Çiller as the country's first female prime minister did little to change this. There is a general expectation that the party or parties which hold power at the centre will use the resources of the state to reward supporters at local level. This has been clearly demonstrated in the tea industry, since the Tea Corporation has been by far the most important conduit for the allocation of state resources to Lazistan. Political considerations have influenced the location of factories and the distribution of the jobs that they create. But it is not only in the tea industry that party politics determines the allocation of state resources. For example, if several counties come forward at the same time with proposals to revamp their extra-mural education services, it is the one with the best political ties (*irtibat*) to the Ministry in Ankara that will obtain the resources for a modern building. A similar pattern at a lower level determines which villages will obtain new asphalt roads.[6] It is considered normal for the party or parties that hold power in the city and smaller towns to privilege their own supporters in the filling of the posts under their control. This has helped to entrench one party power in a number of places, and some concede that the jobs factor may exercise more influence over voting behaviour than a person's left or right wing preferences. Some are critical of the practices referred to disparagingly as *torpil*, but for most people the use of connections to obtain some private advantage in an area of the public sector is not viewed any differently from the equivalent route to a private sector job.[7]

The Motherland Party, the new party formed by Turgut Özal which swept to power in 1983, owed much of its popularity to its promise of a new style of politics, one which would break away from the destructive left versus right polarisation of the 1970s. In practice, however, a radical break proved impossible. Mesut Yılmaz, Özal's successor as party leader and prime minister, came under pressure to show that he could deliver the goods that his constituents in Rize expected. His party did so not by building more tea factories but by making public credits available for new economic initiatives, including some in the tourist sector. In one small town, several party activists appeared to benefit personally from this policy. It was sardonically noted by their opponents that 'the person who holds honey in his hands will lick his fingers' (*bal tutan parmağını yalar*).

[6] In theory all villages should have obtained such a road by the end of the 1990s. Yet by August 1999, out of a total of 6138 kilometres of rural road in Rize province, only 550 had been upgraded with asphalt or concrete.

[7] Thus fathers and uncles are expected to use all the resources at their disposal, including political ties, to secure the careers of sons and nephews. Many people give up other employment, such as a small shop or craft activity, in order to obtain even low-paid positions in the state sector, since these are much more secure and bring a pension after 20 or 25 years. Cf. Dubetsky 1976 and White 1994 on the importance of personal ties in both formal and informal sectors in Istanbul.

Under the Motherland Party the numbers of officials and workers in the state tea factories dropped to something a little closer to economically rational levels. However, even here there was a perception that the party was still playing the game in the time-hallowed way, making appointments according to political criteria. When the Motherland Party was defeated at the polls in 1991 and the Tea Corporation passed under the control of a coalition of its opponents, one of the most popular acts of the new prime minister, the veteran leader of the True Path Party Süleyman Demirel, widely known simply as 'Father' (*Baba*), was to end the freeze on public sector recruitment. Workers were hired according to lists drawn up by the new governing parties, in proportion to their voting strength nationally. People who lived in a village where these parties had no active local members stood little chance of obtaining these very desirable jobs unless they had a personal connection that they could activate. A small minority of positions were filled through the drawing of lots.

The practice of filling public sector jobs not through open competition but through the mediation of the political parties is by no means restricted to unskilled jobs in the tea sector. Doctors and teachers can also be denied appointments in their home regions for political reasons. By the time the left of centre Social Democratic and People's Party came to share power in 1991, it had a long queue of deserving supporters whose needs it was expected to address – people who had been frozen out of state posts ever since the military intervention of 1980. Many supporters of this party felt strongly that this was wrong. Sometimes they added a rueful phrase such as 'well, you know, this is Turkey' (*biliyor musun, burası Türkiye*), and asked us to agree that such practices would not occur in any western European country (an assurance we were unable to give them). With the Motherland Party adapting quickly to the traditional mould of party patronage, only the religious party continued to argue for a radically different model of the way political parties should relate to the state. However, when this party came to share power in 1994 it found itself in the same position as the Social Democrats a few years earlier, with a long list of supporters who had been patently disadvantaged in preceding years. Within a short time, they too were accused by their opponents of unfairly diverting the resources of the state to their own supporters.[8]

It is difficult to organise for political action outside the major parties. This was demonstrated in 1999 when a group of western Hemşinli attempted to gather support to oppose a new hydroelectric scheme in their valley. They argued (correctly, as far as we could see) that the scheme was likely to have highly detrimental environmental consequences and formed a *vakıf* to gather funds and

[8] The Motherland Party has remained by far the strongest party in Lazistan in the 1990s, even assuming control of several *belediyes* with a left-of-centre tradition. In Rize province it took 43.5 per cent of all votes in the general election of 1999 (the religious party held on comfortably to second place). The success of the Motherland Party may seem curious, given that its free market policies have obviously had negative consequences for the region, particularly in the tea industry. It is probably to be explained by the high profile of Mesut Yılmaz, the party leader. His supporters emphasise the prospect of having a local MP in high office, even though they simultaneously insist that he is too honest a politician to break the rules to favour his own region. Many supporters no doubt genuinely believe that his market policies are the right ones for both region and country in the long term.

organise meetings.[9] However, the Motherland Party had explicitly endorsed the intervention, and since no other major party was prepared to take a position, no one was optimistic about the chances of having it reversed.

Cafe society

Politics is only one outlet for male sociability in contemporary Lazistan and a comparatively minor one. There are many others, including those that are similarly dominated by men in most other countries. Most towns have thriving sports teams, with football (soccer) by far the most popular. Committee members tend to comprise prominent local businessmen, some of them also involved in local politics. They are expected to invest some money into the local team, perhaps through improving its facilities or, since elements of professionalism have entered in recent years, financing the acquisition of new players and possibly providing a nominal job in their own business. In the more commercial climate of the 1980s sponsorship became important and Rize's team was taken over by the state Tea Corporation. Even in the smaller towns crowds may number several thousand for local derby matches. Fans occasionally get too excited and the police may have to intervene to disperse rival groups; but by most international yardsticks the standard of behaviour is good.

Activities more specific to Lazistan include those organised in the Kaçkar Mountains by hunting associations, which exist in several county towns. However, it is not necessary to join an association in order to hunt or shoot. Some men travel regularly with one or two friends to the other side of the mountains, where the terrain is more favourable for most activities. Interest in falconry is widespread, particularly among Lazi.[10] These birds are only rarely in action but frequently displayed by their admiring handlers. The best birds change hands for substantial sums of money. As with more conventional sports, the aesthetics of this activity are of interest exclusively to men. Bird owners do not have a formal association but tend to congregate at a particular tea house in a convenient hamlet cluster or in the town.

This conforms to the more general pattern of male sociability, based on the patronage of simple cafes (*çayhane*, *kiraathane* or *kahve*). In these establishments one can while away the hours (or, in winter particularly, the days) for no more than the cost of a few rounds of tea.[11] Such cafes were in the past associated mainly with the towns, but with the coming of tea they have spread to most rural areas. In some interior areas where the winter population is very small, it functions in the summer months only. In more populous areas custom remains lively in winter, when more people have time available. Local gossip is the principal pastime, but conversations range widely. Some premises have a political

---

[9] The *vakıf*, a central institution of Islamic civil society, has no religious significance in this context. It is a common form of association, closely resembling that known as a *dernek* ('association'). Both are formalised in that they require security clearance for their establishment and should in theory submit regular records of their office-holders, their activities and their accounts to the state authorities.

[10] Cf. Marr 1910: 626.

[11] On coffee and tea consumption in pre-modern Lazistan see Marr 1910: 621.

Plate 4.1 Cafe society, Pazar.

Plate 4.2 Pazar: the Club for Hunting and Shooting; in the background a man tends his pet hawk.

or religious affiliation, made obvious by the newspapers available to customers, or by the television channel. Some urban cafes have links to particular villages or to specific occupational groups. They are popular places to watch major sporting occasions and they often have a regular core of backgammon players. Some pensioners 'linger' (*takılıyor*) at different cafes at different times of the day, so friends and family always know more or less where to find them. Some shopkeepers effectively run *ersatz* cafes of their own, calling a tea boy to fetch supplies from across the street whenever they have a customer with whom they wish to maintain a long-term relationship. Cafe life in Lazistan is active throughout the year but ebbs during the daytime hours of the Ramadan fast, when the Teachers' Club is often the only place open. Some cafes close for the entire duration of the fast, but most spring into life when the sun goes down: after eating at home, men gather convivially in their regular haunts until the early hours of the morning.

This attachment to the cafe does not imply an ideal of idle relaxation, in opposition to work. Only a man who has worked hard for many years, whether in the region or outside it, can sit comfortably (*rahat*) in his preferred tea house day after day, and not be criticised for idleness. At the same time, many older men, including those who have officially retired and draw a pension, remain economically active. Younger men often need to visit cafes in order to make the connections that may bring them work. They are an important mechanism for spreading information about where labour is needed, notably to the sharecroppers who pour into Lazistan at the commencement of the tea plucking season.

Not all men frequent cafes regularly. Many who live in rural areas pop in only once a week on market day when they travel down to the coast. Some settlement clusters do not have even a simple tea house; but even in those that do, some men are equally happy to sit for hours by the side of the road or outside a post-office or shop, sharing the news of the community. Some men construct a special small building (*köşk*) for such *muhabbet* on a suitable corner of their land, or they may adapt a granary (*serender*) for this purpose. It is rare for men to avoid company by remaining within their houses. Those who do so are mostly very old and/or infirm, or they have been shunned by other men and excluded from the community.[12]

The basic characteristics of male cafe society have not changed very much in recent years, but consumption has begun to diversify. It is now possible in most cafes to order coffee and soft drinks as alternatives to tea. The number of pastry shops and small restaurants has also increased. Billiard rooms provide entertainment for the young. Older men can now choose between a variety of establishments that serve alcoholic drinks. The steady upward trend in beer consumption accelerated sharply after the impact of the Russian markets, discussed in Chapter 3. For those with money, most conspicuously returning migrants during the months of summer who have their own cars, the coastline of Lazistan now offers a fair number of 'up-market' restaurants, *gazinos* and *müzikols*, where it is easy to spend more in one evening than the patron of a rural tea house spends in a year.

One further form of association in which men predominate is the emerging interest in regional traditions and 'culture'. In one small town a few Lazi men

---

[12] In one case, which we could not verify, this was said to be the fate of a former migrant worker who was thought by his fellow-villagers to be mistreating the German wife he had brought back following his years of working in that country.

have attempted to set up a library and museum to exhibit distinctive features of local architecture, songs and folk poetry. Since they have no official recognition as a minority group these initiatives are necessarily discreet. However, the members of this group are cautiously optimistic about the prospects for more formal consolidation of their association (*dernek*) in the future. Such centres have long existed with official approval in the major cities of the west, notably Ankara and Istanbul. These have stressed not ethnic group affiliation but *hemşerilik*, which usually means common county of origin. Thus both Lazi from coastal villages around Pazar and Hemşinli from interior villages are eligible to become members of the Istanbul association for the people of Pazar. Some of these centres publish newsletters and magazines, and have regular programmes of social events. Although these events are for men and women together, or for whole families, the organisation of the associations is in male hands. Such centres facilitate economic links between migrants, as well as serving to promote social integration in the metropolis and binding members into an ongoing sentimental link to their roots in Lazistan. Clearly the role of a cultural centre within the home region would be a very different one. The larger issues of group identity will be explored further in Chapter 8.

Rotating savings and credit associations

Women do not participate in cafe society. Exceptionally, for example when visiting town or on a long journey, women and children eat in the 'family room' (*aile salonu*) of a small restaurant. Instead, women have their own forms of sociability, mostly away from the public arena and informal. From their homes, the more affluent, non-working urban women, have over the last thirty years developed a new form of socialising that incorporates an economic element. This is derived from the 'reception day' (*kabul günü*) reported elsewhere in Anatolia.[13] In Lazistan the most common name is 'gold day' (*altın gün*), while some refer to it as 'money day' (*paralı gün*). If you hear that 'so and so is having a day today', you understand at once that she is hosting one of these gatherings. The pattern is as follows. A small number (at most a dozen) of women agree to get together on a regular basis (often monthly), visiting each member's home in turn in a cycle that may last up to a year, depending on the exact number of participants. The gathering usually takes place in the early afternoon, when no men are in the house, and it lasts several hours. In preparation, women typically go to the hairdresser's and put on clothes made especially for the occasion. Refreshments, often a full meal, are provided by the hostess. Participants chat, tell jokes, listen to music and dance.[14] Apart from group members, only a few young children and perhaps an elderly relative of the hostess are present. Each participating woman

[13] For discussion of women's 'reception days' elsewhere in Anatolia see Benedict 1974b, Aswad 1974, Fallers and Fallers 1976, N. Tapper 1983, Wolbert 1996. A brief description of the 'gold day' in Istanbul is given by White 1994: 9–10. For a detailed discussion of similar practices among Turkish women in Cyprus see Khatib-Chahidi 1995. For more detail on Lazistan see Bellér-Hann 1996. On rotating savings and credit associations internationally see Ardener and Burman 1995. They are brought into a common framework with mutual aid groups and other forms of informal associations by March and Taqqu 1982.

[14] Elite, *sosyete* women may also gamble (*kumar oynamak*) during these meetings.

contributes the cash equivalent (on that particular day, as verified by local jewellers) of a specified quantity of gold, usually one or two grams; the exact amount depends on the financial strength of the participating families.[15] Lots are drawn to determine who, among those who have not yet benefited in this cycle, will receive the pooled sum. A member who is prevented from attending on a particular occasion sends her contribution to the hostess.

This custom was apparently brought to Lazistan by government officials in the 1960s, when silver was the usual currency. It continues to provide an important mechanism for integrating non-local women into small-town society. Many of the women who participate are well educated and wealthy, able to employ other women to help with their household chores. Group membership is often influenced by the position and work relationships of the husband. For example, wives of officials working in the tea industry may be concentrated in one group, and wives with a link to the Government Building in another. However, groups are seldom completely exclusive. Kin ties are often significant, but an unrelated woman with an outgoing, attractive personality may be welcome if her husband is of sufficient social standing.[16] The gold days provide all women with an opportunity to meet, to talk, and to stay in touch.

Conversation at these meetings ranges from family events and local news to the latest developments in popular television serials and newspaper scandals. It can jump back and forth between the real person of the TV star, as known through other media, and the character she plays. Discussion may confirm views about proper moral behaviour, as prescribed by tradition, but it can also lead to the modification of standards. For example, discussion of the prostitutes associated with the Russian markets was premised throughout on the fact that modest Turkish women were morally superior. However, stories about these markets led to more critical scrutiny of male behaviour than ever before. Without ever questioning male domination *per se*, women's discussion in these years contributed to altering perceptions of the other sex.

A further function of these gatherings is the confirmation and modification of standards of material culture. This applies particularly to the groups known as *sosyete*, whose tastes and behaviour in everything from cooking and crochet patterns to the education of children are followed closely by other groups lower down the hierarchy.[17] Moral effects may be noticed here, too, for some elite women are thought to overstep the acceptable boundaries of modesty, e.g. by paying too much attention to gambling and not enough to religion. But even the critical probably harbour some admiration for the freedom of movement that some of these women demonstrate and their seemingly complete freedom from male interference.

[15] Some groups used a special gold coin with the image of Atatürk, but the currency did not have to be gold at all. Some prosperous families stipulated higher sums in German marks. Sometimes women agreed to tie the sum to the price of a consumer product and there was lively discussion about what it should be. Examples in 1999 included sets of bed linen and mobile telephones.

[16] This is easier for the wife of a bank manager than for the wife of an ordinary primary school teacher.

[17] Those classified as *sosyete* are by no means equally wealthy. In cases of *agha* families whose material fortunes have declined, it is sometimes 'spendthrift' women who are held to blame. Yet the public behaviour, dress code and child rearing customs of such women may nonetheless be held up by other women as models for emulation.

Although the motivation for participation in these groups is not primarily financial, the economic element is also significant. Outside the elite groups, the direct material incentives for participation are considerable since the funds are often used to purchase a substantial item of household equipment. Economic rather than social aspects predominate in the groups that are organised in some work-places, in which colleagues complete the transactions perfunctorily, perhaps over a cup of tea in their lunch break on payday, paid for by the person receiving the funds. In some of these workplace credit associations, male colleagues also take part.

Many women, in all social strata, have only little or no access to their hus-bands' earnings. They typically use the money they obtain through the group to purchase jewellery, usually gold, which is then their personal property. Men have no right to touch this, either in customary or in modern law. This provides women with a personal fund under their exclusive control and an insurance in case of crisis. Husbands accept this, because they share in the prestige that membership brings. Participation does more than confirm the status of a woman in the local community: it is also a statement about the position of her family.[18]

Modified forms of the gold day have begun to penetrate into rural areas. Here the sums of money involved are usually smaller, and the hospitality and entertainment on a reduced scale. There is again a fusion of economic and social motivations. Many women may have a specific practical use for the funds they receive when their turn comes. However, it is difficult to say that this outweighs the pleasure they derive from putting on their best clothes, sitting in the main living room of another house (not the kitchen area where they usually sit during informal visits), and feeling that they are emulating the fashionable women of the town. Like some urban women who lack the financial means to participate in gold days along the lines described above, poorer rural women instead organise 'towel days' (havlu günü), in which each participant contributes an embroidered towel to the pool. This fund typically goes into a daughter's trousseau. It brings a material advantage, but it does nothing to improve the participant's financial status or long-term personal security.

These women's associations have not developed 'from below', out of the tradi-tions of Lazistan, but have been widely disseminated following the examples of outsiders and local elite women. They have become an important vehicle for female sociability and integration, particularly for urban newcomers. A more general source of their attraction is the sense that participation brings a woman into a novel form of contact with other women, and somehow closer to modernity. Despite the ostensible expressed principle of strict equality in the pooling arrangements, the scope for hospitality and display also promotes status competition and feeds back into the growth of a national society of consumers, as noted in Chapter 3.

Mutual aid

The difficulties in disentangling social from economic motivations are also apparent in institutions that do have roots in the Lazistan past, and which have developed new forms 'from below'. Both men and women continue to interact

[18] This is termed 'status-production work' by Papanek 1989.

sociably through work. For example, activities related to mosque-building are conspicuous in both urban and rural areas. In a recent innovation, the men of one village attend Friday prayers in the mosque of another during the tea plucking season and ask at the end of the service if the inhabitants of that village have any surplus tea available. By this they mean quantities in excess of the Tea Corporation's current quotas. In theory such 'surplus' still has a commodity value if it can be sold to a private factory, but in view of the unreliability of the private sector (see previous chapter) people are usually willing to convert this surplus into a gift, if they know that any eventual proceeds will be put to financing mosque work. A year later the donors make a return visit to see the new mosque; they submit a similar request for surplus tea, and receive a similar gift.

In rural areas males are from time to time called upon for minor road works or bridge repairs. Even for more substantial road building, local residents, sometimes summoned by their village headman, the *muhtar*, are expected to turn out to work alongside the staff and bulldozer provided by the state's 'village services' (*köy hizmetleri*) department. Large work groups to establish tea gardens are no longer convened, in part because by the 1990s few districts had much scope for further expansion of the garden area. Only the maintenance of the leaf collection points (*alım yeri*) remains a local responsibility, demanding male labour cooperation. In recent years men have worked together to install *teleferiks* – steel cables used to transport even substantial weights from roads in valley floors to houses that are either completely inaccessible to motor transport or not served by the regular shared taxis.

The labour requirements of house building have also changed in recent years. Most tasks are nowadays carried out by urban-based professionals who do not necessarily possess any qualifications and often depend on the labour inputs of the new immigrant underclass. Rural families still seek economies where they can, for example by using their own trees to save the cost of timber for the roof. Relatives, neighbours and friends will help out with the work in return for food and drink. The household which benefits from the cooperation makes no specific promise to return. The reciprocity is implicit and long-term.

Whereas male labour cooperation is mostly restricted to specific, one-off activities, many rural women work together in more enduring and systematic ways. The generic Turkish term for cooperation is *imece*, but local usage prefers the form *meci*.[19] The gender difference in mutual aid is said to date back to well before the arrival of tea, to the period when women carried out a wider range of agricultural tasks. Maize, the main subsistence crop, was extremely labour-intensive. This work was more tolerable if carried out sociably, by a group of women together. It was also safer to work thus, given that women had moral as well as physical anxieties about working alone. Moreover it often made economic sense, since the variegated topography of the region meant that the cycle of tasks proceeded more

---

[19] For alternative terminology see Paleczek 1987: 149; Özgün 1996: 125. For descriptions of *meci* among the Lazi in western Anatolian migrant villages see Paleczek 1987: 149–55; Özgün 1996: 125–43. For more detail on Lazistan see Solak n.d.: 32; Kesici-Sırtlı 1999: 53–4, Özgün 1996: 125–8. According to Özgün, the term *meci* is used only for all-female groups; male groups and mixed work groups were known among the Lazi as *nodayi*. Brief discussions of *imece* are also given by Schiffauer 1987: 138–45; Onaran-Incirlioğlu 1991: 241–3, and Delaney 1993: 150–55.

slowly in some fields than in others. *Meci* was also popular in the hazelnut groves.

The principles of reciprocity and rotation underlying the classic form of *meci* are basically the same as those which underlie the savings and credit associations. Word is sent out to other households in advance, a cooked meal must be provided by the host, and at least one member of the hosting household must participate in the work. These are not fixed, bounded groups, although there is likely to be considerable overlapping in the course of each agricultural season. Participation in *meci* is an investment of labour resources which creates open-ended reciprocal ties that reinforce pre-existing multi-stranded ties of kinship, neighbourliness and friendship.

The popularity of *meci* has diminished since tea was introduced. The reasons are at least partly given by the nature of the new crop. The fact that plucking periods are unlikely to coincide for each household should in itself be conducive to *meci*. However, due to variety within the gardens of any one household it is usually detrimental to the harvest if all its tea is plucked at the same time. *Meci* became more problematic in the early 1980s when the Tea Corporation introduced quota measures for each registered grower. Households do often supplement their labour resources for harvesting tea, primarily through the return of migrants and through the use of hired labourers and sharecroppers. Exceptionally, male labour is also diverted into supporting what is seen primarily as a female responsibility. Assistance to other households is occasionally offered at the end of a plucking period, when one's own harvest is complete. But if systematic cooperation between households in the harvesting of tea is rare, women still prefer, as in the past, to work in company. Sociability and safety are equally stressed. Some women still express fear of evil spirits (*cin*) which are believed to be lurking in the tea gardens. More prosaically, they need to help each other in lifting large quantities of tea and then again in laying down the load at the collection points. Working in pairs is therefore common. Two sisters may form a partnership that continues after they marry and work in different households. Dyads formed by sisters-in-law are also common in the tea gardens. The common meal of traditional *meci* is more likely to be substituted by a short pause in someone's kitchen for tea and conversation. Little attention is paid to the details of who provides the tea, or which partner may be deriving greater benefit from the cooperation in a particular month, or even a particular year.

The dominant role of tea in the generation of cash income does not mean that traditional *meci* has disappeared altogether. In some areas it persists in its old form as a rotating labour association, usually focused on the vegetable garden and interrupted by a meal. Women also work together in more limited ways in other jobs, notably the collection of firewood (driftwood in the coastal hamlets) and fresh grass for the cow. Both of these tasks are time-consuming and likely to require a long walk away from the hamlet. They are also demanding physically, since each woman returns with a heavy basket on her back (sometimes with additional bundles strapped on top). As with tea, the initial lifting and final unloading of this weight may require assistance. Cooperation in this task may cement close bonds of friendship between in-marrying women. For those who have not moved far from their natal cluster, it may be the main vehicle for maintaining one's previous female relationships.

Other types of cooperation are summed up as 'neighbourliness' (*komşuluk*). This takes basically the same forms in urban and rural areas and consists in a willingness to provide informal assistance whenever this is needed, such as lending food to the woman next door who has just run out of something, or looking after her children while she is in hospital giving birth. In this way women maintain strong ties which they can activate at any time simply by dropping by (or, increasingly in the 1990s, by picking up the telephone). If one woman is unlucky enough to be told at a tea collection point that her tea needs to be sorted before it will be accepted, to approximate more closely the 'two leaves and a bud' norm, neighbours and friends waiting to deliver their own tea will readily lend a hand. On market days women help each other in taking goods to and from the town, and in sharing any extra information to which they gain access. Female labour cooperation is elaborate in the preparations for village weddings, when the mood is usually one of ebullience. In the sombre mood that follows a death, women gather for mourning and cooked food is provided by neighbours for several days to the household of the deceased.

The main difference between *meci* and *komşuluk* is that *meci* is still strongly associated with productive activities carried on outside the house, whether for cash (tea) or as part of the residual subsistence economy, notably wood and fodder collection, and it should ideally have the structural elements of rotation and reciprocity. In some ways it is the structural opposite of the gold day, which is characterised by status competition, formalised hospitality and regulated reciprocity. *Meci* is focused on production not consumption, and it has more informal patterns of hospitality and open-ended reciprocity. *Komşuluk* features even less structuration. It is the informal pooling of resources in the domestic sphere by women who usually know each other extremely well. Tasks such as childminding, or care for the old and the sick, are prominent in this female sphere and therefore open to *komşuluk*. Whereas old people's homes and hospices can be viewed as characteristic institutions of civil society in the modern west, the Lazistan equivalents are still to be found in the realm of the family, and primarily in the caring practices of women.

Gender

In this chapter we have been concerned with civil society as a zone of social activity between the principles of state and market, and between the family on the one hand and modern offices and institutions on the other. Unlike the principles of state and market, which are recognised in local discourse (as when people speak of the state as *devlet baba* or speak out for or against the ideal of the *serbest pazar ekonomisi*), civil society is not a local model at all. The word *halk* is often used inclusively to denote 'the people', but this populist aggregation is remote from current definitions of civil society in terms of intermediary associations and non-governmental organisations. The modern Turkish word for society, *toplum*, is an abstruse term seldom heard in Lazistan, while *sivil toplum* is used only by a few intellectuals in the Western Anatolian cities. Patterns closer to the civil societies of western countries are well established in these cities, where large middle classes participate in a variety of formally constituted associations. A narrow focus on such associations, however, may be misleading even here. The bases of social activity in the poorer districts of Istanbul are found not in formal associations but in ideas about reciprocity analogous to those held by many villagers.[20] In Lazistan, too, the formal institutions are weakly developed and seldom of major significance. It is more important to understand the networks that flourish informally, between neighbours, friends, colleagues and workmates. It is often difficult and not very fruitful to disentangle economic interest from sociability in these networks. They are not civic institutions, they do not mediate or represent, at least not in the usual sense of the political scientist and they contribute to outcomes that contradict the meritocratic ideals of modern western democracies (as when *torpil* is employed to secure personal goals). Yet these networks of informal practices add up to a realm that is autonomous of the state and not reducible to the logic of the market. It therefore falls within civil society as we use this term. There are also good grounds for including in this realm a number of institutions linked to Islam, but we postpone consideration of these until Chapter 7.

The most striking deviation from the models of western political science is the marked influence of gender on most forms of sociability in this region.[21] The Kemalists, as we have noted, were in theory fully committed to gender equality. Although Atatürk's own marriage was short-lived, it is known that he enjoyed the company of westernised Turkish women and actively promoted western models of interaction. Since his death the numbers of women in waged employment and in the most prestigious professions have continued to increase. In numerous sectors the proportion of women is higher than the corresponding figure in most western countries. In the fashionable areas of the big cities gilded youth behaves in ways that appear at least superficially to resemble cosmopolitan norms. Yet in the poorer districts, crowded with new immigrants, the picture is very different. Here most women wear a headscarf, and many a full veil (*çarşaf*).[22] As in many smaller towns and villages of Anatolia, many families see little point in supporting the education of daughters. They are married off young, becoming the responsibility of another household and losing close ties with their natal families. In rural regions the proportion of women in employment remains extremely low.

Lazistan falls somewhere between these extremes. It is a particularly interesting case because of the well-known stereotypes of the position of women in this region. These have retained their fundamentally negative force, despite the praises lavished by Atatürk on the tough peasant women of Anatolia.[23] The region

---

[20] See White 1994; cf. White 1996. For more general discussion of reciprocity in the rural context see Schiffauer 1987.

[21] Of course this strong separation between the worlds of men and the worlds of women is by no means peculiar to Lazistan or to Turkey. Close parallels can be found in other Muslim societies and with non-Muslim Mediterranean societies, and comparisons can be made with patterns of gender segregation in other parts of the world. For further discussion of gender and civil society in Muslim societies see Rabo 1996. Here we confine our attention to the Turkish context, within which the patterns of Lazistan do not differ substantially from those found in most other regions of Anatolia.

[22] We agree with Göle (1996) that it is important to distinguish between full veiling, in many cases a very recent phenomenon, and the persistence of the headscarf; but both are rejected by the Kemalists.

[23] 'In contrast to Ottoman women, who were considered coquettish and alienated from their people,

remains a long way from achieving the conjugal ideals to which the Kemalists aspired. State officials and businessmen are predominantly male. Few women who proceed to higher education return to live and work in this region.[24] Married couples seldom visit each others' houses as couples, and it is expected that each partner will continue to cultivate separate social networks.[25] Visiting as a couple is confined mostly to *sosyete* circles and specific groups such as high-ranking officials and teachers; and even when couples go together, they are likely to chat and to eat in separate single-sex groups. The principle of segregation has been extended into new space that was intended to overcome it: in the municipal parks that have been established in most small towns the young married couples who take their children along tend to split and form separate, single-sex groups.

The modesty code is visible to all from early socialisation. Girls notice that their mother is quick to don a headscarf and to roll down the sleeves of her blouse when a man from outside the immediate family enters their house. Some young girls begin to cover their hair from the moment they enter school, aged six or seven. Though the scarf cannot be worn inside the school, it can at least be worn on the journey there and back. By the time they enter puberty most rural girls and a high proportion of town dwellers are following the same dress code as their mothers. Their movements outside the immediate neighbourhood (*mahalle*) are strictly controlled. Most people in all age groups say that it would be *ayıp* (shameful) for women to behave differently. Most accept that a young female urban office-worker must discard the headscarf on working days; rather fewer accept that she may display her hair freely on other days as well; she is expected to put on a headscarf if she visits elderly relatives in the countryside, or attends a wedding party where the hosts are known to have strong religious loyalties. Girls who refuse the headscarf as a matter of principle are criticised as *ayıp* or *saygısız* (disrespectful).[26]

Boys are more spoiled and enjoy greater freedom to play, while girls are subjected to more discipline and are expected to make a contribution to household tasks at an age when this is not yet expected of their brothers.[27] On hot

---

[23] (cont.) and Muslim women, who were considered to be subordinated by religion and alienated from progress, Anatolian women were brought onto the scene as main figures. Just as populism supported Kemalist nationalism, the Kemalist women's movement glorified Anatolian women in contrast to Ottoman cosmopolitanism. The attributes of Anatolian women, accentuated in the discourses of Mustafa Kemal, still lie in the collective Turkish memory: "It is always they, the noble, self-sacrificing, godly Anatolian women who plough the land, fell firewood in the forest, barter in the market-place and run the family; and above all, it is still they who carry the ammunitions to the front on their shoulders, with their ox-carts, with their children, regardless of rain, winter and hot days." Anatolian women were both the "savers" and the "saved" ones: they were expected to save the republican values from 'degeneration', while these reforms, in turn, saved them from the fanaticism of Islam. Thus, Kemalist women served as a bridge between civilization and nation.' (Göle 1996: 64).

[24] Unmarried women with higher education do sometimes return to their home town after retirement (when they are typically in their mid- or late-forties). They form a small but highly respected section of the category *sosyete*.

[25] Magnarella argued that a 'rather rigid segregation of conjugal roles' (1998: 106) was beginning to undergo major changes in the town he studied in the 1960s.

[26] The key terms *ayıp* (shameful) and *namus* (honour) have Lazuri equivalents in *oşine* and *oncşore* respectively.

[27] For more detailed discussion of the gendered dimensions of socialisation in Turkey see Kağıtçıbaşı 1982; Delaney 1991: 72–98; White 1994: 62–5, 71–3; Göle 1996.

summer days when pre-pubescent boys can bathe freely in the stream that flows through their valley, their sisters must help at home or accompany their mothers to the tea gardens. Even in conveniently located coastal villages, few girls learn to swim. Segregation is strongly enforced from adolescence. Teenagers are not able to socialise with members of the other sex. Sitting together in the public park after classes, or even a chaperoned meeting with a boy in the relative privacy of a pastry house, can provoke parental wrath and neighbourhood gossip. These conventions are broken only by a few young people and by strangers to the region, including relatives making a summer visit from Germany. These girls or young women gather in small groups 'to wander about' (*gezmek*) but after a short period in 'public' space (e.g. at the Russian market) they normally settle down for the evening in the privacy of someone's home. Even when there is no male company, others often criticise such 'loitering' when it is conducted by women. It is entirely acceptable among men. In short, the separation of male and female worlds corresponds to one standard usage of the distinction between public and private spheres.[28]

Pazar has established an annual tea party early in May at the municipal hall, nominally to mark Mother's Day (*Anneler Günü*). Until 1992 the event had been sponsored by the officers of the nearby radar station. When a new commanding officer disclaimed responsibility, it was taken over by the local education authority and in 1992 it was successfully organised by primary school teachers. It was open only to urban women (even if space and resources had allowed for the invitation of villagers, tea plucking obligations at this time would have limited their attendance). The only men present were a few male teachers and musicians. The (female) deputy head of the school gave a welcoming speech and sweets and soft drinks were served. Women sat in groups determined by kinship, workplace and social class. Members of the local elite sat prominently near the stage. The atmosphere was relaxed, an orchestra performed several songs in Lazuri, and some women grabbed the microphone spontaneously and sang. As more and more joined in the dancing, the earlier rigidity of the sitting order was abandoned: locals mingled with strangers, housewives with professionals. The ostensible purpose of this party was charitable. Raffle tickets were sold for the benefit of the school organising the event. When it seemed, towards the end of the party, that many tickets were still unsold, a leading *sosyete* personality intervened to save the day. She took the leftover tickets from the deputy head, purchased a substantial number herself, and simply instructed those around her to buy the rest. The event went down as a great success, and many expressed the view that such entertainments should be held more often.[29]

---

[28] The distinction between public and private spheres is closely related to civil society theory. We maintain, however, that civil society, like the institutions and practices linked to the principles of market and state, embraces both the public and the private, the formal and the informal, for both men and women. For careful discussions of diverging applications of the public/private opposition see Weintraub and Kumar 1997. The dichotomy has figured prominently in feminist studies, including anthropology. Ethnographic work, however, has often undermined the assumption that power differentials can be mapped onto this dichotomy. It is not self-evident that the conversations of women, confined to domestic space, have less impact on community norms and behaviour than the conversations of men in their workplaces and cafes. See Dubisch 1986 for some Greek illustrations.

[29] Its inclusiveness was incomplete. Women from conservative families were not afraid to attend, since they knew it was a single sex party. However, a few women who habitually wore the full veil and

Somewhat paradoxically, the rules of segregation are more relaxed at the major religious holidays, when family visiting is the main activity. But the most striking departure from normality is the cultural festival, which has become a regular annual event in a number of Lazistan counties. One of the most popular events is that held over a weekend in the Hemşinli *yayla* of Ayder, located in a beautiful valley high up in the mountains. It provides summer pasture for a number of Hemşinli villages. The state, motivated by the valley's tourist potential, has built a tarmac access road and a bathhouse at the hot spring. Local people have added some small hotels and shops, and the community is a busy summer base for native and foreign trekkers in the Kaçkars. On the weekend of the festival, those coming from adjacent villages and small towns far outnumber the foreigners. Despite unpromising weather, in 1993 they arrived in droves in minibuses and on the backs of trucks. Some young men came to camp for a noisy weekend, with an abundant supply of alcohol and the latest cassettes from Istanbul to play on their sophisticated audio equipment. Some older people came primarily for the hot baths, having booked their hotel room a year in advance. The majority were day-trippers, who arrived as family groups with large picnic baskets. Few stayed in the mixed group for long. Some of the more entrepreneurial men saw the festival as an opportunity to make money through the sale of food and refreshments, from informal stalls that needed no licence. Groups of men patrolled the edges of the arena, or gathered for impromptu renditions of the communal dance known as *horon*. Some were good dancers, others not, but virtually everyone took part at some point. Women tended to huddle in groups to chat with relatives and former school mates, whom they no longer saw regularly. Everyone enjoyed the performances of visiting folklore troupes. The only performers who did not receive warm applause were the state dignitaries who arrived in a cavalcade of black cars, badly delayed by the chaotic throng in Ayder's narrow street, to make the opening speeches. People had come to be with their friends and families and to enjoy themselves, not to listen to official speeches. In summary, these festivals seem to offer a modern version of the 'communitas' previously associated with the *yayla* and they are popular with men and women of all ages. In addition to their political and economic significance, they deserve also to be seen as significant expressions of civil society in contemporary Lazistan.

[29] (cont.) for whom all forms of music and dancing were a sin (*günah*) did not turn up. Female members of the new local underclass were similarly absent.

5
Patriarchy

Baskets: a key symbol?

The last three chapters have progressively extended the notion of public sphere beyond state and government to include not only the decentralised interaction of the market but also all the diffuse sociability of civil society. In doing so we have seen that each of these realms also impinges on the private and personal. In particular, we saw in Chapter 4 that, compared to most western societies, gender divisions and segregation are marked. In this chapter we explore how far deviations from the ideal type of civil society can be explained in terms of another ideal type, that of patriarchy.[1] Like civil society, this is not a concept used locally. However, people in Lazistan do nowadays talk readily of their traditions and customs, often apparently imagining them as a package, to be contrasted to another package that defines modernity. Each of these packages can be thought of as a bundle of values or ideals, potentially available to all for disaggregation. There is no consensus about the contents of each bundle. Some draw a distinction between one modern variant which emphasises the individual and the free market economy, and an alternative which emphasises the collective responsibilities of the state. But opposed to both of these is the bundle which appeals consciously to tradition, to the past as a source of values. Whether explicitly invoked or not, this bundle has greater salience in the personal and familial relationships of everyday life. At the same time, what is said and represented in symbols and discourse is only a partial guide to actual behaviour, which is also shaped by a range of pragmatic considerations. These are the tensions we begin to explore in this chapter.

After three quarters of a century of Kemalist republicanism the family continues to provide the bedrock for personal and group identity in modern Lazistan, as it does in one form or another all over the world. The dominant values asserted

---

[1] We use this term in a loose way to mean any system of male domination. Carol Delaney finds this 'sloppy' and argues for a more restrictive usage. In her view, patriarchal systems of domination are those which depend on specific cultural ideas of male procreative powers, i.e. men as fathers (1991: 37).

For ethnographic accounts of patriarchy in Turkish rural society see Delaney 1991, Sirman 1990. Marcus 1992 offers a feminist critique based mainly on the literature produced by western travellers to the Ottoman Empire. (On women's position in the Ottoman Empire see also Dengler 1978.) Further discussions can be found in Mansur Coşar 1978, Abadan-Unat *et al.* 1981, Kağıtçıbaşı 1982, Stirling 1993b, White 1994.

Plate 5.1 Woman with basket (empty).

Plate 5.2 Rural girls often start carrying a sized-down basket when very young.

by families in Lazistan, though they are expressed in locally specific ways, are similar to those found elsewhere in Turkey, and in much wider regions of the Middle East, the Caucasus and the Mediterranean. In spite of these close similarities, people in Lazistan talk about the family as a local or regional speciality, as 'our traditions' (*örf-adetlerimiz*).[2] As we have noted, stereotypical representations of Lazistan have long highlighted the exploitation of women.[3] The Kemalist state has seized on this issue. Modernising officials found it convenient to play up the image of a woman struggling under heavy physical burdens while her spouse whiled away his days in the cafe. *Kaymakams* new to the region accosted women in rural areas to measure the weight of the load they carried on their backs, and interrupted the conversation of the tea house to appeal to the men to put an end to such obvious injustice. Campaigns of this sort do not seem to have had much practical impact, though local media representations still return to the theme regularly.[4] These may increase awareness of gender imbalances within the region and even promote reflection on the causes; at the same time they may simply reinforce the prevailing stereotype of female subordination.

While many patterns of behaviour conform closely to discourses of an extreme patriarchy, others do not. This reality varies significantly according to district and social class. The complexities are well illustrated by a popular metaphor that, at first sight, confirms the 'extreme patriarchy' diagnosis. The statement that 'a woman is a basket. You empty it and then fill it again' (*Kadın sepettir. Boşaltıyorsun, sonra yine dolduruyorsun*) might seem to be concerned solely with a woman's reproductive role. Another version of the same saying emphasises her passivity: 'A woman is a basket. You throw the old one away and replace it with a new one.' (*Kadın sepettir. Eskisini atarsın, yenisini alırsın.*) This metaphor is associated with the Lazi, among whom it is well known to men and women of all ages. It is explained, often with a broad smile by women, or with a smile of pained embarrassment by men, as an expression of women's subordination. Both men and women see it primarily as a procreation metaphor which presents the role of women in the creation of human life as passive and secondary. It can be considered a regionally specific variant of the 'seed and soil' metaphor on which Carol Delaney builds her analysis of patriarchal relations in a central Anatolian village.[5] In Lazistan, as elsewhere in Anatolia, men are thought to play the more important role in the generation of new human life, to provide the creative seed, while the woman merely provides a receptacle, or the soil in which this seed may grow. People say that 'a woman is like a field. Whatever you sow will grow.' (*Kadın tarlaya benzer. Ne ekersen o biter.*) Like the basket metaphor, this implies a low evaluation of women. In some respects the Lazistan case would seem to be an even more clear-cut, classical case of patriarchy than that examined in detail by Delaney.[6] The

---

[2] Alongside *örf-adetler*, some people nowadays use the term *kültür*. A few use the term *gelenek-görenek*, a 'pure Turkish' term for 'tradition' that was coined in the course of the language reforms, but has not succeeded in displacing the Arabic-derived *örf-adetler*.

[3] Similar images are found throughout the Black Sea region. See Toumarkine 1995: 35; Küper-Başgöl 1992: 180; Hann 1993.

[4] See e.g. the front cover of the first issue of the magazine *Rize'nin Sesi* (Voice of Rize), 1999.

[5] Delaney 1991. See Dube 1986 for a complementary study of the symbolism of biological reproduction in India.

[6] Delaney's most specific data concerning verbalisation of the gender imbalance in procreation

main function of the woman is to bear children. She herself has no control over this process, an incapacity that extends to all important social issues, e.g. to marriage and divorce, or to household finances and economic strategies.[7]

Baskets are still conspicuous in the economy of Lazistan and they are still strongly associated with women. It is said to be shameful (*ayıp*) for a man to carry a basket.[8] Some people, however, both men and women, give the basket metaphor more positive glosses. In particular, the idea that women lack agency in reproduction is countered by an enhanced view of women's role in production. Compared to women's more limited roles in agricultural production elsewhere in Anatolia, in Lazistan, perhaps due to high male out-migration over a long period, women have long been the main workers on the land. In this context the basket metaphor can become a positive statement about the ability of women to undertake all kinds of heavy work.

The structure of kin groups, residence and customary inheritance rules all continue to show a clear male bias. Wedding rituals symbolise the transfer of a woman's allegiance, and of authority over her, from her natal household to that of her husband. The daughter-in-law is expected to contribute fully to the division of labour in her new household. Great expense is incurred in her recruitment, and – the matter is often phrased in just these terms – she is expected to pay off some of this debt through her labour services (*hizmet*).

A strong emphasis upon male honour and female modesty is the most obvious expression of patriarchal ideology in Lazistan.[9] Women are supposed to be weak (*zayıf*) by nature. Men must take ultimate responsibility for all the actions of their wives. The latter are simply not independent moral agents. It is not safe to leave a woman alone in the company of a strange man. If an unmarried couple are found together, people automatically suspect sexual contact; the county courts tend to uphold this interpretation. The Lazistan concept of honour embraces both ideas about respectability and 'face' (*şeref*) and ideas that emphasise the sexual integrity of the household under its male head (*namus*).[10] Weapons are both a conspicuous symbol of male power and a readily available tool for dealing with situations in which honour in the *namus* sense is compromised; many households have at least a pistol at their disposal.

---

[6] (cont.) are drawn not from her own fieldwork but from that of Michael Meeker in the east Black Sea area, adjacent to Lazistan. See Delaney 1986: 497, 1991: 33; Meeker 1970: 157. Similar ideas were expressed in traditional Albanian society, where a woman was considered 'a sack for carrying things' (Peristiany 1976: 12).

[7] For more detailed discussion see Bellér-Hann 1999a.

[8] Wolfgang Feurstein considers the extensive use of baskets an 'ethnic marker' among the Lazi (1983: 55–6). He also sees the refusal of men to carry them as an assertion of their strong male identity (1983: 36). Turkish folklorists have described baskets as 'the ingenious invention of the people of the eastern Black Sea coast', and 'an inseparable part of woman's life in this region' (*Rize'de el sanatları* 1991: 22).

[9] For samples of the literature on honour and shame in Mediterranean family life see Peristiany 1965, 1976; Davis 1977; Antoun 1968; Bouhdiba 1985; Herzfeld 1980; Gilmore 1987. For Turkey, see the works listed in n. 1 above. See also Meeker 1976, who presents a comparison between the situation he found on the Black Sea coast and that of Arabian society.

[10] Meeker (1996: 51–3) offers an interesting account of *şeref* and *namus* in which he sees them as products of a distinct Ottoman philosophy of citizenship, rather than as merely the local variants of a pan-Mediterranean honour and shame ideology. However, his gloss of *namus* as 'honesty' is inadequate for Lazistan, where it is almost invariably concerned with infringements of the modesty code.

Further evidence supporting the diagnosis of patriarchy is the acclaim that is accorded to a daughter-in-law who produces sons, in comparison with the vulnerability of the woman who produces a succession of daughters. Here, as elsewhere in Anatolia, male domination is vividly demonstrated in everyday rules of respect and politeness. It is not only wives, daughters and daughters-in-law who must treat men with deference. Younger men are expected to show respect to older men, e.g. through more formal terms of address. For a young man to smoke a cigarette in his father's presence, drink alcohol or sit cross-legged is considered disrespectful. For this reason father and son are unlikely to frequent the same tea house.[11] Family members are expected to ask for the head's permission *(izin)* before carrying out an activity that would, in most western societies, fall within the sphere of individual freedom of action.[12] Patriarchs can make binding decisions about such matters as a daughter's education, or the apprenticeship of a son, or the marriage of either.

In short, most of the details familiar from the literature on honour and shame can be found also in Lazistan. This is a deeply rooted constellation of values with a long history and considerable continuing power. However, this model must be contextualised against changing usages and practices. Most of the hard tenets of patriarchy are significantly softened in practice. An assertive daughter-in-law may succeed in imposing her will on others, even on her father-in-law. Women attract more respect as they grow older, just as men do. The curse of a mother is just as powerful as that of a father, perhaps even more so.[13] Daughters are loved and not simply transacted. A daughter returns to visit her parents after marriage and, if the distance allows regular contact, her parents may play an important role in the raising of their grandchildren. The mother who produces only sons may also be pitied, partly because a daughter is considered to be a better carer for aged parents. Old people may choose to live with their married daughter in preference to sons, and this is accepted by the son-in-law. The terms for patrilineage *(sülale)* and tribe *(kabile)* have virtually disappeared from use. *Hısım* (affines) is heard only rarely. Instead the term *akrabalık* serves as a multi-purpose term that includes everyone with whom one has kin or affinal links. The emphasis is on flexibility, rather than following the logic of a patrilineal system. The relative wealth of this region and the continuing high rates of emigration have both worked to undermine traditional patterns of residence. It is unusual nowadays to find married brothers living together in one household. The proportion of couples who must spend their first years of married life under the roof of his parents with little or no financial autonomy has declined, though it remains significant. Fathers who deny their daughters access to education or who try to force their children of either sex into unwanted marriages are unlikely to win the approval of the community.

We do not argue that a patriarchal world view has disappeared. On the contrary, this cluster of values and practices persists and has far-reaching effects. But

---

[11] Cf. White 1994: 63. Similar rules are observed in all female company: young, outgoing brides smoke in secret rather than in the presence of their aged mother-in-law; however, such avoidance rules are more strictly observed among men.

[12] Cf. Delaney 1993.

[13] Cf. Schiffauer 1987: 114, 269, n.3.

even at the level of discourse it has to compete with other clusters and cannot be considered as an all-encompassing system, while at the level of practice it is inevitably further modified. Werner Schiffauer has argued that patriarchal systems begin to disintegrate when migration options give young men the possibility of challenging their fathers.[14] This process accelerated in Anatolia in the 1950s and 1960s, but we must remember that these options have been common in Lazistan over a much longer period. Let us, therefore, resist the temptation to exaggerate the reach of the principle of patriarchy, as symbolised in the basket, and instead look more carefully at what people say and what people do in three key material domains: work, money and inheritance.

Work

Like all other activities, how people secure their material livelihood is shaped by their beliefs and values. Attitudes to work have been frequently discussed by many earlier ethnographers of Turkey and we noted some of its most social aspects in the previous chapter. A widespread representation of the Ottoman empire emphasised the lack of respect accorded to labour and echoes of such 'Orientalist' judgements can be found in more recent anthropological studies of Anatolian rural society. Carol Delaney found that the ideal of men in the village where she worked was 'sitting' (*oturmak*) and that work in any form was despised.[15] Schiffauer confirmed her view that work as such is not positively valued. It is something from which men withdraw at the earliest opportunity.[16] These diagnoses carry a large measure of truth for many groups in Lazistan as well, but they remain partial. New job opportunities have brought new ideas and values along with them. The greatest change has been the introduction of tea. We have noted that most tea is plucked by women, and that some men rationalise this by claiming that female hands, being smaller and more dextrous, are better suited to this task. Some men are reluctant to carry baskets, or indeed any weight on their backs, as women do. This may be related to the symbolic associations of baskets with women's reproductive function. Some are also reluctant to carry fertiliser sacks. These are normally delivered by lorry or taxi, but from the village roadside it is usually women who must pick up and carry the 50 kilogram sacks to a place of storage, or directly to the tea gardens.

On the other hand, it is also the case that most male hands are otherwise engaged when tea is plucked. In particular, they work long hours in noisy and strenuous conditions, including night shifts, in the tea factories. At these peaks men also work as lorry drivers transporting tea from the villages to the factories. They are employed as 'experts' at the collection points in villages, weighing and registering the tea delivered by producers, and helping to load it onto the lorries. It would be misleading to suggest that what the men are doing is not work at all. When male labour power is available for plucking it is normally used. Men of all

[14] Schiffauer 1987.
[15] Delaney 1991: 115.
[16] Schiffauer 1987: 106–18. Schiffauer's persuasive general argument is that ideas about work cannot be disentangled from the duties that one owes to the head of a household.

Plate 5.3 Men and boys operate the new carts, while women continue to carry loads on their backs.

ages can be observed both plucking tea and carrying it on their backs in baskets or sacks to the collection points, the tasks that are alleged in the stereotype to be beneath their dignity. Many of these men are sharecroppers or seasonal migrant labourers who originate outside the Lazi region.[17] Local men will wish to avoid this company if they can, but if they are not otherwise engaged they will normally join in, unless they are too old or infirm.[18] Unmarried youths are certainly expected to help. In recent years the spread of the *teleferik* and of various forms of hand carts (*el arabası*) have partly displaced baskets and alleviated the transportation problem for both tea leaves and fertiliser; use of these technologies tends to mean more work for men.

It is unusual for men to carry firewood or animal fodder. Most agricultural as well as household tasks are linked primarily to women: animal husbandry, vegetable production, cleaning, washing, cooking, needlework, and caring for the aged, the sick and children all fall within the female sphere. Milking is normally considered a woman's job, for which even unmarried girls are not considered to be qualified, although they may have to deputise for their mother on occasion. Unmarried girls do not normally go to collect firewood but learn how to do so during the period of their engagement (*nişan*). Informants state that this age-related division of labour has nothing to do with prohibitions but is an attempt on the mother's part to spare her daughters drudgery and hard work while they are at home. Domestic activities such as embroidery and knitting for the trousseau are not classified as work.

All maritime jobs, freshwater fishing, hunting, trade and commerce, driving, and all forms of migrant work are predominantly associated with men. The list of tasks associated with rural men includes the construction and maintenance of houses, mosques, productive plots, paths and roads. Given the frequency of major storms in this region, these are recurring jobs, even for a villager who is not expanding his garden area or engaged in house-building. Although they do not milk cows, the slaughtering of animals is an exclusively male responsibility.[19]

The coming of tea is thought to have eased the labour burden for both men and women, especially the latter. Its cultivation is not less demanding than maize production, but giving up their traditional subsistence economy has enabled most households to reduce the number of animals they keep and reduced the workload accordingly. We received very varied answers when we asked villagers about how the coming of tea had modified traditional divisions of labour. Some said that women still worked harder, as they had done in the past. Some, however, said that its impact had been egalitarian. Some, both men and women, summarised their division of labour as 'separate but equal' (*ayrı ama eşit*). The same verb for 'to work' (*çalışmak*) was used for women's agricultural activities as

---

[17] When sharecroppers and labourers are employed the owners of tea gardens are normally in the area to supervise. This activity may be undertaken by women as well as men; this being at hand to supervise is popular among 'non-working' housewives who spend most of the year in more cramped urban accommodation.

[18] Men who take on women's work may then be humorously described as *kılıbık* ('hen-pecked') by neighbours, even though domestic power (including control over the purse) often lies with the male in this type of household. Cf. Schiffauer 1987: 108.

[19] Turkish symbolic associations of milk with women and blood with men have been elaborated by Delaney (1991).

for male wage-labour.[20] Answers on the whole contradicted the idea, so wide-spread outside the region, that the women of Lazistan undertake all manner of difficult tasks while men lounge indolently in cafes.

It is increasingly common for men and women to share tasks. The preparing of new tea gardens is in theory a man's job, but in practice men and women often do this work together. Pruning may also be done jointly. Many couples undertake shopping trips together, perhaps including a restaurant lunch. Some men enjoy cooking. If a man cooks, he does this for pleasure, in his leisure time, and it does not form part of his domestic obligations. It is the same if a man takes responsibility for shopping. Some rural men do so gladly because this gives them the excuse for a lengthy sojourn in a tea-house, either in the market town or in a smaller settlement that he passes on his way. However his wife may accede to the arrangement gladly if she is able to consume just as much tea and conversation in the time that she is alone at home. Men do not join the group of women who sell garden produce at the weekly market, but they do sometimes sell animals. Even in the larger towns the 'modern' husband willing to share household chores such as washing and cleaning remains very much the exception.

Underpinning many gendered aspects of the division of labour is an implicit distinction between skilled and unskilled work, with women being associated with the latter.[21] Women's work confines them to the familiar ground of the neighbourhood or village, while male activities often take them far outside their region.[22] However, this is precisely the basis on which many rural women build high self-esteem. As a Lazi girl explained, 'There is no job in this village that a woman cannot do, and there are plenty of jobs that only we do.'

Work is a central value for both men and women.[23] The woman's right to be maintained by her husband is a part of what Deniz Kandiyoti terms the 'patriarchal bargain'.[24] Failure to do so gives grounds for divorce. Idleness may cause a man to lose his wife, but a girl who is considered lazy is unlikely to make a good marriage.[25] As one woman explained, 'the best candidate to become someone's second wife [by religious marriage unrecognised by the modern secular legal system, a position regarded as degrading and feared by most women] is a girl who does not work' (*en iyi kuma adayı çalışmayan kızdır*). Women seldom allege that their men are lazy, and in this sense may be said to have internalised the 'bargain'.

---

[20] Some avoid this verb and simply say that 'women do the tea, wood and grass' (*kadınlar çay, odun ve ot yaparlar*). Some will only consider tasks in the vegetable garden as work if the woman is producing systematically for the market.

[21] Variations according to social class and economic position must also be borne in mind: in well-to-do families which rely on seasonal migrant labour, managerial tasks often devolve to a woman.

[22] Cf. Delaney 1991: 232–9.

[23] Cf. Yalçın-Heckmann's discussion of the Kurds of Hakkari, 1991: 169.

[24] Kandiyoti 1988. She explains this idea as follows: 'Like all terms coined to convey a complex concept, the term *patriarchal bargain* represents a difficult compromise. It is intended to indicate the existence of set rules and scripts regulating gender relations, to which both genders accommodate and acquiesce, yet which may nonetheless be contested, redefined, and renegotiated.' (1988: 286 n 1.) It will be clear already that this 'bargain' or 'pact' takes a different form in Lazistan from the 'classic patriarchy' described by Kandiyoti. In particular, women are in a different position by virtue of the fact that they are the prime acknowledged workers on the land and therefore the prime earners of agricultural income. In terms of her ideal types, the women of Lazistan are closer to Africa than to Anatolia. Recently Kandiyoti has subjected the term to further searching critique (Kandiyoti 1998b).

[25] Cf. Schiffauer 1987: 114.

Relatively few Lazistan households, even in *sosyete* circles, are rich enough to live comfortably without work. People who continue to work even when rich enough to retire attract admiration. So do those who study hard with the aim of obtaining qualifications for a prestigious profession. Within the category *sosyete*, however, there is a small leisure class where patriarchal values appear to be thoroughly subverted. These households reverse traditional domestic roles: while the women go out to gamble, men stay at home to mind the children. These men are seen (with considerable exaggeration) as pitiful and 'hen-pecked' (*kılıbık*), dominated by their wives, who are ever ready to gamble away the family's wealth. This perceived reversal of gender roles attracts condemnation and the women are seen as the main culprits. They are not criticised for not working, but for being too open (*açık*), too free (*serbest*), oblivious to both religious morality and to community expectations. Similar comments were sometimes made about the trader-tourists, whose visible poverty was often attributed to a failure to work properly.[26]

There is no single 'mental model' of work in contemporary Lazistan. Strong gender differences in the division of labour persist, but diligence is expected and valued among both men and women. Neither men nor women are expected to engage in physically demanding work when the next generation is old enough to undertake the relevant tasks. The early age at which many people can draw pensions, either from the state or privately, is consistent with traditional preferences.[27] Nonetheless many elderly people continue to work hard to the end of their lives. Tea has both entrenched a traditional division of labour and, in the eyes of many local people, alleviated the greater burden traditionally falling onto women.

Money

Another key area for exploring the domestic 'balance of power' between men and women is the allocation and control of household finances, a sensitive topic in most societies. We probed this subject among families we knew well in different parts of the region. In some cases male control was so complete that a woman was called to account even for the small sums she earned from selling the vegetables she had grown or the milk she had produced. In other words, she had no financial autonomy whatsoever. In other cases control by the senior female seemed equally complete: husband and sons handed over their wage packets and pensions, and had to ask for funds from her in order to visit the teahouse or engage in any other expenditure. Most households fall between these extremes, but practical contingencies usually conspire to favour male control.

Most households have multiple sources of income. Regardless of residence pattern, most augment the goods and cash generated in agriculture (primarily tea) with income from trade, government employment, factory employment, remittances or pensions. Total income depends on many factors, including the

---

[26]In some cases this was phrased in terms of faults in the socialist system, which did not allow its citizens to work properly. Turkish capitalism was not faulted in this way.

[27] Proposals in the late 1990s to raise retirement ages (to sixty for men and fifty-five for women) were very unpopular in Lazistan.

Plate 5.4 Sümer, 1982: the men of a hamlet working together.

Plate 5.5 A young married couple work on their new house together.

size and location of landholdings, the composition of the household (the age, gender, and number of children), education and qualifications, and the assistance of migrant workers. Household composition depends on the pattern of births and the phase that has been reached in its developmental cycle. Having unmarried teenaged daughters means not only a ready supply of labour for one's own tea gardens but also the possibility of using them to bring in extra cash by working as day labourers on other people's plots. However, their impending marriages will involve many expenses. With marriage these girls will be lost to the household, both as unpaid family labour and as potential cash earners. The contributions of sons usually cease when they separate from the paternal home. Some migrants, however, continue to support their parents long after they have established their own households.

Many factors outside one's control can have an impact on the household economy: inflation, bankruptcy, unemployment, health problems and the payments practices of both public and private sectors of the tea industry are all important variables which affect budgeting. Even at times of apparent economic stability, households must constantly be ready to face new challenges. Cash flow is not evenly distributed throughout the year. Due to the seasonal nature of tea cultivation and related industries, cash is most plentiful in the autumn months. Larger purchases, such as household durables, clothes, a manually operated cart or a cable lift, tend to be concentrated in this season. Those who remain in the countryside throughout the year stock up with flour, rice, pasta, sugar, olives, oil, lentils and even tea (many families, however, obtain their supplies of tea by one means or another from their local factories). This bulk shopping is necessary in upland villages, where severe weather conditions can paralyse communications for weeks. Many families in the middle and lower income brackets have difficulties in the winter and spring, if they have to meet all outgoings from just a single pension or salary. Urgent needs for food, clothes, medical care or education can be funded by credit, which then means that when cash starts coming in again in the summer, some or even all of it goes to pay off debts. Money needs to be set aside for family expenses, notably weddings and the daughters' trousseaux (which is gradually built up over the years). Poorer families pickle vegetables in the summer, to avoid having to purchase for high prices in the winter months. Many people say that, although their diet is now more varied than it was before the introduction of tea, they now eat less meat than they used to.

Some features are common throughout Lazistan, as well as no doubt further afield. Wherever a male household head is absent for most of the year as a labour migrant, women have control over household budgeting, including their own earnings from agriculture. Sometimes this control is shared with an older son, who in time takes over budget management from his mother. Men earning a regular salary as government employees or factory workers tend in all districts to hand over a certain amount of their earnings to their wives for household management.

Intra-regional differences, however, are also significant. In the county of Fındıklı we found that women exercised a lot of control over family budgets.[28] Later work in Pazar led us to modify this picture. Women's participation in tea production, often to the complete exclusion of men, does not necessarily assure

[28] Hann 1993: 138 n.7.

them access to the resulting income. The tea money, the main source of income for most rural households, is paid out at the processing factories or at the tea collection points. Payment can be made to persons other than the garden owner formally registered. Each household has at least one tea registration booklet (*çay cüzdanı*) issued by a nearby factory, in which the household's sales are recorded. When freshly plucked tea is taken to the collection points, the family *cüzdan* is handed over to the official representing the factory, who notes the date of sale and the amount of tea that has been delivered. If there is only one *cüzdan* in the household, it is always in the name of the household head, who in most cases is a man. Women's actual contributions thus remain invisible, at least on paper.[29] Payment, however, normally takes place several weeks later (and often later still in the private sector). When a factory is ready to make the payment it broadcasts an announcement in the town by loudspeaker. In the easterly counties it is often the women producers who queue up at the factory gate to collect the money due to them. However, in the more westerly districts, such as Pazar, the money goes predominantly to men. People explain the difference in terms of differing world views. People in the easterly districts are considered more liberal and modern in their attitudes to the modesty code, in matters such as women's clothing and smoking. In contrast, the western parts are perceived as more conservative, devout and even fanatical (the exact terms used reflect the regional affiliation and world view of the person speaking). Inhabitants of Pazar insist that their stricter adherence to Islam and the modesty code prevents them from allowing their women to queue up in a public place, sometimes for hours, in the company of strange men. Yet this can be critical in determining women's access to cash.

This intra-regional difference in women cultivators' ability to gain access to tea income is confirmed in women's ability to participate in financial decisions. In Fındıklı many families report that women and men make such decisions together, or that the wife holds the purse strings. In Pazar, however, the general pattern is that male household heads control cash income, and either give a regular housekeeping allowance or retain all cash, taking upon themselves responsibility for shopping and giving money to others on an *ad hoc* basis when they make a trip to town. Where tea payments are collected by a man, he may deduct a sum for his own 'pocket money' and hand over the remainder to his wife for custody. He is more likely to do so if he has another regular source of income that he may never discuss in detail with his wife, such as income earned in forestry, or from a small shop, or from a pension following years of migrant labour. In this pattern each partner has prime access to a distinct revenue stream. However, even if the woman is the acknowledged custodian of pooled money, it does not necessarily mean that she has full control over such money. Usually all large items of expenditure on the household and its individual members will be negotiated between the spouses.

Some women generate cash by producing for the market, for example from selling vegetables, dairy products, eggs, animals, or from embroidery or sewing. Relatively poor rural Lazi can find customers for their milk by informal

---

[29] Households with substantial tea gardens usually have several *cüzdan*s in the names of different household members, which may include women. This facilitates their selling to private factories, once they have exhausted their quotas with the Tea Corporation.

networking. However, in Pazar villages these earnings and a woman's ownership of a cow and her right to sell it are occasionally disputed. In one such story it was related that 'Hasan needed money. So he told his wife that he thought that the cow was ill. She agreed to let him call a vet whom he had bribed to say in front of his wife that the cow was very sick. After this he easily managed to persuade his wife to let him sell the cow (which was perfectly healthy) at the market. Although he obtained good money for the cow, he deceived his wife into thinking that he had received next to nothing.'

Social and economic differences cut across the intra-regional variation. In Pazar rural families tend to follow the 'pool allocation pattern' while the 'housekeeping allowance pattern' seems more characteristic of wealthier families.[30] However, these are ideal types and lived reality is more complex. A man may agree to give his wife a housekeeping allowance, but the amount and regularity of such handouts may vary considerably because of the seasonal nature of tea work, both in the factories and in plucking. The housekeeping allowance may metamorphose into pooling, which can in practice mean the concentration of cash in the hands of the man. Even in poorer families where pooling is the basic principle, not all kinds of cash are pooled. Tea money can be pooled without the household head giving up any of his pension or salary. A woman may pool her income from selling milk, but she is more likely to retain it and use it for personal expenditure, put it aside for unexpected crises, spend it on 'extras' for the children, or put it towards a daughter's trousseau.

For example, Selma (20) was the second oldest daughter in a family of seven girls and two boys. She was unmarried, and lived and worked at home. The earnings of the girls who worked in the family tea garden were collected and controlled by their father. Her father, who sent allowances home during the many years he worked in Istanbul as a waiter, received a small pension. After returning to Lazistan he ran a cafe in town, but it was not very profitable. The family's major income was from tea, and they had to be careful in their budgeting. They also needed to prepare the trousseaux of six unmarried daughters. In this family the household head retained his pension and any surplus from his cafe for personal use. He was also able to influence the uses made of the tea money, but only by consultation with his wife. Selma described the economic management of the household as follows:

> It is our father who controls all the money we have. He has to make sure that we have food and basic necessities throughout the year. If everybody in the family controlled his/her income independently, there would be chaos and we would lose out eventually. We all live together. It is obvious when one of us needs something, and if our parents have the money they will get it for us.

This account suggests full internalisation of the 'patriarchal bargain'. When the need for certain items, such as underwear for a girl, was not obvious to the father, this was communicated to him by the mother.[31] Although these girls were required to work in the family's tea garden with no direct remuneration, when

---

[30] See Dwyer and Bruce 1988.

[31] Schiffauer reports that girls were forbidden to ask for money from their father for items that were closely related to their bodies, for which women had to pay from the income they earned from selling fruit, yoghurt, eggs etc. (1987: 122). In Lazistan many women have no option but to obtain the money needed from their husbands.

plucking was finished in their own gardens they sometimes took on work as day labourers in the neighbour's tea garden and used the wages earned as they pleased. Like the father's pension, which constituted his personal spending money, and tea money, which was largely used for paying off debt and purchasing foodstuffs and clothing, these monies were 'earmarked'.[32]

There is little uniformity in treatment of the earnings of unmarried children living in the parental home. Lazi parents are said to be more indulgent with their children than the Hemşinli, and sometimes daughters are treated more leniently than sons. Some say that salaried young people should keep all or most of their earnings, although girls are often expected to use at least part of this money to build up their trousseau and sons to make an equivalent long-term investment, such as buying a car or putting it aside for building a house. Mothers may encourage their daughters to buy clothes and jewellery for themselves, but voluntary contributions to the general household budget are seldom declined. Such contributions may take the form of food purchases, which it is often convenient for the son or daughter to make on the way home from the workplace. In prosperous families even younger girls may be remunerated for work. Saliha was 13 and still a primary school pupil when she voluntarily started picking tea with her mother in their nearby gardens. She kept a mental note of the amount she picked and, although she did not receive any cash for her work, her mother spent the appropriate amount on golden jewellery for her daughter.[33]

The appearance of foreign prostitutes in the early 1990s led to an increase in female control over household budget and decision-making in at least some families. With husbands keeping more for their 'personal needs', some women, formerly meek and subservient, were provoked into new strategies to ensure greater financial security and independence for themselves and their children. Selma's mother, whose income had previously been under the control of her husband, decided at this point to open her own bank account, as a consequence of what she considered to be his excessive spending. He retained his pension and small business in the town, but she acquired full control over their tea income. At about the same time, and for similar reasons, Fatma and her husband Aziz made a transition to genuinely balanced pooling arrangements. Previously she had been entirely dependent on him and the money he brought in from his tea factory job. She managed to persuade him to give up the unprofitable sideline that he ran from a small shop in the town, and to transfer the premises to her name. She then invested her wedding gold to launch a new business selling furniture, linen and mattresses, and managed everything herself.[34]

Inheritance

Control over household finances is bound up with inter-generational transfers of money and goods. The basic principle is that parents have full responsibility for

[32] Cf. Zelizer 1989.
[33] Cf. Delaney 1991: 175–6; White 1994: 70–83. The perception of Lazi mothers as particularly indulgent towards their daughter implies a degree of female control over household budgeting.
[34] See Bellér-Hann 1995b.

both daughters and sons until they are married. Working children are expected to make a financial contribution as long as they are living at home, and some continue to do so after marriage and the establishment of a separate residence. Prosperous families, on the other hand, often provide generous financial allowances to their children up to the point of their marriage, which is then the occasion for a more comprehensive financial settlement.

The general principles of inheritance throughout Lazistan are that land and houses, by far the most significant forms of wealth in the region, should be inherited on an equal basis by sons. Traditionally and today it is usually the youngest son who remains in the parental home and assumes greater responsibility for the care of ageing parents. However, it seems likely that there has always been a lot of variation in residential arrangements, as well as in the transfer of material goods and in the division of land, both formal (legally registered) and informal. The fringe benefits of a public sector job may make a big difference. One son may, for example, have his accommodation needs met throughout his working life by the provision of a low-rent state flat or house (*lojman*), while others have urgently to build new private homes. The construction, even in rural areas, of three or four storey buildings allows for further options: the top floor apartments are often left incomplete, to be finished as and when needs and resources dictate.

Land is the supreme good in Lazistan. The introduction of tea has given it high value as a commodity, but this is realised only in quite exceptional cases, when a family dies out or all members leave the region permanently. The timing of its division (*taksim*) is variable. People say that in the past it was more common for the estate to remain intact until the death of the patriarch, even if he was infirm and both management and labour were undertaken by the families of his married sons. Nowadays sons are likely to be allocated their share when they move into separate accommodation. The shares of migrants may continue to be managed by the patriarch, or by a brother or other relative. Division is normally accomplished orally in the presence of witnesses, such as the *muhtar* and one or more village elders. Few bother to record the transfer of ownership at the government building, which does not maintain a full land register. (It is more important, given the introduction of quotas, that gardens be registered with the Tea Corporation; however, this institution is concerned with the size of gardens, not with their ownership.)

Turkish women in law enjoy the same rights of inheritance as men. However, the Kemalist civil code is not the most decisive source of legal ideas in the lives of rural and small town people.[35] Women themselves say that they do not expect to receive an equal share because, if they did, the property devolving to their husbands would necessarily be diminished as full allocations were made to his sisters. People agree that if family land is sold, for whatever reason, then women should receive a full equal share along with their brothers; but as land seldom goes on the market this principle remains hypothetical. Women's exclusion from the inheritance of land is not stated openly, since most people know this flies in the face not only of modern legislation but also of Islamic norms. Informants therefore

[35] See Magnarella 1998. See also Abadan-Unat *et al.* 1981: 13; cf. Toprak 1981b: 288.

say that daughters may inherit land but, in practice, they willingly (*isteyerek*) give up their share in favour of their brother(s). They often add that a woman benefits from the fact that her husband's property will include his sisters' 'voluntary donations'. Men stress that women are 'not forced' to comply (*zorlama yok*). For a woman to claim her share is considered shameful (*ayıp*), and such action may lead to permanent friction between her and her natal family. The important thing is that a woman should be decently provided for at marriage, and that she has the security of knowing that she can always return to her father's house. Treating her as an individual with a claim to an equal share in the family estate would have the effect of cutting her off from this source of security. In addition to the jewellery she receives at marriage, nowadays from both sides, her parents make a significant contribution to the furnishing of the new household. An effort is made to ensure that all children are fairly treated.[36]

In cases where there is no male heir, the estate will usually pass to one or more in-marrying sons-in-law (*iç güvey*), though the extent to which this is found in Lazistan is variable. In some eastern districts, it is common to divide up the estate among the daughters. Here, widows often retain control of all aspects of household management for many years, even when a married son is present in the household and ready to take over. A widow normally inherits one third of an estate, the remainder going to her children or, if she has none, to her late husband's male relatives. Whether or not she remarries, she does not have the right to dispose of her husband's house. People say that this is in line with Islamic family law, which is more appropriate than the codes of the secular state.

Cases that reach the courts are always exceptional. Many court files merely record a dispute that does not proceed further, presumably because a settlement has been reached informally. The largest categories in the files that we examined in Pazar in 1992 concerned fathers bringing cases against their sons alleging inadequate support following the formal transfer of land to the younger generation, and women who, for one reason or another, find themselves in poverty and claim land against their brothers, usually following their father's death. The courts normally confirmed both types of claim. In one case Meryem A. (b. 1928) brought a suit against her stepmother, her father's second wife, and her step siblings demanding her share of her father's land. Her father had had seven children: Meryem was his only child by his first wife, who had died long before; there were six more children, two sons and four daughters, from his second wife. The case was settled in court, when the defendants agreed that Meryem should have her share. The estate was divided into 28 equal portions (*pay*), of which a quarter was declared by the court to be the property of the widow, Meryem's stepmother. The remaining three quarters were then equally divided into seven parts, each of the seven children receiving three portions. The judge himself remarked that in practice none of the other four daughters were likely to claim their shares, which would therefore devolve to their brothers.

In another case Hatice B. alleged that Sinan B., elder brother of her late husband, had in effect disinherited her from four *dönüm* of prime tea land in their

---

[36] However, daughters may in practice be treated differently – for example, if a particular match requires more generous provision than was made for a sister, or if the resources of the family should change unexpectedly.

village which the two brothers had exploited together. The brothers had sold this land before Hatice's marriage. According to Sinan the proceeds had gone towards the costs of her wedding and other financial support, but she claimed that her brother-in-law in fact used up most of the money on gambling. Later, Sinan had rebought this land, but he insisted that his sister-in-law, by now a widow, had no right of ownership or possession (*hiç bir zilliyet ve tasarrufu kalma mıştır*). At this point the legal arguments became camouflaged in an antiquated language closer to Ottoman than modern Turkish, and hardly penetrable by local people. The key point was that Hatice had married her husband with the religious rite (*dini nikah*) only, because she was a minor at the time in the eyes of the state. The judge nonetheless ruled that half of the disputed land should be divided up among Hatice's four children, though she herself did not receive a share.

Another case was directly related to the Russian markets and resolved before reaching court. When a married man with two teenaged sons expressed his intention to sell his inherited tea land in order to purchase a car, his wife was adamantly opposed to the plan. She alleged that he wanted the car only to facilitate his illicit encounters with 'Russian' prostitutes. She therefore appealed to the husband's three married sisters, urging them to claim their share of the patrimony if her husband persisted with his plan. They did so, while making it plain that in principle they did not dispute his right to alienate the family land. He could, for example, use the proceeds to buy other property, or to pay for the education of his sons. But the sisters supported the view of the wife that the planned car purchase was morally unacceptable.

Intra-regional differences

Some of the variation in the extent to which women can assert themselves in the households of contemporary Lazistan is determined by the personalities of individual men and women. However, the social patterning is also significant and we have outlined some of the factors that shape the domestic balance of power. Contrary to expectations we did not find the urban–rural distinction to be particularly important. This boundary is blurred, partly because so many families and households have a residential base on both sides. Those who live throughout the year in towns, especially if both partners work, are more likely to pool income and share decision-taking. But many urban women do not have regular wage work and live under the close control of husbands and fathers-in-law. Assumptions of peasant conservatism and more patriarchy in the countryside are inappropriate in Lazistan, in part because so many villages are now within daily commuting range of the towns and have similar employment and income profiles.

But geographical location is important in other ways. Local people themselves, both indigenes and immigrants, saw a significant distinction between the western parts of Lazistan, particularly the environs of Rize, where male control was said to be strongest, and some of the easterly parts. Some people suggested a precise dividing line in the Lazi zone between the districts of Ardeşen and Fındıklı, and we found some grounds to support this suggestion. To the east, in the districts of Fındıklı and Arhavi, many Lazi took pride in having achieved higher levels of education and culture (*kültür*) than their neighbours. Arhavi in particular had a reputation as a 'Little Istanbul', or even a 'Little Paris'. A more egalitarian division of labour and greater financial autonomy for women formed one facet of this reputation. The village of Sümer, where our first impressions were shaped in 1983 and 1988, falls into this eastern zone. Further differences included a stricter observance of the modesty code in the western districts than in the eastern ones, demonstrated for example in the more conservative dress code followed by women in Pazar and Ardeşen. Some families in Sümer with only modest gardens and relying exclusively on family labour have allowed women to assume a financial and managerial role in the family that is rare even among more affluent families in the west of the region. Some prosperous families release their women from manual work and lavish substantial sums upon them, but still do not allow them a significant decision-taking role. For at least some women an increase in wealth, particularly if it is linked to a move to new urban surroundings, can cause increased social isolation and reduce the autonomy they enjoyed when they were directly involved in rural production.

In addition to this east–west differentiation, the introduction of a crop which brings much higher yields in coastal areas has, as we have noted, reversed the previous pattern of north–south relations. Tea can still be grown in the interior, but yields and consequently income become progressively lower. Continuities with an older, more emphatically patriarchal peasant society were visibly stronger in some upland areas, where families had more children and often stayed together longer under the parental roof. This was the only part of the region where we came across men with a clear sense that they headed not just a household but a larger lineage group.[37] In practice, here too women could exercise a very considerable degree of autonomy, especially if their menfolk were constrained to spend the greater part of the year in remote cities as migrant labourers. But when the men were at home they made their dominance explicit in ways that we seldom noted in coastal areas. Women did not joke or banter, as they often did elsewhere, but fell meekly silent whenever the men were present.

In the more prosperous tea-growing communities nearer the coast, such explicitly subordinate behaviour was characteristic not of the local people but of newcomers who have moved into the region from adjacent parts of Anatolia to augment the labour force. This new underclass has grown up on the basis of an older pattern of social inequality which partly coincides with the east–west spatial differentiation. Thus lower population densities east of Ardeşen enabled the *agha* families to plant larger tea gardens, exceeding the area that they could farm with family labour alone. These districts therefore contain a higher proportion of sharecroppers, including some who have come here from the western districts of Lazistan itself. The more 'balanced' gender relations found here among locals must therefore be set against the increased prevalence of an 'unbalanced' pattern among recent immigrants. More and more local women have given up the

---

[37] One man in a Lazuri-speaking village claimed that he was head (*reis*) of a *kabile* comprising fifty-eight persons, twenty-three of whom had lived together over many years in a multiple-family household, before the brothers eventually built separate houses and divided their land. This man explained that he did not exercise day-to-day control outside his own household, but insisted that he was fully involved in all key decisions in the larger group, including house-building and marriage strategies.

burden of work on the land and begun to work out new models of conjugal relations. The model to which most have aspired is the one that they see as more western and more modern, the one that is promoted not only by the state but by the everyday images of the media and the national consumer society in which they live. This is a formidable combination. In practice, since their employment options are extremely limited, the main forms of socialisation open to women in the small towns remain the 'days' discussed in the previous chapter. Meanwhile the burden of hard manual labour has been passed on to others. Ironically, the traditional Lazistan stereotypes of female exploitation may now have a lot of purchase among the new rural proletariat, but less and less on an indigenous population that is concerned to differentiate itself from these newcomers.

Namahrem

The preceding sections suggest the need for a critical and differentiated assessment of patriarchy at the level of sociological realities, but the fact remains that the whole of contemporary Lazistan has a strongly gendered civil society. In a discourse found throughout the region, segregation and the modesty code are often explained by local people, and especially by women, with the concept of *namahrem*. This concept shows the influence of religion in the regulation of everyday behaviour and the constitution of society, but in a manner that is quite different from the links that Carol Delaney posits between procreation beliefs, Islamic cosmology and patriarchy. The primary meaning of *mahrem* is given in Redhouse's Turkish– English lexicon as 'Who is not familiar or intimate; used especially of those men and women who are not blood relations and therefore are debarred from familiar social relations with each other'.[38]

Within the Turkish context Göle connects the concept of *mahrem* to veiling and to the world view of Islam:

> The honor of a woman is directly proportional to the distance she is away from 'abuse', or the possibility of sexual harassment. It is veiling itself that ensures the required distance. A look invites lust and causes sedition; a lustful gaze leads to an illicit act (*haram*); and it is illicit to look at a woman if her clothes cling to her body. The emergence of women into the outside world depends upon certain rules. Cohabitation of women and men is forbidden, for it is among the reasons for the increase in cases of adultery (flirtation). It is forbidden also for a woman to stay alone with a man (*halvet*) who is not a family member because it is a possible sin and a possible imputation against her honor. It is only proper to shake a woman's hand when she is old enough to be 'delivered from lust'.[39]

While Göle's work is highly relevant for understanding the concept of privacy (*mahremiyet*), most of her discussion centres on contemporary forms of veiling as a political statement of young Islamist women. This is different, Göle emphasises, from the traditional Muslim women's wearing of the headscarf, which is 'confined within the boundaries of traditions, handed down from generation to

[38] Redhouse Dictionary 1974: 2066.
[39] Göle 1996: 53.

generation and passively adopted by women'.[40] It is this latter issue that interests us in the small town and village context of Lazistan, where rural and small town women who passively adopt the headscarf far outnumber the well-educated urban Islamists. Nevertheless, the latter have received far more attention in the scholarly literature, perhaps because of their high visibility and close connections to the political face of Islam. The 'traditional' women have been largely excluded from discussions of veiling, even in anthropological accounts.[41]

We argue that female covering and normative behaviour are encapsulated in the concept of *namahrem*, which plays an important part in women's self-definition and in the general discourse of personhood and social relations. In her seminal article on the concept of *namahram* in Iran, Khatib-Chahidi gives this definition:

> *Mahram* is the legal term denoting a relationship by blood, marriage or sexual union which makes marriage between persons so related forbidden. It is a permanent prohibition which remains unaffected by divorce or death. *Mahram* also has a wider meaning: uppermost in the mind of the average Iranian when the term is used is the fact that *mahram* persons are those with whom one can mix freely and be on informal terms.

She proceeds to define *namahram*: '*Na-mahram* literally denotes any person of the opposite sex whose kinship does *not* represent an impediment for marriage. By extension *na-mahram* is sometimes used to denote people of the opposite sex whom the speaker does not know.'[42]

In republican Turkey many city dwellers have little more than a vague idea of these meanings and *nahmahrem* is not prominent in the literature on honour, shame and the modesty code in Anatolia.[43] Yet to most Sunni Muslims in Lazistan it is as central as it is for the Shiite population with which Khatib-Chahidi was concerned in Iran, both regulating the use of physical space and providing the ground rules for sexual relations and marriage. The fundamental prohibitions are everywhere the same, but compared with the Iranian case, in Lazistan greater flexibility is achieved by making some *namahrem* categories mutable. With a small number of close relatives, sexual congress is incestuous and therefore utterly unthinkable, though people stress marriage, rather than sex, in their explanations. The taboo applies equally to married and unmarried women. A married woman who engages in unlawful sex is committing adultery (*zina*), which is certainly a sin (*günah*). The violation of the incest taboo, however, results in a much higher degree of pollution and is more likely to be classified as *haram*. The effect of the taboo is to allow a woman greater intimacy with persons in this category, who are typically men with whom a woman must share space on a daily basis, with whom it would be virtually impossible to observe the prohibitions that must be followed with all *namahrem* males.[44]

---

[40] *Ibid.*: 4.

[41] Küper-Başgöl discusses the issue of veiling within the context of Turkish feminist discourse (1992). Veiling and related issues are also discussed by Seufert (1997b) and Özdalga (1998).

[42] Khatib-Chahidi 1981: 114.

[43] Major monographs on Turkey make no explicit mention of the concept of *namahrem*, although female modesty and the gendered division of space that it encapsulates usually occupy a central place in the discussions (Stirling 1965, Meeker 1970, Paleczek 1987, Delaney 1991, White 1994). An important exception is Sauner-Nebioglu's recent monograph (1995). The term is well known elsewhere in the Islamic world (Khatib-Chahidi 1981, Mumtaz and Shaheed 1987, Bellér-Hann 1999a).

[44] We follow local usage in explaining the idea of *namahrem* primarily from the female standpoint. The positive form *mahrem* is not used.

Thus a husband is non-*namahrem* (*namahrem olmaz*) because of the marriage tie, and he is the only male in this category with whom she may (indeed must) have sexual relations. The other males in the category include her father, brothers, sons, grandfathers, uncles, nephews, and the corresponding relatives on the husband's side. Stepfathers, half brothers, etc. are also normally included. In line with Koranic prohibitions, the taboo is extended to milk siblings (*süt kardeş*), persons suckled by the same woman. Since none of these men may marry or have sexual intercourse with her, it is possible for a woman to be relatively relaxed and informal in their presence (appearing without a headscarf, with sleeves rolled up, joking and laughing). In the presence of all other men, whether relatives or strangers, a woman is confronted by a potential sexual/marriage partner. They are therefore *namahrem* to her. Her hair and all other parts of the body considered to have sexual significance must be covered, she must speak and behave respectfully.[45]

Namahrem 'maps' are redrawn not only by marriage and divorce but also by births and deaths, which can have multiple repercussions for *namahrem* relations. The marriage of a sister turns a woman's new brother-in-law, previously *namahrem* (unless, for example, he is a close relative of her husband) into non-*namahrem*. A woman's husband is non-*namahrem* as long as they are married, but from the moment of divorce an ex-husband and his close relatives revert to the status of *namahrem*. The death of a husband also entails reclassification of her husband's male relatives (necessary if, as was formerly quite common, the widow was to marry his younger brother). The marriages and divorces of a woman's siblings also necessitate realignments of her *namahrem* map.

In traditional Iranian houses the courtyard favoured the observance of *namahrem* rules, since people in the rooms surrounding the courtyard could see who had entered, while they could not be seen by the newcomer. Lazistan village houses, however, are not surrounded by a high wall or fence. Space is shared in the hamlet and women are heavily involved in agricultural work. In this context, where first cousins are regarded as potential marriage partners, *namahrem* rules have to be continuously reinforced. Many people explained *namahrem* ideas by reference to the living arrangements in the *yayla* or summer pasture, where the same point applies with greater force, since sleeping arrangements are necessarily different from those of multi-roomed houses. People lie down side by side in the summer house known as the *mezra*. Members of extended families often have to sleep next to each other, 'like sardines in a tin', and a full segregation of the sexes is impossible. However, male and female can be safely juxtaposed if they were non-*namahrem* to each other.

The large measure of consensus among informants concerning *namahrem* relations gives way to some disagreement and uncertainty over the exact status of

---

[45] The traditional female dress code in Lazistan was formerly quite different from the rest of Anatolia, where issues such as the headscarf have become highly contentious in recent years. (see Göle 1991, Delaney 1991, Özdalga 1998). Full veiling (i.e. wearing the *çarşaf*) seems never to have been practised. Elderly people recall that women used to wear a large woolen shawl called *atkı*. Some recall that this was forbidden in the wake of Atatürk's reforms: women were threatened that it would be torn into pieces if they wore it. This seems to be an example of how reforms were reinterpreted, or misinterpreted, at the local level since, although Atatürk prohibited men from wearing the *fez* and discouraged veiling among women, women's clothing was never the object of legal sanctions.

milk brothers and of paternal and maternal uncles. The Koran makes it clear that a woman is forbidden to marry either a maternal or a paternal uncle, and some people say that these should therefore be considered non-*namahrem*, persons with whom intimacy can be maintained. Yet some informants suggested that both the maternal uncle (*dayı*) and paternal uncle (*amca*) were *namahrem* to the woman. The fact that one is forbidden to marry one's uncle and yet still not allowed to be intimate with him indicates that perhaps sex and marriage are not quite the same thing after all in this context. Others differentiate between uncles: 'you can safely lie down next to your maternal uncle in the *mezra*, but you could never do this with the paternal uncle.'[46]

The prohibition against milk siblings is laid down in the Koran, but it is also well-known in the Caucasus among Christians.[47] Many women say that a milk brother is closer than one's own brother, which would certainly render milk brothers non-*namahrem*. However, others insist that the milk brother is *namahrem*, a stranger with whom no intimacy should be allowed. Creating milk siblings is said to have been common in the past as a deliberate strategy to preclude later marriage. In one poor upland village, where village endogamy appeared to be the norm, we were told that villagers were deliberately trying to avoid the creation of milk ties because this would limit the number of eligible marriage partners. The prohibitions can be extended to relatives of the actual milk siblings: for example, a girl's 'milk paternal uncle' (*süt dayı* – a man suckled by the same woman as her mother) is often said to be non-*nahmahrem*. Some said that the taboo extended to seven degrees of kin. Whereas a death or divorce immediately alters the list of males considered *namahrem*, nothing can weaken the bonds created by milk. This is perhaps a clue to explaining why the mother's brother should be perceived as closer in this context.

The closer proximity of the maternal uncle is somewhat at odds with the patriarchal ideology that attributes prime significance to male seed in procreation. So is the fact that a woman is likely to be blamed if a child turns out to be unhealthy, deformed or weak, a puzzle not resolved by Carol Delaney. One solution offered in Lazistan is to say that 'the child takes after his maternal uncle' (*Çocuk dayıdan çeker*).[48] Shifting the blame onto the closest male relative on the mother's side salvages the idea that men play a more important role in the formation of a child, while exempting a father from blame in cases of misfortune. However, this also implies a higher valuation of female nurturing than is allowed for in simple, unilateral models of patriarchy and 'generative power'.[49]

Thus the idea of *namahrem* as the basis of the modesty code does indeed

[46] Sauner-Nebioglu's recent study among migrant villagers from Lazistan in western Anatolia mentions the same contradictory attitudes towards the maternal uncle. According to her findings the paternal uncle is always regarded as a non-intimate, a stranger to the woman, while the maternal uncle is considered an intimate. This privileged position of the maternal uncle is expressed by these migrants in terms similar to those we found in Lazistan: 'you can share a bed with your maternal uncle, he is a *mahrem*'. (1998: 121–2).

[47] Luzbetak 1951: 56. See also Paleczek, who discusses this relationship under the heading 'fictive relatives' (1987: 83).

[48] Another formulation is: 'the child turned out wrong because of his maternal uncle' (*Çocuk dayıdan bozuktur*). Such sayings, like the basket metaphor discussed in the previous chapter, have lost a lot of their currency and cannot be elicited without embarrassment.

[49] For an elaboration of this argument in the context of procreation ideas see Bellér-Hann 1999.

reinforce deference and obedience to male authority. The paternal uncle is more of an authority figure than the mother's brother. Lazistan women mount no overt challenge to the dominant patriarchal principles. Yet their discourse of *namahrem* also makes plain the importance of shared substantive nurturing. *Namahrem*, when discussed from the male standpoint, the standpoint that has dominated the anthropological literature on honour and shame, is all about female chastity and male honour.[50] However, to women this paradigm, which gives every individual a binary classification that impacts on all their social interaction, contains a message about the high value of uniquely female capacities, a message moreover that carries the full legitimation of the Koran.

[50] It is worth stressing that these key terms do not translate readily into local concepts. The term *ırz* is reported by Meeker from Of as approximating chastity (1996: 51–3); but it is not used in the Lazi region. The word *iffet* is occasionally used by elderly people with above average education, but seldom by villagers.

6
Marriage

The marital bond

Marriage is the institution that forms, links and reproduces families and it is therefore absolutely central to social life. Because marital decisions reflect the most important dimensions of social differentiation – age, class, ethnicity and pre-existing kinship – the practices and values associated with this institution are an ideal field in which to explore further the questions of power and control that we began to consider in the previous chapter. Marriage is assumed by virtually all to be the desired condition for a person's adult life and to embody their traditions *par excellence*. We therefore begin with a general review of these, before proceeding to investigate the balance of continuity and change in specific domains: material payments associated with marriage, cousin marriage, and wedding celebrations; finally we shall consider cases in which marital ideals are not fulfilled: divorce, remarriage and multiple marriage.[1]

The traditional norm in Lazistan, as in most of Turkey, was that young people, marrying for the first time, had little say in the choice of partner. This is often recognised as the sharpest point of contrast with the west. In both town and countryside and among all social groups, marriage is still considered too impor-tant a matter to be left to the whims and sentiments of the young. It is primarily the responsibility of a father to ensure that his children, both boys and girls, make satisfactory marriages. Improved communications have merely widened the radius within which he may seek to discharge this responsibility. Emigrants to Istanbul and also to Germany often find their spouses through contacts arranged by their parents back in Lazistan. The suitability of the other family is assessed as carefully as possible. Material conditions weigh heavily, but lack of wealth may be offset by a prestigious family history, especially if this is linked to a good education and employment prospects. In both town and countryside, a son-in-law who has established a profitable business is much more attractive than one with no viable route out of the dependencies of the parental home. The prospect of inheriting land is valued but, given the decline in the relative profitability of tea growing, unless the estate is very large, it is usually much more important to have a non-farm job (*iş sahibi olsun*). Girls who have undertaken some form of

---

[1] For comparative discussion of marriage in Turkey see Stirling 1965; Erdentuğ 1969, 1971, 1975; Öztan 1974; Mansur Coşar 1978; Magnarella 1979; Abadan-Unat 1981; Timur 1981; Ansay 1987; Paleczek 1987; Schiffauer 1987; Delaney 1991; White 1994.

post-secondary education and have white-collar jobs in the towns are similarly sought after.[2] Social comparability and compatibility of the two families is important. *Sosyete* circles are largely endogamous and this is the only class in which some women stay permanently single. Intermarriage between local people and members of the new underclass is rare.

In short, marriage in Lazistan is not, and probably never has been, the private affair of two individuals. It is a contract between their respective families, negotiated on the assumption that both sets of parents care deeply about the long-term happiness and security of all of their male and female children. The age of marriage is variable.[3] Most men marry within a few years of completing their military service. It is nowadays rare to marry earlier, though many immigrants to the region still do so. The number of men who delay marriage until they are into their thirties seem to be increasing: statistical data for 1989 in Pazar indicated an average age of marriage for men of 28, and for women, 23.[4] Both figures are certainly higher than past norms, but precise comparisons are impossible because before the 1950s marriages were often registered only after the birth of children, and a good many were never registered at all.[5] A woman who is still single as she approaches twenty-five is likely to be a concern to her family, especially if she has younger sisters (it is still unusual for the order of marriage to deviate from birth order).

There exist, and probably always have existed, informal mechanisms which allow the preferences of young individuals, and even love, to be taken into account. Boys can suggest a girl they would like their father to consider. Girls do not find it easy to be 'proactive' but they do have an informally acknowledged right of veto. The asymmetry is linked to the basic assumption that negotiations be initiated from the male side. Negotiations may, however, nowadays be prompted by a declaration of interest from either of the young persons concerned. If the parents refuse to act on this information, which implies converting a 'love marriage' into an 'arranged marriage', the only remaining option to the couple is elopement (*kız kaçırma*).[6]

There are basically two types of elopement: it can occur with the girl's consent or without it.[7] The latter, in effect a form of rape (*zorla kaçırma*), has become extremely rare, though informants suggested that it was still quite common in the first half of the century, particularly among families which had difficulty in paying the brideprice (*başlık*) and where the social difference between the two families was considerable. Parents usually acquiesce in an elopement by consent, and they may even organise a retrospective wedding celebration. However, the loss of prestige may be considerable, particularly for a family of high social standing which

---

[2] Cf. Stirling and Onaran-Incirlioğlu 1996.

[3] In exceptional cases, usually when the marriage has been agreed when both partners are small children (*beşik kertme*), it could in the recent past be contracted between children as young as eleven.

[4] Calculated from the local marriage registers. The national figures were 24.8 for men and 21.8 for women (Behar 1995: 100).

[5] For discussion of misreporting see Hancıoğlu 1997: 5–8.

[6] Statistics for the incidence of arranged marriages must therefore be treated with caution. Cf. Ergöçmen 1997: 94–5.

[7] The same distinction is made in Lazuri.

has previously made it plain that it regards the proposed partner as socially inferior.[8] It may take several years and the birth of several healthy grandchildren before everyone is back on speaking terms, usually through the mediation of a brother or other close relative. Many elopements depend on aid from a trusted senior member of the man's family, who provides accommodation and sometimes even financial support for the new couple. This household acts as moral guarantor, ensuring that the religious wedding ceremony is concluded before sexual relations take place. Thus, such elopements by no means undermine all traditional moral norms. The new couple requires the support and tacit approval of other family members if they are to succeed in thwarting the will of the parents.

Emine, a Lazi girl from Pazar, eloped with the Hemşinli Osman in this way in the mid-1970s. A village boy, he had spotted her in the streets of the market town and tried to persuade his parents to arrange a marriage. His parents made discreet enquiries which revealed that, although her family had roots in a local village, Emine had been raised in a western Turkish town where her father had worked for many years as a tailor. His parents concluded that, being used to urban comfort, she would not be willing to work on her prospective in-laws' land or live in a village, and they declined to pursue the matter. Osman therefore made Emine's acquaintance in secret, and the two agreed to elope. They stayed for a week in the flat of his cousin in Istanbul, still sleeping separately. When suitable accommodation had been found, they quickly completed both the secular and religious marriage ceremonies. Two months later they returned to Pazar, where Osman obtained an apartment in the town and a permanent job in a tea factory. These favourable circumstances helped to reconcile the two families superficially, but Emine never received her trousseau, there was no wedding party, and the couple received no significant financial help from either family. Both Emine and Osman considered this to be fair treatment, in view of their violation of marital conventions.[9]

The elopement of Sevtap and Kaya came about because her parents objected to his heavy drinking and lack of regular employment. A partial reconciliation took place some months later, but the bride's side refused to take part in their belated wedding party. Other cases led to long-term hostility and even to violence. When Ali fell in love with Gönül, her brother opposed their marriage because he had long been in love with Ali's sister, who had meanwhile become engaged to someone else. Ali and Gönül were planning to elope when her brother kidnapped Ali's sister (*zorla kaçırma*). Ali's family responded by smashing the windows of the shops owned by Gönül's family in town, and his relationship with Gönül was destroyed.

Most elopements involve high risks, particularly for the girl.[10] If there is no reconciliation, she has no guarantee of shelter with her parents in the event of

---

[8] See Toroslu 1974 for more general discussion of elopement in Turkey. For statistics see Ergöçmen 1997: 94.

[9] Even when the girl's side is prepared to release her trousseau after reconciliation, the offer may be turned down by the young couple, who think it shameful (*ayıp*) in the circumstances of an elopement. It is then passed on to an unmarried younger sister or another female relative. Emine was the eldest of ten siblings. When, twenty-five years after her own elopement, her youngest sister followed suit, the parents blamed Emine for establishing an unfortunate precedent.

[10] Cf. Schiffauer 1987: 206.

later marital problems, such as domestic violence. Meryem and Aziz eloped to Istanbul, before returning a few months later to his village. There was no reconciliation, even though her village was close by.[11] When Meryem was badly beaten she took refuge at her paternal uncle's. This did not lead to friction between the two brothers: such support is tacitly expected in cases where the father is not himself willing to help a disobedient daughter. The intensity of his personal indignation varies, but long-lasting rage is the socially expected behaviour.

Many marriages still take place within small rural communities, where the list of eligible partners is relatively short. When people look elsewhere it is common, when a suitable girl has been identified, to use the services of a 'go-between' (görücü). The go-between can also act as a matchmaker and bring complete strangers into contact. She typically visits the family of the potential bride in the company of one or two other women. The girl herself may be informed, or she may know nothing of the purpose of this visit. Further visits are made by the boy's female relatives, and then by male kin. At this point either party may withdraw from negotiations without anyone's honour being offended. If all continues to go well, there follows a formal visit by the parents of the groom to request the girl's hand. If this 'requesting of the girl' (kız isteme) ends in 'cutting the word' (söz kesme), a small party is held there and then.[12] Alternatively, particularly in wealthier families, celebrations may take the form of a later engagement party to which many friends and relatives will be invited.

The point at which the prospective couple see each other for the first time is highly variable. Where both parties are village neighbours or residents in the same small urban neighbourhood, this is not an issue. In other cases the prospective groom may join his kinsmen on one of their early visits, perhaps going not to the bride's home but to the nearby home of a relative, which is considered 'neutral' territory. In town the first such arranged meeting is likely to be in a pastry shop. The young girl is always accompanied by a female relative, who sits close by. A boy may also seek to observe the girl from a distance, and complain if there is something that is not to his liking. This right is less frequently granted to a girl. A more conservative family may allow the prospective husband and his parents merely to walk past their daughter in the street, or perhaps to meet up with her sisters, who will pass on an account to the potential bride. Meetings may also be engineered by family and matchmakers. Havva was aged twenty-seven and had declined several offers when she was taken one day by her married sister to visit her father-in-law in hospital. There, as planned by the families, she met a nephew of the sick man. The nephew had a major speech impediment but Havva, well aware that she was already considered to be old, found him acceptable. Their marriage was a happy one.

Even in the 1990s we came across cases where the only sight the couple had of each other right up to the day of the civil ceremony was a passport-sized

---

[11] One of the several reasons why her parents refused to forgive her elopement, even after the birth of her third child, was the fact that it took place when she was in the last year of high school. It was interpreted as a negation of all the sacrifices her parents were making to educate her.

[12] Some informants remember a further ritual called the 'visiting the groom' (enişte görmek) which typically took place sometime between the engagement and the wedding. A mixed party of the bride's male and female relatives (but not the bride) went to visit the groom, where they were fed and entertained. The visitors placed a necklace of hazelnuts around the groom's neck.

photograph. It is increasingly viewed as risky not to allow the couple to see each other before the engagement (*söz kesme*), since a refusal at this point brings serious consequences for both families. Any breaking off of an engagement diminishes the marital opportunities of the girl, and possibly of her younger sisters as well. She may be obliged to accept a man from outside the region, or a widower or a divorcee, or even to become the second wife (*kuma*) of a man who has not legally divorced his first wife (see below). Nonetheless, it occasionally happens that women do break off an engagement. In one case, a girl had not seen the man she was supposed to marry before their engagement and she disliked him so much when she saw him that she called off the marriage, in full knowledge of the difficulties this would create in the search for an alternative. (She eventually found a husband in another town, who was probably unaware of the story.) In another case, a girl broke her engagement on the eve of the Ramadan holiday, *Şeker Bayramı*. In the course of several visits to the boy's household following the engagement, she had found out that his family, with whom she would be expected to co-habit for several years at least, was extremely quarrelsome. Her refusal provoked the young man's father to shoot (but not kill) not only the girl but also her brother and sister, for which he was duly imprisoned. The case was not classified by the community as a matter of sexual honour (*namus*) but more in terms of loss of face, honour in the sense of *şeref*.[13]

Payments

Close attention is paid to the material provision that each side will make for the new couple. Until recently, in many parts of Lazistan a *başlık* payment was made by the family of the groom to the family of the bride.[14] The connotations of this 'brideprice' are nowadays considered awkward, even by those most deeply attached to their traditions. How can a society aspire to be modern and yet transfer women by means of payment, as if they were commodities in a market-place?[15] These payments did not, of course, lead people to confuse women with other commodities. Nevertheless, the embarrassment felt about this custom in modern Lazistan creates some difficulty in obtaining reliable information. When we first broached the subject, it was common for people to deny that *başlık* had ever been paid in their village. One woman who denied the very existence of the custom divulged a few months later, after getting to know us better, that a substantial sum had been paid under this rubric at her own marriage, a mere fifteen years earlier.

We attempted to explore intra-regional diversity in *başlık* payments by circulating a questionnaire to village headmen. Many were similarly coy in their responses and the exercise brought meagre results. In interviews, people would

[13] Cf. Meeker 1976: 244–5; also Schiffauer 1983: 70; 1987: 30.
[14] Brideprice payment was common practice among South Caucasian peoples (Luzbetak 1951: 86). For the *başlık* in modern Turkey see Benedict, who notes (1974c: 24) that this form of wedding payment was widespread in the Black Sea region; he links this to the significance of women's economic activities. See also Stirling 1965: 185–9, Schiffauer 1987: 27–30, Delaney 1991: 118–20, Yalçın-Heckmann 1991: 246.
[15] Cf. Ergöçmen 1997: 95.

insist that this payment had nothing to do with the purchase of women, and that more money was spent on a daughter's trousseau than ever came in to family coffers through *başlık*. Most exaggerated the time that had elapsed since the custom had died out. Closer enquiries revealed that, in spite of a nationwide proscription, it had persisted, at least among certain social groups, in many parts of Lazistan until the early 1980s.[16] Only in certain Lazi districts east of Ardeşen did people have no recollection whatsoever of *başlık* payments. Here, the practice had ceased by the early twentieth century, if indeed it had ever existed (many people rather doubted the possibility). Apart from *başlık*, other payments made to the bride's side included 'presents' (*hediyeler*, sometimes *bahşiş*) to her parents and money to her mother known as 'milk right' (*süt hakkı*). This was a symbolic payment for the mother's services in the raising of the bride. Like similar payments due to the bride's maternal uncle (*dayı hakkı*) and to one of her brothers, usually the youngest (*kardeş hakkı*) it has all but disappeared.[17] If they persist, the payments are nominal sums, made either in the course of the celebrations at the engagement party or at the wedding.[18]

The major material transfer to the bride herself is her trousseau (*çeyiz*). This tradition seems to be a relatively recent one in Lazistan. Many older women say that they did receive something from their parents' home when they married, and this *might* have been termed a trousseau, but it was extremely basic: perhaps no more than a towel or a pair of socks. As some women put it, they were too poor for anything better. Elaborate trousseaux became fashionable only after the successful introduction of tea. Nowadays virtually all girls prepare a chest full of bed linen, tablecloths, headscarves, prayer rugs, handmade lacework and three or four dresses. In richer families these may be accompanied by carpets and curtains. Lacework is also a relatively new fashion. Many of the items sewn, embroidered, or hand-painted for the trousseau represent new skills, disseminated through the courses of the extra-mural education department. Mothers start building up the trousseau when a girl is still very young, and she will begin working on it herself at around the age of ten. Those expected to stay in education for longer can avoid some of the pressure of preparing a big trousseau. It is assumed that the money they will earn later through their job will enable them to buy items of equivalent value, or to have them made by others.

A contemporary dowry consists of much more than the contents of the wedding chest. The girl's family is expected to provide all the furniture for a bedroom (a double bed, a wardrobe, chests of drawers, dressing table, several sets of bedding, covers, large carpet and curtains). In 1992 an average small-town family would reckon to spend up to 6 million TL on these items (roughly $900). A girl should also have her own modern sewing machine. A wealthy family is also likely to provide electrical equipment, such as a vacuum cleaner, television and refrigerator (known collectively as 'white goods', *beyaz eşyalar*). Knowledge, or presumed knowledge, of the amount of money spent circulates widely. These

---

[16] Cf. Paleczek 1987: 295.

[17] A similar custom prevailed among Muslim Georgians, whose wedding prestations also combined bridewealth payment and gifts of gold jewellery to the girl's side (Magnarella 1979: 43, 47).

[18] Cf. Benedict 1974c: 18. In one case that we documented, however, dissatisfaction on the part of an elder brother with the refusal of the groom's side to pay him what he saw as his due led to the cancellation of a planned union.

items are not publicly displayed, but the bride is usually happy to show off her handiwork to visitors (perhaps in return for a token tip, *bahşiş*). A recent innovation is for the bride to receive some gold from her own family; they may also present the groom with an item of similar value, such as an expensive watch.

Expenses are even more substantial on the groom's side. The costs of the wedding itself are often said to be in the order of the cost of a new car. They include the costs of hired cars, the bride's hairdressing bills (perhaps for the engagement party as well as the wedding) and her wedding dress (perhaps also an engagement dress). By agreement, some of these costs (up to one third) may be covered by the side of the bride, particularly if they have special preferences as to the form the celebration should take. The groom's side will also contribute a complete set of living room furniture (large dining table and chairs, cabinet, two armchairs, sofa and carpet, adding up to about 10 million TL). An agreed list of additional personal goods for the bride, such as a leather handbag, a purse, a pair of boots, several dresses and a winter coat, is also covered by his side in the run-up to the wedding. The bride, usually accompanied by female relatives, points to the style of her choice, whilst either the groom himself or other family members stand by to pay the bills.

The other major outlay is the gold that the groom's side presents to the bride (*altın takmak*). Older people recall that, before the introduction of tea, in prosperous families the bride received a large silver coin or five smaller ones (*beşibirlik*). In 1992, even small-town families of relatively modest means reckoned on spending at least 10 million TL on gold for the bride. The precise amount is guided by knowledge and gossip about what others have paid, and many weddings are delayed while the groom's side struggles to come up with the sum stipulated. In poor upland villages the demands may be as little as one bracelet or a pair of earrings. (Inability to meet higher demands may help to explain the persistence of village and hamlet endogamy.) The gold is transferred either at the wedding or at the engagement party (in which case the same items of gold may be handed over a second time at the wedding). Sometimes only part is transferred at the engagement and the residue at the wedding. Whatever the details, the payment can be interpreted as a form of 'indirect dowry' which augments the security of the woman in the event of hardship, such as being widowed or divorced.[19] In Lazistan people say that it is a payment for a girl's virginity: 'the gold is a girl's honour' (*altın kızın namusudur*). This gold is not returned to the husband's side if the couple divorce, not even if the fault lies unambiguously with the wife. It is, however, returned if the marriage is not consummated. A man who takes a virgin girl as his second wife must, even if no legal wedding takes place, transfer some items of gold, while a man who marries a widow or a divorcee has no such obligation.

[19] This can be viewed as a continuation of the Islamic *mehr*. On the Ottoman *mehr* see Duben and Behar 1991: 114. According to Güriz, it is understood by women as a 'means of security' (*güvence aracı*) (1974: 100). We did not hear the term *mehr* used in Lazistan, although Paleczek found the form *mahr* in Fevziye, a Lazi migrant village in Western Anatolia (Paleczek 1987: 90). Cf. also Moors, who found that Palestinian women mostly converted their *mahr* payment to gold, over which they exercised considerable control (1991: 118). This payment, made only to the wife, is a fundamental feature of Islamic marriage law; it was traditionally paid in kind as well as in money (Öztan 1974: 47).

Many of the groom's close kin assist in meeting these formidable expenses, which, even allowing for the great rise in incomes, nonetheless impose at least as large a burden on the household as did the *başlık* payment in the past.[20] Those who give the most valuable items of jewellery usually receive a small packet from the bride as her acknowledgement of the relationship, the 'bridal bundle' (*gelin bohçası*). It contains small items of her handiwork: socks and a shirt for men, headscarves, pillowcases, handkerchiefs and towels for a woman. The preparation of these bundles takes time and some expense, though much less than the value of the gold the bride receives.

Real estate (*taşınmazlar*) normally figures in wedding prestations only when a girl is given in marriage as a second wife (*kuma*). According to the state's legal codes this woman has no rights of inheritance after a deceased husband, nor even rights over her own children. In the negotiations that precede the marriage it is therefore usually agreed that some land, a house or a flat is transferred to her name by her future husband, as a form of compensation.[21]

There are of course many variations around these norms. In addition to meeting the costs usually expected of the male side, his family may also be willing to pay for items normally covered on the bride's side, such as bedroom furniture and kitchen equipment, in order to secure an exceptionally attractive girl who comes from a significantly poorer family. The groom's family may be excused living room furniture expenses if the couple is taking up residence with his parents. The stipulations affecting the bride's side are seldom relaxed, even if the furniture they provide has to be put into storage until the new couple is ready to move into their own accommodation; by this time it is expected that the groom's side should also have fulfilled its obligations.

All of these financial matters should be negotiated well before the wedding, but problems and recriminations are not unusual. Turgut's parents arranged for him to marry within his village the daughter of a family considered to be *sosyete* in terms of tastes and aspirations, though not in terms of wealth. The girl's parents wanted a modern, low-cut wedding dress and a wedding celebration in the municipal wedding hall (*düğün salonu*) in town, with music and entertainment. Turgut's family, which had a reputation for piety and adherence to older traditions, opposed this. They challenged the dress and obtained the concession that it would be more modestly cut. They bought not only the living room furniture but also the bedroom items, and on top of this they offered generous amounts of gold and clothing. The girl's father, however, demanded an extra 5 million TL to cover additional items that he had already purchased for his daughter. When Turgut's family declined to pay, the young couple violated custom and spent their wedding night in the bride's house rather than the groom's. Turgut's mother had difficulty in coping with the alienation of her son and the loss of prestige this development brought. She concluded that her new daughter-in-law had cast a spell on him, and even after the birth of two sons there has been no reconciliation with his parents.

---

[20] By 1999 total average wedding expenses on the male side were said to be running at around 2 milliard TL on the groom's side, including gold purchases and up to one and a half milliard on the bride's side, a significant increase on 1992 levels in real terms.

[21] As is the practice elsewhere in Turkey: see Güriz 1974: 129.

Cousin marriage

Marriage to a first cousin was not always discouraged in the Christian tradition, and has remained widespread in the Islamic Middle East. The case of modern Lazistan is instructive because it shows how people have resisted the systematic efforts of their governments to eradicate a deeply rooted social practice. Yet its roots in this region are probably not ancient at all, at any rate among the Lazi, whose closest linguistic relatives in the Caucasus have strong traditions of 'marrying out'.

According to one estimate, 23 per cent of women of childbearing age in Turkey in 1983 were married to kin (*akraba evliliği*).[22] The proportion has declined in recent decades but remains high, not only in more remote, 'tribal' areas but also among certain urban groups, particularly recent migrants.[23] It is not to be dismissed simply as a backward custom, found only in remote places and among the poor. People in Lazistan recognise that quite normal families as well as elite families from *sosyete* ranks also arrange marriages within their kin group. The main reason is usually said to be the desire not to alienate property outside the family: 'the property should not go outside' (*mal dışarı gitmesin*), 'the property should stay in the family' (*mal aile içinde kalsın*), 'the inheritance should not be split up' (*miras bölünmesin*). The practice is thought by some to be responsible for a high incidence of mental and physical handicap. Some link it, in the case of elites, to a less visible tendency to social decadence.

Though the property dimension may well be important and in some cases decisive (notably where a bride has no brothers), it does not reveal the whole picture.[24] Cousin marriage fits well into a patriarchal system. Marriages between two brothers' children are much more likely to be determined by men alone, without significant consultation with wives or with the cousins themselves. The context of kin obligations makes it extremely difficult to refuse a brother's request for your daughter.[25] The request is sometimes made when the children are extremely young, or even at the daughter's birth. The cousins themselves may be unenthusiastic, particularly if they have grown up together in the same hamlet, living virtually as brother and sister. They may have difficulty in consummating the marriage, in which case an early divorce is likely.[26] However, the pressure to

---

[22] Akkaya 1994: 145. This figure covers women aged between 15 and 49 who, at the time of the survey in 1983, were married to or had been married to a relative. The proportion for the Black Sea region was slightly lower than the national average, 22 per cent. A more precise figure for cousin marriages was not obtained. The same source gives an estimate of 30 per cent for 1968 and believes that kin marriage in general is in continuous decline.

[23] Cf. Paleczek 1990 and Stirling and Onaran-Incirlioğlu 1996, who document and explain an *increased* incidence of cousin marriage among urban migrants.

[24] Cf. Holy 1989: 112–13.

[25] Cf. Yalçın-Heckmann 1991: 235.

[26] However, strong attraction may also occur. People say that first cousins may 'naturally' fall for each other and develop strong feelings of jealousy towards others. Elopement by first cousins is by no means unknown. In one unusual divorce case, the female plaintiff complained that her husband had completed a religious marriage with his father's brother's daughter before his secular marriage to the plaintiff, that the cousins had even had a baby, and that the sexual relations had continued after they were both legally married to non-relatives. Some young people, male and female, emphasise the advantages of first cousin marriage in making for a more harmonious relationship in the first years of marriage, when the new couple is living with his parents and the relationship with the mother-in-law can often prove difficult.

enter such a marriage and to make a success of it can be considerable: in addition to relationships of economic dependency and the moral authority of the father, one may come under pressure from a sibling whose own marriage is contingent on one's own and may even be planned simultaneously, perhaps even to a sibling of the cousin that you are marrying.

A patriarchal bias emerges if one asks people whether some types of cousin marriage are 'closer' than others. The usual answer is that marrying a father's brother's daughter (amca kızı) is the closest. Next closest is marriage to a father's sister's daughter (hala kızı), followed by mother's brother's daughter (dayı kızı) and mother's sister's daughter (teyze kızı). All four types occur in Lazistan and as far as we could judge they were in most districts equally distributed. Some name the last type as the least objectionable because it is generally believed that 'blood ties' (kan bağı) are not so close between the children of two sisters as between those of two brothers.[27] Others say that marriage between the children of two brothers is the most desirable form, and many believe it to be the most common in practice.[28] Many people merely express a general preference for marrying kin, not differentiating between cousins, nor indeed distinguishing cousin marriage from other, more distant forms of kin marriage. All are subsumed in the category akraba evliliği.

The state is not interested in differentiation but advances arguments about the dangers of genetic inbreeding to persuade people to give up all forms of kin marriage. The press regularly runs features about cousins unable to produce children, or whose offspring are seriously handicapped. Many, particularly younger people, accept these arguments from biology. In one state campaign in the early 1980s the risk that a first cousin marriage would produce a seriously handicapped child was given as 30 per cent.[29] A popular newspaper alleged that one in every ten babies born to first cousins was crippled.[30] A 'Commission to Fight Kin Marriages' was founded in Fındıklı in 1983 by the kaymakam, with strong local support.[31] Its stated goals were to make available the latest scientific information about the harmful effects of close marriages and to work out strategies for dissuading people from such marriages. However, in Lazistan as a whole the majority is far from convinced. Whatever the newspapers report, for the actors themselves it is far from obvious that cousin marriages are more likely to result in deformed offspring than other marriages. The government's message is

[27] Cf. the observations of Sauner-Nebioglu among Lazi migrant villagers in western Anatolia: 1998: 122–3.

[28] Meeker's analysis of cousin marriages in the Of region near Lazistan reveals a more ambiguous attitude to FBD and other types of close kin marriage, which he compares with the situation he found in another Middle Eastern society (1976). Meeker (1970: 90), Paleczek (1987: 293) and Yalçın-Heckmann (1991: 227) all found other types of cousin marriage to be as prevalent as father's brother's daughter.

Marriage records do not indicate kinship between the marriage partners but it is reasonable to assume that a high percentage of unions between people of the same surname took place between children of two brothers. The proportion of same surname marriages in Pazar in the early 1990s was almost the same as forty years earlier, at 12–13 per cent.

[29] See Bulvar 3 May 1983, Karadeniz 15 May 1983, Bulvar 3 May 1983. Cf. Kesici and Sırtlı 1999: 89.

[30] Bulvar, 3 May 1983.

[31] See '"Akraba Evliliği ile Mücadele Komisyonu" çalışmalarını sürdürüyor' in Hürriyet 1 July 1983. The initiative was set up in the wake of nationwide publicity during 'Disabled Week' (Sakatlar haftası), 10–16 May 1983.

therefore often seen, particularly by older people, as an unwarranted intrusion into the intimate matters of family life, an attempt to break with a tradition (*örf-adet*) that many families wish to uphold. Even local doctors expressed their doubts to us: some had married cousins themselves, and they challenged the quality of the scientific evidence on which the government campaigns were based.

Why should people wish to maintain such customs? The answer seems to lie not so much in matters of money and property as in less tangible issues of trust and honour. As some phrased it, when you married a cousin, 'you knew exactly what you were getting'. In the words of a local lawyer: 'Our marriages are well-thought out. We do not marry strangers, so we know where we stand with our partner, and the chances of things going wrong are minimal.' Everyone is reluctant to enter into affinal ties with people of whom they have no close knowledge. Even for parents who think of themselves as modern, the prime duty of a father to ensure a successful lifelong union is thought to conflict with the idea that young people should make their own decisions on the basis of personal attraction. The more 'modern' parents may allow their children more say in the matter, but the surest way to obtain peace of mind in an increasingly urbanised and anonymous, mass society is still to arrange a marriage as close to home as the incest laws will permit.

In terms of the prime goal set, cousin marriages seem to be successful. They do, like other forms of arranged marriage, provide a stable and caring environment for children. While few people explicitly commend cousin marriages nowadays, many will bring the conversation around to a contrast between the stability of marriage in Turkey and the high divorce rates of contemporary western societies. They see the latter, with all their negative consequences for both adults and children, as the price you end up paying if you give young persons more freedom to choose their marital partners for themselves.

Weddings

Most weddings in modern Lazistan have three components. The modern state requires formal registration at its Population Office (*Nüfus Müdürlüğü*) in each county centre. This can be processed by the *muhtar*, who is then responsible for notifying the county office. This formality is devoid of ceremony. On the basis of the paper issued by the Office or by the headman, an *imam* can conduct the religious wedding (*imam nikahı*). The interval between the civil registration and the religious wedding may be virtually nil, or it may be several months; a few days gap seems to be the most common. Almost everyone considers the religious wedding the most critical step.[32] It usually takes place in the bride's house and does not require the couple's presence; they can be represented by male family members. The ceremony is private and its exact timing is kept a secret to prevent malevolent magic. Although weeks or months may have passed since their engagement, it is only after the performance of the religious ceremony that the couple may have physical contact. Until this point, at least in the western

---

[32] Güriz lists a number of reasons why the religious ceremony may be preferred to the legal ceremony (1974: 124–7).

districts of Lazistan, even to hold hands and kiss is proscribed. Following the religious ceremony, a wedding party *(düğün)* is organised, typically a few days later, and this completes the social recognition of the marriage in the community. The timing may vary. Where one of the parties is not a resident of the region, e.g. following migration to Istanbul, the families may agree to hold the main reception in the metropolis.

Most weddings take place in the summer, regarded as the most pleasant season on the Black Sea coast, in spite of the work that has to be undertaken on the land. They tend to be concentrated between the peak tea plucking periods. The period between the two Muslim religious holidays is thought by some to bring bad luck and is therefore avoided. Many families nowadays organise a henna party *(kına gecesi)* for their daughter on the eve of the wedding celebrations.[33] This is increasingly paralleled by a similar party at the groom's house. Such parties are attended by men and women, with the usual segregation. If the wedding party itself is to be held on public or commercial premises in the town, these parties are seen as a substitute for the hospitality that was formerly provided over several days at the groom's house. Misfortune, notably a recent death in one or other of the families, may lead to cancellation of the wedding party or its replacement by a quiet gathering with religious prayers at the groom's home.

On the day of the wedding the bride goes to the hairdresser's and dresses in a European-style white wedding dress. When she is ready she is collected by the groom and his relatives. In some houses she is seated on top of the wedding chest containing her trousseau, positioned just inside the front door of her house. There is a humorous verbal exchange between her future father-in-law and one of her male relatives (often her paternal uncle). She is handed over to the groom's party only after the latter have paid out the small cash payments (in theory previously agreed) known as *süt hakkı, dayı hakkı,* and *kardeş hakkı.*

In the past the party would then have proceeded to the groom's parental home for a reception including one or more substantial meals. Nowadays more and more families choose an option which they see as more modern, and also less exhausting and expensive for all concerned, an evening *salon düğünü.*[34] All of the coastal towns can offer suitable facilities: some have municipal halls, some privately owned restaurants, and most both. The largest of these can accommodate several hundred guests. Music is made by a small orchestra, or by a single musician with a synthesiser. These parties are attended by all and sundry; with buses and shared taxis readily available for hire, even the more remote villages are within reach. Older people tend to remain in family or neighbourhood groups throughout the evening, but younger people take advantage of the opportunity for more extensive same-sex socialising. Most Pazar weddings are held in the wedding hall of the municipal building, constructed in the 1970s, when such weddings became fashionable. The hall is colourfully decorated, with the stage at the front used to display bouquets, mostly sent by local businesses connected to the

---

[33] This is said to be a relatively new practice in the eastern districts of Lazistan, imported rather like the *güns* discussed in Chapter 4. Like the *gün,* it is now spreading from the towns into the more affluent villages, but it is not yet widely practised in poorer upland villages.

[34] For discussion of the comparable changes in a western Anatolian town see N. Tapper 1985, 1992.

families and by those involved in any of the material transactions occasioned by the wedding. The groom's father is the 'owner/master of the wedding' (*düğün sahibi*) and he does his best to welcome all guests. The opening music tends to be a noisy mixture of standard modern Turkish styles. Eventually, some time after 8 pm when most guests have arrived, the new couple appears and opens the dancing, to general applause. They are soon joined by others, but the modern western style dancing is generally segregated at this point. Later the musicians play more tunes considered local, which in this context means the Black Sea region, and there is sometimes a separate *kemençe* performance.[35] The bagpipes (*tulum*) are also a popular complement to modern electrified music. In Pazar it was considered especially appropriate for accompanying the circular *horon*, which is nowadays often danced by men and women together. Occasionally, songs are sung here in Lazuri. The music may be interrupted to allow a talented or simply extrovert individual to sing. On one occasion, Turkish folk songs were sung by the mother of the groom, a widow who busied herself with guests all evening as 'mistress' of this wedding. Token refreshments are distributed (often a single carton of fruit juice) and small children may be given balloons to play with.

The highlight of the wedding comes when the couple are invited to the microphones at the front to receive gold and other gifts, most of them previously agreed between the two families. The Master of Ceremonies (often a relative of the groom, though the task can be undertaken by a stranger for a fee) reads out congratulatory telegrams before the cutting of the wedding cake. The bride and groom tackle this task jointly, but their knife usually turns out to be blunt. It begins to cut only when relatives have placed a sum of cash on top of it. The music and dancing continue until about 11 pm when guests start going home.

This modern style of celebration has obvious practical advantages, particularly in terms of the numbers of guests who can be invited. However, many people still feel that a real wedding party should last longer and be held in the house of the groom, 'according to tradition'.[36] A village wedding still takes up at least most of a day. After the bride is collected in the morning, usually by car, a full meal is served. The bride wears a white wedding dress, sits next to the groom, and displays all her newly acquired jewellery. Tradition requires that the bride and her parents should look serious, even sad. She sits next to her new husband, but there is no conversation between them. The social hierarchy determines the order in which people are served, starting with senior males. Male and female groups are located in different parts of the house, or outside it if the weather permits. The men often gather inside disused maize granaries, where they chat and sip *rakı*. If they join the women at all, it is later in the evening when the music begins. If there is to be dancing, it should be initiated by the newly married couple. However, men and women usually dance separately.

Family members often disagree as to the form the wedding celebration should take and various compromises are possible. One recent adaptation is to hold the

[35] This small fiddle is the main indigenous string instrument of the Black Sea region. In coastal districts it has been almost entirely replaced by the *bağlama* (*saz*). See Picken 1975, Stokes 1993.

[36] Some conservative families criticise the *salon düğünü* on religious-moral grounds. They say it is shameful for a bride to shake hands with so many strangers, to wear the fashionable low-cut wedding dress, and to have her hair exposed to strangers.

party in a conveniently located tea collection centre (*alım yeri*), which offers more space than is available inside the home and is therefore more conducive to dancing. One family from a village near Pazar with a reputation for conservatism married a daughter to a distant relative in western Turkey. Since the wedding was to take place at the groom's residence, the family agreed to arrange a larger than usual engagement party in the municipal wedding salon. The girl wore a large headscarf covering her bosom, gloves, and a plain loose dress rather than the figure-hugging white costume favoured by most young people nowadays. While this gave rise to some comment, it did not interfere with the usual pattern of music and dancing.

Conservative attitudes, either on the part of bride-takers or bride-givers, do sometimes cause disappointment among the guests. For example, people like to inspect the gold the bride has received from the groom's family and are disappointed if this is not permitted. Sometimes the bride's parents are reluctant to attend the wedding. One couple met for the first time when registering their marriage at the Population Office in Pazar. The girl's side had stipulated that there was to be no music and dancing, because her grandfather had only recently made the pilgrimage to Mecca. When female relatives of the groom began to dance to taped music, the bride's brother burst in and switched the machine off. When they tried again, the bride's father condemned them strongly for not adhering to the agreement that the two families had made prior to the wedding. He said that he would like to take his daughter back home, if it wasn't already too late. The bride herself was helpless. She had not been seen in this village previously, and was criticised by local women for being slightly older than the normal marrying age, and not particularly attractive.[37]

Another Lazi village wedding party which we attended proceeded more smoothly. It illustrated many features regarded as traditional. Although the bride came from another Lazi village, she was the groom's father's sister's daughter (*hala kızı*) and therefore 'not a stranger' (*yabancı değil*). The party was held in an *alım yeri*, beautifully decorated, which happened to be right next door to the groom's house. Food was served outside, though women and children also ate informally in small groups inside the house. The meal consisted of a number of dishes, including soup, vegetables and meat, followed by rice and a sweet dish. Women also sat at small tables around the walls of the *alım yeri*, leaving the central space empty. Dancing was initiated by adolescent girls before the arrival of the new couple. There was no break in the music when the bride and groom arrived. The bride was required to step on a vine-shoot, supposed to ensure fertility as well as longevity. One of her male relatives, an elderly man, lay on the ground pretending to be ill. A male relative of the groom helped him up and carried him; he did not need any money for a 'cure'. Eventually the couple entered the *alım yeri* by passing under a 'gate' of human hands. They immediately started dancing, to great applause.

Meanwhile, outside the bride's maternal uncle was sitting at the head of a long table known as the *mangal sofrası*, with close male relatives of the groom

---

[37] Some weeks later we asked the same women how the new bride was settling in. They had not had a chance to get to know her well, they said, but they praised her for her hard work and, in particular, her ability and willingness to carry heavy loads on her back.

attending to his demands in the ritual known as *mangalcılık*. He demanded that the bride's side produce cigarettes (he stipulated an American brand), pistols, alcohol, sweets and honey. He demanded *rakı* using the usual Turkish euphemism 'lion's milk' (*aslan sütü*). To the feigned dismay of the bride-givers, and the delight of the onlookers, a bowl of fresh yoghurt was presented instead. Although we were told that women sometimes organise their own *mangalcılık*, on this occasion they were not even involved as onlookers. The entire performance was drawn to a close after half an hour, as previously agreed; apparently in the past it could last much longer.

Shortly after this, at a table at the end of the *alım yeri*, the bride was formally presented with her gold.[38] The venue was crowded by now, mostly with women, and many of those who had previously been chatting outside tried to squeeze in for this part of the proceedings. The Master of Ceremonies was the groom's paternal uncle. With microphone in hand he called people forward to present the bride (and in some cases, the groom) with gold or money. Beginning with the bride's side, people were identified not by their names but by their relationship to the new couple. The value of the gift was always made clear and it decreased with the closeness of the relationship. Gifts of money to the bride sometimes complemented a gift of gold made to the groom, and vice versa. These included sums in deutschmarks and dollars as well as Turkish lira, all of which were pinned onto the couple's clothes. The sums mostly fell between $15 and $30. This was followed by more dancing, faster and wilder than before, though still segregated. Several men fired their pistols in the air. Although this is against the law, a local policeman participated enthusiastically in this part of the proceedings. Indeed, he was said to be the source of ammunition for all the others. The celebrations continued until dawn and the bride's immediate family stayed in the groom's house overnight. In this case, unusually, the religious ceremony only took place the following evening, and the consummation of the marriage that same night.

The banter of *mangalcılık* is claimed as a tradition by both Lazi and Hemşinli.[39] In addition to items such as those in the example given above, the bride's side typically demands money to pay for their own fares home. Some people say that the ritual should take place twice, first when the bride's male relatives are seated at the wedding table, and again for her relatives on the female side; the bride and groom should be present throughout at the head of the table. In practice nowadays it is only performed once and, as in the above example, the new couple may not be present. On the other occasion that we witnessed a performance it was again the bride's relatives on the maternal side who constituted most of the audience, attended by three male relatives of the groom. The leading role was played by an extrovert *yenge*, wife of the bride's brother. When the groom's *dayı* (referred to as the *mangal başı*) attempted to serve food to these guests, the *yenge* turned her plate upside down. Everybody followed her example; the groom's plate

---

[38] As in the *salon* wedding, the public display is carefully scrutinised, to be borne in mind in future negotiations. It is common to hear allegations of exaggeration and to be told that poorer families have secretly borrowed items of gold for the occasion, to avoid losing face in the community.

[39] Solak (n.d.: 30) may therefore be justified in treating this as a regional phenomenon, rather than one tied to a particular ethnic group.

was turned over by a woman sitting next to him. The *yenge* announced that she was not going to give the bride away and accept food (as a symbol of concluding the deal) until she had received some valuable presents. She demanded a watch, which was quickly found for her. Then she asked for sweet dishes, whereupon several trays of *baklava* were put in front of her. Then she asked for honey, which was supplied, and for pistols, which were given in the form of children's toy guns. Eventually she asked for money to cover her travel expenses. She received the equivalent of $25, a sum greatly in excess of actual costs, which was quickly handed over to the groom. The groom's relatives played their part by showing some reluctance to come up with the items demanded and reacting with humorous comments such as 'for that amount of money you could fly all the way to Germany'. The *yenge* also denigrated the quality of the goods she was given. On seeing that the honey must have been bought on the 'Russian market' she described it, to everyone's delight, as 'the *gogos*' product', *gogo* being at this time the term used to describe foreign women engaged in trade and prostitution. These exchanges, on this occasion crossing the usual gender boundaries and introducing new, highly topical materials, are followed with enthusiasm. Some people fear that the prevalence of the salon wedding will lead to the disappearance of this ritual.[40]

After the wedding ceremonies the couple are expected to spend the night in the groom's house. Most brides are virgins at this point and their knowledge of sexual relations is likely to be very limited. Male knowledge may not be much greater, though we were told that relatively few men are virgins at marriage. One common path is to be taken to a brothel in Ankara or Istanbul by an older relative. It is also common for men to acquire sexual experience during their military service. Some women confess to being frightened on their wedding night and liken their defloration to a rape. Stories circulate, among men and women, of brides who have to be tied down before intercourse. In villages near Rize and Of, until recently, other newly married women would gather on the following morning to inspect the bedclothes and dance in celebration.[41] The Lazi region seems to have no comparable tradition. However, in some Pazar villages it was the custom until the early 1970s not to complete the furnishing of the couple's bedroom until the nuptial night. One of the bride's sisters-in-law would then take the bride to see the new bedroom. She then would leave the bride on the pretext of going to fetch a glass of water, and the groom would return in her place. The following morning the sister would discreetly inspect a piece of white cloth placed on the nuptial bed and show it to the mother.

Within the Lazi zone there is a further striking difference between the more conservative, western counties (Pazar, Ardeşen) and the more 'enlightened'

---

[40] Among Georgian villagers in western Anatolia and some Lazi in the same area a similar ritual seems already to have disappeared. It was called *sofra tutulması* and took place after the bride was taken to the groom's house:

'Singing to music, they [bride's male kin] ordered all kinds of exotic foods and dishes, for example specially prepared fish or fruit which was out of season. In order to find these foods, the groom's kin had to travel to neighbouring villages or Inegöl. Even then they often were unable to meet the demands of their affinal guests and consequently experienced embarrassment. After dinner, the guests, if satisfied, danced to the same music they had used to sing out their dinner orders. Hayriye informants told me that this ritual was so demanding, that the villagers dropped it by consensus.' (Magnarella 1979: 50).

[41] Cf. Meeker 1970: 219.

counties to the east. Although it is everywhere expected that a girl should be a virgin when she first sleeps with her husband, there are differences in the timing of that moment. In the western counties it normally follows the religious ceremony and the wedding party, the community's recognition of the new relationship. In Arhavi, Fındıklı, and Hopa, however, it is solely the religious ceremony that matters for this purpose. The new couple may sleep together after the religious ceremony, which in some cases can precede the wedding by up to several months. It is said to be not unusual for brides to be in the early stages of pregnancy at their own wedding party. This may take place with the approval of both sets of parents. In some cases the groom's mother may prepare the nuptial bed, while in others there is no explicit endorsement of sexual relations, but the new couple will be allowed opportunities for intimacy if they wish to take them.[42] Some informants defend this apparent liberty by arguing that frequent meetings between the young people following the formal agreement of the two families necessitate an early religious ceremony. Once the couple are allowed to see each other regularly, they are bound to violate the unwritten rules of *namahrem* by joking, laughing, holding hands. A religious wedding changes the relationship between the young people into one which allows intimacy, including sexual relations. Pressures for a stricter attitude seem to have increased in recent decades, and some people in the eastern districts regret this. They interpret this unusual liberty as a manifestation of trust between the families. Whether this east–west difference can be linked to the earlier spread of Turkic and Islamic influences in the western parts of the Lazi region must remain a matter for speculation.

The new bride, if she is to live in the husband's parental home, is expected to submit to the authority of her mother-in-law and work under her guidance.[43] She can expect to be treated on a par with the unmarried daughters of the household and to be allowed to visit her own family regularly (beginning with a prescribed visit on the third day after the wedding). Many women return for extended visits of up to several months, particularly if their husbands have work that takes them away from home. This pattern is interrupted only when the new couple have their own separate accommodation. It is not necessarily broken by the arrival of children. However, the standing of the daughter-in-law rises appreciably when she becomes a mother, particularly when she gives birth to a healthy son. This remains the ultimate purpose of every marriage.

Multiple marriages and divorce

The discussion so far has focused on marriages in which both partners are young and are marrying for the first time. In this last section we consider a spectrum of

---

[42] Once sexual intimacy has commenced it is regarded as unthinkable that either party could step back from the proposed marriage: such a step would be classified as a *namus* offence and dealt with by violence, though no one could recall any such cases. In the western districts even the breakup of an engagement can be enough to create a *namus* issue leading to violence, and such cases are relatively frequent.

[43] The new pattern of dual residence may involve the new couple acquiring an apartment in the town for the winter months but continuing to form a single household with the husband's parents in their village house during the summer.

cases in which the ideal of marriage as a lifelong exclusive partnership is not attained.

The most common circumstance is the premature death of a spouse. Ideally a widow should not remarry and stories are told extolling the virtues of women who lose their husbands while still young and attractive, but who choose to remain single. In fact, many such women have little or no choice. Having lost her virginity, a widow is unlikely to be asked to marry an eligible bachelor. The choice is more likely to be between remarriage to an elderly widower, or to a divorced man, or someone with a physical disability, and marriage to a man who already has a legal wife, i.e. becoming a *kuma*, a relation not recognised by the modern civil code. When a woman remarries, her children normally stay with her deceased husband's parents. In reasonably well-to-do villages and in towns it is increasingly feasible for a widow with children to continue living with her in-laws. However, her position is not an easy one. Widows are more limited in their daily actions than their married counterparts, for whatever they do can be misinterpreted. As one woman put it, 'A widow cannot speak or laugh aloud, because others will accuse her of wanting to draw attention to herself. She cannot visit neighbours too frequently, because she may be suspected of wanting her neighbour's husband. If she calls on her married sister too often, they will say that she is after her brother-in-law.' In poorer villages a young widow can only afford not to remarry if she has at least one male child on whom she can expect to depend in old age; even then, she is better advised to remarry to secure her own future financially.

A widower has fewer difficulties in remarrying (living alone for a man is thought to be a pitiable condition), but in practice he too is likely to face problems. If he has sons by his deceased wife, they will lose out if their father remarries, since the new wife will inherit one-quarter of his estate. The consequences are even worse if she bears sons herself. Yusuf was thirty-five and had married a cousin, older than himself, at the age of twelve. The couple then had five children before the early death of his wife. The eldest son (eighteen in 1992) tried to prevent Yusuf from remarrying for economic reasons. Yusuf considered these objections legitimate and, rather than simply exercise his patriarchal right, he tried hard to persuade his son to understand his situation. He failed, however, and after Yusuf remarried his relationship with his son deteriorated sharply. Widowers often prefer a woman nearer their own age who is unlikely to want more children. Friends and relatives, male and female, will help in the search for a suitable partner. Often a go-between (*görücü*) is engaged. Divorced men and women proceed in similar ways, though divorce carries an additional social stigma for women.[44]

Polygamy, the taking of a second and even a third wife without divorcing the first, continues with the approbation of custom and Islamic law, which allows up to four wives at any time.[45] Some villagers assert that, provided a husband treats all his wives equally, religious law allows him up to seven wives. In practice most

[44] See Ansay 1987. For more detailed discussion of divorce in Turkey see Levine 1982; Starr 1992: 96–101.

[45] On Islamic marriage law within the Ottoman Empire see Aydın 1985. On Islamic marriage in modern Turkey see Güriz 1974. For further discussion of the co-wife's position in rural Turkey see Stirling 1965: 110–11.

people agree that treating even two wives equally is virtually impossible. Most women abhor the institution, but a few men and women are prepared to defend it. They argue that it prevents prostitution, and that historically, when males were in short supply, e.g. after a war, the institution served to ensure that all women were under proper male control and protection.[46] The second wife may obtain more economic security than she enjoyed previously, through the transfer of property to her (nowadays carried out using the legal machinery of the state).

The main cause of polygamous marriages is the inability of the first wife to produce a male heir. The problem can be tackled in other ways: the adoption (*evlat edinme*) of a brother's or sister's son is an acceptable, and for most women desirable alternative.[47] But in the absence of this option, polygamy is an alternative in which the first wife is expected to acquiesce, given her own failure to produce an heir.[48] The following case was set out in an open hearing (*duruşma*) of a divorce lawsuit in Pazar. Musa, a fifty year old Lazi man, wanted to divorce his forty-five year old wife Havva after more than thirty years of marriage. They had five daughters, four of them married. The youngest unmarried daughter, aged eighteen, was a witness for her mother. Musa wanted to divorce his wife on account of 'incompatibility' (*geçimsizlik*). During questioning it transpired that Musa had already married another woman by religious ceremony, with Havva's consent. In fact, having failed to produce a son herself, she had arranged this marriage.[49] Musa had then settled with the *kuma* in one part of the house, while the other part was occupied by Havva and the youngest daughter. Musa had stopped sleeping with Havva and gave no more money to her, although he did give small amounts to his daughter upon request. This was a violation of Islamic law, which insists that the husband treats his wives equally in every respect. He had transferred a part of his tea gardens to Havva, but she argued in court that this did not generate enough income to make a living. Divorce (*boşanma*) was granted on grounds of incompatibility (*geçimsizlik*) between husband and wife, and between the two women. However, Havva was not awarded any more of his land or other property. The judge emphasised that she had consented to her husband's second, polygamous marriage and implied that she had knowingly brought about her own trouble. He did not take account of the fact that it would have been difficult for her to do otherwise, given the force of customary law in the shaping of public opinion. She became worse off as a result of the judge's decision, for although she retained the area of tea that he had transferred, she lost her right to reside in Musa's house and was obliged to return to her elderly parents' house, where her married brother was also living.

[46] On the basis of his study of nineteenth-century Ottoman population registers for the eastern Black Sea region, McCarthy argues that polygamy in this area was 'well suited to the migration pressures and demographic situation of the time.' (1979: 323)

[47] This strategy is frequently followed by Turkish villagers. Like other Anatolian villagers (cf. Stirling 1965: 42) few in Lazistan bother to register such adoptions legally. The biological parents believe they are performing a meritorious deed (*sevap*) in giving a child and thereby helping to save a marriage, bringing the kin group closer together, and at the same time improving the inheritance prospects of their own existing children.

[48] Cf. Mansur Coşar on the 'conflict and insecurity' that polygamy creates for women (1978: 127).

[49] Some first wives may try to control the selection of the *kuma* in order to ensure that the woman who joins her household is a good worker, and/or that she has some physical or social disability which makes it likely that she is used for procreation and nothing else.

In another case, the first wife became a cripple, following many pregnancies which had resulted in seven surviving daughters but no sons. Shortly after the husband married a *kuma*, they persuaded the first wife to consent to divorce in return for a modest material settlement. She then moved to Istanbul to stay with one of her daughters, while the *kuma* stayed in the village and was converted into a legal wife after the birth of two sons. Another woman who divorced her husband of twenty years after he brought a *kuma* into their house ended up by herself becoming the *kuma* of another man. One *kuma* who had a minor physical handicap gave birth to two sons and two daughters and was able to live under one roof with the first, legal wife, without difficulties. In another case where the two women proved to be compatible, kin links between them were created by a marriage arranged between the *kuma*'s nephew and a daughter of the first wife.

It is unusual to come across *kumas* in the towns. One forty-eight year old labour migrant to Germany returned to Pazar and married again in the hope that she would bear him a son. He made financial provision for her by buying her a flat. When after several years of marriage she had produced no children, her husband abandoned her and rejoined his first wife in Germany. Migrant workers who have taken a second wife in Germany are normally condemned, but there may at the same time be some sympathy for men who have to experience long-term separation from their partners.[50]

It is difficult to gauge the overall frequency of illegal second marriages. Most villages that we visited had one or two households that contained a *kuma*, or had done so in the recent past. Informants emphasised that the typical *kuma* was a woman with some imperfection, which could range from physical deformity to mild forms of mental illness or tainted honour resulting from a broken engagement or loss of virginity before marriage. Some *kumas* are recruited when still minors from the large families of tea sharecroppers. A poor man may see this as the best way to secure his daughter's future and he may hope that it will open up a range of useful social contacts for himself and others in his family.[51] A second wife may also be acquired through elopement. Regardless of whether she eloped or was given away by her father, if the girl was a minor at the time of the consummation of their marriage, the first wife has the right to accuse her husband of raping a minor. This would almost certainly result in the husband's imprisonment. However, not many women are aware of this right. No reliable statistics are available, but one judge in Pazar suggested that marriages performed solely by religious ceremony could form up to 10 per cent of all marriages in the county. Other officials considered this to be an exaggeration.

In line with the rest of Turkey, divorce seems to have been rare in the past in Lazistan, and (despite anecdotal evidence about a recent rise linked to the phenomenon of the Russian markets) it remains so.[52] In the past it was enough

---

[50] Migrants often fail to register their *first* marriage, usually because one or both of the parties is too young. In such cases the second wife, married outside the region, has the rights of a legal wife and it is the first wife who is technically the *kuma*.

[51] Although sharecroppers are more numerous in the eastern counties, we formed the impression that *kuma* relationships involving permanent local residents are more prevalent in the west of Lazistan.

[52] At 0.35 per 1000 population, Turkey's 1976 Crude Divorce Rate was the lowest among Mediterranean countries (Levine 1982: 325). By 1990 the national rate had risen to 0.92, but the rate for Rize and the Black Sea remained at 0.33–0.34.

to follow the procedure of Islamic law, which allows a man to divorce his wife by a formal repudiation (*talak*), but this has disappeared in the last half century.[53] Whether a *kuma* is in the frame or not, the main reason why most men prefer to avoid legal divorce is financial. Divorced wives may be eligible for maintenance from their ex-husbands, which can be substantial, especially if the couple also has children. Men are also fearful of losing custody of their children to their former wives. In practice, the woman often comes under pressure not to pursue cases through the courts. If she does go to court, she is pressured to accept a financial settlement that takes no account of the land owned by her husband. Again, customary law tends to take precedence not only over the secular legal system but also over Islamic law, according to which the value of the land should be taken into consideration. The woman is unlikely to remain in possession of the marital home, but will move back to her father's house, or to the house of another male relative, or to that of a married child.

Small children usually stay with their mother, but she is likely to ask that any older children should remain with her husband and his parents, a request that the court always grants. A divorcee with children will find it more difficult to remarry. Nonetheless, various strategies are possible. One thirty-five year old mother, left by her migrant worker husband for another woman, took her two daughters back to her father's house. She helped to pluck their tea and received her share of the resulting income. She made up her mind not to consider divorce and remarriage until her daughters had completed their education and themselves been married. Apart from being a respectable and prudent course of action, she admitted, this was at the same time a form of revenge on her husband, who could not marry the woman with whom he was cohabiting until she consented to legal divorce. In the meantime he had to pay her and the children substantial maintenance.

County court files give some hint of the reasons that lead people to divorce.[54] In a majority of cases (55 per cent) women were the petitioners.[55] Of the examined cases, 58 per cent ended in divorce, 20 per cent were rejected, and the remainder were either declared invalid, withdrawn by the plaintiff, or still in progress. The four main justifications for divorce in Lazistan, as elsewhere in Turkey, are: incompatibility (*geçimsizlik*), adultery (*zina*), wilful desertion (*terk*) and 'other'.[56] *Geçimsizlik* is a blanket term which also covers cases where the actual problem is the absence of children. According to the national statistics, almost half of divorces occur in childless couples.[57] The proportion was lower in

---

[53] On the provisions made by Islamic law for this type of divorce see Aydın 1985: 113–14.

[54] This section is based on scrutiny of 137 divorce files and 17 related legal documents in the county of Pazar between 1989 and 1991. Not all of the examined cases ended in divorce: on some occasions the case was closed and the couple reconciled. On other occasions the case was closed because the parties failed to turn up for the hearing. As in inheritance cases, described in the previous chapter, the courts seem frequently to be used as an escalation intended to engineer an informal solution. Many cases cite multiple causes of divorce, hence the figures given add up to more than 100 per cent.

[55] Cf. Starr (e.g. 1992: 92), who argues on the basis of her work in western Turkey that, from the 1950s onwards, women began to make more use of the legal system, including divorce laws, to secure their rights.

[56] *Boşanma İstatistikleri* 1990: Table 1.

[57] *Boşanma İstatistikleri* 1990: Table 2.

Pazar and only in 3.6 per cent of cases did a man explicitly state that the lack of a *male* child was the key issue. Seventeen per cent of the examined cases were initiated by women explicitly because of a husband's *kuma* relationship. Eleven per cent of cases were brought by women wishing either a divorce or maintenance payments from a man who was either married or cohabiting while working in a distant city, or in Germany.

Other reasons for pursuing divorce are suggestive of the conditions and practices that more and more women are unwilling to endure. In 15 per cent of the examined cases women complained about the difficulties of sharing accommodation with their husbands' families, a situation usually described as 'lack of peace' (*huzursuzluk*). Multiple family households normally contain the groom's parents and his unmarried siblings. In some cases it was not so much her husband that the petitioner wished to divorce as his family. In such cases some specific evidence of maltreatment or economic exploitation was required by the court to warrant the granting of a divorce.

More than 20 per cent of all cases brought by women featured complaints about a husband's gambling and/or drinking, frequently linked to domestic violence and deprivation for the wife and children. An inveterate gambler might even appropriate his wife's gold, which both for customary law and for the state courts is the wife's exclusive property. This too was subsumed under the rubric of incompatibility (*geçimsizlik*) or severe ('violent') incompatibility (*şiddetli geçimsizlik*).

The same concepts figured in the cases filed by male plaintiffs. Here *geçimsizlik* covered 'neglect of wifely duties' (*kadınlık görevini yapmamış/kadınlık vazifelerini yerine getirmez*), which figured in 13 per cent of all cases brought by men. It was sometimes coupled with accusations that the wife had neglected the children. Leaving the house without the husband's permission or going to places disapproved of by the husband (*kocasının mahzurlu bulunduğu yerlere izin almadan gitmesi*) was a complaint in 9 per cent of cases. Insults (*kötü hakaretler*) were cited by both men and women in 5 per cent of all cases. Women were occasionally accused of gossiping about family secrets. In a few cases where male plaintiffs filed the case, it turned out that the husband had already taken a *kuma*.

If a woman leaves her husband's house and takes her gold with her, it is generally assumed that she does not intend to return. A husband in this position may request the court to issue an 'admonition' (*ihtar*) for her to return (4 per cent of cases brought by men). He may also pursue attempts at reconciliation by other means. He may, for example, try to fetch his wife himself, or send other members of his family, perhaps the *muhtar*, the *imam*, and other people of standing in the community to reason with her. In line with customary practice, women may expect such attempts to be made, and some of those filing for divorce specifically complained that their husband had taken no initiatives towards a reconciliation.

In 20 per cent of all cases, almost half of them marriages between first cousins, family pressure (*aile baskısı*) associated with an arranged marriage was blamed for the incompatibility of the partners. In a further 3 per cent of all cases either the husband or the wife complained that they had not been aware before the marriage that their partner had a serious physical or mental deformity.

Both men and women may request divorce on grounds of adultery (*zina*).

According to state law, any wife whose husband has taken a second wife by Islamic law may accuse him of adultery. A husband may bring a case on the basis of neighbourhood (*mahalle*) gossip: if two witnesses confirm that his wife has spent even a few minutes alone with a strange man, the plaintiff is considered to have a strong case. However, in the examined divorce cases only five men alleged that *zina* had been committed by their wives, while two women brought this complaint against their husbands. These low figures are at least partly due to the fact that adultery is treated as a criminal offence in Turkey, which is punishable with up to six months' imprisonment. In practice, unless there is some compounding offence, a fine and/or the payment of damages to the injured party is the more usual punishment. However, many cases of adultery never lead to divorce cases. The offence is a violation of honour (*namus*), which may lead to violent death and hence to a criminal trial. Courts recognise local sensitivity to the honour code and tend to impose fines rather than imprisonment whenever it is possible to do so.

In certain cases the court took action on behalf of a disadvantaged woman, even where no legal marriage contract existed. Fatma (b. 1959) could not technically seek a divorce from her cousin Zafer (b. 1958) because their arranged marriage took place in 1974 by religious ceremony only, when she was too young to marry legally. They had three sons, but after the birth of their third child she alleged neglect, swearing and violence on the part of her husband. Eventually Zafer took his eldest son and went to live in Istanbul, where he became engaged to another woman. Fatma was left with two children and no financial support. Because her natal family had insufficient resources to support her, she was forced to pluck tea for strangers as a sharecropper, while Zafer's family owned large tea gardens. Even though her marriage had no status in the eyes of the state, she was awarded substantial damages against Zafer.

The evidence considered in this section concerns exceptional cases, but the climate that it reveals also bears upon the vast majority of marriages that never trouble the courts. It suggests that, at the foundations of social life, a cluster of patriarchal ideals and practices retain much of their force in this western part of the region. Men, especially if wealthy, have considerably more scope to remarry following divorce, regardless of 'fault'. Women can return to their parental home if they are abused or betrayed by their husbands, but this resource is insecure, and some parents cannot afford to welcome their daughters back. If they do, it is likely to be only as a temporary expedient before she can be offloaded again, this time to anyone who will take her. In control over property, as in custody of her own children, the cards are all stacked against the woman. Whatever the state's legal code might proclaim, her own family, instead of assisting her to pursue her rights as a citizen, often connives with general patriarchal pressures.

7
Islam

Variable zeal

In the last two chapters we have shifted the emphasis away from realms associated normally with the public sphere and focused on the familial, the personal and the unequivocally private. Public and private are thoroughly intertwined in the shaping of social identitites, and we see this even more clearly when we turn now to examine religion. Islam has been highly successful in resisting the fate that has befallen other religions in modern times. Whereas most Christian societies have experienced far-reaching secularisation or a sort of compartmentalisation that separates belief from the practical affairs of the world, Islam maintains a more pervasive hold over its followers. It is not surprising, therefore, that some anthropologists have seen in Islam the basis of a 'local model', or even an ultimate source for the encompassing ideology of patriarchy.[1] Others, however, have drawn attention to divergences between 'orthodox' teachings or theology and popular beliefs and practices; they have shown that Islam everywhere is both influencing and being influenced by modern phenomena such as universal literacy, strong national identities, high rates of migration and consumerist globalisation.[2]

The vitality of Islam in Turkey, in spite of three quarters of a century of Kemalist secularism, has attracted considerable scholarly attention.[3] Even though the inhabitants of Lazistan are Sunni Muslims, the dominant group in the country as a whole, local understandings of Islam and the degree to which religion in fact shapes modern lives vary considerably within the region. In Rize, Lazistan's largest town, the religious party has been the main rival to the Motherland Party. Islam is highly visible on the streets. Few women go without a headscarf (başörtü) and a conspicuous minority is fully veiled.[4] Large new mosques have recently been constructed here and in several of the smaller towns. Religious inscriptions are prominently displayed in commercial premises. During Ramadan in 1983 it

---

[1] Delaney 1991.
[2] See Eickelman 1998. See also Ahmed 1992, Ahmed and Donnan 1994 and, for Turkey, Tapper 1991a.
[3] The most stimulating assessments of the role of religion in republican Turkey have been those of Şerif Mardin: see in particular Mardin 1989. Many of the issues discussed in this chapter are addressed in the collection of papers edited by Richard Tapper (1991b) and by Shankland 1999a. The importance of religion in contemporary Turkish politics is analysed by Toprak 1981a, 1990.
[4] For a description of various degrees of covering see Özdalga 1998: xiii–xvii.

was almost impossible, in a town of almost fifty thousand people, to find an open restaurant during the hours of the fast. In these ways the importance of Islam became firmly stamped on our minds at the very beginning of our research.

We were therefore surprised, when we moved from Rize to the village of Sümer, to find that some people here were not observing the fast at all; or, if they were, they said they were doing so for 'social reasons', or because it had been 'demonstrated scientifically' that to fast for one month each year was healthy for the body.[5] This village, though well above average in size, did not in 1983 have a single *imam*. We lived in the main hamlet, quite close to the largest mosque, but there was no *müezzin* available to issue the call to prayer. The reason, people said, lay at least in part in the failure of local people to press the authorities into sending anyone. Any *imam* allocated to Sümer would have to be an outsider, since in the county of Fındıklı religious education was not highly valued, and few local children took part in summer Koran courses. In short, although we noted that some of the families we came to know did observe the fast and their daily praying obligations, religion did not seem to be the major force in the community that preparatory reading and impressions elsewhere in Turkey had led us to expect.

Further fieldwork in the 1990s has forced us to abandon the quest for simple generalisations about 'religion in Lazistan'. From our base in the county of Pazar, positioned midway between Rize and Sümer, we were again impressed by the strength of religiosity. We found that a particular style of radical Islam was strongly asserted in a few places, and we shall discuss this phenomenon in more detail below. Everywhere we looked, religion seemed to be a vital force in shaping both individual lives and social relations. New mosques and *Imam-Hatip* schools were being constructed all over the region. They were sponsored by local associations called *vakıfs* and *derneks*, archetypical vehicles of 'civil society' that we found to be lacking in the secular sphere. By the 1990s Sümer, too, had a resident *imam* and new mosques under construction. However, religious zeal was still less conspicuous in eastern counties, in comparison with more western parts of the region. This religious boundary coincides with the one we noted at the end of the previous chapter between Ardeşen and Fındıklı: to the west, a strong tendency to religious conservatism and even extremism is acknowledged by the inhabitants and confirmed by indicators such as women's dress and attendance at Koran courses; to the east, it is tempting to conclude that Kemalists have succeeded in fashioning a society in which religion's place is closer to the place it occupies in the industrialised societies of western Europe.

This variation within the region probably reflects very old differences, but it is hardly possible to reconstruct the processes of religious change. The Lazi were Christian before their conversion to Islam, which was completed in the seventeenth century. This past had disappeared from their collective consciousness by the nineteenth century. Lazi attitudes towards religion are represented inconsistently in travellers' accounts. In 1834 Eli Smith wrote: 'Among fruits the worst are *cheraz* [Kiraz] (cherries), so among Muslims the worst are the Laz.'[6] At the same time

---

[5] Cf. Tapper and Tapper 1987b: 65.

[6] E. Smith and H.G.O. Dwight (from their *Missionary Researches in Armenia*, London 1834, 1834; quoted in Toumarkine 1995: 48). As so often, it is impossible to be sure if the authors are using Laz in the ethnic sense (Lazi) or in the looser regional usage.

the area also had a reputation for sectarian fanaticism.[7] Similar contradictions persist today. The religious devotion of the Lazi was questioned by a Rize intellectual, who suggested that Ramadan was not properly observed in the region (*Ramazan Lazistan üzerinden uçar*).[8] Hemşinli apparently had a saying that 'Even a saint should not be allowed into one's courtyard if he is a Lazi (*Lazdan evliya, sokma avluya*), implying that the Lazi were insincere and unreliable Muslims.

Atatürk's republic proclaimed 'laicism' as one of its cardinal principles and interpreted this as meaning state regulation of religious activities. The Ministry for Religious Affairs in Ankara has ultimate responsibility for the education of clerics and their deployment to mosques, in much the same way that secular civil servants are given their postings.[9] Like their secular equivalents, *imams* who are public functionaries (*kadrolu*) receive a salary from the state and are entitled to a pension after twenty-five years of service. Each county has a *müftülük*, which is the local organ of official religious affairs.[10] This system operates throughout Lazistan, but it does not succeed in confining religious life to the private sphere as the state would wish. Even where such goals are more completely realised, as in Fındıklı and Arhavi, the role of Islam in people's lives should not be underestimated. We shall first consider some of the commonalities, aspects of Islam that seem to be important throughout the region, before turning to some specific contemporary developments in western districts.

Shaping lives

Religion impinges on everyday personal and social existence. Our account here is built up from our observations and from local accounts, not from books and theology. This local knowledge is fragmentary and contingent. Even when it appears to provide a coherent world view, religious knowledge usually draws on a range of popular, locally rooted ideas as well as orthodox doctrines transmitted at the mosque or in Koran courses.

Prayer is a daily obligation for the Orthodox Muslim, both man and woman. During most of the year only men pray together in the mosque, usually once a week on Fridays. They may visit the mosque to pray individually at other times. They also pray at home. With the exception of *Mevlud* rituals (and, for some urban women, communal praying during the month of Ramadan) women's daily prayers are private. Even if they pray at the same time as their husbands, they do so separately. There is great variety in daily observances. Many rural and urban women in Pazar county who go around 'covered' (*kapalı*, i.e. always wearing a headscarf) certainly perform them with some degree of regularity. If devout (*dine*

[7] Toumarkine 1995: 48.

[8] 'Ramadan flies over Lazistan' (i.e. without anyone noticing it).

[9] See Shankland 1999a. For the full historical background see Berkes 1964.

[10] In 1992 the *müftü* of Pazar was responsible for 70 mosques in the county. In addition there were three permanently established Koran courses in the county, two in Sinanköyü (one for male and one for female pupils) and one in the village of Melyat (male only). The qualifications gained on these courses do not suffice to qualify one as a *kadrolu hoca*: since 1965 one needs at least a secondary school (*lise*) graduation certificate. The recently founded *Imam-Hatip* secondary school in Pazar, with approximately 250 students, including one girl's class of 25, does meet this requirement.

bağlı) women miss a prayer, e.g. due to work, they make up for it after their evening prayer (*kaza*).

The social influence of Islam is pervasive in Lazistan in the holy month of Ramadan.[11] It affects everyone, whether or not one observes the fast, and irrespective of how one rationalises this decision. Most people in both town and countryside do fast (*oruç tutmak*) throughout the day. Heavily pregnant women with urgent work to carry out in their tea gardens in the 1983 Ramadan would not consume even a glass of water in the course of a long hot day. Some said they felt pressure from family members, particularly the mother-in-law, and this in spite of the fact that local health workers argued that expectant mothers were exempt from the normal requirements. In some cases their own family members said the same, but the women insisted on fasting anyway.[12] Other women who missed fasting days while having their periods (this is a ritual prohibition) made up for these days conscientiously when the fast was officially over. According to the estimates of the *müftü*, in 1992 90 per cent of women fasted in the district of Pazar, compared to approximately 80 per cent of men. Those with time to spare do a lot of extra praying during this month. Men visit the mosque more frequently, and women, mostly the daughters and wives of local merchants and craftsmen, many of them fully veiled (i.e. wearing the *çarşaf*) attend the late night service of Teravih.[13] Some pious women who do not attend excuse themselves by saying that to go to the mosque at all would risk infringing the modesty code: they might be observed by men on arrival or when leaving. Most consider participation in this communal praying to be meritorious. They follow the instructions of the *imam* with close intensity. Since the *Teravih namazı* includes twenty *rekat*, the service lasts for well over an hour, after which the women go home in groups accompanied by their participating male relatives.

Sosyete women tend not to go to the mosque but some sponsor Koran readings in their home, typically given by a young *imam* who has only recently completed a Koran course himself, for the benefit of their friends and relatives. These women take pains to appear as devout as possible. During the fast they confine their socialising to the late evening, after breaking the fast (*iftar*) in the company of their families at home. They commiserate with each other on the difficulties of observing the fast. Some give up gambling completely in this period.

The special atmosphere of Ramadan is also created in mundane ways, e.g. by the flat bread, *Ramazan pidesi*, which bakers produce in this period. In music and video shops certain products available throughout the rest of the year are discreetly withdrawn from the shelves. Some small businesses, not only cafes and restaurants, close completely for the month. Shopkeepers, especially those running

---

[11] Together with profession of the creed, fasting during the month of Ramadan is often seen as sufficient for a minimal definition of a Muslim. Regular prayers, generosity in almsgiving, and the pilgrimage to Mecca follow in order of importance (the last is an obligation only for those who can afford it).

[12] It is generally accepted that the sick (including pregnant women) are in principle exempt from fasting requirements, as are the very old, children and travellers. Some parents were nevertheless proud of children who voluntarily observed the fast, even if just for a few days.

[13] This is a special service performed after the evening worship during Ramadan. Rural women do not attend the mosque, not even during Ramadan. In town only a devout minority does so. The women's quarter in the mosque is separated from the main part by a wall, not just by a curtain, and women enter through a separate gate. They listen to the *hoca's* voice through the loudspeaker.

Plate 7.1 The Feast of Sacrifice (Kurban): seven families slaughter a cow and divide the meat into equal portions.

commercially successful operations, come under pressure to show charity towards the poor and to contribute to good causes, such as the funding of a mosque or of a Koran course. The religious party usually initiates donations to national and international causes, e.g. by inviting contributions in 1992 towards relief of suffering in the war zone in neighbouring Azerbaijan.

The other major religious festival, like Ramadan acknowledged by the state with a three-day public holiday, is the Festival of Sacrifice (Kurban). The religious significance of this holiday seemed to be less well understood and it is not preceded by elaborate prayer cycles and fasting. Rationalisation of religious obligations sometimes takes unexpected forms, as when officials claim that they slaughter an animal each year because they know this to be 'an ancient Turkish custom'. Most families that make a sacrifice (in rural areas this means the large majority) do so with proper attention to the Islamic ritual and have at least some awareness of its meaning.[14] A sheep is the most common sacrifice, but several families (ideally seven) may combine to slaughter a cow. A woman can sacrifice in her own right if she possesses at least 80 grams of gold. Meat is weighed and distributed in equal portions among those participating. Families too poor to be able to afford to make a sacrifice themselves receive meat from relatives or neighbours. Meat is also sent to urban neighbours, including those known to have sacrificed themselves. This is explained as a recent development, to show that one is on good terms. After the holiday most animal skins are donated to mosques, to provide more funds for worthy causes. Secular officials encourage donation of the hide to the state's disposal service; in 1992 the proceeds were earmarked for the Turkish Air Force.[15]

Both the Ramadan and Kurban festivals are occasions for family almsgiving (*zekat*). Donations, calculated according to family size, are made by the head of the household two or three days before the holiday, although the timing may vary. For example in 1991 Fuat, who has a wife and three children living at home, gave TL 50 000 to a children's Koran course next door to the tea factory where he was employed (TL 10 000 for each family member). Very poor families receive gifts in kind, such as one kilogram of sugar or flour. People of limited means have no obligation to give.

The two main movable feasts demonstrate the strength of Islam publicly. Some businesses open as normal from the second day, but it is considered shameful (*ayıp*) to perform any non-urgent work on the first day of a religious holiday. Many migrants take additional leave at this time in order to visit family in Lazistan. Both of these holidays are more important in family life than the major public holidays of the annual secular cycle, which are one-day affairs, seldom marked by general visiting and hospitality. Their religious significance has not been lost and some families take this opportunity to visit cemeteries and have *suras* read from the Koran at the graves of their relatives. This reading can be done by anybody who reads the Arabic script, e.g. a high school student who has attended a Koran course. Men and women often go separately to tidy the graves of their relatives and say prayers.[16]

---

[14] Cf. Delaney 1991: 298–303.
[15] Cf. Shankland 1999a: 74–6.
[16] This contrasts with the situation in Eğirdir, Western Anatolia, where 'after burial, little attention is

Islam in the secular republic has also lost little of its importance in the ritual marking of the human life cycle. As elsewhere in the Muslim world, birth rituals are the least emphasised.[17] The baby is usually not taken out of the house during the first forty days of his/her life. After forty days are over *(bebek kırklandı)* both mother and child undergo a full ritual bath *(gusül abdesti)*. During this period the woman is still perceived as polluted and sexual relations with her husband are prohibited. Much attention is paid to names. Although modern, secular first names have made great inroads with boys, as we noted in Chapter 4 it is common for more traditional names to be used within family circles. When Sevim, a little girl, was sick regularly throughout her childhood, her family decided that they should switch to an Islamic name taken from the Koran. They knew that to use non-Islamic names was sinful, and therefore considered the sickness a punishment. After she was renamed Fatma at the onset of puberty, her health was said to have improved dramatically.

The first major ritual in a young male's life is his circumcision *(sünnet)*. In Lazistan this is usually conducted, as elsewhere in Turkey, before the boy is ten years old, and sometimes when he is as young as two. The main change of recent years is that fewer families now go to a specialist *sünnetçi* in Rize. Many turn instead to a qualified medical doctor, who carries out the operation in the privacy of their homes. The *imam's* presence is important but, depending on the family's means, the occasion is commonly turned into a general social celebration.[18] Whatever the scale of the hospitality, the boy is clad in distinctive white uniform for the day. His nerves are tempered by pride, if he is old enough to understand that this ritual will transform him into a man. In some parts of the region the municipalities organise circumcision *en masse* every year at a local hospital. This reduces the cost to their families, though some participants may still arrange for an additional private reception. Such celebrations are said to be a relatively recent custom in this region. Nowhere in Lazistan is the boy paraded around town on horseback accompanied by musicians, as practised elsewhere in Anatolia.[19]

Apart from wedding rituals, discussed in the previous chapter, rituals commemorating death are the most conspicuous in contemporary Lazistan, especially in rural areas. As soon as news of a death is received women gather in the house of the deceased. They say prayers and they mourn, but they also get on with

---

[16] (cont.) paid either to the grave itself or to the theological ambiguities posed by the decomposition of the corpse' (Tapper and Tapper 1987a: 85). In some Lazistan villages food, usually sweets, are left on graves for the dead (the sweets are in fact later collected by children, but this is nonetheless considered a meritorious deed, though disapproved of by the religious authorities).

One still sporadically comes across beliefs concerning the return of the spirit of the dead *(hortlak)* on Friday night to check that the members of his household are living as good Muslims and that they remember him and pray for him. If this is being done, the spirits of the dead are content and return to their graves. If, however, they find that religious duties have been neglected, they cry and curse, and misfortune falls on the house.

[17] The celebration of children's birthdays with a cake and friends and family invited is becoming popular, primarily among urban civil servants and the elite. It is regarded as a European custom and associated with modernity and secularism.

[18] Large receptions are common among senior state officials and, increasingly, among local elites as well. Among poorer families there may be no party at all.

[19] There is no ritual corresponding to circumcision in the life of a young girl. Delaney (1991: 87) sees adoption of the headscarf as the female equivalent, but this comparison was found implausible in Lazistan.

more practical tasks: the preparation of the body, and whatever assistance is needed by the bereaved family. Cooked food is provided by relatives and neighbours for at least three days following a death, during which it is forbidden to cook in the house of the deceased. Funerals are normally held promptly and linked to the regular Friday prayers whenever possible. Women do not attend. Instead they gather again in the house of the dead and wail loudly.[20] Lazi women mourn both in Lazuri and in Turkish. Men carry the body to its final resting place, which is very often a corner of the family's own land. Burial space adjacent to mosques is nowadays extremely scarce, and in any case many families prefer the idea of burial plots on family-owned land. Many urban residents are taken by cortege back to their settlements of origin for burial. Following general Islamic practice, bodies are placed directly into the earth wrapped in a seamless white shroud (*kefen*).

The death is thereafter commemorated in the family through a ritual known as *Mevlud*, based upon the Ottoman author Süleyman Çelebi's poem about the Birth of the Prophet. *Mevluds* are commonly held on the forty-first or fifty-second day after the death, and then annually on the anniversary of the death.[21] The liminal period of forty days' mourning is taken literally. One young widow who came to attend her husband's funeral in Pazar was criticised for returning to Istanbul before the forty days were over (*kırklarını beklemeden*). The general pattern for a *Mevlud* is that the *imam* comes to the house, where as many as fifty people may assemble by invitation.[22] Both men and women may participate in the recitals but a degree of segregation is always observed, stronger in the west of the region than in the east. Women may be confined to a separate room where they can barely hear the voice of the *imam* as he recites the famous poem; often they are hidden by a curtain. Hospitality may extend to meat dishes (*etli yemekler*) and a sweet drink (*şerbet*) and sweets (*Mevlud şekeri*) are always provided. Alternatively, *Mevluds* may also be held in a mosque, where gender segregation is similarly observed and only sweets are distributed. Although *Mevlud* has no status in Orthodox Islam, the rules applied are the same as those followed at prayer and Koran recitals. Men and women should not see each other, because their attention would then be diverted from the object of the gathering.

Although most *Mevluds* are still strongly associated with the commemoration of the dead, they have experienced a general efflorescence in recent decades.[23] It

[20] Women's mourning sometimes approaches the level of ecstasy. This contrasts with the observations of the Tappers, who found that in Eğirdir: 'Sorrow and mourning are severely discouraged (women say, 'if you cry, the pain will be the deceased's, not yours'), and the bereaved are encouraged to help themselves and the soul of the deceased through positive ritual activities.' (Tapper and Tapper 1987a: 86)

[21] There was uncertainty, among both lay persons and *hocas*, about the timing of the commemoration of the dead. While most agreed that the forty-first day after death was correct, others insisted on the ritual significance of the fifty-second day, which is thought to be the time when the flesh separates from the bone.

[22] Most participants are close relatives and neighbours. However, others may also be invited. One pious townswoman whose husband works in a tea factory situated next to a Koran course for boys invited all its pupils to a *Mevlud* held in memory of her father-in-law. She believed that this lent an extra quality to the religious merit gained.

[23] *Hocas* trained elsewhere in Turkey are said to be responsible for its recent popularity. Nancy and Richard Tapper (1987a) have sought to explain the popularity of this ritual among women in terms of the high value it places upon a specifically female role – that of giving birth. No such interpretation was ever advanced to us in Lazistan. However, in some exceptional cases *Mevluds* were organised for women alone.

is now common to organise a *Mevlud* when moving to a new house, or as an alternative to a secular wedding party. A wedding with *Mevlud* (*Mevludlu düğün*) is usually preferred when the groom is a *hoca* or when a recent death among the relatives of either party would render secular wedding celebrations inappropriate. *Mevluds* have not, however, been linked to the circumcision ritual, which is felt to be somehow inconsistent with their sacred character. A *Mevlud* can also be organised as an expression of gratitude when a prayer has been answered, for example when a male child is born, when a son returns safe and sound from his military service or from migrant labour, when someone recovers from a severe illness, or when a daughter advanced in years manages after all to find a husband.

The supreme ritual accomplishment for any Muslim is the pilgrimage to Mecca (*Hac*). The formidable expenses involved mean that, even in a prosperous region such as Lazistan, only a small minority of the faithful can hope to undertake this journey. Nowadays the pilgrimage is regulated by the state and travel to Mecca is by air only. This has reduced the numbers of pilgrims in the 1990s.[24] Many more men make the journey than do women, and it is virtually inconceivable that a woman should go before her husband (it is more likely to be years later). Women say that they should wait until they arc past childbearing age to avoid the possibility of ritual pollution.

A pilgrim who returns from Mecca commands great social prestige, which is extended to include the wife of the male pilgrim. The fact that they have already gained merit through their husband's pilgrimage may account for the reluctance of some pious women to undertake the pilgrimage at all, even when the possibility is open to them. One Pazar lady, well known for her modesty and piety, turned down the possibility of accompanying her husband: she felt that she would find it difficult to cover herself up completely for such a long period. The youngest men we knew to go on the *Hac* were in their early forties. The community generally recognises the pilgrim's distinction by referring to him thereafter as *hacı*, though this is not quite automatic. In the case of a relatively young man who has made the journey thanks to the wealth he has accumulated while working in Germany, or thanks to his family's ability to pay, and not from any exceptional religious commitment, the recognition is likely to depend upon the post-pilgrimage lifestyle. If he refrains from alcohol and gambling and goes regularly to the mosque, the epithet *hacı* will be bestowed, not grudgingly or ironically, but with genuine respect for the holiness that is assumed to derive from his completion of the sacred journey.

The popular stream

The social impact of Islam goes deeper than this cursory outline of the major Islamic rituals would suggest. *Mevlud* rituals, though not strictly speaking orthodox, are highly standardised and have effectively been incorporated into the canon. These forms of religious knowledge, including the daily prayers, are

---

[24] Not only are costs higher, but people regret that they no longer have the opportunity to make brief visits to other famous Islamic cities, as they could in the days when the journey was made by bus overland.

transmitted primarily by family members, but also in school and in state-approved Koran courses. Many schoolchildren, including the children of state functionaries, both in towns and villages, attend courses during the summer holidays, usually for several successive summers before the onset of puberty. If a woman *hoca* is available, girls are instructed by her, but this is rare. In addition to learning to read the Arabic script and reciting parts of the Koran, the course aims to communicate guidelines for acceptable moral conduct, that befitting a good Muslim. Sensitive topics such as the prohibitions surrounding menstruation and the importance of ritual ablution for women and men are also discussed in the courses.[25]

Outside these channels, however, religion also impinges on everyday life in forms that are widely acknowledged to be non-orthodox. It is difficult to sustain a sharp dichotomy between 'orthodox' and 'popular' Islam, since a good deal of popular knowledge regarded as Islamic blends Koranic teachings with unorthodox cosmology and practices. Similar forms of syncretism are well documented for other parts of the Muslim world. We are not concerned here with the persistence of 'pagan' survivals and their separation from a later Islamic 'layer'.[26] Nor do we approach the popular stream of Islam as the antithesis of orthodox teachings and embodied in mystic orders.[27] Popular religion here does not stand in structural opposition to 'official Islam', but is rather a natural extension of it. The assumptions which have relevance for individuals' world views and daily actions are constantly reshaped by a variety of sources, including religious meetings, media broadcasts, newspapers and the trickling down of orthodox teachings through Koran schools.[28] Not everybody subscribes to all the currents of this 'popular stream'. Our presentation is fragmentary, for it was not our aim to tease out a comprehensive set of Muslim 'patterns of interpretation'. People dabble in the popular stream in casual and contingent ways according to changing needs and circumstances, and nothing would be more misleading than to create an image of 'the traditional Muslim'.[29]

---

[25] For details of school instruction see Kurt 1989. For a summary history of religious education in Turkey see Bilgin 1998: 72–5. For many boys and girls instruction received in the form of prohibitions and prescriptions at such religious sessions is the only source of information concerning sexuality and reproduction. One informant defended this aspect of religious education by saying that 'it is not shameful to talk about anything that qualifies as religious'. (*Dini şeylerden bahsetmek ayıp sayılmaz.*) State primary and secondary schools provide rudimentary religious education from age 9 to 10, emphasising the basic elements and humanistic teachings of orthodox Islam, without touching upon the rituals and observances that shape most people's lives. These secular sources play no more than a minor role in the shaping of religious awareness. The very fact that girls and teachers cannot wear the headscarf in school immediately renders the institution inadequate for delivering a strong religious message to girls.

[26] Feurstein (1986b) has identified pre-Christian layers in the folk beliefs of the Lazi, notably the *koncolozi*, which is a kind of sea monster that can poison food. (One prevents this by covering all food pots.) However, like other beliefs concerning the 'mountain man' (*dağ adamı*) and the *çinka*, ideas about the *koncolozi* have all but disappeared. They were viewed as quaint, perhaps useful in tales told to children, but not to be confused with the spirits and fairies of popular Islam. A Muslim shrine near Ardeşen is apparently located on the site of one of five pre-Islamic *oxvames* (sacred places for praying) (Toumarkine 1995: 93–4); but this history has no significance for the Muslims who visit it today (see below).

[27] This is the approach followed by Özdalga 1998.

[28] The mystic line, however, also forms part of our investigation. As we shall see, some local people also participate in Sufi orders, but they are viewed by most other locals with considerable suspicion.

[29] Cf. Seufert 1997b: 247–9.

Ideas about creation are derived directly from the Koran and are broadly consistent with popular beliefs elsewhere in the Islamic world. Adam was created from earth (*toprak*) whereas his adversary, Satan, together with the evil spirits (*cins*), was created from fire. Eve, the first woman, was created by God from Adam's spare rib to become man's companion (*eş*). This is held to explain why women need men's protection constantly. Some hold that the navel was created when the Devil spat on Adam's stomach. When Adam wiped the saliva away, he created the dog, which stands closer to man than any other animal. The Devil tempts man through man's own body, namely his stomach, in the shape of fire (i.e. sexual desire – *nefis*) as well as externally, e.g. in the form of beautiful women. Fire is completely absent in Paradise (*cennet*).

This world is often referred to as false (*yalan*) and temporary (*geçici*), where people are only guests (*misafir*). Hell (*cehennem*) is envisaged as an enormous pit (*çukur*), somewhat like the sea, in which water is boiling constantly. Above it is a bridge as narrow as a hair (*sırat köprüsü*). Anyone who can cross it gets to Paradise.[30] Sinners, however, will fall into the boiling water, where they are beaten by the angels (*melekler*) as punishment for their sins. After the expiation of all his or her sins a person is allowed into Paradise. Some men were not sure what happened to women after death, but women themselves were certain that they too had the right to enter Paradise. It is imagined as a green space, flat all around.[31] People here have nothing to distract them from the pursuit of happiness. Angels, created by God from light and invisible to the human eye, wait on people and perform specific duties allocated to them by God. Men often mention the presence of beautiful girls (*huri kızlar*) and imply sexual pleasures, but women deny the possibility of carnal desires. They identify these girls with the angels, who serve both men and women.[32] Most women further believe that the polluting fluids and discharges associated with reproduction will cease to exist.[33] Food and drink will be consumed for pleasure: they are not digested but rather evaporate. One remains attached to one's this-worldly spouse, everyone will regain his or her youthful appearance, and those who die single will at last be able to marry.

Angels also have various functions in this world. It is widely held that you should not cut the fingernails of babies before the first birthday because this is the job of the angels. If you inadvertently put some food into your mouth during Ramadan, this, too, is said to be the angels' doing. (*Bunu sana melekler yedirdiler.*) It is not sinful, provided one notices in time and does not swallow. Angels are also thought to be responsible for recording humans' good and bad actions. Each person has two such angels. The one on the right shoulder records the deeds by which you gain religious merit (*sevap*), while the one on the left puts down all your sinful actions (*günah*). Awareness of this distinction provides an ever-present moral guide through life.[34]

Sevap is the broad category of meritorious deeds, by no means confined to the

[30] For Turkish villagers' images of Hell and Paradise, see Delaney 1991: 310, 316.
[31] This is particularly significant in the local context, where women often have to carry heavy baskets on steep hillsides.
[32] Some men insist that each man will be served by seventy-seven such beauties.
[33] This implies the possibility of sexual pleasure without consequences and side effects. Women, however, limit such images to the confines of marriage, even in Paradise.
[34] Cf. Stirling 1965: 230–1.

fulfilment of a religious obligation. Organising or attending a *Mevlud* is described as *sevap*, although it is not a prescribed duty. Applying henna on one's hair and hands is also *sevap*, though dyeing one's hair is a sin, *günah*. Although epilation is not proscribed during Ramadan, many women believe it to be *günah* and hasten to have it done before the holy month begins. Religious obligations such as performing the full ablution are occasionally distinguished as a 'duty' (*farz*), but women tend to use the word *sevap* much more frequently. Either term can be used for a woman's financial contribution to the slaughtering of an animal at Kurban. Other religious obligations are generally described as *sevap*. For example, some women see breastfeeding as *sevap*, because it is through the smell of the mother's milk that children will recognise their mothers in Paradise.[35]

Günah includes the violation of prohibitions such as *namahrem*, which we discussed in Chapter 5. A woman who does not cover her hair and one who kills (e.g. if she slaughters an animal when there is a man available to do so) are both committing a *günah*. The concept of killing includes abortion, which is described by some women as a 'big sin' (*büyük günah*) because not only are you committing murder, but you induce someone else to commit a sin in the process. The distinction between the degrees of sin often seems arbitrary. The category of *haram* overlaps with *günah* and many people cannot explain the difference. Theft and adultery may, for example, be classified as *günah* by some and as *haram* by others. One man said that the money he earned through lending his bull to other peasants could only be used to feed the bull, and if it were spent on anything else, this would be *haram*. Consuming alcohol is similarly classified, but men like to point out that drinking wine is a more serious offence than consuming *rakı*, since only the consumption of wine is explicitly forbidden. Neglect of the ritual obligations concerning cleanliness, such as the full ablution after sexual intercourse, and letting bodily hair and nails grow, are sometimes described as *mekruh* (abominable) as well as *günah*. A failure to utter the formula '*Bismillah*' before cooking or eating is also *mekruh*.[36] The term *cenabet* denotes a state of impurity, which can be brought about by touching food after intercourse without ritual ablution, or by having intercourse during menstruation. To breastfeed in this impure state is also seen as highly dangerous. Menstruation (*aybaşı*) is regarded as polluting, as its popular designation implies (*kirlenmek* – to become dirty). It too must be followed by a full ritual bath. It is widely believed that the prayer and the fasting of a menstruating woman are not accepted and therefore ineffective. Some women, however, maintain that it is always legitimate to listen to a *hoca's* words (and therefore, for example, take part in a *Mevlud*). Menstruating women are permitted to cook and bake, but it is said that the dough prepared in such a state may not rise.

Some men link women's greater susceptibility to pollution to their basic physical and mental inferiority. However, some female informants put forward other interpretations. They agree that women are highly vulnerable to physical and therefore moral contamination, but they describe men as *inherently* dirty. Whereas a

---

[35] Hanefi jurists classify breastfeeding one's own baby as a religious, but not a legal obligation for Muslim women (Aydın 1985: 53).

[36] In one moderately religious family the young son's regular uttering of this phrase was a source of pride for the parents and considered *sevap*.

woman's heart is clean (*temiz*), that of a man is dirty (*pis*). Thus, they say, a woman can become a saint (*evliya*) if she were to pray non-stop for forty days, but a normal man would not reach this status if he were to pray for four hundred years. Without challenging male superiority directly, some women thus imply that men are at least 'equally imperfect'.

For many people, especially in the rural areas, the spirit world is a powerful reality, as has been reported for other parts of Anatolia and the wider Muslim world. An elderly man in Arhavi recalled that in his childhood some women had made a wish (*dilek bağlamış*) by tying pieces of cloth on trees and bushes near a stream and praying.[37] No such practices survive in the region today. It is, however, common to make a wish and solemn vow (*vadetmek*), and to fulfil one's promise if one's wish comes true. Such wishes include the birth of a child, or more specifically of a son, recovery from a dangerous illness, or the appointment of a son to a post in his home town. The promise usually takes the form of a prayer (*dua*) but may also involve the sacrifice of an animal, or fasting outside the month of Ramadan. Failure to keep one's promise will bring punishment by spirits (*cinler, periler*) in the form of bad dreams or illness.

The terms *cin* and *peri* are used interchangeably in Lazistan.[38] The main evidence for their existence is their explicit mention in the Koran. *Cin*s are said to be made out of fire (for this reason they are frightened of water), and this links them directly to the Devil. This would suggest that all *cin*s are evil, but in fact the picture is more complicated. Many people speak of two types of *cin*s, Muslim and Christian. Only the latter perpetrate evil deeds against humans. Muslim *cin*s can also be troublesome, but they are generally regarded as 'soft' (*yumuşak*) and much less of a threat. Some good spirits may be harnessed to provide people with useful services. If one reads the *Cin Suresi* from the Koran three times and then looks over one's right shoulder, one's three wishes should come true. If, however, one looks over the left shoulder by mistake, one becomes paralysed (*çarpınır*). *Cin*s are often thought to act upon higher orders. Apparent accidents are seen as a result of supernatural activities, sometimes as punishment for an evil deed or blasphemous words. A man who swears crudely and subsequently experiences any physical problem or accident, however minor, will interpret this as a warning from the supernatural.

All *cin*s are invisible to the human eye, awaking at night and sleeping by day. They lead a life similar to humans, get married, have children, but do not have to work in this world, a situation which is remarked upon as a reversal (*ters*) of the human condition. In Paradise, by contrast, humans can see them but they cannot see humans. Then they will have to work, while humans will be exempt. In this world a human is in greatest danger from *cin*s after dusk. The *cin*s often lay their tables near rubbish heaps, so people are well advised to avoid such spots, for misfortune will befall anyone who accidentally touches it. Special prohibitions prevent vulnerable persons, such as young brides, pregnant women and women during the first forty days after birth, from going outdoors at all after dusk. If they

[37] Cf. Kriss and Kriss-Heinrich 1962, I: 39.
[38] Cf. Strasser 1995: 91. Strasser offers extended discussion of *cin/peri* ideas in the adjacent province of Trabzon and considers to what extent deviations from Koranic ideas can be attributed to pre-Islamic influences.

do, they should not transgress the gutter (*damlık*), which is a favourite hiding-place of *cins*. If the bathwater of new babies is poured away, or their nappies and clothes left outside after dusk, the baby may be paralysed by an evil spirit. They are particularly dangerous at times when a person is in transition from one social role to another and it is plausible to see them in this sense as guarantors of social order.[39] In some cases a *hoca* or blower (*üfürükçü*) may be able to help by praying or blowing upon the patient, but on occasions the evil spirit may prove to be stronger and the condition can last for life. A particularly strong and harmful Christian *cin* can be exorcised by a Christian priest. Evil spirits may also appear in the form of nightmares, in which they often take on a fearful shape such as an enormous head without a body, or that of an animal which represents bad luck, notably a snake. In such cases the *hoca* uses a bowl of water, prays over it and then asks the patient to look into it (*suya bakmak*). The patient usually sees the fearful shape in the water, and is then cured. Various methods of healing can be used in combination.

Many people, but especially women, are troubled at some point in their lives by evil spirits. Typically, a woman thinks she hears the voice of a close male relative, such as her father or her husband, after darkness has fallen. If she goes out or responds to such false calls, the *cins* may get hold of her and keep her until she is paralysed.[40] Occasionally *cins* may frighten women working in the tea gardens, especially when they go aside to find an isolated spot to relieve themselves. Some *cins* appear as beautiful women to tempt men.

Popular religion is often resorted to in times of personal misfortune and in circumstances in which an illness is not responding well to treatment, or no treatment is available. One common strategy in times of crisis is to turn to magic (*sihir olayı*), which in most cases means consulting a charm specialist (*nuskacı*).[41] The charm (*nuska*) is pinned to the sufferer's clothes, where it is supposed to combat evil spirits. Women who pay money to *hocas*, both female and male, for the writing of such charms do so with a strong dose of scepticism, but with the simultaneous conviction that it can do no harm and might be worth trying. Charms can be prepared for almost any difficulties that people face in their lives, from passing examinations to solving marital difficulties and producing male offspring. Many women resort to charms for physical ailments, for depression, and for solving problems with their children. One woman visited a female *hoca* on five successive days when experiencing difficulties in her pregnancy. The *hoca* told her to collect water from seven different springs, from which she had to drink every day during her treatment. On each visit the *hoca* both wrote a charm and blew upon her. Charms are commonly prepared for crying babies and for children showing signs of problems, such as a stammer, disruptive behaviour, and other mental or physical disorders. As well as their use in healing and correcting, charms may also be written preventively to ensure future success, e.g. in school or in a business enterprise. They are often worn together with the charm against the evil eye, an eye-shaped blue bead (*nazarlık*).

[39] Strasser 1995: 92.
[40] People are often unclear if *cins* are responsible or if blame should be attributed to the spirits of the dead who, as elsewhere in the Muslim world, are thought to trouble the world in the form of evil demons. Cf. Kriss and Kriss-Heinrich 1962, II: 16.
[41] Cf. Kriss and Kriss-Heinrich 1962, II.

Charms may be prepared by anyone who is accepted as a religious specialist by his or her clientèle, regardless of how the techniques were learned. One Lazi woman in her mid-eighties had learned her skills from her mother-in-law, a *hoca*. Unlike most other practitioners, she did not accept money for her services. Instead one gave her a packet of biscuits or some fruit. She worried that her activities might attract the authorities' attention, especially since she lived (on account of her son's job) in a house for government employees (*lojman*). However, she regularly took the risk because she believed that to use her knowledge in a good cause was meritorious (*sevap*). She wrote charms only for children, and believed that to interfere in the marital conflicts of adults would be sinful. Her texts were cut out from a handwritten copy of the Koran which she inherited from her late mother-in-law. She did not know the Arabic script herself. The charm consisted of a small piece of paper torn from this book and inserted, together with a bead, into a piece of linen, which was then sewn in a triangle shape. She then took a small packet of biscuits or a bag of sugar cubes brought by the client, and read a prayer over them, usually the forty-one *Yatsı*. Even the piece of cotton used for sewing the *nuska* together and for tying the bag of food was taken from an old knitted scarf that had already been 'read upon'. Some of the biscuit or sugar was fed to the child, who was then told to wear the *nuska* at all times.[42]

While all magic associated with children is good, jealousy, hatred and revenge are important motives for *nuska* writing in the world of grown-ups. A woman may ask for a charm to take revenge on another woman, or on a man who has jilted her, or on her hated mother-in-law. A charm can be commissioned to turn a young man against his family. Many domestic conflicts are explained in terms of magic (the subject is even acknowledged in the county court divorce files discussed in Chapter 6). Love charms are used by both men and women, though belief in their efficacy is more readily acknowledged by women. If the person who is in love addresses the other while wearing a charm prepared for this purpose, or holding it under the tongue, his or her love should soon be reciprocated. Similar results can be achieved by making the person drink some water in which the *nuska* has been soaked.

Some informants distinguish between *hocas* who only perform 'good' magic and those who use their skills for sinful purposes (*kötü hoca*). The latter was feared when, at the end of an engagement party in Pazar in 1999, a charm was found left on a table. No one could understand the writing, but it was natural to suppose that someone wished to spoil the planned marriage. Mistrust of bad *hocas* leads some people to try to solve their problems by themselves. One woman explained that, whenever her baby cried, she took a full ablution, put on a clean

[42] This lady believed that a *nuska* would also work for a Christian, except that in this case one should not use a Koranic text, but simply a piece of paper with the name of the child and of the parents. This *nuska* should be taken to a church, where a priest should make the sign of the cross over it and read any piece of sacred scripture.

In conversations with us, Christianity was often invoked for comparisons. It was usually spoken of with respect, sometimes even with reverence. People stressed that 'we are all the servants of the same God' (*hepemiz aynı Allahın kuluyuz*). Compared to the Koran, which has remained the same for well over a thousand years, the Bible is thought to exist in multiple, and therefore unreliable, versions. Both Moses and Jesus are known and revered as prophets, but Mohammed was the last of God's messengers and is therefore to be seen as the revealer of the ultimate truth.

nightdress and read the *Kureyş Suresi* from the Koran three times, followed by the *Fatiha* once. Afterwards she blew upon her child (a practice usually performed by *hocas*) and this, she claimed, always brought the desired result.

Belief in bad magic performed by binding (*bağlamak*) is widespread among both men and women.[43] In particular, if during the religious wedding ceremony (*imam nikahı*) anybody who is ill-disposed to the new couple ties a knot on a piece of string, buttons up his or her coat, ties shoelaces, or simply crosses the legs or arms with evil intentions, this can prevent the new couple from consummating their marriage by rendering the bridegroom incapable of sexual intercourse. Therefore any kind of tying or jobs which include tying (embroidery, knitting, sewing) should be avoided in the bride's household during the days preceding the wedding. If the damage has been done, a *hoca* may help by symbolically untying the knot and through prayers. Another way of casting a spell on the new couple is to commission a bad *hoca* to perform magic by preparing a *nuska* which, in addition to the written charm, includes a piece of clothing or some hair belonging to one of the young couple. This *nuska* is then thrown into the sea or burnt, and the result is said to be the same as with *bağlamak*.

While male impotence is thus explained by supernatural interference (black magic), female barrenness (*kısırlık*) is seen as an inherent biological fault, and as preordained by God. Accordingly, women cannot resort to simple magic to cure it or to ensure the birth of a male child. They may, however, visit shrines (*türbe*), such as that in the Lazi village of Angvan (new name: Seslikaya), near Ardeşen.[44] Locals know little about the history of the shrine, except that a certain Hasan Efendi lies there. He was a devout Muslim who acquired fame through his teachings and became a saint (*evliya*).[45] Women (seldom men) also bring children with various forms of difficulty on a pilgrimage (*ziyaret*) to say prayers at this shrine. Other remedies may also be tried. A child who is late walking may be taken to the mosque on a Friday and his ankles tied together. The first man to leave after the Friday prayers is asked to cut the string. Some people have such a child step on the grave of an ancestor. Childless women may try tying seven pieces of cotton of different colours around the waist, but almost everyone would consign practices of this sort to the realm of superstition (*batıl inanç*).

Belief in the evil eye (*nazar*) is also widespread. It is described as a harmful cross-shaped light that shines from some people's eyes, and it is especially dangerous to children, young women and animals. It is thought, by women and men, that most of the persons with this power are female, and that the cause behind it is conscious or unconscious jealousy (*kıskançlık*). Fear of jealousy is articulated in the widespread view that it is responsible for many untimely deaths. The only generally approved measure one can take against the evil eye is to have a *nuska* written. Using the evil eye bead (*nazarlık, mavi boncuk*) on either children or animals is rejected by *hocas* as a sign of ignorance (*cahillik*), while some people go further and say it is actually sinful (*günah*). In spite of this the use of the bead is common, sometimes in combination with the written charm. Some

[43] Cf. Schiffauer 1987: 21, 259
[44] Cf. Kriss and Kriss-Heinrich 1962, I: 48. See also N. Tapper 1990: 236–55; Marcus 1992: 130–4.
[45] The inscription on the stone memorial inside says *Molla Osman'n oğlu* (Son of Molla Osman) and the date is 1208 A.H./1793–4.

explain it away as mere decoration. Protection unseen by the outside world is also common: unmarried girls, brides and newly married women may secretly stick forty-one pins inside a garment (a coat, a cardigan) for this purpose. Houses, farm buildings and even fertile tea gardens are protected by animal skulls hung in a prominent position. These skulls usually derive from the sheep that is sacrificed when a new house is built or a new tea garden planted. A thorny wreath decorated with pieces of red ribbon and/or eggshells may also be used.

The *falcı* or fortune-teller is still visited in rural Lazistan, especially by unmarried women or young married women with anxieties about their future. People also go to enquire about the outcome of family quarrels, or to seek assistance in finding lost objects. The *falcı*, who may be male or female, uses methods very similar to those of *hocas* and *üfürükçüs*, including 'looking into the water' (*suya bakmak*) and 'reading from books' (*kitaptan okumak*). Answers are notoriously vague enough to allow the *falcı* to claim success, whatever actually happens. Some people who make use of *nuskas* draw a line and insist that the *falcı* is pure superstition, whereas the *nuskacı* is efficacious by virtue of possessing religious knowledge.

All of these beliefs and practices are passed on from generation to generation. They are condemned by orthodox *imams*, but legitimated by a minority, some of whom are themselves prominent writers of *nuskas*. Some of the best known in Lazistan originate just outside the region, in the Of and Çaykara counties of Trabzon, a region long famed for its zeal. Other *imams* point out that these *Oflu hocas* often lack the rudiments of a proper Islamic education. Some were poor, with large families to support from a modest state salary. A little extra income from the writing of charms may be preferred to tea-plucking on a sharecropping basis, which a good many *imams* do in this region.[46] Some *imams* are as forthright in condemning their colleagues as any anti-clerical Kemalist, alleging that they deliberately exploit the anxieties of gullible people for their personal gain. However, one Çaykara *imam* whom we knew seemed very genuinely to believe in the spirit world, in the power of magic, and in his own capacity to mitigate its negative effects. He claimed an impressive success rate in alleviating some medical complaints, while insisting that he advised those he could not help to seek modern medical treatment.

The militant tendency

The beliefs and practices discussed above are seen both by devout adherents and by Kemalist critics, as rooted in the past. However, the proliferation of Mevlud rituals is evidence that the established religion is capable of evolving new ritual forms. We turn now to other, more radical forms of innovation. Even when it looks deep into the past for sources of inspiration, this radicalism must be set in the contemporary Turkish context. Its leaders, commonly and tendentiously

---

[46] A poor *imam* who works in this way may earn more respect than one who does no physical work and expects others in the community to assist with all the worldly needs of his household. People may be disdainful of an *imam* who is thought to care too much for modern fashions, e.g. in dress and hair styles. In one village people spoke dismissively of their *sosyete hoca*.

called fundamentalists, are best seen as religious modernists. They are sharply critical of what we have termed the 'popular stream'. In the models and behaviour of many supporters, however, popular, orthodox and radical streams may from time to time converge.

A radical stream of Islam has been increasingly prominent in the realm of party politics since democratisation was introduced in 1950, initially through the Democratic Party, and later through more specifically religious parties. These parties have been regularly closed down by the secular authorities, most recently in 1997; but up to now they have always managed to reappear stronger than before in terms of support at the polls. The religious party established itself as the second party in the local elections held in Lazistan in 1994, and again in the national elections of 1995, polling more than one quarter of the votes in Rize province.[47] In the 1990s the party supplied the mayor of Rize and extended its strong base in the western counties to counties east of Ardeşen, where it had previously struggled to gain a foothold.

To be able to operate the religious party must formally accept the basic principle of 'laicism', as established by Atatürk. Local leaders consider that this principle (laiklik) has been misinterpreted in Turkey, where it has come to mean hostility towards religion (din düşmanlığı). Religious party activists call for the implementation of modern western European standards, by which they mean a genuine separation of religion from the state. In other respects, of course, the west is not a model to be emulated. Religious party activists point to the proliferation of television programmes imported from western countries, and argue for the need to counter this trend with Islamic broadcasting. In their newspapers and other publications they seek to present Islam as a modern force better able to provide corruption-free public services than any secular parties. They frequently draw on concepts of science in presenting the Islamic message as thoroughly modern and intellectually sophisticated.[48] The religious party has targeted young people with considerable success, especially in rural areas. Each county town has a branch of the National Youth Foundation (Milli Gençlik Vakfı) which serves the activists as a social club. The public meetings organised by the religious party are better attended than those of any other political organisation.

The arguments of Islamic intellectuals are inevitably adulterated and distorted in the hands of activists at the level of the village and the urban mahalle. Here the activists tend to tap into old sources of tension, even as they apply new techniques of mass communication to spread awareness of dangerous forces. For example, they distribute leaflets and photocopied articles which prove that eating pork is at the root of sexual jealousy, and that it is responsible for giving so many foreigners their supremely ugly faces. Sexual jealousy is attributed to the activities of Jewish businessmen, who secretly contaminate food and cosmetics (especially lipstick) with pork fat. The grass roots activists often invoke the rich

[47] For an analysis of the nationwide success of the Welfare Party in 1994 see Salt 1995, Shankland 1996. In Lazistan the party could not overtake the popularity of the Motherland Party, whose leader Mesut Yılmaz was regarded as Rizeli, but it took votes away from all other major parties. Its support faded slightly in the elections of 1999 when the voters of Lazistan, in line with the national trend, turned in record numbers to the Nationalist Action Party.

[48] See Tapper 1991b and Shankland 1999a. The latter includes a translation of substantial sections of Necmettin Erbakan's The Just Economic Order.

spirit world noted in the previous section. They invoke the concept of *namahrem* to criticise men who wear shorts and T-shirts, and they prevent their own children from participating in sports. The development of the Russian markets, and in particular the immoral activities of non-Muslim women, contributed in the early 1990s to a rhetorical emphasis on the loss of collective honour, though many activists continued to date the moral decay from Atatürk's coming to power. Disasters such as landslides, earthquakes and mining accidents are regularly interpreted as divine warnings.

The prevailing Sunni orthodoxy of historical Lazistan has been modified in the republican period by the spread of sectarian currents (*tarikats*) not previously known in the region. Among the most influential of these have been the movements of Bediüzzaman Said Nursi and that of Süleyman Hilmi Tunahan.[49] Through their devotional and mystical literature, they have provided invaluable resources to those who object to Kemalism's regulation of religion as if it were just another division of the state's bureaucracy. The movements emphasise spirituality, but also continuity with the Ottoman Islamic past and the values of equality and social justice. They were well established in some of the towns of Lazistan by the mid-1950s, possibly even earlier. In the early 1990s there was an active *Nurcu/Süleymanci* group in Pazar, with a membership of 40–50.[50]

This county also contained an exceptionally dynamic rural *tarikat*.[51] Hamdi *hoca* was born in the Lazi village of Sinanköyü around 1950. The village has a reputation in the surrounding county for violence: blood feuds were common until the last generation, and everyone remembers the murder of a headman in the 1960s by a co-villager who did not approve of the route planned for a new access road.[52] But Sinanköyü also had a reputation for piety, exhibited in high levels of participation in mosque services and also in the pilgrimage to Mecca. It is said that Hamdi had no state education beyond primary school. Although his family was strongly religious, they had not previously produced an *imam*; his grandfather had run a successful bakery in Izmir. Hamdi spent his formative years in Istanbul, where he came under the influence of a holy man known only as Mahmut, said to originate in the town of Adıyaman in South-Eastern Anatolia. The details are not clearly known, even to other local *imams*, but most seem clear that Hamdi is the charismatic head of a Sufi *tarikat*; religious officials classified him as a follower of the *Nakşibendi* order, but some of his students used a narrower designation *Mahmutçu*.[53] Hamdi returned from Istanbul to Lazistan in

---

[49] The Nurcu movement has been the subject of a magisterial analysis by Şerif Mardin,1989. For more general discussion of the rise of *tarikat* in recent years see Shankland 1999a.

[50] Most were members of the officially registered 'sponsoring associations of the religious high school' (*Imam-Hatip Lisesi Koruma Derneği*). Religious officials at the *müftülük* saw them not as a threat but as a support to their own work.

[51] We were unable to gather more than fragmentary data about this group because its leader, though receiving us courteously and immediately bestowing suitable Islamic names upon us, was less than forthcoming in answering questions. Given the history of his initiative and the scope of his aspirations, his reticence in front of strangers was understandable. The names in this section are fictitious. Some of the material in this and the following sub-section is discussed in more detail in Bellér-Hann 1994.

[52] The feud between the two sides lasted for over ten years and was eventually concluded by an official reconciliation in the Rize prison, in the presence of religious and government officials. Peace was concluded with the ritual sacrifice of an animal (*Ardeşen Sesi* 1974(2): 107).

[53] For an overview of the Nakşibendis see Mardin 1991.

1969, having decided to dedicate his life to spreading the true message of Islam in his native region. The resources of his family were modest, but they made land available for the building of a school, to supersede the temporary Koran courses held each summer in the mosque.[54] It is unclear where additional funds have been obtained: those who are unsympathetic claim that all his initiatives have been sponsored by extremists in Iran, but it is likely that his pious foundation (*vakıf*) also attracts donations from within Turkey.

From very modest beginnings Hamdi's school expanded rapidly. His first premises are described in a printed *vakif* leaflet as consisting of one room with a mud floor and windows without glass. Initially he had fifteen pupils. In 1979 he started building a new school on a piece of his own land, which came to form the basis of his pious foundation. The five-storey building for male students was completed in 1984. It was followed one year later by a three-storey building erected some distance away, close to Hamdi's own house, for female students. By the 1990s these schools were thought to be teaching approximately 300 pupils. Most were boarders who paid a monthly fee, but poor children were supported by the foundation. Their ages varied. Officially, no one could be admitted without having completed five years of secular primary education.[55] Their length of stay was not rigidly determined and varied from just a few months to as long as ten years. Teaching, as in other Koran courses, concentrated on reading the Koran in Arabic and *Hafızlık*, the memorising of the sacred text. Some students proceeded to the *Imam-Hatip* school and became state-employed *kadrolu* specialists. However, Hamdi kept some of his best students to teach in his own schools. Since many did not have a stable family background, and some had no family at all, Hamdi was active in arranging their marriages.

This entire initiative took place 'from below' and outside the regulatory framework of the state: in this sense at least, it is an exemplary civil society initiative. Much of the early construction work for the schools was apparently undertaken by the voluntary cooperative labour of the pupils, although by 1992 we found that major tasks were carried out by hired workers rather than pupils. (This also applied to Hamdi's own, relatively modest tea gardens, although his Kemalist critics in the town nearby insisted that he exploited the labour of his students for his own private gain.) Sinanköyü has a separate mosque, where services are held by a *kadrolu imam* who has no official link to these Koran courses. Hamdi's school figured on a list of approved Koran courses drawn up by the *müftü* of the county. The *müftü* acknowledged, however, that they are entirely different not only from the summer courses provided in most villages, but also from the few other all-year-round schools that exist in other settlements. They were in some ways more like a shrine, and often visited as such.

Hamdi experienced considerable harassment from the authorities in the early years, including a short spell of imprisonment. Since the political situation stabilised in the middle of the 1980s he has been left alone. By the time of our fieldwork he had built up a formidable reputation in the county and those adjacent

[54] Hamdi has never worked for the state as a *kadrolu imam* though according to some he does receive a salary from the state as the Director of a Koran course.
[55] The changes of 1997, noted in Chapter 2, made it theoretically impossible for these schools to recruit pupils before the completion of eight years of regular state schooling.

to it. He was much in demand as a preacher.[56] When he visited the county town he sometimes stood prominently in the back of a truck – physically a very large man, with robes flowing, he cut an impressive figure. Although his wife had not trained as a *hoca*, his son, daughter, and their spouses had all had thorough religious education and were teaching at his school. Whether or not, as his critics alleged, he experienced lapses of personal vanity, Hamdi's dedication to his cause could not be doubted. Graduates of his courses organised groups and networks to spread the message further afield. About one quarter of his female students and somewhat fewer boys were said to be from the local community (Sinanköyü and its immediate neighbours), and his impact on this formerly turbulent village is respected by both insiders and outsiders. Even those who pilloried him as an *Ayatollah* who had turned his village into a 'mini-Iran' conceded that it had, since his initiatives, become a more peaceful and prosperous place. The village certainly felt very different from most other villages. Unlike neighbouring villages of similar size it had no cafe or any other secular social life. The main Koran course building dominated the skyline and, quite apart from the numbers of students in Islamic dress, local people, too, seemed to dress more carefully than most villagers. Some women wore a full veil (as distinct from the ubiquitous *başörtü*) when they worked in the fields and tea gardens.[57]

Conflicts with external officials have flared up occasionally, for example when Hamdi flatly refused to grant access to his girls' school to a team of family planning instructors with a briefing to visit all educational establishments for teenaged girls. After pressure from the county health authorities, he was forced to give way and allow the instructors to deliver their talk, but he limited the time to precisely one hour and allowed no time for questions and discussion. Some local doctors have commented negatively on the children's nutritional state. Some also allege extensive use of tranquillisers and sleeping pills, evidence in their eyes of the psychological damage caused by excessive doses of religion, but no such charges have been proven.

Tensions were also occasionally expressed within the village. We were witnesses to a verbal exchange between two local girls on their way home for lunch. One, a student at the course, was wearing a headscarf underneath her black veil. The daughter of the village headman (who herself wore just the normal headscarf, and whose sister was attending the same course) challenged what she perceived to be the exaggerated piety of the other girl: 'Aren't you ashamed that the edge of your headscarf is showing? If you are so religious, you should also take care that your headscarf is hidden. Showing off your headscarf is also

[56] We never heard Hamdi himself preach, although we heard some of his disciples. People told us that he placed more emphasis upon spirituality and even mysticism; he did not employ the populist anti-western rhetoric used by many religious party activists, though in his conversations with us his deep-seated distaste for the west was made abundantly clear.

[57] Some supporters of Hamdi argued that women should not be allowed to undertake work outside their houses, but this was obviously unrealistic given the traditions of his region. We did not hear any women endorse this claim.

Women were obliged to lift their veil for identification purposes by a *jandarma* official at the general election in 1995. Sinanküyü voted overwhelmingly for the religious party. According to the official, who was also present at the count, there were loud gasps of surprise and disapproval for each ballot paper that supported a rival party.

Plate 7.2 Distribution of certificates at the end of a women's sewing course organised by the Adult Education Department in Sinanköyü.

namahrem!' The student retorted angrily that the headman's daughter should not make such shameful remarks, especially in front of strangers.

By 1992 an accommodation had been reached with the state that satisfied both parties. At the mosque, Hamdi and the *kadrolu imam* took it in turns to lead the main weekly service, and their relations were harmonious (though this had not been the case with at least one previous *kadrolu imam*). Relations with the teachers at the state primary school in the village were also good, because these did not attempt to interfere with the Koran courses and turned a blind eye to some behaviour in their own school that would not be accepted elsewhere (such as young girls wearing headscarves). Adult education courses (noted in Chapter 2) were viewed with suspicion by Hamdi and his colleagues, but the courses in embroidery and needlework were popular with local women. They eventually went ahead without obstruction. Hamdi did not attend the celebration held to mark the end of the course in 1992, and he would probably have disapproved of the artificial Christmas tree that the state officials positioned at the entrance to the exhibition of the women's work.[58] However, his mother, along with several other veiled women, did attend and the *kadrolu imam* was on hand to utter an appropriate grace for the array of state officials before their festive meal.

Although Sinanköyü remained exceptional, Hamdi expanded his activities to other villages and towns in the 1990s. He himself transferred his main residence to a new Koran course on the coast just outside Çayeli, west of Pazar, leaving the schools in Sinanköyü to be run by his daughter and by former students. A large new school in another Pazar village was denied state recognition as a Koran course when it failed to muster the requisite minimum number of twenty pupils, though in 1999 teaching continued on an unauthorised basis for girls, under the leadership of one of Hamdi's former pupils.

In general, women have less scope to cultivate and express a radical commitment than men, who can demonstrate their piety through regular attendance and additional voluntary work at a mosque. One of the most interesting changes in many parts of Turkey in recent years has been women's visible demonstration of their faith through the adoption of a full veil (*çarşaf*) in preference to the customary headscarf. These women practised their faith intensely, both individually and in new community groups. One significant group in this region was led by Safiye, a young woman who had given up a science degree course at university in order to study at Hamdi's school in Sinanköyü. In some ways she resembled the veiled Islamist women discussed by Nilüfer Göle, who subvert the usual opposition between progressive and reactionary by completing their university courses.[59] Safiye, however, felt the need to make the choice between Islam and secular higher education. She opted out of the latter, but continued to study at the Koran course, where she acquired a thorough knowledge of the Arabic script and language. She was an avid reader and expanded her intellectual horizons well beyond the theology taught at the course. In this way Safiye and others like her subverted not the dualism addressed by Göle but the basic category of 'educated'. They became a significant group in Lazistan in the 1990s, making an impact on other women in towns and in villages not only through their very

[58] These were bought at the 'Russian markets' and became a popular ornament on such occasions.
[59] Göle 1996: 96.

visible demonstration of their commitment to Islam but also through their extensive informal networking and especially through unofficial religious gatherings held during the holy month of Ramadan.[60]

' One of the sermons (sohbet, vaız)[61] delivered by Safiye in a private house during Ramadan in 1992 was attended by about sixty women, mostly from the lower and middle business class of the town. The contents resembled the populist blend conveyed by the religious party. While everyone else sat on the floor, Safiye, who wore a beautiful yellow silk dress and many golden bracelets, and whose gold earrings were visible beneath her thin headscarf, sat in a large armchair in the corner. Several young colleagues from the Koran course, squatting beside her, took it in turns to guide the prayers, and one of them recited two suras from the Koran. After a further communal prayer, Safiye launched into a lengthy sermon. She began by commenting on the immodest dress habits of the women of the region, including some of those present at this meeting, and attributed this laxity to Atatürk's revolution. Previously, all women would have been covered (kapalı).[62] She criticised westernising forces in the mass media and asked why a Muslim culture (kültür) should be fed the corrupting products of a Christian one. It was wrong to claim that modern science and technology were exclusively western products: she knew that the west had stolen many ideas from Muslim scientists. She also attacked capitalism, and more specifically, the practice of usury, which favoured only the rich. She noted the hypocrisy of certain politicians who posed as good Muslims in order to attract votes, but when in power behaved as if they were Christians or Jews.

Safiye frequently addressed morality and family values, illustrating her points with short stories and anecdotes. One story concerned a Swiss Christian woman who, after reading the Koran, had allowed her daughter to marry a Muslim. He turned out to be a bad Muslim, who drank alcohol and gambled. The Christian had to remind him of his own ideals. Another anecdote concerned the Turkish girl who, dressed only in a two-piece swimming costume, had won a beauty contest in Belgium soon after the foundation of the republic. This was the greatest of all Christianity's victories over Islam, for never before had a Turkish woman been so debased. Whereas an Ottoman gentleman would not even find it proper to divulge the names of the female members of his household, in Atatürk's country these 'beautiful jewels' had become corrupted. An influx of outsiders, by which she meant the wives of officials, and especially of army officers, was partly to blame for this degeneration in Lazistan.

The meeting continued with several popular hymns (ilahis) and the reading of a satirical anti-secularist poem, which had everyone laughing. After a further

[60] They have even spread into eastern counties such as Fındıklı and Hopa. Here, however, they are much criticised by the majority of men and women who see the radicals not as independent moral agents, but as pitifully deceived by scheming leaders (and, in some cases, attracted by unspecified material incentives).

[61] Normally sohbet in modern Turkish has a broader meaning and can apply to many forms of secular discussion or conversation; but in this context it is a synonym for vaız, sermon or 'admonition'.

[62] In conversation later, Safiye agreed that the kapalı women of the past did not cover themselves fully, as with the contemporary çarşaf. She said that formerly covering had been a matter of local custom, whereas in the case of her and her friends it was the conscious (şuurlu) expression of their religious convictions. Cf. Göle 1996: 88.

Plate 7.3 Public meeting of the religious party, Pazar, 1992.

Plate 7.4 A young girl at the same political meeting. Her banner reads: 'May the hands that reach out for the headscarf break off!' (or 'Hands Off the Headscarf!')

Koran recitation, which Safiye elucidated in Turkish, taped religious music was played and the women began to disperse. Some stayed a little longer to exchange religious books and hymn texts.[63]

Safiye and her colleagues from the Koran course were considered to be 'knowledgeable' (*bilgili*) and 'better than us' by other women attending, who acknowledged that they themselves were ignorant (*cahil*) in comparison. This is how Safiye herself saw things, too. Like her colleagues, she had had a revelation: although born and brought up as a Muslim, she had in effect 'converted' (*dönmüş*) to a full Islamic way of life. This dramatic moment happened when she first visited Sinanköyü, out of curiosity, and walked past the buildings of the Koran courses. The main charge levelled against these women, for example by other women who dropped out after attending meetings once or twice only, was that they were extreme (*aşırı*), and the main evidence for this was their use of the *çarşaf*. No one challenged the contents of the sermon, not even those passages where the former chemistry student had given her scientific confirmation of the widespread view that the husbands of those women who went about uncovered (*açık*) were immune to sentiments of jealousy due to their consumption of pork products. Even some of those repelled by what they see as 'fanaticism' (*yobazlık*) nonetheless admired these young women for their religious knowledge and their dedication.

Other female *hocas*, not associated with Hamdi's sect, were also active. Hülya was a young woman of 25 who had been born and brought up in Ardeşen, but then taken to Istanbul as child. Here she stayed as a boarder at a full time Koran course. Although she would have liked to continue her studies there, she returned to Lazistan when her parents arranged a marriage with a state-employed *hoca* from the same county. When her husband was appointed to Pazar, she began to teach local women on an informal basis. As a *kadrosuz hoca* (not in the state's employment) her classes were necessarily unofficial, but thanks to her husband's employment she obtained support from the county *müftü*. He arranged an apartment in which she could pursue her work as a *hoca*. Hülya rejected the younger preachers associated with Hamdi as too 'extreme'. Although her own teaching covered very much the same ground, and she too belonged to those whose education had taken place in the 'invisible' sphere of religious schools, she did not identify with Safiye and her circle. Some other women we knew in the local context, who also donned the veil, did so not so much because of an inner conviction or because they had had a thorough religious education. In some cases they simply yielded to family pressure: wives and daughters of *hocas*, or of extremely pious men, were especially prone to start veiling themselves fully. The veiled women's homogenous appearance concealed almost as much diversity as found among women dressed according to 'modern' dress codes.

If in the early 1990s the female version of the militant tendency was nevertheless perceived by other, more conventional women as forming a united front, this had much to do with the social impact of the Russian markets, as discussed in Chapter 3. For example, in 1991 radical women criticised the annual beauty

---

[63] Much in demand were the works of Emine Şenlikoğlu, a former fashion model who had given up this sinful career after a revelation. For further discussion of the themes of Islamic women's literature see Acar 1991.

contest sponsored in Rize by the Tea Corporation. It eventually proceeded amid considerable tension. The winner was a *lise* student – who remained fully veiled throughout the competition. The following year the competition was cancelled after attracting just three entrants. *Çarşaf*-clad women and even younger girls were conspicuous in organising public demonstrations outside government buildings, sometimes in alliance with male activists of the religious party and sometimes in their own right. Their banners alleged a link between the prostitution business and the spread of AIDS, though the disease was said by doctors to be unknown at the time in that region. They claimed to be speaking for all women of the region in urging a return to traditional morality. As so often the emphasis was on clothing and the modesty code: 'may the hands that reach out for the headscarf (i.e. to remove it) break' (*başörtüsüne uzanan eller kırılsın*). Another slogan read: 'We are not an advertising tool, we want our personality/identity' (*Reklam aracı değiliz, şahsiyetimizi istiyoruz*).

Discourses, realities and moralities

Dualistic world views are asserted across a wide spectrum of opinion, from radicals through regular *kadrolu imams* and the mass of believers to the tiny minority of atheists. They are frequently expressed in a spatial dichotomy between east and west. Islamists typically describe the west in terms of moral debauchery. Its society is corrupted and spoiled (*bozulmuş*). In contrast to the strong values held in Turkey, the west has abandoned family relations (*aile bağlantısı yok*). The diagnosis is often propagated with fanciful images: England is a country which has legalised gay marriage, while Germany is a country with forty million dogs. This east/west dichotomy is also employed to contrast justice and privilege, on the one side the poor (*fakirler*) and on the other the Mercedes culture of elites (*sosyete*). The west is associated with capitalism, an inhumane form of economic organisation that is responsible for widening social differentials wherever it spreads. The embracing of free-market doctrines by Turkish governments after 1983 inevitably created opportunities for this critical strand. Critique was stimulated by the behaviour of prominent public figures: the wife of Prime Minister (later President) Özal was sometimes perceived as an Imelda Marcos figure, indulging a luxurious lifestyle at the expense of poor taxpayers. As we have seen, even small provincial towns have their identifiable stratum of *sosyete*, associated with smart clothes and cars, luxuries and gambling, Marlboro cigarettes rather than home-produced Maltepe. On top of all this, the depravities of the Russian markets provided the inhabitants of Lazistan with the most striking confirmation of what can happen when a society drifts away from its moorings in religion. These ex-communists, like western capitalists, were quite simply barbaric (*barbar*), while civilisation (*medeniyet*) was only to be found in Islam.

A widespread Kemalist view, well represented among influential groups such as teachers, uses a similar east–west dichotomy in diametrically opposed ways. Proponents argue that it is the continued strength of Islam which is hindering social progress in Turkey. They see a correlation between the strength of religion and economic backwardness. With the partial exception of their own region, the whole of eastern Anatolia is characterised as backward (*geri kalmış*), reactionary (*irticai*), conservative (*tutucu, eski kafalı*) and ultimately fanatical (*bağnaz, yobaz*). In contrast, western Anatolia is held to show reassuring signs that Turkey is capable of emulating western models of modernity. Urban society in cities such as Istanbul and Izmir is seen as modern (*çağdaş*), progressive (*ileri*) and *sosyal*; 'social' in the positive sense that people develop a wide range of social contacts and are no longer locked into repressive family relations. Some members of this group see all religion in terms of superstition (*batıl inançlar*) and cite the examples of local *imams* who supply poor gullible people with magical charms. The new type of religious activist is classified as 'educated ignorant' (*okumuş cahil*) and criticised for inciting others, especially highly impressionable young people, to acts of flagrant desecration, such as attacking statues and pictures of Atatürk in public places. These activists are *barbar*, while those who categorise them in this way maintain a self-image as civilised, *medeni*.

Both the religious and the Kemalist world views have undergone new twists and emphases in recent decades. The same governments that promoted a market economy after 1983, i.e. more capitalism and westernisation, also allowed religion more scope than previous republican governments. The building of an *Imam-Hatip* school in Pazar in the early 1990s was condemned by some teachers, though it proved to be very popular. In Lazistan as in many other parts of Turkey the Motherland Party's period in office between 1983 and 1991 was a period of religious efflorescence. In addition to new mosques and schools, new religious bookshops appeared in small towns where no other kinds of literature were available.

Another dichotomy often employed by those who deplored these trends was between closed (*kapalı*) and open (*açık*) societies. We have already come across this opposition in a different context: a woman is described as *açık* if she does not cover her head with a scarf. Applied to whole communities, a *kapalı* village is one in which all women wear scarves de rigueur – such as Sinanköyü, discussed above. Some of its neighbours are said to be more *açık*: if you ask in what way, since many women appear to be dressed exactly as in Sinanköyü, people say that male mosque attendance is weaker and that the other village has a more *sosyal* character, evident in the existence of one or more cafes. The eastern districts of Lazistan are generally agreed to be less *kapalı* than the western. In Fındıklı and Arhavi you may even come across rural women picking tea without a headscarf, dressed in jeans and T-shirts. This – admittedly rather rare – spectacle is applauded by the Kemalists, but denigrated by Islamists. The two camps agree on the designation of the poles of the dichotomy, differing only as to which pole is positively evaluated.[64]

These dichotomies provide people with mental models. We, as analysts, can adapt them to make models of our own. For example, we can suggest that the

[64] The east–west dichotomy within Lazistan seems to have strengthened since the 1970s. In 1973 in the Pazar *lise* girls in their final year had to be banned from entering the school in mini skirts. At the same time a conservative *kaymakam* in progressive Fındıklı banned schoolchildren from attending cafes in his town. See *Ardeşen Sesi*, 22 June 1973, 1: 44; *Ardeşen Sesi*, 19 March 1974, 2: 116.

pursuit at national level of 'free-market', 'open' economic policies was conducive to a groundswell of resentment that contributed to more conservative, 'closed' social practices, notably veiling. This was not an argument we ever heard put forward in Lazistan. We did hear, from a *kaymakam*, the metaphor of the Turkish state as a ship, pointing definitively, at least since the inception of Atatürk's Republic, towards the west. Many passengers, however, he commented with a tinge of sadness, have all along been determined to carry on facing east.[65] In recent years (the official elaborated on his metaphor) some passengers have been running on deck towards the east. A group of them had seized the bridge and was trying to set the ship on a new course. But, as befitted his position, the *kaymakam* did not think that this group stood any chance of succeeding in changing the direction of Atatürk's ship of state. At most they might slow down its rate of progress. He pointed to the other groups of passengers who clearly approved of the ship's current navigating officers – in other words, those who had embraced the values of western society. The contest between religion and modernity had to be kept in balance, and that was an important part of his job as a *kaymakam*. He had authorised the building of a number of new mosques, but also a number of *gazinos*, restaurants, cafes and beer-gardens, which in the long run might have more impact on the society of the region.

These dichotomous discourses are inadequate for understanding the disparate elements to be found within contemporary Islam, and how these are in turn related to other models, such as those of Kemalist secularism and civil society. The neat dichotomies of discourse disintegrate when confronted with social realities. The east–west continuum does not square with the fact that the extreme of immorality is represented by prostitutes who also hail from the geographical east; these are not easily lumped into one category with western capitalists. The fact that, within Lazistan, it is the westerly counties that are unanimously considered more *kapalı* poses a further puzzle.

Three general possibilities may be considered. First, it can be argued that the cleft between Islam and Kemalism is so deep that no reconciliation is possible. People live with the daily experience of a contradiction between the traditional and the modern, but they are powerless to mediate it. Aspects of Islam that are new and modern, far from forging a bridgehead to the modernity of Kemalism, are accentuating awareness of the basic contradiction. In intellectual and political discourse the diagnoses of polarisation and dislocation have become sharper in recent decades. Arguably this has been reflected in the political stalemate of the 1990s.

A second possibility is that three quarters of a century of Kemalism have sufficed to bring about a new synthesis. Far from bifurcation, according to this diagnosis we can speak of a new unity, whether or not this is appreciated by the actors themselves. In the words of Richard and Nancy Tapper: 'Turkish Islam and Turkish republicanism/nationalism today are both expressions of a single underlying ideology of social control.'[66] Their diagnosis of 'accommodations' is consistent with the empirical results of other anthropologists and with many of

---

[65] This is a variant on a common theme. Cf. White: ' "Turkey is like a bus headed West with all the passengers running East" – An Istanbul taxidriver' (1994: 1).
[66] Tapper and Tapper 1987b: 72.

our own findings in Lazistan. For example, a poem written by a strongly religious villager in the district of Pazar emphasises the need to defend national unity and confirms a suggestion, made by the Tappers, that in some contexts Atatürk may be interchangeable with the Prophet himself. In the handwritten version presented to us, the Prophet's name was crossed out each time it occurred, and that of Atatürk substituted for it, as in this stanza:

Let's not deviate from the words of the government,
Let's follow in (the Prophet's) Atatürk's footsteps
Those who deny this should cry
Do not do this, brothers, pity the fatherland.[67]

The danger in emphasising synthesis, however, is that continuing ambiguities and contradictions are overlooked. A third possibility places the stress on fluidity and dynamic variations in social identities. Sometimes people may have a sense of unifying synthesis, sometimes it is the sentiment of contradiction that prevails. Some people who articulate the basic dichotomy also express its lack of purchase on their lives. Most people distance themselves from all polar positions. As a local government employee put it; 'We are living between two extreme trends. One is represented by the extreme religious faction, the other by atheists. We cannot identify with either of them, we are caught in between.' Mainstream Islam and mainstream Kemalism are not the poles of the dichotomy here. Rather, the poles are 'the bearded', 'the black ones' and 'the *tarikatçı*' on the one hand, and 'the Marxists' and 'the communists' on the other. Islam and Kemalism are neither separate and somehow equivalent churches, nor do they fuse into a coherent synthesis. Rather, people behave pragmatically on the basis of imperfect information and guided by a jumble of models. Some of these exude elements of absolute, unconditional certainty, more so for some than for others, more in some districts than in others, and more in some stages of the life cycle than in others;[68] but no single model can suffice for negotiating social life in its entirety.

People live out these combinations in the course of their lives. The most fundamental patterning derives from the factors of gender and age, followed by social class, education and occupation. It is difficult in practice to maintain the purity of a polar position. Officials and other professional people might seem, to judge by their words and their public lifestyles, to be the epitome of the decadent west. But the doctor who enjoys his *rakı* in the urban *gazino* also visits his parents in their village home at the weekend, where his behaviour and reputation are quite different. Even a *kaymakam* has to alter his lifestyle when his mother-in-law comes to visit at the end of the Ramadan fast. A *sosyete* woman meticulously says her afternoon prayer during Ramadan, before setting out for a long evening of gambling. A religious party activist goes to much trouble and expense to ensure that he and his family can watch the new commercial TV channels, despite the bad reception in his valley. And so on.

The messages given to children are often confused. At one extreme, there are

[67] From the poem *Cana kıymak* by a Lazi villager.
[68] Schiffauer 1987 has a good account of the greater attention paid to Islamic norms by the more elderly peasants of the village he studied. Women, too, including urban women who think of themselves as modern and even as enlightened (*aydın*), tend to wear the headscarf and pray more frequently as they age.

those who aggressively dismiss Atatürk, in the full knowledge that, to others, such sentiments are sacrilegious. We did not enjoy the experience of being spat upon by a rural child of primary school age when, in answer to his question, we confessed that we were not Muslim. At the other extreme, plenty of urban children no longer attend Koran courses at all. They celebrate their birthdays in the western manner, and religion plays no visible role in their family life. However, most children are no more able than adults to maintain a polar position, if only because their teachers vary considerably. Some observe the fast in Ramadan, some do not. The beginning of the afternoon session of the main primary school in Pazar regularly clashed with the midday call for prayer from the central mosque, situated next door. Thus the call to prayer mingled with the chanting of the national anthem. The loudspeaker systems were of roughly equal strength, and neither side could unplug the other.

In other contexts the outcome is different. In Hamere, a village with a reputation for being 'enlightened' (aydın), we attended a henna party where modern Arabesk tunes were being blasted across the valley when the evening call to prayer intruded, also amplified from a tape; unperturbed, our young hosts simply disconnected the mosque's loudspeaker, and the party continued. In neighbouring Sinanköyü even weddings have no music and there is nothing to disturb the amplification of religious messages. However, not everyone in this village was equally enthusiastic about Hamdi hoca. The elected headman in the early 1990s was a man of leftist, secular bias, though like many others he has transferred his loyalties to the Motherland Party. His reasons, he admitted, were a combination of local patriotism and the hope that this party would channel more state resources into Lazistan. The headman worked for many years in Istanbul, where he drank alcohol. He carried out most of his headman's duties from the tea-house he rented in the county town. However, he sent his youngest daughter to attend the Koran school organised in the village by Hamdi hoca because he believed that this would provide her with a good general education. The girl was intelligent and willing to study, but thin, often sick and therefore hardly able to work hard in the fields. In these circumstances the Koran course seemed preferable to commuting daily to school in town, and better than her giving up school altogether.[69]

While Kemalists have treated religion and science as two unconnected realms which should not interfere with each other, some of the 'old-fashioned' hocas as well as their clients perceive religious healing and modern medical practices as complementary. Their claims should not be hastily dismissed. A doctor trained at Ankara University who worked in the county town nearest the village of the county's best known Oflu hoca acknowledged that the reassurance and optimism which the latter was capable of generating could, in themselves, produce impressive results in patients to whom he, the medical doctor, had little or nothing to offer. There were certain circumstances, he conceded, when a sick person might be better advised to spend his or her limited resources on a charm (nuska), or on a visit to the only significant türbe (shrine) in the area, that at Angwan. The doctor, a staunch Kemalist, could never bring himself to give this advice to a patient, but to us he was prepared to admit the positive role that religion might

[69] This information was confided in conversation over some cans of beer that he had smuggled into his village home.

Plate 7.5 Hamdi, founder of the Koran courses in Sinanköyü, and his village headman.

play in the alleviation of suffering. Many people seek complementary sources of relief. An urban mother who found her infant sons a terrible strain was unconvinced by her doctor's assurances that their behaviour was entirely normal. She visited a woman with a reputation for writing powerful charms and pinned a charm to the underclothes of her more troublesome child, though she was embarrassed if visitors noticed it. Many young mothers use a small gold medallion featuring Atatürk's head to ward off the evil eye. When the seventeen-year-old son of another urban family had a nervous breakdown, he was unable to talk, read, write or recognise anybody. He was taken to doctors and psychiatrists in Rize and Trabzon, but there was no improvement. Eventually, his worried parents, though they thought of themselves as enlightened, took him to a well-known *hoca* to heal the boy with magic. The *hoca* wrote a charm and immersed it in water but the boy refused to drink it. Eventually, his favourite science teacher from school came and persuaded the boy to drink this water. A young librarian who thought of herself as modern, claimed not to believe in paradise and hell, miracles and superstitions, but only in God. At that point another woman who had just bought a crystal vase at the Russian market joined our conversation. The vase suddenly cracked and disintegrated, without anyone touching it. The librarian was adamant that this was a case of *nazar* or evil eye – one of us must have been subconsciously jealous of her colleague's acquisition of this bargain. She claimed that the Koran confirmed the scientific reality of such causation.

The best evidence that most people prefer not to understand their world in terms of stark dichotomies is that of many decades of democratic voting. If it can be safely assumed that most of the people we have been calling Islamists vote for the religious party, it seems likely that the majority of committed Kemalists sympathise with the political left. Yet some of these Kemalists, particularly those loyal to Bülent Ecevit, have seen merit in some of the theses of the religious party activists – notably in their radical social egalitarianism and anti-Americanism. They may even welcome the election of a mayor from the religious party, provided he can be classified as a 'modern Muslim' and not as one of 'the bearded ones'. But the majority of voters in Lazistan have not been attracted by either leftist or Islamist positions. They have voted for parties which maintain the compatibility of Islam with both a free market capitalist economy and a pluralist, democratic political system.

The President of the Rize Province branch of the minuscule Socialist Party lived in retirement in Pazar. His hardline Marxist views had not changed since his formative years in a Village Institute in the 1940s. His career as a teacher had been interrupted by harassment and imprisonment. He had a very clear perception that religion was a form of false consciousness, deceiving the majority of people as to where their true interests lay. His own wife was deluded in this way, since she prayed five times a day, as all good Muslims should. But, he said, she was nonetheless a socialist, because she agreed with his diagnosis of Turkey's social ills in terms of the class struggle and so on. Others in his family, including his sons, did not accept this analysis. They did not visit very often.

At the other end of the political spectrum, dogmas are constantly modified in practical life. Hamdi *hoca* owns a car and many household conveniences. One shopkeeper with a Kemalist orientation delighted in telling stories of all the clerics who had purchased their consumer durables from his store, taking advantage of a hire purchase arrangement that contradicted Islamic trading ideals. The religious activists are very diverse. One senior *imam* in the Pazar *müftülük* argued that Turkey needed to become more European. He himself had visited Germany, where it was allowed to wear religious clothing in public, and where the state gave more active encouragement to churches. In Turkey, *laiklik* had, in his view, meant state encouragement of atheism, and low standards in religious education. Within Lazistan, he believed that the more *açık* counties of Fındıklı and Arhavi were better places to live and bring up children than the more reactionary western districts. This *imam* was critical of both extremists such as Hamdi and of those of his colleagues who write charms, such as the *Oflu hoca* noted above. However, the latter was using the income he obtained from his charms to support the education of his sons at an English-speaking university in Ankara.

High school students often have difficulty in reconciling what they have been taught in school and in Koran courses with what they read in the secular press and watch on television. A few girls entertained 'feminist' ideas and defied parental authority in small ways, e.g. by smoking whenever out of parental sight, and by visiting a seaside cafe without a male relative escorting them. Some, however, felt uncomfortable in their fashionable modern clothes, and had a constant feeling of guilt. They stressed the need to be modern Muslims, which to them had nothing to do with observing the dress code and daily prayer. Within a few years, however, the girls who made these arguments had been married by their respective families to close kin.

There is a definite affinity between patriarchal authority and religious conservatism. These elements combine in many families to frustrate individual aspirations in other directions. For example, some girls who would have preferred to attend a regular state secondary school had been enrolled instead at the *Imam-Hatip* school by their devout families. However, the norms of patriarchy and religious conservatism do not always point to the same decision. One girl had to withdraw from the Koran course at Sinanköyü, very much against her will, because she was under the authority of her elder brother, who had decided that she should return to their home. A fellow pupil was shortly afterwards married off to a local man with moderate views. She was obliged to give up attending Hamdi's Koran course and her full veiling, in other words to conform to the norms of mainstream family life.

In pointing to some of the real-life complexities which undermine the polarising dichotomies that are common in discourse, we do not mean to suggest that any of the various models on which people draw outside of their religion has a comparable moral force. On the contrary, many ardent Kemalists emphasise their respect for this aspect of religion, which is consistent with the aim of the secular state to confine religion to a differentiated private domain. Only tiny numbers of people declare themselves atheist (*dinsiz*). Such a stance is equated with 'immorality' (*ahlaksızlık*) and not tolerated. Atheism is one of the charges brought against the foreign prostitutes who are said not to know God (*Allahı tanımazlar*), or not to know the meaning of shame (*ayıp mayıp ne olduğunu bilmezler*). People who, in some utterances, condemn all religion as fraudulent superstition, may still be concerned to teach their own children the difference between primitive folk religious practices and the enduring values that constitute the substantive moral core of Islam. They may reject the Islamists' exaggerations concerning western family life, but nonetheless view the greater promiscuity and high divorce rates of the west as unattractive features, which Islamic morality should continue to combat.

Small-town commercial life, as we noted in Chapter 3, is a moral minefield. To survive as a shopkeeper or merchant one is in effect obliged to give priority to material interests (*çıkar*), and thereby to transgress the ideals of Islam. Consumers understand this, and they vent their criticism only on those who hypocritically pretend that this is not so. For example, one can hardly sustain a claim to piety if one opens one's restaurant business during Ramadan. Some traders tell cynical stories about the sophisticated cheating practised by some ultra-devout Rize businessmen; they say that, when placing orders in Istanbul, they would rather deal with a Jewish supplier rather than a fellow-Muslim. The *hacıs* who charge over the odds are pilloried. Few wealthy businessmen, it is pointed out in Pazar, have donated money to the religious party: more have supported the Motherland Party, with its highly secularised, *sosyete* leadership. The moral tensions in the economic sphere have increased under the market-oriented initiatives of this party, quite apart from the dramatic impact of the Russian markets.

Classical studies of the social and sociological effects of religion, deriving from Max Weber, often invoke a dichotomy between a religion's external social effects and its internal, subjective impact on individuals. In the literature on rural Turkey it is sometimes argued that Islam emphasises criteria for proper public behaviour, but rather neglects questions of responsible moral action by individuals.[70] The strong emphasis placed on female clothing supports such an analysis, and we have seen this to be a prominent theme for religious activists in contemporary Lazistan. The reaction to the Russian markets may also be understood in this 'external' sense, as primarily a concern with the correct ordering of society.

However, this dichotomy, too, seems much too simple to sustain. Fallers formed the impression on the basis of his fieldwork in the 1960s that 'Turkish Islam is very moralistic.'[71] In the generation that has elapsed since, the 'puritanical' elements, and the appeal to an individual conscience, have been strongly emphasised by Islamic intellectuals. As Meeker has pointed out, they reach conclusions 'which serve as an orientation for personal thought and action.'[72] This is not to argue that Islam is being 'privatised'.[73] Contrary to Kemalist plans, it has not proved possible to confine religion to the private sphere: it retains and in some highly visible ways it has increased in public salience in recent years. But it *also* has immense impact on individual moral behaviour, backed up of course by the persistence of ancient popular ideas: bad deeds will be punished by fire.

[70] Schiffauer 1987 argues that more individualist, protestant meanings of morality are missing from Islam.

[71] Fallers 1974: 97.

[72] Meeker 1991: 190.

[73] We therefore disagree with Toprak (1995: 2), who argues that the Kemalist state has 'succeeded in privatising Islam for the majority of Turkish citizens.' Cf. Casanova 1994 for a discussion of 'public religions' and recent processes of 'deprivatisation' in a comparative framework.

8
Ethnicity

Minorities and muddling through

In the Gellnerian model with which we began, the nation-state is endowed with a single homogenous high culture. This model therefore never has to deal with any problem of cultural minorities. At the other extreme, Clifford Geertz has recently outlined a view of the world in which virtually every country is endlessly fragmented. He prefers to steer away from the terms ethnicity and nation, perhaps because they draw too strongly on a holistic, integrating notion of culture of which he disapproves. Yet his own work, we suggested in Chapter 1, has contributed to the popularity of this notion; and even in his recent work the multiple minority identities ultimately recoalesce, if not into a 'seamless unity' then at least into 'an irregular, rickety and indefinite whole'.[1]

Geertz is certainly justified in complicating the Gellnerian model of modernity, which is heavily skewed to certain European experiences and operates at a very high level of abstraction. But a Gellnerian is also correct in responding that Geertz provides no explanation for the special force of nationalism and ethnicity in constituting the wholes of the modern world and for why they do not always appear rickety and indefinite to their members. In the case with which we are dealing here, the social realities of contemporary Turkey are more complex than Gellner might like to admit. Civil society in his 'Atlantic' sense and 'modular' individuals are largely missing in Lazistan.[2] Yet we have argued that Kemalism has been successful in promoting a new national identity that provides the decisive frame for all other forms of social identity in the country. We therefore suggest that, at least in this field, some elements of the approaches of Gellner and Geertz need to be combined; but we disagree with both in preferring to dispense altogether with the notion of 'a culture'.

A truly homogenised society is very hard to imagine. Why should we privilege the much contested concept of ethnicity when we discuss problems of minority recognition? We have neglected ethnicity so far in order to foreground other factors that contribute to social identities in this region. Minorities do not have to be defined in ethnic terms. At this point it may be useful to summarise the main factors we have considered so far in exploring and differentiating the contemporary population of Lazistan. These factors are highly diverse, partly because we

[1] Geertz 2000: 255.
[2] See Gellner 1994a.

194

have taken the region as our unit, rather than any one village or town. We argue that social life as it is now lived in this region cannot be squeezed into a single model or reduced to a few structural polarities. People do of course use simplifying heuristics in their discourses, to help them to make sense of their lives. Sometimes the discourse will translate into specific action, as when women protest to state officials about the immorality of 'Russian' prostitutes. However, the fit between discourses and behaviour is often loose: the very same women buy goods on the Russian markets and form more nuanced opinions about the foreigners they meet there.

To approach personhood and sociality it is necessary to examine not only the models of local people, as given in their discourse and in symbols, but also a range of often confusing social practices. It is necessary, to adapt a recent metaphor of Geertz, not merely to assemble a file card inventory of social identities, but to 'cross-index' these cards and to recognise in doing so that the identities are constituted in the course of interaction.[3] A good deal of the literature on modern Turkey has in effect denied this complexity and exaggerated the dichotomy between, on the one hand, the forces of Kemalism (associated with modernity and secularism) and, on the other, the forces of tradition, including Islam and a core of patriarchal practices rooted in the family. It is hard to escape from this way of thinking. Michael Meeker, for example, in seeking to overcome simplified contrasts between Kemalist and Islamist world views, shows how both are struggling in different ways to resolve the basic dilemmas of the mass, anonymous society.[4] However, his analysis is itself built on a contrast between this mass society and the allegedly more personal character of social life in the past, when languages of 'familiarity and intimacy' were more significant than the abstractions of nation and God. Such dichotomies are seductive. They lead us to overlook the extent to which people resolve and transcend them in their everyday experience. Rather than diagnose dissonances, absences, or a 'void in the psyche' brought about by the imposition of Kemalism, rather than see this 'project' as obliterating the shared 'natural', socially unifying meanings of Islam, closer attention to the micro-specificities suggests that the people of Lazistan have on the whole succeeded remarkably well in reconciling new forms of sociality with an enduring insistence on the importance of the personal.[5]

What are the most significant group boundaries in this region at the end of the twentieth century? Social worlds are undoubtedly wider and more open-ended today than they were before the republic, though we should remember that the communities of this region have been open to the world for a much longer period. Nonetheless distinctions are often drawn between natives of the region and strangers to it. As a result of Kemalist modernity, two new minority groups

---

[3] Geertz 2000: 254.

[4] See Meeker 1997.

[5] The term 'project' is used by Mardin in his 1997 critique of Turkish social scientists, who with few exceptions have failed, in his view, to recognise the continuing importance of Islam in creating the cultural foundations of social life. As with Meeker's suggestion of 'void' (1997: 184), the extension of this diagnosis to the whole country seems questionable. It may be close to the mark as a characterisation of limitations of many republican intellectuals, and it may be an apt characterisation of the predicament of particular groups, such as migrant workers or civil servants of rural origin; but it is not the correct diagnosis for most inhabitants of contemporary Lazistan.

are especially conspicuous. The first, much larger than ever in the past, is made up of state officials, ranging from elite university graduates to low-level police functionaries and rural midwives. This group is not sharply bounded, for the proportion of state officials recruited locally has increased over the years, and some immigrant officials have married and settled in Lazistan. The second new minority is made up of the day labourers and sharecroppers who have entered the region in large numbers, primarily to assist with the plucking of tea leaves. This group, too, is internally diverse, and it is not found in all districts. Some have become permanent residents and a few have managed to purchase land as well as a house or flat and become integrated into the new community. Significant numbers of sharecroppers originate within the boundaries of Lazistan, but these are not sharply differentiated from immigrants from other parts of the Black Sea coast or the Anatolian interior.

The opening of the state border with Georgia and, a few years later, the influx of petty traders from all over the former Soviet Union led to a new drawing of the insider/outsider boundary. The opening to the Caucasus, for the first time in living memory, and the rhetoric of Black Sea Economic Cooperation had unintended consequences. Far from weakening longstanding ties between Lazistan and central and western parts of Turkey, the appearance of the trader-tourists and the associated phenomenon of prostitution seem to have strengthened higher levels of identity as Turks and as Muslims. The seasonal labourers who appeared a little later in the 1990s, mainly from Georgia and Azerbaijan, were viewed more positively and formed a distinct new minority.

Residential patterns generate further distinctions, notably between permanent residents of the region and those who return for part of the year only, usually for a combination of holiday and tea garden management. Those who live in the county towns are usually better off than those who live permanently in rural areas. None of these distinctions, however, is particularly rigid, since most families maintain links with close kin outside the region and many families own a town flat as well as a village house. The town *mahalle* can emulate the intimacy of the village. Some migrants who are only seldom seen in the region in the course of their working lives nonetheless eventually settle permanently in their home village or its county centre.

Older forms of social hierarchy, that is, those which existed prior to the dissemination of tea, have left their mark. It is not simply that certain family names have prestige because of the wealth and power they enjoyed in the past: some elite families have managed to convert the bases of their past domination into new forms of power, e.g. by using their large landholdings to create tea estates, or by astute investments in urban commerce and utilisation of their inherited real estate. However, some formerly influential families have failed to adapt in any of these ways, and this too is recognised and commented upon.

There is a pervasive sense that society has changed radically over the last half century. Our initial approach to these changes in this book was in terms of two complementary, sometimes conflicting, principles: state and market. Each has generated new forms of social differentiation, which have in turn encountered criticism and resentment. Some Kemalists are short-stay officials who interact socially only with others like themselves and make it plain that they look down upon 'provincial customs'. They are often resented and despised. Equally, those who are thought to take the market principle to excess, to manipulate credit facilities in order to line their own pockets, are also reviled and brought to account, at least in gossip. Although the market principle has gained in signifi-cance since the 1980s, the extent to which it supports a new class structure remains limited. Houses and cars are the most visible signs of modern social differentiation, both in the towns and in the countryside, and some of their owners form an identifiable minority and lead more reclusive lives than hitherto. However, the great majority of urban businesses remain small and family-run, as are the great majority of tea gardens; many households combine these activities, and most economic transactions retain a marked personal element.

We saw that venues for intimacy and solidarity are everywhere available. The main institution is the cafe, increasingly supplemented by small restaurants and newer establishments that also serve alcohol. These, like the political parties and a variety of small associations, also town-based, are dominated by men. Women socialise separately, notably through the 'days', which are beginning to spread into some rural districts. Considerations of class and status shape the formation of these groups. Labour cooperation continues to play a significant role for many rural women. Overall, we argued that social integration in Lazistan depends less on the institutions of a 'civil society', in the sense of formal mediating institutions, than on the persistence of traditional, gender-specific patterns of sociability. The ideas and practices that regulate personal and familial life have much in common with the 'honour and shame' codes found in neighbouring Caucasian, Middle Eastern, and Mediterranean societies. Adherence to traditional norms governing marriage and inheritance is a source of pride, but here too there is always room for debate, choice and diversity. The decision-taking power of women is not uniform across the region or between different social groups. The forms of marital payments have varied, as has the organisation of weddings. The more modern *salon* experience can be interpreted as a sign of the loss of an older intimacy, but many who choose it say they do so in order to make sure that more of their friends as well as relatives will be able to attend, while engagement parties and stag nights are popular new forms allowing more intimate celebration. The prolifera-tion of the wider, weaker networks does not necessarily undermine the strong local networks of kin and community.

The core of the personal lifeworld and the most likely suspect, if one insists on specifying some ultimate foundation for culture or ideology, is to be found in Islam. We showed some of the ways in which this continues to shape and give meaning to lives. However, here too we noticed differentiation and regional variation. Islam is no monolith. The recent emergence of a 'fundamentalist' colony within the region and the appearance on the streets of women in çarşaf have provoked debate and criticism, from those who see themselves as devout Muslims as well as from secularists. Instead of seeking in Islam, or in some notion of traditional patriarchy, or in the two together, an all-encompassing culture that continues to define the person and inter-personal relations, we argue that it is necessary to see how these interact and cross-cut the differentiating principles of state and market and all the other social distinctions to which we have drawn attention. We see persons as engaged in continuous flexible adaptation throughout the life-course of a variety of principles or models in a process that, given the uncertainties and constant need to make compromises, is best described as 'muddling through'.[6] Persons are constituted in the course of these continuous adaptations. The concept of 'muddling through' lacks analytic elegance and sophistication, but that is precisely what makes it so useful as a description of how the people of Lazistan resolve tensions that, far from being unique to Turkey, may be inherent in all modern societies. Instead of locating the people of this region firmly within the framework of another distant culture, 'muddling through' makes them seem more like ourselves. Of course the variation and cross-cutting are not arbitrary and chaotic; some clusters of ideas and practices show consistent affinities. There are patterns, but they are more complex than a simple contrast between Islamic and Kemalist will allow. For Geertz, these 'intersections of outlook, style or disposition' add up to a 'rickety' but still ordered cultural whole.[7] We argue that, to the extent that this is so, the order is derived not from any deep shared *culture* but from the frame within which all these intersections take place, the *society* created by the Kemalist state-nation.

Lazi and Hemşinli

Our argument, then, is that social identities are formed in the course of muddling through, but within a national frame as specified by Gellner. How does ethnicity fit into this frame? Is this not one further source which, like Islam, deserves some sort of special recognition? Outside of their families and the personal networks in which they invest so much, and their state-nations, are there no intermediate secular collectivities with which the people of Lazistan strongly identify? The answer cannot be a collectivity called Lazistan, the name of an Ottoman sub-province which ceased to exist as an administrative unit more than seventy years ago. As we explained in the Introduction, this name is merely a convenient label for the arbitrarily selected territory of our investigation. There is no evidence that Lazistan was a focus of group loyalty in the past either.

So, just who exactly do they say and think they are? The aggressive modernist question implies a single, all-encompassing answer, that there is one type of identity that trumps all other types. For Kemalists this is, of course, national identity. In the language of nationalism, and ethnicity, it is usually assumed that each person has one pre-eminent attachment. The world can then be represented as a map of ethnic groups and nations, the main difference between these terms being that an ethnic group does not control its own state. Social scientists have been using this vocabulary for a long time. The terms ethnicity (ethnic group) and nation have been adapted to avoid the difficulties of earlier categories to identify group belonging, notably 'race' and 'tribe'. Ethnic groups and nations are

---

[6] 'Muddling through' was the expression used by the American anthropologist Steven Sampson in his analyses of survival strategies in socialist Romania: see Sampson 1984. It is attributed by Scott (1998: 327) to Charles Lindblom. 'Muddling through' is not to be confused with 'postmodernist' analysis of the fragmentation and 'hybridisation' of identities, particularly when this emphasises wilful experimentation or 'playing' with identities.

[7] Geertz 2000: 254–5.

conventionally defined not with respect to primordial racial exclusivity or evolutionary sophistication, but in terms of culture.

This was not the vocabulary and these were not the axioms when Lazistan was an Ottoman sub-province. The principal basis of social identity then was religion. *Millet* referred to confessional orientation and did not necessarily reveal language or any other significant cultural features. Kemalist success in establishing and disseminating the new national identity does not preclude the persistence of other kinds of allegiance and we noted the continuing force of local patriotisms in Chapter 2. We turn now to consider more carefully the ethnic identity categories that were introduced in Chapter 1, which go unrecognised in the hierarchical structures of the state.

Modern states normally adopt one of two options in dealing with ethnic diversity. Either the state recognises ethnic minorities as part of its efforts to codify and control them, or it denies their very existence by assimilation strategies or worse. The former course was followed in the nationalities policies of the Soviet Union and China, originally formulated by Stalin. These conceded few political rights but brought impressive results in other fields, for example in promoting minority education in small, endangered languages. In the case of larger regionally based groups, such as Ukrainians or the Uyghurs in China, these socialist minority policies facilitated the consolidation of a relatively 'thick' alternative identity to that which dominated in the state, thereby contradicting Gellner's ideal type in which a single 'high culture' has a monopoly. Other forms of minority recognition were implemented in the policies of postcolonial India towards its castes and tribes. The basic problem with most forms of multiethnic polity is that such interventions by the state can lead to the rigidification and over-simplification of dynamic complex processes. Sometimes the state officials construct the very categories into which subjects are then slotted. They 'folklorise' minorities and consign the tribal and peasant traditions to the museum.

But states which follow the alternative, unitary model and fail to acknowledge ethnic differences at all are open to even stronger criticisms. The Turkish model of the unitary and indivisible state, strongly reaffirmed in the constitution of 1982, is basically in line with the course pioneered by post-revolutionary France. It can be viewed as a sustained effort to achieve that 'congruence' of polity and culture stipulated by the Gellnerian model. But just as France, despite beginning the task many centuries earlier, still has minorities of Bretons and others, so it is increasingly recognised that the Turkish state is unlikely ever to bring about a fully homogenised Anatolia.

No administrative entities and no emigrants' associations are founded on the basis of an ethnic identity as Lazi or Hemşinli, and yet these identities somehow linger. With the exception of Arhavi, which apart from a few newcomers is exclusively Lazi, and the new small county of Hemşin centred on the town with the same name, all of the counties between Pazar and the state frontier contain both Hemşinli and Lazi. They also contain pockets of Georgians. Both the expanding towns and the depopulating rural areas contain immigrants who do not belong to any of these categories. In this context we can consider them as 'unmarked' Turks, though of course they too may attach importance to their local or regional origins. The western counties of Lazistan have experienced relatively little recent immigration from outside the region and are in ethnic terms overwhelmingly 'unmarked' Turkish.

Rize is the largest city in this region and the identity *Rizeli*, which is promoted by the state, cuts across the ethnic boundaries. In principle it applies only to the administrative province. It therefore includes the Lazuri speakers of Pazar, Ardeşen and Fındıklı, but excludes the Lazuri speakers of Arhavi, Hopa, and Borçka. It includes the Hemşinli of Pazar, nowadays monolingual in Turkish, but excludes the Hemşinli of Hopa. Yet we found that the categories Lazi and Hemşinli cropped up more frequently than Rizeli and we were keen to understand what these classifications might mean, of both self and others. When someone said 'I am a Lazi' (*ben Lazım*), was this a qualitatively different declaration of identity from the statement 'I am from the place Çayeli' (*ben Çayeliliyim*)? Was the former a claim to a unique ethnicity, while the latter merely specified a local variant of Turkish national identity?

Classification as Lazi or Hemşinli is generally understood to refer to descent, but as we have noted the history of these groups has been almost entirely forgotten. People allow for the fact that some have become group members following migration into the Lazi homeland, intermarriage and a process of assimilation. The primary supplementary criterion for group membership is then linguistic competence. Almost all who profess Lazi identity have some knowledge of Lazuri. Those who have not been taught this language by their parents are nonetheless aware of its existence, and would not dispute that this language is central to the group's identity. Essentially the same criterion applies in the Hemşinli case. Those in the western districts have not spoken any language other than Turkish for a long time, and the Hemşinli tongue is said to be close to extinction in the easterly districts as well. Nevertheless, knowledge that this group once had its own separate language in the past provides a basis for the continued assertion of a collective identity.

Many people can reel off other differences between Lazi and Hemşinli. They typically begin with location and mode of subsistence: most Lazi villages lie closer to the coast and have weaker traditions of animal husbandry. Lazi are associated with the coast and anchovies, Hemşinli with transhumance and the consumption of dairy produce. People then go on to identify differences in clothing, house building, in music and dance, and in the size and structure of the family. However, as most readily concede, none of these criteria are very convincing today. Since the rise of tea as the dominant cash crop, very few Lazi make their living from the sea, and few Hemşinli are dependent on pastoralism. The Lazi have been better placed to take advantage of opportunities in tea, but many Hemşinli have been able to adapt at least part of their landholdings for the new crop. In any case, differences between the coast and the interior do not correspond, and probably never have corresponded, to ethnic group differences. It is likely that multiple families stay in one household for a longer period in the more upland parts of the region, but this applies to the Lazi who live in these areas as well as to the Hemşinli. Lazi villagers in the neighbourhood of Çamlıhemşin share summer pastures with Hemşinli. Moreover, for several generations there have been Hemşinli hamlets within Lazi coastal villages, again with economic profiles identical to those of their Lazi neighbours.[8] In the region as a whole, living standards have

---

[8] Lazi *aghas* are said to have sold land to Hemşinli for as little as a *teneke* (tinplate) when the coast

risen for both groups, not only due to tea but due to similar migration strategies.

If realities have become confusingly similar, discourses still point to a range of largely unverifiable stereotypes that highlight group differences. There is a large measure of agreement about these images. Hemşinli are seen, both by themselves and by Lazi, as more calculating planners, as more 'cold-blooded' (*soğuk kanlı*) and genteel (*efendi*).[9] The explanation sometimes given is that they were compelled to take up large-scale labour migration before most Lazi.[10] They managed to enter the modern world more rapidly, achieve higher levels of education and civilisation, and find employment in the state sector. Others say that Hemşinli qualities of diligence are much older, and it is intuitively plausible to expect a stronger disposition to think ahead and plan for the future among pastoralists than among coastal people who, at least in the past, could take an abundant supply of fish for granted.

Images of the Lazi, including self-images, are quite different and closer to the general regional stereotypes about 'Laz'. While his neighbour is a prudent planner, the Lazi concentrates on the short-term. He is hot blooded (*sıcak kanlı*), nervous (*sinirli*), and always on the move (*hareketli*), in search of some new opportunity. Where the Hemşinli is fat (*şişman*), a condition still associated with the pastoral mode of subsistence, the Lazi is thin (*zayıf*). The Hemşinli is also said to be soft (*yumuşak*) in contrast to the tough, bold (*sert, mert*) character of the Lazi. This contrast is usually illustrated with reference to the honour code. While a Hemşinli will try hard to find a peaceful solution to a problem of *namus*, the typical Lazi will start a fight or reach straight for his gun. Women and guns are linked: both should be gripped as tightly as possible! In some Lazi villages the names of local bandits (*eşkiya*) are still remembered.

There is also a more vulgar level of stereotyping, as when Hemşinli make fun of the large nose of the Lazi, while Lazi complain about smells and a lack of hygiene among the Hemşinli.[11] Jocular proverbs may indicate past rivalries but there is no sign that these continue in the present. Nowadays they are simply outlets for inter-household tensions.[12] Some allegations may be taken more seriously, especially any

[8] (cont.) around Ardeşen was drained in the late Ottoman period; this land now contains extremely fertile tea gardens.

[9] There is some evidence, especially in the county of Ardeşen, that violent crimes are more common in Lazi areas. The stereotypes are significantly different in the more eastern counties. In Hopa, the Hemşinli are often said to have reacted more slowly than their Lazi neighbours to the opportunities of the republican period; their backwardness is demonstrated, in the eyes of neighbouring Lazi, by higher rates of first cousin marriage. The Lazi of Arhavi, having little direct contact with Hemşinli themselves, also challenge any suggestion that the latter are more 'advanced' or 'civilised'. They tend to see their Eastern Hemşinli neighbours as rowdy troublemakers, an image that was borne out when they were allegedly responsible for some minor disruption at the end of the Arhavi Festival in 1992.

[10] For evidence that Hemşinli migrants preceded Lazi in seeking work as bakers and pastry-cooks in Batumi and other cities of the Russian empire see Marr 1910: 618.

[11] Large noses are a genuine source of concern to some Lazi men and plastic surgery in Istanbul is apparently common. Some people suggest that a desire to attract 'Russian' women lies behind an increase in demand for the operation in recent years. See 'Laz burnu Karadenizli'nin kaderi değil' (The Laz nose is not the Black Sea man's destiny), *Rize Kaçkar* 1992: 1(6) 2.

[12] Some Hemşinli women quoted the following verse (with Lazi women also present, to everyone's great amusement):
Kaynana iyisi
Derin olsun kuyusu.

questioning of the other's religious devotion. There is a ready riposte for allegations of dubious descent: if a Lazi calls a Hemşinli 'converted Armenian' (*dönmüş ermeni*), the Hemşinli will retort with an accusation of 'converted Mingrelian' (*dönmüş Megrel*), and vice versa.

Whatever long-term patterns they may disguise, the evocation of such stereotypes helps to maintain some sense of groupness. Stereotypes are mentioned most frequently in support of a continuing preference for endogamy and the claim that, historically, rates of intermarriage have been low. This claim may be exaggerated, since there certainly was some intermarriage even before the introduction of tea and the improved communications that have facilitated mixing in recent decades.[13] According to the Hemşinli, they were reluctant to take Lazi women as brides, but generally willing bride-givers. Lazi formulated the same norm in terms of their willingness to incorporate Hemşinli girls as brides, coupled with a reluctance to allow their daughters to marry into a Hemşinli community, where they would have to work harder to meet the demands of animal husbandry. Many emphasised differences in physique. Hemşinli women lived on a protein-rich diet of meat and dairy products, while the Lazi depended on maize bread, augmented by some fish. Hemşinli girls were stronger, better used to harsher weather conditions, and therefore more desirable marriage partners. However, it was sometimes alleged that the Hemşinli used to deter Lazi men from marrying their daughters by insisting on a high brideprice.

Feurstein found in the 1970s that, although Hemşinli hamlets were to be found within the administrative confines of a Lazi village, it was inconceivable that a Hemşinli could establish a household within a Lazi hamlet (*opute*).[14] This is no longer the case, though such mixing is still unusual because land and houses are so rarely transferred on the market. Analysis of marriage records in the mixed

[12] (cont.) *Ne kadar derin olsa,*
  Görünür muncirisi
('The good mother-in-law's well should be deep. No matter how deep, her nose will stick out of it.') Here the Hemşinli daughter-in-law inserts the Lazuri word for nose, *munciri*, in place of the standard Turkish term. Lazi women present retorted by alleging that 'the Hemşinli's bum is full of lice' (*Hemşinli götleri bitli*).
Lazi are also charged by their neighbours with a lack of hospitality:
  Lazlar lazlar melezler
  Hoşmeni yemezler
  Birbirine gitse
  Hoş geldin demezler.
('The Lazi are mongrels, they do not eat *hoşmeni*. When they visit each other, they do not say "welcome".')

[13] That the stated preference could be broken is suggested by a well-known legend that explains the origin of the bagpipes (*tulum*). The story describes the elopement of a Hemşinli youth with a Lazi girl. The preference for endogamous unions among Lazi villagers, which we noted in Chapter 6, contrasts with the strongly exogamous customs of Muslim Georgian villagers in western Turkey: see Magnarella 1979: 28; Paleczek 1987: 85.
  At the western extremity of the Lazuri-speaking belt, the Lazi villages of Melyat and Surminat adjoin the monoglot Turkish village of Örnek. When we asked about the bases of group distinctiveness, people said that, apart from language, there were none. There had been an evenly balanced exchange of women between these villages as far back as anyone could remember. Intermarriage with local Hemşinli (also Turkish monoglots) was less frequent, but this was simply because they were further away and less well known. Evidence of past Lazi-Georgian intermarriage is given in Marr 1910: 554. Lazi-Greek intermarriage is noted by Brendemoen 1990b: 56.

[14] Feurstein 1983: 12.

county of Pazar reveals a significant increase in the frequency of mixed unions in recent decades.[15] In the 1940s as many Lazi men married Hemşinli women as vice versa, but in the 1950s it seems that the proportion of Hemşinli men marrying Lazi women rose. The ratio was more balanced again by the 1990s. We found no evidence that inter-ethnic marriages were more likely to lead to marital problems or divorce. A Hemşinli woman who married into a Lazi village might never become fluent in Lazuri, but she soon learned enough to get by.

There is no friction between these identities today. In the counties with mixed populations, Lazi and Hemşinli mingled in the same cafes and shops without difficulties. Some people suggested that there was a preference in the past to shop and conduct other business with someone from your own group, but this has died out. The Lazi who runs the most dynamic pharmacy in Pazar has engaged a Hemşinli assistant, and agrees that this has helped to bring him the custom of Hemşinli villagers. The strategy is presented not in terms of mobilising ethnic solidarity but in terms of loyalty to a common locality (*hemşerilik*). Hemşinli have a virtual monopoly in some branches of the local economy (e.g. bakeries, fruit and vegetables), but this dominance is not perceived in ethnic terms.[16] The prevailing view is that the two groups 'harmonise with each other' (*Hemşinli ve Laz birbirine uyuyor*). There is some confusion about whether particular terms and customs originate among Lazi or Hemşinli, but it is generally agreed not to matter very much.[17]

Although language is commonly said to be the major or indeed sole 'objective' marker of Lazi distinctiveness, Lazuri is not necessarily to be seen as a unifying medium. It exists in at least four quite different variants. Indeed so different is the Lazuri of Hopa from that of Pazar (not only in pronunciation, but also, we were told, in up to fifty per cent of the actively used vocabulary) that Lazi from these districts often find it easier to converse with each other in Turkish. Many Lazi do not have a high opinion of their language, which they perceive as a *patois* rather than a language potentially on a par with Turkish or with Georgian. This view is heard more frequently in the western counties, where people say that their command of Lazuri is limited or 'corrupted' (*bozuk*) in comparison with that of the eastern districts. Beyond acknowledgement that they speak a related dialect, Lazi in Pazar and Ardeşen do not feel that they have much in common with the residents of the eastern Lazi districts. For example, few bother to visit each other's festivals. The same seems to apply in the case of the western and eastern Hemşinli. Hamlet, county and national level identities all seem more meaningful, and the east–west intra-regional distinctions that we have noted in numerous contexts seem unconnected to the ethnic divisions. In summary, both the Lazi and the Hemşinli have forgotten a great deal. They have forgotten their settlement history and the fact that they were formerly Christian. They have largely forgotten any

---

[15] The data are not unproblematic, since in the 1940s and 1950s only a small percentage of marriages were officially registered. Marriage registers do not report the ethnicity of the marriage partners but give only the village for each partner; for this reason, mixed villages were excluded from the calculations. For further discussion see Bellér-Hann, forthcoming.

[16] The strongest group in the grocery sector in Pazar is neither Lazi nor Hemşinli but a group of immigrant families from a village south of Rize.

[17] For example, the term *mezra* (summer camp in the *yayla*) and the custom of *mangalcılık* (discussed in Chapter 6) are claimed by both Lazi and Hemşinli.

group-specific knowledge they once had concerning housebuilding, animal husbandry, etc. They are well on the way to forgetting their languages. They have forgotten almost everything, except the group names and the above-mentioned stereotypes. These hardly seem sufficient to give persons their 'basic, most general identity', as Fredrik Barth defined ethnicity.[18]

Ethnogenesis or ethnocide?

Ernest Gellner, was well aware of the persistence of minority identities such as those of the Lazi and the Hemşinli, even though they did not fit into his general model. They were like a time machine, he used to say, in which the basic scripts of nineteenth-century national movements might be rehearsed all over again, on a smaller scale. The basic choice was whether to follow the path of full assimilation into the larger and more developed entity that ruled your valleys from a remote capital city, or whether to strike out and construct something new by reworking elements of folk culture into a standardised national culture. The intellectuals who carried out these tasks usually claimed to be the 'awakeners' of their nations. Gellner, however, saw these ethnogeneses as novel creations, the fabrications and inventions of the intelligentsias.

His interpretation of the Lazistan situation would run something like this. The linguistic and cultural diversity of the Ottoman Empire, exemplified in the *millet* system, was unsuited to the requirements of a modern industrial society. It has therefore been replaced by a more viable system, that of the Turkish state-nation. Through radical reforms of the means of communication and education, a much more homogenised society has been created in Anatolia. It is characterised by an ethos of equality and tremendous mobility, both geographical and social. Lazi and Hemşinli seem to have accepted the invitation to join the national society, as indicated by the many prominent positions they have obtained in Ankara and Istanbul. This view holds out little prospect for the persistence of Lazi or Hemşinli cultural distinctiveness. Such identities are too small to survive in the modern world. Gellner understands the motives of those parents in Lazi areas who do not encourage their children to speak Lazuri because they believe that this will impede their fluency in Turkish, and thereby their chances of making social and economic progress in the national society. In certain superficial ways, local distinctiveness may persist and even be strengthened. Folk dancing may flourish as never before, and local dishes of cabbage (*karalahane*) and maize bread (*mısır ekmeği*) are available at the new restaurants dotting the coastline. But behind this façade of distinctiveness, the substantive reality is one of increasing functional integration into the society of the modern state-nation.

Some people in Lazistan endorse this analysis and say, usually without much sign of regret, that Lazi and Hemşinli have been 'assimilated' (*assimiley olmuş*). Others explicitly reject this term. They insist that you cannot be assimilated into something that you have been a part of from the very beginning.

Other social scientists and also international organs such as UNESCO have been less sanguine about these processes than Ernest Gellner or the Lazi

---

[18] Barth 1969: 15.

themselves. They have used a more emotive term, *ethnocide*, to capture what is perceived as the destruction of a people's cultural identity. It differs from *genocide* inasmuch as people are not physically killed, but the destruction of their cultural identity is nonetheless seen as a violent and immoral action. This term has not, so far as we know, been adapted into Turkish and we did not hear anything like it in Lazistan. However, in Turkey too the word *etnik* is acquiring significant currency among intellectuals and by 1992 there were a handful of people in Lazistan 'interested' (*meraklı*) in the Lazi as an *etnik grup*, as defined by common descent, language and culture.[19] These enthusiasts were local people with at least secondary school education and diverse jobs. They had a loose network of contacts in other parts of the country, including links with university staff conducting research into the history and traditions of their homeland. In one town efforts have been made since the 1970s to build up a library, and a 'museum of Lazi culture'. Those involved have tentatively sought official recognition, but always been advised to wait because of the delicacy of 'separatist' issues elsewhere in the country. Every year they were proud of their festival, one of the largest and best attended in the east Black Sea region; but they pointed out that the contents did not include any recognition of the Lazi as a people with a specific identity of their own. They were sceptical when a government minister made a promise, at a festival in their town in 1992, to create a new cultural centre for the town, for they had heard similar promises before.[20] In the meantime these men were getting together informally, translating into Turkish poems that they themselves collected in villages, and cultivating contacts with Lazi researchers in Istanbul, in Georgia, and elsewhere.

In another county we once heard a Lazi doctor argue cautiously in a gathering of local state officials that it would be in the country's interests to grant more recognition to ethnic minorities. He emphasised that no Lazi entertained any separatist political ambitions by jesting to the group that, since the Lazi were already so strong in the corridors of power in Ankara, not to mention the property markets of Istanbul, why on earth would they wish to secede from the state? But despite the attempted humorous tone, his words cut no ice with the audience, which seemed greatly embarrassed by the doctor's remarks. One after another the others present emphasised that Turkey was one unified country, and that only malicious foreigners had an interest in promoting divisions, as a means of retarding the country's development. The doctor did not press his point further.

It has proved easier to make such arguments at the other end of the country. In the mid-1990s a Lazi group in Istanbul produced half a dozen issues of a journal called *Ogni* which argued that the Lazi had a distinct culture (*kültür*) that should be recognised by the state and a language that should be properly written down and taught to future generations. Soon after it was launched, the editor was arrested and accused of separatism. He was acquitted. The contributors were careful to avoid any political provocation and the contents of the journal emphasised the

---

[19] Some were reluctant to use this term, perhaps for political reasons. Others said that, whereas minorities such as Kurds and Armenians could properly be described as ethnic groups, the Lazi were simply a distinct cultural and linguistic entity *within* the Turkish people.

[20] A major new library and adjoining facilities were in fact established in this town by 1999, but they contained nothing on the Lazi.

regional as well as the ethnic dimension.[21] Nevertheless, *Ogni* was discontinued after the publication of the sixth issue. Although the reasons for its eventual demise are not clear, its troubled history indicated that any publication documenting distinctive ethnic groups was perceived as a threat by the Turkish authorities.[22]

However, the collapse of *Ogni* has by no means put an end to the recent wave of cultural activism of Lazi in Istanbul.[23] Similar ground was covered in the journal *Kafkasya* (Caucasus), launched in 1997, which also carried articles about Lazuri and Lazi culture and book reviews of notable foreign language publications. A Lazi festival has recently been established in Sapanca in western Anatolia and a Lazuri alphabet for children, first published in 1935 in Stalin's Georgia, has been reprinted in Istanbul.[24] An organisation established in 1993 to promote ethnic identity, shared history and cultural values is continuing its activity.[25] A rock group called *Zuğaşi Berepe* ('Children of the Sea') gives concerts, partly in Lazuri, and has released a cassette.[26] Financial backing is said to come from businessmen with Lazi roots and the leading activists in Istanbul are said to be teachers and lawyers. The latter give guidance on how far cultural rights can be claimed without the risk of fines and imprisonment. Aksamaz has summarised the orientation of these Lazi intellectuals as follows:

> Lazi intellectuals do not endorse/approve of ethnic nationalism, neither do they sympathise with ethno-political organisations. However, they are sensitive to questions which concern the survival of their language. Lazi intellectuals are pursuing in their publications a dissemination policy appropriate to the solidarity of the peoples belonging to the culture of the Caucasus. Lazi intellectuals believe in universal values. They do not want new wars, internal and external migrations, hostility, dissension or new borders. They want a pluralist, participatory Turkey with all democratic institutions and rules, where they can speak and develop their own language and express themselves without fear.[27]

[21] For example there were articles on the position of women, local politics and economic matters; see Bellér-Hann 1995a.

[22] For an interview with the owner and editor of *Ogni* see *Azadi* 19–25 December 1993. No. 4, Another interview with a Lazi intellectual concerning *Ogni* was published in *Alaşara* 3. 1995, pp. 11–12. A notable forerunner of *Ogni* in the 1970s was the newspaper *Karadeniz Haber*. In the late 1990s some Hemşinli intellectuals in Istanbul launched a journal with an agenda roughly comparable to that of *Ogni*. It had an even shorter life. On the other hand a journal called *Hemşin*, devoted solely to regional (*yöresel*) topics, has appeared since the 1960s without disruption. It may be significant that Hemşin doubles as a place-name, and can therefore be accepted as a local or regional marker. Moreover, while Lazi have a distinctive ethnic marker in their Caucasian language, linguistic difference is a thing of the past for the great majority of Hemşinli. Their most visible 'marker' is their women's colourful headgear, which can conveniently be classified as a mere detail of folklore.

[23] In addition to substantial publications, such as Özgün 1996, Aksamaz 1997, Amicba 1993, Ersoy 1994, and Vanilişi and Tandilava 1992, journals aimed at wider audiences have translated international scholarly work on the Lazi and the Caucasus; see Allen 1995; Aksamaz 1995a, 1995b, 1996; Saxokia 1995; Hewitt 1996; Lomouri 1996.

[24] Zitaşi 1994.

[25] Reported in *Cumhuriyet*, 22–28 January 1993. The initiative was attacked in *Hürriyet*, 5 February 1993, p. 4 (German edition).

[26] For an interview with members of the rock group see *Cumhuriyet*, 19 March 1994. Apparently the group has given concerts in Lazistan itself, but it is based in Istanbul. A CD entitled 'Lazuri Birabape – Heyamo' (Lazi Songs – Heyamo) was released by Birol Topaloğlu in 1997.

[27] Aksamaz 1997: 45. Aksamaz has translated some of our earlier articles into Turkish, even though our perspectives do not always coincide with his own. See Bellér-Hann 1999.

There is no consensus among the activists about how best to promote the Lazi cause. Some favour putting it forward within the framework of Black Sea identity in general, others stress 'the Pontic synthesis', drawing attention to the Greek heritage of the Black Sea region, while a third discourse focuses more narrowly on Lazi identity itself, emphasises ties with the peoples of the Caucasus, especially Mingrelians, and connections with ancient Colchis as the original homeland. The question of ties with today's Georgians remains open.[28] These on-going debates are, for the most part, waged by second- or third-generation migrants in Istanbul who speak little or no Lazuri, and whose visits to the 'homeland' are short and sporadic. Theirs is the expression of a new identity rooted in knowledge of difference as perceived in the big cities. It is hard for these activists to connect with the concerns and identities felt by the people who live permanently in Lazistan, even if they have close relatives there. The great majority of people in the Lazi counties are completely unaware of this activity in the diaspora.[29]

Ogni also published contributions from a longstanding advocate of Lazi culture, the German scholar Wolfgang Feurstein, who has conducted research into the language, material culture and mythology of the Lazi since the early 1970s. His conviction that the Lazi are an endangered people is diametrically opposed to the constitutional stand taken by the Turkish authorities. Alongside scholarly publications, Feurstein has worked on the production of a romanised Lazuri alphabet and pedagogical materials to enable more Lazi to become literate in their mother tongue.[30] He encourages the duplication of these materials, which are taken to Turkey by returning labour migrants. However, few Lazi in the home region are aware of the existence of these materials and many continue to scoff at the very idea that Lazuri could be written down and taught in schools alongside Turkish.

Feurstein's position is not one that we can endorse, but it is impossible not to feel a lot of sympathy with his goals.[31] He does not presume, as an outsider, to tell the Lazi who they really are. He does not see his efforts, and those of other intellectuals inside Turkey, as a process of ethnogenesis, the creation of a new ethnic identity. On the contrary, as he sees it people deserve the opportunity to hold on to an identity that has been theirs for centuries. He argues that the Lazi are an *Ethnie* or *Volk*. Close examination of their material culture demonstrates, in his view, that they share a common 'Colchian' heritage with Mingrelians. This

---

[28] We thank Alexandre Toumarkine for sharing information concerning the evolving discourse of Lazi intellectuals in Istanbul.

[29] We have, however, recently been informed that Lazuri songs are now played by local radio stations within the homeland – in slots devoted to local folklore.

[30] Much of Wolfgang Feurstein's work on the Lazi remains unpublished, notably his dissertation (1983); for a concise summary of his stance see Feurstein 1991, 1992a, 1992b, 1992c; his Lazuri alphabet is presented in Feurstein 1991.

[31] The emphasis of Feurstein's work has changed over the years. In some of his earlier work he presented the Lazuri-speaking belt as the exclusive homeland of the Lazi, overlooking the presence of Hemşinli and others in their midst. The group he organised at that time in Germany was called *Lazebura*. Since 1992, however, he has been the principal *animateur* of a *Verein* called *Kulturkreis Katschkar*, which addresses not only the Lazi but all the other long-established peoples of the southern Caucasus. For further comparative discussion of Feurstein's activities see Hann 1995a, Hann 1997. The volumes in which these articles appear offer useful guides to the current state of play in the scholarly literature on questions of identity, ethnicity and nationalism; the first is multi-disciplinary, the second is exclusively anthropological.

affinity has not, in Feurstein's analysis, been 'essentially' weakened by centuries of interaction with Greeks, Turks and Armenians, nor by Islamisation. This evolved Lazi identity now faces the threat of extinction because Turkish nationalism refuses to acknowledge its existence. Feurstein argues that the modern Turkish state (for example, through chauvinist historians such as Kırzıoğlu, whose work was noted in Chapter 2) is denying its minorities their rights to express their cultural identity. He sees himself as contributing to the efforts of Lazi intellectuals themselves to widen the sphere of choice for the Lazi. A Gellnerian would see them all as 'awakeners', as the forgers of a common ethnic identity for people who have not experienced this form of groupness hitherto. It might, however, be held that Gellner's model is no longer appropriate since he did not explicitly address the issue of continued linguistic and ethnic diversity in states that have experienced several generations of national homogenisation.

Feurstein's work has attracted admiration and support from the distinguished Scottish journalist Neal Ascherson, who has a generic sympathy with the causes of small nations. After visiting Lazistan and interviewing Feurstein at his home in Germany, Ascherson devoted one of his columns in the *Independent on Sunday* to a portrait of Wolfgang Feurstein as a man undertaking a noble mission, bringing not just an alphabet but a new sense of nationhood to the Lazi. How could anyone fail to support the rights of the Lazuri language and the Lazi culture?[32] Our response was to write to the newspaper criticising the journalist's romantic exaggerations and political naivety. We pointed out, as we have argued in this book, that identities are multiple and complex. At present, few Lazi see themselves as constituting an *etnik grup*. They feel more strongly about other belongings: to localities, to counties, to their country and to the universal community of Islam, and these by no means exhaust their options. Just before Ascherson's article appeared in 1993, the best football team in Britain, Manchester United, had been knocked out of a European competition by Turkey's best, Galatasaray. This team is based in Istanbul, some eight hundred miles away from Lazistan, yet it enjoys the passionate support of many Lazi (as well as of the Kurdish leader Abdullah Öcalan). The example is not trivial: sports offer a good illustration of the kind of identification that Gellner expects a modern state-nation to develop. In short, we suggested that it was a mistake to place such great weight on just one type of identity in the modern world. Ascherson implied that the Lazi were all busy discovering their folk poetry and looking forward to the day when laws would be promulgated in their own language. But this was very far indeed from the realities we had observed. We also suggested that to promote the cause of the Lazi in this way could easily lead to a denial or foreclosing of currently popular identity options – including the option of following the fortunes of your favourite football team in your favourite mass circulation newspaper.

We do, of course, understand why people should be concerned for the Lazi. In not recognising the language and denying Lazi the right to organise cultural associations, the Turkish state is imposing constraints that go against the grain

[32] Neal Ascherson's article about the Lazi in the *Independent on Sunday* was published on 7 November 1993; an abbreviated version of our response appeared in the following issue. Ascherson has included parts of his material in his volume *Black Sea* (1995). His text is discussed in more detail in Hann 1997.

Plate 8.1 Girls dressed in Hemşinli costume dance the *horon* at the opening of the tea 'campaign', 1992, Pazar.

Plate 8.2 Traditional Lazi village house, Fındıklı.

not only of current European thinking about language policy but also the ethical codes of anthropology, the study of human diversity. How can anthropologists stand back and watch as the distinctiveness of the Lazi is obliterated by the relentless pressure of the modern Turkish state? There is no easy resolution to this dilemma. Many anthropologists have become actively engaged in the causes of 'threatened cultures', but such engagement is problematic when the people themselves emphasise only the benefits that they have gained from the processes of modernisation. Does the existence of a group name, a language, a body of oral literature and perhaps a few other traits of difference, mainly in material culture, add up to the human social equivalent of an endangered species? For Feurstein, the Lazi constitute a *Volk* and have done so over many centuries on the basis of their unique independent culture (*eigenständige Kultur*). By careful study of the language and of surviving folk tales he can gain insight into the ancient roots of the culture, perhaps into ethnogenesis of the Lazi *Volk*. This can be termed the Herderian style in anthropology, based on a romantic notion of culture as an evolving organic whole. Similar notions are found in various schools of 'national ethnography', whose work contributed to the formation of national ideologies in many parts of the world, notably in central and eastern Europe.

An anthropological analysis based on Malinowskian methods is bound to yield quite different results. Malinowski, too, subscribed implicitly to the holistic Herderian perspective that assumed the world to be composed of neatly bounded units. Functionalist anthropologists could thus produce synchronic accounts of 'the so and so', and congratulate themselves on having overcome the errors of speculative evolutionism and diffusionism. At the same time, the Malinowskian emphasis upon fieldwork led to the dominance of 'presentist' approaches. The anthropologist enquired into what people did, said and thought at a particular time, and disregarded the ways in which all of these things have been shaped by the past. Our approach to the Lazi has been basically synchronic in this sense. In the highly mobile and interdependent social worlds of the late twentieth century, we have found that the identifications that matter to Lazi people cover a wide range, from those given by birth to those acquired by adopting particular careers, consumer styles, places of residence etc. Somewhere in all of this a subjective identification as Lazi remains significant, but it is a small subset of a thick portfolio of identities. People do not think about it much and they have trouble in explaining exactly what it means to them. As we have seen, it is nowadays difficult to pinpoint any beliefs or practices that distinguish the Lazi from their neighbours. Only a few stereotypes of group attributes are readily elicited, to be set alongside the uneven persistence of their language. Lazi do not use narratives of the past to claim group unity: some say their ancestors must have come from the Caucasus, others suggest that it might have been Central Asia. The Lazi themselves, it would seem, are fundamentally presentist, lacking a Herderian sense of their group as a solidary entity moving and developing through time. The suggestion that the present Lazuri-speaking population constitutes an entity with its own unique 'spiritual culture' is foreign to the Lazi themselves.

From this perspective, ethnogenesis is not something which took place back in the mists of time, which a patient scholar can try to illuminate and to recon-struct. Rather, it is the process getting underway now, as groups of enthusiasts set about giving the Lazi a sense of unified identity that they have never possessed in the past. With this diagnosis we line up with Ernest Gellner and 'modernist' theories of national identity. We do not, however, follow an extreme presentist view that neglects altogether the weight of the past and its influence on the shaping of identities. Historical evidence, where it is available, must be taken carefully into account.[33] Sometimes that evidence will show that specific claims, perhaps strongly and sincerely held by large numbers of people, are in fact spurious. Many Lazi see keeping *atmaca* as a distinctive custom of their group, and they feel uncomfortable, perhaps somehow diminished, when told, by a local teacher who has investigated the matter, that this practice almost certainly originates among Circassians. Awkward moral issues arise in dealing with the evidence of the past, but that is no reason for distorting or suppressing that evidence.[34] Neal Ascherson implicitly accepts such a standard when he makes it clear that he has little sympathy with the 'revival' of the Don Cossacks in the wake of the collapse of the Soviet Union. In this case Ascherson recognises 'contradiction' when he sees it, and refers despairingly to 'the bazaar of ethnic and linguistic nationalism which is selling quick identities all around the Black Sea.'[35] Yet he believes the Lazi case to be authentic and convincing, though at present it hardly commands greater popular support than that of the Cossacks. Clearly Ascherson believes, as does Feurstein, that the persistence of a different language in this case gives the Lazi a stronger right to assert their difference. We would simply say that, thanks to the persistence of Lazuri, Lazi intellectuals have the more promising materials to work with as they elaborate their claims to distinctiveness. They cannot be sure of success. The aspirations of Lazi activists, currently ignored or repressed by the Turkish state, have to cope with the difficulty that so many Lazuri speakers, like so many Kurds, have preferred to adopt the dominant language and the national allegiance it implies.[36]

Those who hold that the ethnocidal policies of the Kemalist authorities are to blame for the failure of the Lazi people to realise their true identity as an ethnic group or nation are implying that they have been somehow taken in, duped by Turkish nationalist propaganda. Yet historical evidence suggests that the accommodations of Lazuri speakers date back to Ottoman times, when they gave up their religion, gave up rules of exogamy, and began to identify ever more strongly with the imperial state and to use its main language.[37] Like Frenchmen who have forgotten that their ancestors were Normans, Franks, or whatever,

[33] The most eloquent exponent of historically informed approaches to nationalism is Anthony D. Smith. See e.g. Smith 1986: Ch. 1 for an exposition of how his approach differs both from the modernism of Gellner and the 'primordialism' of other scholars.

[34] Thus the historical accounts of Bryer and Feurstein are always to be preferred to those of Kırzıoğlu, quite irrespective of how many Lazi may have read and accepted the latter's accounts of their past.

[35] Ascherson 1995: 103.

[36] For comparative discussion of language policies see Weinstein 1990, Coulmas 1991. It is highly probable that Turkey will come under increasing pressure from other European governments to protect small languages and to respect 'minority rights' more generally. In 1992 the Council of Europe approved a 'European Charter for regional or minority languages' which spoke of 'inalienable' rights to use such languages, in the public sphere as well as privately. As of 1999 Turkey had not signed or ratified this Charter or its associated Convention. (For the full texts see *Nationalities Papers* 27 (1), Appendices A and B: 139–66).

[37] Cf. Benninghaus 1989a.

there are plenty of Turks who have forgotten their origins in groups such as Lazi or Hemşinli. Neither they nor the people who identify today as Lazi deserve to be patronised or treated as children by outsiders. At the moment there is little interest in the home region in pursuing the kind of recognition that Feurstein and Istanbul activists are seeking: the freedom to produce dictionaries, to teach the language in local schools and to establish a museum or two. If the activists were free to operate more openly, more Lazi might be receptive to such initiatives, especially if they thought that a little 'heritage chic' would stimulate tourism and be good for their businesses. It would be wrong, however, to insinuate that people feel some inner craving for improved recognition of Lazi identity. However paradoxical this may be for a phenomenon that is by definition collective, ethnicity, if it is felt at all, is confined to the private sphere. The explicit assertion of such an identity *could*, however, become a strong public force, analogous to the militant tendency in religion and qualitatively different from 'muddling through' between the other identifications we have considered, if ethnicity develops further as a focus for reflection and debate in Turkey as a whole.

9
Conclusion

'Countries vary, but civilisation is one, and for a nation to progress it must take part in this single civilisation.' – Mustafa Kemal (Atatürk), 1924.[1]

'The cultural is the social viewed from another perspective, not a distinct analytic entity.'[2]

The regional balance sheet

The storms that brew when weather systems collide with the Kaçkar Mountains wreak havoc on the people of the coastal zone and their environment. The new roads into the interior are regularly blocked or washed away. Even the main road along the coast is occasionally closed by landslides, particularly the cliffs in the vicinity of Arhavi. The harbour constructed in Hamsılı in the 1960s has long silted up. Over decades, political parties promised before each general election that they would fund the necessary dredging work but the job was never done. In 1999 the promise was linked to the new motorway construction but villagers have become sceptical and many now give their votes to the religious party.

The topography and remoteness of Lazistan have posed challenges to the planners of high modernity, and the best efforts of the harbour and road builders to tame nature have not been entirely successful. What can we conclude about the efforts of the social engineers? At times in the twentieth century, especially after 1950, Turkey was a plausible exemplar for poor non-western countries wishing to develop and to modernise their societies. At the end of the century it is just as commonly perceived as an exemplar of James Scott's analysis of 'how certain schemes to improve the human condition have failed'.[3] Economic growth has held up well, but governments have lacked stability and human rights have not been respected. A sense of potential unfulfilled is commonly expressed in Istanbul and Ankara too, and disillusion is by no means restricted to supporters of the religious party. What went wrong? Was it a mistake to break so drastically with the past and to transplant so many institutions from the west? Şerif Mardin, for example, argues that the Kemalists, with their rational and bureaucratic principles, failed to address the heart and the sentiments of traditional Ottoman-

---

[1] Quoted in Lewis 1961: 287.
[2] Goody 1992: 30.
[3] Scott 1998.

214

Turkish society. In particular, the attempt of these Jacobins to curtail the influence of Islam was a recipe for enduring social dissonance.[4]

But just how radical was the Kemalist rupture? We have tried to present a more nuanced account. Kemalism was certainly radical at the level of institutions, but it could not sweep aside deep-seated continuities, both at the level of ideas and everyday practices, notably in the ideology of patriarchy. The programmes of the modernist officials were softened and subverted. The central state was in some ways 'domesticated', it was integrated into the constitution of social and personal identities. Kemalism was not, to use Scott's term, '*métis*-friendly'. On the contrary, Turkish modernity drove a coach and horses through most fields of local, 'practical knowledge', in Lazistan as elsewhere. The tea monoculture, and the disappearance of the old crafts and housebuilding techniques, have destroyed vast resources of traditional knowledge. Yet 'social cognition' in the sense of Paul Stirling has expanded. People may no longer know the traditional forms of fishing and hunting, but they learn how to get jobs and buy real estate in Istanbul, how to protect the value of their cash savings, and how to discriminate between alternative religious orientations. Personal and kin networks are at least as vital in these processes as formal qualifications, and the rules are essentially the same wherever you go in the country. Some observers may be saddened by this standardisation, but the inhabitants of the peripheral region that we have examined in this book do not see themselves as prostrate before the centralised state. They are better approached as proud members of a vibrant state-nation than as passive victims of an undiluted ideology of high modernity.

Scott does not discuss Turkey in his *tour de force*. He is careful to qualify his position and to note that some state interventions can be beneficial. But he holds on tenaciously to the dichotomy between state and society, a dichotomy that has been basic to western political theory and prominent in a good deal of political anthropology. We do not find this dichotomous approach to be much help in accounting for the experience of modernity in Lazistan. There is a sense in which the Kemalist state 'discovered' the new national society and committed most of the sins identified by Scott in other cases. Democratic controls did not exist in the early phase of the republic and they have remained imperfect. The defects and drawbacks have been identified by countless commentators, both Turkish and foreign. As for anthropologists, most feel uncomfortable with the terms that mattered most to the Turkish modernists, terms such as progress, emancipation and freedom. There is too little agreement on their meanings, or on the methods used to promote them. None of these terms has especially strong echoes in contemporary Lazistan; but neither does *métis* or anything resembling it. A concept with rather greater resonance here is *medeniyet*, usually translated as 'civilisation'. This is a term with an important place in both Mardin's traditional stream and in the Kemalist stream, an indication that the disjuncture between the two may not be quite as great as he claims. Many people in Lazistan say that their level of *medeniyet* has continued to rise in recent decades, and that it is much higher than that of stricter, 'fundamentalist' Islamic countries.

Despite some critical disillusionment in recent decades, very few inhabitants of the region discussed in this book would write off Turkey's modernisation as a

---

[4] Mardin 1989, 1996.

failure. By many criteria, not least in comparison with socialist passages to modernity, a comparison which in the 1990s they have been able to make themselves at first hand, the Turkish republic has enjoyed a very substantial measure of success. Let us summarise the main points of our analysis. In this region the state was the prime mover in what seemed for a long time to be a remarkably coherent development strategy, based on tea as a cash crop. Later the state principle conceded more and more ground to the principle of the market. While these moves were welcomed by entrepreneurs, the application of liberal policies in the tea sector caused major problems. The new 'Russian markets' attracted hostility as well as customers, but all along the people of Lazistan have become more closely integrated into a national, consumer-oriented society, which filters the forces of globalisation.

The fluctuating balance between the principles of state and market has affected most aspects of 'civil society', but here the continuities are pronounced. Men and women participate in some formal groups, for the most part separately, but their informal networks are much more significant. The family remains the strongest source of identity and gender divisions remain deeply entrenched, though simple generalisations about women's subordination are risky. We saw also that Islam continues to play a vital role in the moulding of the person in modern Lazistan. It is explicitly rejected only by a tiny minority. A rather larger minority wishes radically to expand the role of religion into other areas of social life and 'fundamentalist' views have gained strength in some parts of Lazistan in recent years.

How can all these factors be brought together into one balance sheet? People hold different opinions about them. The same individuals hold significantly different views at different points in their lives. Perhaps most people in modern Lazistan live every day of their lives in something of a muddle of ambiguities and contradictions. (If so, would this make them any different from most other human beings?) We met very few people who rejected the specifically Turkish version of modernity that has been achieved in Lazistan over the last three quarters of a century. If pressed to draw up a balance sheet, many people emphasise the material gains they have made. This region has profited more than most others from state funding. The entire tea economy can be judged as an extravagant waste if assessed strictly according to the criteria of the international market place. The Tea Corporation is derided by neo-liberal radicals in the private sector as a great machine for pumping public money into Lazistan. But as a result of this economic transformation the old poverty has been almost completely eradicated. Inequalities remain, but people are better housed and fed, and everyone has access to medical and educational services that never existed previously. The buoyant market economy has provided opportunities for serious money-making only to a relatively small entrepreneurial stratum, but it has provided almost everyone with previously undreamed of comforts and consumption possibilities. People are more mobile than ever before thanks to modern arteries of communication, but migration has become one option among others rather than the only available survival strategy.

On the debit side, leaving aside the dubious economics of the tea industry, there are many who believe that the advent of this monoculture has damaged the natural ecology of their beautiful region. The Black Sea itself has been damaged, perhaps irreversibly, through over-fishing and pollution. The social impact of these changes has not been severe in Lazistan, which has become less dependent on the sea than at any time in its history. The losses that people notice more pertain to intangibles, to knowledge and 'the quality of life'. People speak about a 'spoiling' (*bozulmuş*) of human social relations and a decline in traditional values. The ease with which money can be made from tea has made people lazy, especially in some of the more eastern counties, where the owners of large estates put out all the work to sharecroppers. People who formerly prided themselves on their diligence and energy have grown flabby. Too many local youth are pampered, say their parents and grandparents. In Lazistan these concerns are often connected to a concern with sexual morality and honour. In particular, the influx of tourist-traders from the east created a sense of moral crisis. This was the background against which some people became committed in a new and deliberate way to the principal bulwark of their spiritual civilisation, Islam.

But even those who make this turn are far from seeking to turn back the clock. Many of those who campaign vigorously for the religious party say that they want more rather than less modernisation in Lazistan. They claim that their party is less prone to corruption, and more committed to an egalitarian distribution of resources: ideals that they see as both rooted in Islam and thoroughly modern. Here a more general chord is struck. People in Lazistan tend to compare themselves not with the poor farmers of the Anatolian interior, but with the urban dwellers in the west of the country who exemplify Turkish modernity. Compared to Istanbul and Izmir, young people in Lazistan are conscious of living on the periphery. They know little of the poverty that preceded the arrival of tea, but they see that the region is still losing population, that many of their villages are depopulated in the winter months, that few employment possibilities are offered locally, and that it is much more difficult for them to pass the examinations for entry into higher education than it is for more privileged pupils in the big cities. Others voice concerns about health issues – malaria is no longer a problem, and goitre is nowadays rare, but the dampness of the climate is held responsible for high rates of rheumatism, among both men and women, and state medical provision is compared unfavourably to that available in the more western regions. In short, rather than being anti-modern or precociously post-modern, what most people seem to want is *more* modernisation. They desire closer integration into their national society, and an end to the pattern of westwards migration which continues to lure many of the most able away from their homeland, often permanently, and thereby to intensify the sentiment of peripherality among those who are left behind.

Modernity, culture, civilisation

A further purpose of this study was to explore changing social identities. Many of these are by no means specific to this region and even those which are also raise issues of more general concern, and not only to academics. This applies especially to that form of identity known as ethnicity. However this is defined, a modern ethnic group is something quite different from an Ottoman *millet*. At the beginning of the twenty-first century ethnicity is still very much an external discourse for most inhabitants of Lazistan. But many people in this region do identify themselves as Lazi, Hemşinli or Georgian, even if these categories go unrecognised by the state. There are signs that the global discourse of ethnicity is gaining ground in Turkey. Paradoxically, the nationalist ideology of the Kemalists has created fertile soil for new seeds of this kind. Both 'national' governments and 'ethnic' activists advance strong claims for cultural unity. Unfortunately, however, there has been much confusion in the anthropological literature concerning the core concepts of ethnicity and culture. We too have written loosely throughout this book about the 'linguistic and cultural diversity' of Lazistan, but in fact language is almost the sole basis for 'ethnic' differentiation, and even this basis has been seriously eroded.

We have argued that Kemalism has succeeded in establishing the country *Türkiye*, the 'state-nation' as we have termed it, as the prime *societal* framework for the overwhelming majority of its citizens (not to speak of a substantial part of the diaspora). Granted, supra-national forces have an impact on Lazistan, notably in consumption patterns, and granted, some local and regional specificities remain significant. Nonetheless modern Turkey approximates quite closely to Ernest Gellner's ideal type of modernity, which conceives society as a sharply bounded block, united by a dominant literary language and educational system. This can be termed a 'societal culture', though the latter word is arguably superfluous in this context. The anthropologists who have done fieldwork in small towns and villages elsewhere in Anatolia would quickly feel themselves at home in Lazistan. This was not inevitable. Historical evidence suggests that the people of this region became firmly oriented towards Istanbul and Ottoman Turkish civilisation from the fifteenth century onwards, but the present integration into Turkish society is nonetheless based on contingencies. If different political boundaries had been negotiated in the early 1920s, comparable processes of modernisation would have integrated the population of Lazistan eastwards and they would now be communicating in Georgian and Russian.

Does this homogenisation mean that modern Turkish society has a unitary and sharply bounded culture? Gellner's answer is yes. The culture of Lazistan, in his macrosense, differs little from the societal culture. It is true that the material culture (including agri*culture*) shows regional specificities, and that some of the value orientations are linked to universal Islam and not confined to Turkey. Yet even this aspect of spiritual culture is felt by many to be congruent with the national society: being a Muslim is inseparable from being a Turk.

Gellner's model takes national cultures as the hallmark of industrial modernity but it does not explain why some nationalisms are so much stronger than others. Nor does it help in understanding why, after several generations of strong nationalism in Turkey, activists should now be advancing claims for ethnic recognition on behalf of Lazi and Hemşinli, people who have been among the leading material beneficiaries of Kemalist modernisation. It is clear that these people have experienced radical changes over the centuries: in their religion, in their marriage customs, and (especially in the Hemşinli case) in their language habits. The homogenising tendencies did not originate with Kemalism but they have

Plate 9.1 Old Lazi village house and granary, near Çamlıhemşin.

Plate 9.2 The festival at Ayder, 1993.

intensified in this period, especially after the introduction of tea and the improvement of communications. Yet there evidently remains a sense in which one can speak of 'the Lazi', given that they have a common self-designation, and that this has a basis in Lazuri, their language. Despite the considerable diversity within this group, in economic adaptations, in religion, and also in language (dialects), it is possible to imagine the standardisation of the language and homogenisation of Lazi culture according to basically the same recipe as that followed earlier by the social engineers of the Turkish state-nation, only now on a smaller scale. Should such efforts be encouraged in order to preserve Lazi distinctiveness in future generations? Is it possible to conceive that this could lead one day to a *thick* Lazi societal culture, in the way that, say, Uyghurs have developed a thick societal culture within the Chinese state?

Our position is that local people themselves should be able to determine what kind of identities they wish to cherish and develop. If Lazi wish to strengthen their sense of groupness as Lazi, and perhaps forge new links with their linguistic relatives over the border, the Mingrelians, it would seem churlish to prevent them from doing so.[5] In any case, experience suggests that attempts to deny such aspirations, once they exist, are likely to prove counterproductive. In our view, 'concessions' by the state in the field of minority rights would have no far-reaching repercussions for people's inner sense of self. Lazi would still wish to maintain and develop the extensive repertoire of identities they have built up within the modern Turkish state.

Our definition of Lazistan corresponds neither to the ethnic definition, which would draw a line where Lazuri speakers begin at Melyat, nor to the loose, popular sense of Laz, which would draw it anywhere between Trabzon and Sinop. We are especially uncomfortable with drawing a sharp line at Melyat because the continuities between Lazuri speakers to the east and the 'unmarked' Turks of rural Çayeli to the west are overwhelming. Our conception of Lazistan corresponds loosely to the boundaries of an Ottoman sub-province but we emphasised the arbitrariness of these. There is no sharp geographical or cultural boundary west of Rize, only gradual changes in landscape and settlement forms as you move closer to Trabzon, changes that continue as you move further west, to Giresun and Ordu. The east Black Sea as a whole has some measure of unity, but no sharp line can be drawn at Samsun or Sinop either.

The ethnic boundaries between Lazi and Hemşinli persist in stereotypes and symbols but play virtually no role in determining social interaction. At the Ayder festival in August 1993 (discussed briefly in Chapter 4) we asked villagers about *horon* dance styles and were told that Hemşinli, Lazi and 'unmarked' Turks all danced in the same way. Lazi did not regard this as a festival hosted by the Hemşinli, just because Ayder was traditionally a Hemşinli *yayla*. It was a Lazi festival too. Some Lazi girls wore the bright orange and black headscarf (*puşi*) that is usually seen as Hemşinli costume. The festival exuded the techniques that nationalists have used in the promotion of cultural homogeneity; but every question we asked revealed the essential hollowness of such programmes. The state

---

[5] Simplification of the procedures for foreign travel, to enable the Turkish citizens of Lazistan to move more freely and see their neighbours in the Caucasus with their own eyes, would at least help to overcome some of the wilder stereotypes about these people that have arisen in recent years.

was promoting a celebration of the folk customs not of the Lazi or the Hemşinli, but of the entire Black Sea region. Artists were brought in from far afield, including a troupe of male folk dancers from Akçaabat near Trabzon with a national reputation. But schoolchildren were also recruited to perform dances that were described as local, and selection for these groups did not depend on ethnicity. Lazi secondary school pupils had no difficulty in donning Hemşinli costumes if required. All performers were warmly received apart from the state officials, but this was indifference and hardly a sign of subversion or resistance to authority.

The Ayder festival was inaugurated and orchestrated 'from above' but, like the Kemalist project in general, it has been shaped and creatively adapted by ordinary people. The people of Lazistan have been developing their own 'local specificities of modernity'[6] for a long time, but they have not done so in ethnic terms. Instead, we have noted many other registers of identity, some of which unite and some of which divide. The former category has at least four modalities. First, the people of this territory share the same religion: Islam unites the people of Lazistan not only with each other and with the rest of Turkey, but potentially with a vast global community ('Islamic culture'). Second, in the regulation of their interpersonal lives the people of Lazistan have held on to many practices that predate Kemalist modernity, many of them rooted in ideas concerning honour and shame, the core of which is to be found in all neighbouring regions, Christian as well as Muslim ('traditional culture'). Third, they have long been among the most loyal Turkish patriots, supporters of secular power-holders in the remote cities of Istanbul and Ankara ('national culture'). Fourth, they have become participants in a new global community, based on fast communications and consumerism ('global capitalist culture').

Other factors are divisive. Contrary to Gellner's ideal type, which emphasises equality of opportunity in the new societal culture, we have pointed to structures of social exclusion, particularly the emergence of a new underclass ('culture of poverty'). We touched upon, differences in status, occupation, and educational levels.[7] The groups which form according to these 'class' criteria do not correspond to ethnic boundaries. Finally, many people have retained specific local identities to their market centres and to their villages and hamlets ('local culture').

No essentialising concept of 'ethnic culture' is powerful enough to transcend these multi-levelled and cross-cutting sources of identity. The persistence of Lazuri does not mean the persistence of a separate and intact folk culture, as a few activists now argue. On the contrary, if a Lazi folk culture gains recognition in the new century, it is bound to diverge radically from the beliefs and practices which evolved among Lazuri speakers in Ottoman and republican eras. The Lazi will need to acquire what Gellner calls an 'ironic' perspective on their own culture.[8] Even those who have grown up with some Lazuri will have to *learn* this culture. It will need to be viewed as a further phase of social engineering, and not as a *natural* reaction to the *métis*-unfriendly programmes of the Kemalists.

Culture remains the foundational concept of modern anthropology, but it has become increasingly problematic. The term became relativised and distinguished

[6] Kandiyoti 1997: 129.
[7] For detailed analyses of inequality in modern Turkey see Özbudun and Ulusan 1980.
[8] Gellner 1998: 190.

from civilisation in an age when distinctive customs, beliefs and practices could be tied more easily than they can today to territory. For Malinowski culture was not to be studied in terms of separable traits but as an integrated whole, as a 'reality *sui generis*'.[9] He himself paid close attention to material artefacts, to 'instrumental reality' and biological needs, but he pointed also to knowledge and 'mental habits' as an ultimate source. We prefer the formulation of Jack Goody, cited at the head of this chapter, because it points to the need to examine the social relations that lie behind beliefs and practices.

Unfortunately, the culture concept has been prone to essentialist and idealist biases. We have criticised the usage of the ethnographer Wolfgang Feurstein in the preceding chapter. Feurstein argues that the Lazi are an *Ethnie* or *Volk* whose fundamental links are to their eastern neighbours in the Caucasus; twelve hundred years of 'historical-political' orientation towards the west have not 'essentially' altered their culture. His approach emphasises material artifacts but he also argues that the Lazi share basic value orientations and 'spiritual culture'. We have also referred regularly to the work of two Chicago-trained anthropologists who have carried out fieldwork in neighbouring regions of Anatolia and built up their ensuing analyses on core cultural concepts. The ideas they stressed (honour in the case of Michael Meeker, procreation beliefs in the case of Carol Delaney) were not quite identical and our own focus upon ideas of *namahrem* is slightly different again. But we do not see any of these ideas as revealing the deep structures or innermost core of 'a culture'. They are important persisting ideas but they provide no ultimate key to understanding changing social identities. Finally Ernest Gellner is a self-confessed 'modernist' who rejects both the 'ethnographic antiquarianism' of Feurstein and the idealism of the American culturalists. Yet he, too, in the tradition of Herder and Malinowski, bases his model on the assumption that all human communities, the modern as well as the preindustrial, have their unique integrated cultures. The age of nationalism merely brings a new 'high' and consciously asserted form of cultural identity. This ordered, holistic approach perhaps served anthropology well in the past. It helped Malinowski to make sense of the Trobrianders, almost a century ago, but it does not seem to us to be of much use in the modern world, and certainly not in this corner of the Black Sea.

Anthropologists have studied culture in hugely various ways, from 'subcultures' to the alleged rise of 'global' or 'world' culture. Outside anthropology the term is used even more loosely: a culture can be attributed to anything at all, from a business corporation to motorway service stations, from Holocaust commemoration to mass sports. Our strategy has been to restrict usage of this problematic term to a minimum. We often need an adjective to describe behaviour that is not determined biologically or genetically, but *social* is usually sufficient. It will not do to argue that the four main linguistic communities in this region in late Ottoman times were four distinct cultures. These were not separate, self-sufficient groups, but people who interacted constantly. They no doubt exchanged 'cultural traits', and it might be argued that they were united by 'distinctive Ottomanist socio-political culture',[10] just as they were united later in the new 'societal

---

[9] Malinowski: 1937: 623.
[10] Meeker 1996: 49.

culture' of the Kemalists. But it is unclear what the term culture adds in these various usages.

Even if the concept of culture could be given a clear scientific definition that all anthropologists agreed upon, the term is hardly theirs to control any longer. The greatest danger, evident in other disciplines of the social sciences and everywhere in the world around us, is that culture is simplistically linked to language, ethnicity and national identity. This linkage was arguably implicit all along in the ideology of Kemalism, and may now be widely accepted in Turkey.[11] Kemalism has proved unable to devise an alternative basis for citizenship in the modern state. Given these tendencies, we conclude by joining the increasing number of anthropologists who argue that the culture concept is now more of a hindrance both to anthropological understanding and to the pursuit of more progressive, humanistic political programmes.[12] Perhaps the master concept of the discipline should be neither culture nor society, since in the age of nationalism both have acquired the unfortunate connotations of bounded units, but rather civilisation, with its unbounded richness. This opens an alternative way to justify recognition of Lazi distinctiveness: not because this is warranted in terms of a relativist, plural concept of *kültür*, but because it is consistent with the civilisational aspirations of Kemalist modernity, with the expansion of *medeniyet*.

[11]However, for most people in Lazistan at the end of the 1990s the prime meaning of *kültür* still seemed to be 'high culture' – in effect, it is a modern word for *medeniyet*.

[12]Our criticism of the culture concept extends to liberal theories of 'multiculturalism', as conceived by Taylor 1992 and many others. In our analysis, the Lazi and Hemşinli do not warrant recognition as separate 'cultures'. We recognise that some other potential communities in contemporary Turkey have weaker affinities to the state-nation than the people of Lazistan, both subjectively and objectively, but even in these cases it is unhelpful to think in terms of different cultures; all the various different groups and sub-groups of Kurds and Alevis are, like everyone else, engaged in a mesh of cross-cutting ties and 'muddling through'.

For recent scholarly contributions to the debate see *Current Anthropology*, Vol. 40, Supplement, February 1999. See also Kuper 1999.

Bibliography

Abadan-Unat, N. with D. Kandiyoti and M. Kıray (eds) 1981. *Women in Turkish Society*. Leiden: E.J. Brill.

Abu-Lughod, L. 1991. 'Writing against Culture' in R.G. Fox (ed.) *Recapturing Anthropology. Working in the Present*. Santa Fe: School of American Research Press.

Abu-Lughod, L. (ed.) 1998. *Remaking Women: Feminism and Modernity in the Middle East*. Princeton, NJ: Princeton University Press.

Acar, F. 1991. 'Women in the ideology of Islamic revivalism in Turkey: three Islamic women's journals' in R. Tapper (ed.) 1991. *Islam in Modern Turkey. Religion, Politics and Literature in a Secular State*. London: I.B. Tauris. pp. 280–303.

Adjarian, H. 1898. 'Étude sur la langue Laze' in *Mémoires de la société de Linguistique* 10: 145–60; 228–40, 364–401, 405–48.

Ahmed, A.S. 1992. *Postmodernism and Islam. Predicament and Promise*. London: Routledge.

Ahmed, A.S. and H. Donnan (eds) 1994. *Islam, Globalization and Postmodernity*. London: Routledge.

Ahmed, L. 1992. *Women and Gender in Islam. Historical Roots of a Modern Debate*. New Haven: Yale University Press.

Ak, O.N. 1999a. '1486 Tarihli Tapu. Tapu Tahrir defterine göre Fetihten sonraki Rize' in *Rize'min Sesi* 1 (1): 17–20.

—— 1999b. 'Lazistan sancağı merkezinin Rize'ye taşınması ve sancağa dair malumat' in *Rize'min Sesi* 1 (2): 17–19.

Akkaya, Ç. 1994. *Türkei-Sozialkunde. Wirtschaft, Beruf, Bildung, Religion, Familie, Erziehung* (Schriftenreihe des Zentrums für Türkeistudien 9). Opladen: Leske & Budrich.

Aksamaz, A. I. 1995a. 'Türkiye'de bir Kafkasya Dili: Lazca' in *Alaşara* 7–8: 14–15.

—— 1995b. 'Kafkasya kültür kökenli bir topluluk: Lazlar' in *Birikim* 71–2: 128–38.

—— 1996. 'Kafkasya'dan Anadolu'ya Lazlar' in *Alaşara* 11: 1–3.

—— 1997. *Kafkasya'dan Karadeniz'e Lazlar'ın Tarihsel Yolculuğu*. Istanbul: Çiviyazıları.

Akşit, B. 1991. 'Islamic education in Turkey: Medrese reform in late Ottoman times and Imam-Hatip schools in the republic' in R. Tapper (ed.) 1991. *Islam in Modern Turkey. Religion, Politics and Literature in a Secular State*. London: I.B. Tauris, pp. 145–70.

Allen, W. 1995. 'Eski Lazistan' in *Tarih ve Toplum* 143: 48–51.

Amicba, G. 1993. *Ortaçağ'da Abhazlar, Lazlar*. Istanbul: Nart Yayıncılık.

Anderson. B. 1983. *Imagined Communities*. London: Verso.

Andrews, P. (ed.) 1989. *Ethnic Groups in the Republic of Turkey*. Wiesbaden: Otto Harrassowitz.

—— forthcoming. *Ethnic Groups in the Republic of Turkey*. (Expanded, two volume edition), Wiesbaden: Otto Harrassowitz.

Ansay, T. 1987. 'Family Law' in T. Ansay and D. Wallace Jr (eds) 1987. *Introduction to Turkish Law*. Dewenter: Kluwer Law & Taxation Publishers (3rd ed.) pp. 139–56.

Ansay, T. and D. Wallace Jr (eds) 1987. *Introduction to Turkish Law*. Dewenter: Kluwer Law and Taxation Publishers (3rd ed.)

Antoun, R. T. 1968. 'On the modesty of women in Arab Muslim villages: a study in the accom-modation of traditions' in *American Anthropologist* 70: 671–97.

Ardener, S. 1964. 'The comparative study of rotating credit associations' in *Journal of the Royal Anthropological Institute* 94: 201–29.

Ardener, S. and S. Burman (eds) 1995. *Money-Go-Rounds. The Importance of Rotating Savings and Credit Associations for Women.* Oxford/Washington DC: Berg.

Ascherson, N. 1995. *Black Sea.* London: Jonathan Cape.

Aswad, B. 1974. 'Visiting patterns among women of the elite in a small Turkish city' in *Anthropological Quarterly* 47 (Jan.): 9–27.

—— 1978. 'Women, class and power: examples from the Hatay, Turkey' in L. Beck and N. Keddie (eds) *Women in the Muslim World.* Cambridge, Mass.: Harvard University Press, pp. 473–81.

Aydın, M. 1985. *Islam-Osmanlı Aile Hukuku.* Istanbul: Marmara Üniversitesi Ilahiyat Fakültesi Vakfı Yayınları. No. 11.

Banks, M. 1996. *Ethnicity; Anthropological Constructions.* London: Routledge.

Baran, I. 1999. ' Rize'li olmak' in *Rize'nin Sesi. Aylık Kültür, Sanat ve Haber Dergisi* 1 (1): 7.

Barth, F. (ed.) 1969. *Ethnic Groups and Boundaries. The Social Organisation of Cultural Difference.* London: Allen and Unwin.

Başgöz, I. and H. Wilson 1968. *Educational Problems in Turkey, 1920–1940.* Bloomington and the Hague: Indiana University Press.

Behar, C. 1995. 'Recent trends in Turkey's population' in Ç. Balım *et al.* (eds) *Turkey: Political, Social and Economic Challenges in the 1990s.* Leiden: E.J. Brill, pp. 97–106.

Bellér-Hann, I. 1994. 'Women, religion and beliefs in north-east Turkey', in *Proceedings of the Colloquium on Popular Customs and the Monotheistic Religions in the Middle East and North Africa. Budapest 1993. The Arabist.* Budapest Studies in Arabic VIII. Budapest: Eötvös L. University, pp. 257–82.

—— 1995a. 'Myth and history on the eastern Black Sea coast' in *Central Asian Survey* 14 (4): 487–508.

—— 1995b. 'Prostitution and its effects in northeast Turkey' in *The European Journal of Women's Studies* 2 (2): 219–35.

—— 1996. 'Informal associations among women in north-east Turkey' in G. Rasuly-Paleczek (ed.) *Turkish Families in Transition.* Frankfurt am Main: Peter Lang, pp. 114–38.

—— 1999a. 'Women, work and procreation beliefs in two Muslim communities' in P. Loizos and P. Heady (eds) *Conceiving Persons: Ethnographies of Procreation, Fertility and Growth.* London: Athlone.

—— 1999b. *Doğu Karadeniz de Efsane, Tarih, Kültür* (transl. Ali Ihsan Aksaumaz). Istanbul: Çiviyazıları/Mjora.

—— forthcoming. 'Hemşinli–Lazi relations in north-east Turkey' in H. Simonian (ed.) *The Hemshins. Peoples of the Caucasus and the Black Sea Series.* London: Curzon.

Benedict, P. 1974a. *Ula. An Anatolian Town.* Leiden: E.J. Brill.

—— 1974b. 'The *kabul günü*: structured visiting in an Anatolian provincial town' in *Anthropological Quarterly* 47 (Jan.): 28–47.

—— 1974c. 'Hukuk Reformu Acısından Başlık Parası ve Mehr' in A. Güriz and P. Benedict (eds) *Türk Hukuku ve Toplumu Üzerine Incelemeler.* Ankara: Türkiye Kalkınma Vakfı Yayınları, pp. 1–39.

—— 1976. 'Aspects of the domestic cycle in a Turkish provincial town', in J.G. Peristiany (ed.) *Mediterranean Family Structures.* Cambridge: Cambridge University Press, pp. 219– 43.

Benninghaus, R. 1989a.'The Laz: an example of multiple identification' in P. Andrews (ed.) *Ethnic Groups in the Republic of Turkey.* Wiesbaden: Otto Harrassowitz, pp. 497–501.

—— 1989b. 'Zur Herkunft und Identität der Hemşinli', in P. Andrews (ed.) *Ethnic Groups in the Republic of Turkey.* Wiesbaden: Otto Harrassowitz, pp. 475–97.

Berkes, N. 1964. *The Development of Secularism in Turkey.* Montreal: McGill University Press.

Bilgin, B. 1998. 'Religionsunterricht an den allgemeinbildenden Schulen in der Türkei' in H. Coşkun und S. Ağdemir (eds) *Bildungsdiskussion in der Türkei und in Deutschland. 8 Jahre Schulpflicht Religions-unterricht.* Ankara: Hacettepe-Taş, pp. 56–75.

Birken, A. 1976. *Die Provinzen des Osmanischen Reiches* Wiesbaden: Dr Ludwig Reichert Verlag.

Bohannan, P. and G. Dalton (eds) 1962. *Markets in Africa.* Evanston, IL: Northwestern University Press.

Borofsky, R. (ed.) 1994. *Assessing Cultural Anthropology*. New York: McGraw Hill.

Bouhdiba, A. 1985. *Sexuality in Islam*. London: Routledge and Kegan Paul.

Bozdoğan, S. and R. Kasaba (eds), 1997. *Rethinking Modernity and National Identity in Turkey*. Seattle: Washington University Press.

Braude, B. and B. Lewis (eds), 1982. *Christmas and Jews in the Ottoman Empire*. New York: Holmes.

Brendemoen, B. 1990a. 'The Turkish language reform and language policy in Turkey' in G. Hazai (ed.) *Handbuch der türkischen Sprachwissenschaft* Teil 1. Budapest: Akadémiai Kiadó, pp. 454–93.

—— 1990b. 'Laz influence on Black Sea Turkish dialects?' in B. Brendemoen (ed.) *Altaica Osloensia. Proceedings from the 32nd Meeting of the Permanent International Altaistic Conference, Oslo, June 12–16, 1989*. Oslo.

Bryer, A. 1966–7. 'Some notes on the Laz and Tzan' in *Bedi Kartlisa* 21–22: 174–95 and 23–24: 161–8.

—— 1969. 'The last Laz risings and the downfall of the Pontic Derebeys, 1812–1840' in *Bedi Kartlisa* 26: 191–210.

—— 1980. *The Empire of Trebizond and the Pontos*. London: Variorum Reprints.

—— 1988. *Peoples and Settlement in Anatolia and the Caucasus, 800–1900*. London: Variorum Reprints.

Bryer, A. and D. Winfield 1985. *The Byzantine Monuments and Topography of the Pontos* (2 volumes). Washington DC: Dumbarton Oaks Research Library and Collection.

Campbell, J. 1964. *Honour, Family and Patronage*. Oxford: Oxford University Press.

Casanova, J. 1994. *Public Religions in the Modern World*. Chicago: Chicago University Press.

Çelikoğlu, A. 1973. 'Karadeniz ve Karadenizli' in *Arhavi*, Özel Sayı 4.

Cohen, A. (ed.) 1974. *Urban Ethnicity* (ASA Monographs 12). London: Tavistock.

Comaroff, J. (ed.) 1980. *The Meaning of Marriage Payments*. London: Academic Press.

Cordan, B. 1998. '8-jährige chulpflicht in der Türkei: ziele und inhalte' in H. Coşkun and S. Ağdemir (eds) *Bildungsdiskussion in der Türkei und in Deutschland. 8 Jahre Schulpflicht Religionsunterricht*. Ankara: Hacettepe-Taş, pp. 20–32.

Coulmas, F. (ed.) 1991. *A Language Policy for the European Community*. Berlin: Mouton de Gruyter.

Cumhuriyetimizin 75 Yılında Rize. 1998. Ankara: Rize Il Özel Idaresi ve Istanbul Rize Kültür ve Sosyal Yardımlaşma Vakfı Başkanlığı.

Davis, J. 1977. *People of the Mediterranean. An Essay in Comparative Social Anthropology*. London: Routledge & Kegan Paul.

Davison, R. 1990. *Essays in Ottoman and Turkish History, 1774–1923. The Impact of the West*. Austin: University of Texas Press.

Delaney, C. 1986. 'The meaning of paternity and the virgin birth debate' in *Man* 21(3): 494–513.

—— 1991. *The Seed and the Soil: Gender and Cosmology in Turkish Village Society*. Berkeley: University of California Press.

—— 1993. 'Traditional modes of authority and co-operation' in P. Stirling (ed.) *Culture and Economy. Changes in Turkish Villages*. Huntingdon: Eothen Press, pp. 140–55.

—— 1995. 'Father state, motherland, and the birth of modern Turkey' in S. Yanagisako and C. Delaney (eds), *Naturalizing Power. Essays in Feminist Cultural Analysis*. New York, London: Routledge, pp. 177–99.

Dengler, I. 1978. 'Turkish women in the Ottoman empire: the classical age' in L. Beck and N. Keddie (eds) *Women in the Muslim World*. Cambridge (Mass.), London: Harvard University Press, pp. 229–44.

Deringil, S. 1998. *The Well-Protected Domains. Ideology and the Legitimation of Power in the Ottoman Empire 1876–1909*. New York: Tauris.

Dilley, R. (ed.) 1992. *Contesting Markets: Analyses of Ideology, Discourse and Practice*. Edinburgh: Edinburgh University Press.

Dodd, C. 1969. *Politics and Government in Turkey*. Manchester: Manchester University Press.

—— 1983. *The Crisis of Turkish Democracy*. Beverley: Eothen Press.

Dragadze, T. 1988. *Rural Families in Soviet Georgia. A Case Study in Ratcha Province*. London and New York: Routledge.

Dube, L. 1986. 'Seed and earth: the symbolism of biological reproduction and sexual relations of production' in L. Dube, E. Leacock and S. Ardener (eds) *Visibility and Power. Essays on Women in*

228 Bibliography

Society and Development. Delhi: Oxford University Press, pp. 22–53.

Duben, A. and C. Behar 1991. *Istanbul Households. Marriage, Family and Fertility, 1880–1940* (Cambridge Studies in Population, Economy and Society in Past Time). Cambridge: Cambridge University Press.

Dubetsky, A. 1976. 'Kinship, primordial ties and factory organization in Turkey: an anthropological view', in *International Journal of Middle East Studies* 7 (3): 433–51.

Dubisch, J. (ed.) 1986. *Gender and Power in Rural Greece*. Princeton, NJ: Princeton University Press.

Dumézil, G. 1937. *Contes Lazes*. Travaux et Mémoires de l'Institut d'Ethnologie, 27.

Dumézil, G. 1967. *Documents Anatoliens sur les langues et les traditions du Caucase. IV. Récits lazes en dialecte d' Arhavi (parler de Şenköy)*. Paris: Presses Universitaires de France (Bibliothèque de l'École des Hautes Études, Sciences Religieuses. Bd. LXXIV.)

Dwyer, D. and J. Bruce (eds) 1988. *A Home Divided. Women and Income in the Third World*. Stanford: Stanford University Press.

Eickelman, D. 1998. *The Middle East and Central Asia. An Anthropological Approach*. Upper Saddle River, New Jersey: Prentice Hall (third edition).

Eickelman, D. and J. Piscatori (eds) 1990. *Muslim Travellers: Pilgrimage, Migration and the Religious Imagination*. London: Routledge.

Erdentuğ N. 1969. 'Türkiye'nin Karadeniz Bölgesinde Evlenme Görenekleri ve Törenleri', Part I, in *Antropoloji* 4: 27–58.

—— 1971. 'Türkiye'nin Karadeniz Bölgesinde Evlenme Görenekleri ve Törenleri', Part II, in *Antropoloji* 5: 231–66.

—— 1975. 'Türkiye'nin Karadeniz Evlenme Görenekleri' in *Antropoloji* 7: 5–16.

Ergöçmen, B. A. 1997. 'Women's status and fertility in Turkey' in *Fertility Trends, Women's Status, and Reproductive Expectations in Turkey. Results of Further Analysis of the 1993 Turkish Demographic and Health Survey*. Ankara: Hacettepe University, Institute of Population Studies, pp. 79–104.

Eriksen, T. H. 1993. *Ethnicity and Nationalism: Anthropological Approaches*. London: Pluto.

Ersoy, H. 1994. *Rus gözüyle Kafkasya ve Kafkasya'lılar*. Istanbul: nart.

Evans-Pritchard, E. E. 1937. *Witchcraft, Oracles and Magic among the Azande*. Oxford: Clarendon.

Fallers, L. 1974. *The Social Anthropology of the Nation State*. Chicago: Aldine.

Fallers, L. and M. Fallers 1976. 'Sex roles in Edremit', in J. Peristiany (ed.) *Mediterranean Family Structures*. Cambridge: Cambridge University Press, pp. 243–61.

Featherstone, M. (ed.), 1990. *Global Culture: Nationalism, Globalization and Modernity*. London: Sage.

Featherstone, M. S. Lash and R. Roberston (eds) 1995. *Global Modernities*. London: Sage.

Feurstein, W. 1983. 'Untersuchungen zur materiellen kultur der Lazen'. Unpublished MA thesis. Universität Freiburg.

—— 1984. *Lazuri Alfabe; Lazca Alfabe; Entwurf eines Lazischen Alphabetes* (Parpali 1). Gundelfingen: Lazebura.

—— 1986a. 'Lazische ortsnamen und ihre bedeutung' in F. Thordarson (ed.) *Studia Caucasologica I. Proceedings of the Third Caucasian Colloquium, Oslo, July 1986*. Oslo: Norwegian University Press, pp. 51–68.

—— 1986b. 'Die gestalt des Waldmenschen (<Germakoçi>) im volksglauben der Lazen' in F. Thordarson (ed.) *Studia Caucasologica I. Proceedings of the Third Caucasian Colloquium, Oslo July 1986*. Oslo: Norwegian University Press, pp. 69–86.

—— 1991. *Nananena Lazca ders Kitabı Lasisches Schulbuch* (Parpali 2). Freudenstadt: Kaukasus-Verlag.

—— 1992a. *'Lasen' in Die Völker der Erde. Kulturen und Nationalitäten von A-Z*. Gütersloh/ München: Bertelsmann Lexicon Verlag, p. 206.

—— 1992b. 'Völker der Kolchis. Aspekte ihrer mythologie und möglichkeiten eines vergleichs' in C. Paris (ed.) *Caucasologie et mythologie comparée. Actes du Colloque international du C.N.R.S. – Ive Colloque de Caucasologie (Sèvres, 27–29 juin 1988)*. Paris: Peeters, pp. 127–37.

—— 1992c. 'Mingrelisch, Lazisch, Swanisch: alte sprachen und kulturen der kolchis vor dem baldigen untergang' in G. Hewitt (ed.) *Caucasian Perspectives*. Unterschleissheim/ München: Lincolm Europa, pp. 285–328.

—— 1994. 'Bir Alman gözüyle Lazlar' in *Ogni* 1 (2): 19–22.

Feurstein, W. and T. Berdsena 1987. 'Die Lasen. Eine Südkaukasische minderheit in der Türkei' in

Pogrom 129 (3): 36–9.

Fox, R. G. (ed.) 1990 *Nationalist Ideologies and the Production of National Cultures* (American Ethnological Society Monograph Series 2). Washington: American Anthropological Association.

Friedman, J. 1994. *Cultural Identity and Global Process*. London: Sage.

Gachechiladze, R. 1995. *The New Georgia: Space, Society, Politics*. London: UCL Press.

Geertz, C. 1963. *Peddlers and Princes. Social Development and Economic Change in Two Indonesian Towns*. Chicago: University of Chicago Press.

—— 1966. 'The rotating credit association: a "middle-rung" in development' in I. Wallerstein (ed.) *Social Change: the Colonial Situation*. New York: Wiley, pp. 420–46.

—— 1979. 'Suq: the bazaar economy in Sefrou' in C. Geertz, H. Geertz and L. Rosen (eds) *Meaning and Order in Moroccan Society*. Cambridge: Cambridge University Press.

—— 2000. *Available Light: Anthropological Reflections on Philosophical Topics*. Princeton: Princeton University Press.

Gellner, E. 1965 *Thought and Change*. London: Weidenfeld and Nicolson.

—— 1983. *Nations and Nationalism*. Oxford: Blackwell.

—— 1988. *Plough, Sword and Book: the Structure of Human History*. London: Collins Harvill.

—— 1992. *Postmodernism, Reason and Religion*. London: Routledge.

—— 1994a. *Conditions of Liberty: Civil Society and its Rivals*. London: Hamish Hamilton.

—— 1994b. 'The new circle of equity' in C. M. Hann (ed.) *When History Accelerates. Essays on Rapid Social Change, Complexity and Creativity*. London: Athlone, pp. 229–37.

—— 1995. *Anthropology and Politics. Revolutions in the Sacred Grove*. London: Routledge.

—— 1997. *Nationalism*. London: Weidenfeld and Nicolson.

—— 1998 *Language and Solitude. Wittgenstein, Malinowski and the Habsburg Dilemma*. Cambridge: Cambridge University Press.

Gilmore, D. (ed.) 1987. *Honor and Shame and the Unity of the Mediterranean*. Washington, DC: AAA.

Glavanis, K. and P. Glavanis (eds) 1989. *The Rural Middle East*. London: Zed.

Gökalp, Z. 1959. *Turkish Nationalism and Western Civilization*. London: Allen and Unwin.

Göle, N. 1992. *Modern Mahrem. Medeniyet ve Örtünme*. Istanbul: Metis Yayınlar.

—— 1996. *The Forbidden Modern. Civilization and Veiling*. Ann Arbor: The University of Michigan Press.

Good, M. 1978. 'A comparative perspective on women in provincial Iran and Turkey' in L. Beck and N. Keddie (eds) *Women in the Muslim World*. Cambridge, Mass.: Harvard University Press, pp. 482–500.

Goody, J. 1992. 'Culture and its boundaries: a European view' in *Social Anthropology* 1 (1): 9–32.

Grønhaug, R. 1974. *Micro-macro relations: social organization in Antalya, Southern Turkey*. Bergen: Department of Anthropology.

Günay, T. 1978. *Rize Ili ağızları*. Ankara: Kültür Bakanlığı.

Güriz, A. 1974. 'Evlilik dışı birleşmeler ve bu birleşmelerden doğan çocuklar' in A. Güriz and P. Benedict (eds) *Türk Hukuku ve Toplumu Üzerine Incelemeler*. Ankara: Türkiye Kalkınma Vakfı Yayınları, pp. 93–162.

Güriz, A. and P. Benedict (eds) 1974. *Türk Hukuku ve Toplumu Üzerine Incelemeler*. Ankara: Türkiye Kalkınma Vakfı Yayınları.

Güvenç, B. 1993. *Türk Kimliği: kültür tarihinin kaynakları*. Ankara: Kültür Bakanlığı.

Hale, W. 1981. *The Political and Economic Development of Modern Turkey*. London: Croom Helm.

—— 1996. 'Turkey, the Black Sea and Transcaucasia' in J.F.R. Wright, S. Goldenberg and R. Schofield (eds) *Transcaucasian Boundaries*. London: UCL Press, 54–70.

Hall, J.A. (ed.) 1996 *Civil Society: Theory, History, Comparison*. Cambridge: Polity.

—— (ed.) 1998 *The State of the Nation. Ernest Gellner and the Theory of Nationalism*. Cambridge: Cambridge University Press.

Hancıoğlu, A. 1997. 'Fertility trends in Turkey: 1978–1993' in *Fertility Trends, Women's Status, and Reproductive Expectations in Turkey. Results of Further Analysis of the 1993 Turkish Demographic and Health Survey*. Ankara: Hacettepe University, Institute of Population Studies, pp. 1–78.

Hann, C. 1985. ''Rural Transformation on the East Black Sea Coast of Turkey: a note on Keyder' in *Journal of Peasant Studies* 12(4).

230 Bibliography

—— 1990a. *Tea and the Domestication of the Turkish State*. Huntingdon: Eothen Press.

—— 1990b. 'Second thoughts on smallholders. Tea production, the state and social differentiation in the Rize region', in *New Perspectives on Turkey* 4: 57–79.

—— 1990c. 'Second economy and civil society', in C. M. Hann (ed.), *Market Economy and Civil Society in Hungary*. London: Frank Cass, pp. 21–44.

—— 1995. 'Intellectuals, ethnic groups and nations; two late twentieth century cases', in S. Periwal (ed.) *Notions of Nationalism*. Budapest: Central European University Press, pp. 106–28.

—— 1997. 'Ethnicity, language and politics in north-east Turkey', in C. Govers and H. Vermeulen (eds) *The Politics of Ethnic Consciousness*. London: Macmillan, pp. 121–56.

Hann, C. and I. [Bellér]-Hann 1992. 'Samovars and sex on Turkey's Russian markets' in *Anthropology Today* 8 (4): 3–6.

Hann, C. and I. Bellér-Hann 1998. 'Markets, morality and modernity in north-east Turkey', in T. Wilson and H. Donnan (eds) *Border Identities: Nation and State at International Frontiers*. Cambridge: Cambridge University Press, pp. 237–62.

Hann, C. and E. Dunn (eds) 1996. *Civil Society: Challenging Western Models*. London: Routledge.

Hannerz, U. 1992. *Cultural Complexity. Studies in the Social Organization of Meaning*. New York: Columbia University Press.

Heper, M. 1985. *The State Tradition in Turkey*. Beverley: Eothen Press.

Herzfeld, M. 1980 'Honour and shame: some problems in the comparative analysis of moral systems' in *Man* (N.S.) 15: 339–51.

Hewitt, G. 1996. 'Güney Kafkasya ve Megrel-Lazlar'ın Kültürel Hakları', in *Birikim* 85: 84–92.

Heyd, U. 1950. *Foundations of Turkish Nationalism*. London: Luzac and Co. and the Harvill Press.

Heyd, U. 1954. *Language Reform in Modern Turkey*. Jerusalem: Israel Oriental Society.

Hills, D. 1964. *My Travels in Turkey*. London: George Allen and Unwin.

Hobsbawm, E. and T. Ranger (eds) 1983. *The Invention of Tradition*. Cambridge: Cambridge University Press.

Holisky, D.A. 1991. 'Laz', in A. Harris (ed.) *The Indigenous Languages of the Caucasus. Vol. 1: The Kartvelian Languages*. Delmar, New York: Caravan Books, pp. 395–472.

Holy, L. 1989. *Kinship, Honour and Solidarity. Cousin Marriage in the Middle East*. Manchester: Manchester University Press.

Horten, M. 1918. *Die Religiöse Gedankenwelt des Volkes im Heutigen Islam*. Halle a. S.: Max Niemeyer.

Jarvie, I. 1964. *The Revolution in Anthropology*. London: Routledge and Kegan Paul.

Kafesoğlu, I. 1985. *Türk-Islam Sentezi*. Istanbul: Aydınlar Ocağı.

Kağıtçıbaşı, Ç. 1982. 'Sex roles, value of children and fertility' in Ç. Kağıtçıbaşı (ed.) *Sex Roles, Family and Community in Turkey*. Bloomington: Indiana University Press (Turkish Studies 3), pp. 151–80.

Kalafat, Y. 1990. *Doğu Anadolu'da Eski Türk Inançların Izleri*. Ankara: Türk Kültürünü Araştırma Enstitüsü (TKAE Yayınları 112).

Kandiyoti, D. 1988. 'Bargaining with patriarchy' in *Gender and Society* 2(3): 274–90.

—— 1989. 'Women and the Turkish State; Political Actors or Symbolic Pawns?' in N. Davis and F. Anthias (eds) *Women – Nation – State*. London: Macmillan, pp. 126–49.

—— 1991. 'End of empire: Islam, nationalism and women in Turkey' in Kandiyoti (ed.) *Women, Islam and the State*. London: Macmillan, pp. 22–47.

—— (ed.) 1996. *Gendering the Middle East*. London: I.B. Tauris.

—— 1997. 'Gendering the modern: on missing dimensions in the study of Turkish modernity' in S. Bozdoğan and R. Kasaba (eds) *Rethinking Modernity and National Identity in Turkey*. Seattle: Washington University Press, pp. 113–32.

—— 1998a. 'Some awkward questions on women and modernity in Turkey' in L. Abu-Lughod (ed.) *Remaking Women: Feminism and Modernity in the Middle East*. Princeton NJ: Princeton University Press, pp. 270–87.

—— 1998b. 'Gender, power and contestation: rethinking "Bargaining with patriarchy" in C. Jackson and R. Pearson (eds) *Feminist Visions of Development*. London: Routledge. pp. 135–51.

Karabasa, S. 1997. 'Rize'de Yaylacılık' in *Rize*. Ankara: Kültür Bakanlığı (T.C. Kültür Bakanlığı Yayınları 1898, Tanıtma Eserleri Dizisi 72), pp. 183–8.

Karaca, D. 1991. 'Rize Kültürüne Genel bir Bakış' in *Yeşil Cennet Rize'nin Sesi* 1 (2).

Karpat, K. 1963. 'The people's houses in Turkey, establishment and growth' in *Middle East Journal* 17: 55–67.

Karpuz, H. 1993. *Rize*. Ankara: Kültür Bakanlığı (Kültür Bakanlığı Yayınları 1406 Tanıtma Eserleri Dizisi 48).

—— 1997. 'Rize Il Merkezi ve Ilçelerindeki Tarihi Eserler', in *Rize*. Ankara: Kültür Bakanlığı (T.C. Kültür Bakanlığı Yayınları 1898, Tanıtma Eserleri Dizisi 72), pp. 80–108.

Kazamias, A. M. 1966. *Education and the Quest for Modernity in Turkey*. London: George Allen and Unwin.

Kazgan, G. 1981. 'Labour force participation, occupational distribution, educational attainment and the socio-economic status of women in the Turkish economy' in N. Abadan-Unat with D. Kandiyoti and M. Kıray (eds) *Women in Turkish Society*. Leiden: E.J. Brill, pp. 131–59.

Kazmaz, S. 1997. 'Rize Halk Kültürü', in *Rize*. Ankara: Kültür Bakanlığı (T.C. Kültür Bakanlığı Yayınları 1898, Tanıtma Eserleri Dizisi 72), pp. 138–60.

Kesici, A. and Y. Sırtlı 1999. *Mapavri'den Çayeli'ne*. Çayeli/Rize.

Kesimal, O. 1999. 'Müteahhit 'Yeşile zarar vermeyeceğiz' diyor, çevreciler Katliam var' diye dünya'yı ayağa kaldırıyor. Vadide fırtına koptu' in *Merhaba' 99 (Karadeniz gazetesi'nin ücretsiz ilavesi)* 88: 84–5.

Keyder, Ç. 1987. *State and Class in Turkey. A Study in Capitalist Development*. London: Verso.

Khatib-Chahidi, J. 1981. 'Sexual prohibitions, shared space and fictive marriages in Shi'ite Iran' in S. Ardener (ed.) *Women and Space. Ground Rules and Social Maps*. London: Croom Helm.

—— 1995. 'Gold coins and coffee ROSCAs: coping with inflation the Turkish way in northern Cyprus' in S. Ardener and S. Burman (eds) *Money-Go-Rounds. The Importance of Rotating Savings and Credit Associations for Women*. Oxford/ Washington DC, pp. 241–61.

Kinross, Lord 1965. *Atatürk*. New York: William Morrow.

Kıray, M. 1964. *Ereğli, ager sanayiden önce bir Kasabası*. Ankara: Derlet Planlama Teşkilatı.

—— 1981. 'The women of small towns', in N. Abadan-Unat with D. Kandiyoti and M. Kıray (eds) *Women in Turkish Society*. Leiden: E.J. Brill, pp. 259–74.

Kırzıoğlu, F. 1946. 'Gürcü Profesörlerine Cevab' in *Hürses Gazetesi* 17–22 January 1946, Istanbul.

—— 1972. 'Lazlar/Çanarlar', in *Türk Tarih Kongresi VII*, Vol.1, pp. 420–45.

—— 1976 'Gürcistan'da Eski Türk Inanç ve Geleneklerin Izleri' in *I. Uluslararası Türk Folklor Kongresi Bildirileri, Istanbul 23–30*, Ankara 1976, pp. 141–66.

—— 1986. *Milli Tarihimizde Rize Bölgesi* (lecture delivered in Rize, 19 December 1986) typescript.

—— 1990. 'Milli Tarihimizde Acara ve Batum Sancağı Bölgesi Tarihi', lecture delivered in Rize Kültür Sitesi Salonu, 2 May 1990, typescript.

Kluge, T. 1913. 'Materialien zu einer Lazischen Grammatik nach Aufnahmen des Dialektes von Trapezunt' in *Nachrichten von der Königlichen Gesellschaft der Wissenschaften zu Göttingen. Phil.-hist. Klasse*, pp. 264–324.

Koch, K. 1855. 'Kolchis und das Land der Lazen', in K. Koch (ed.) *Die Kaukasischen Länder und Armenien*. Leipzig: Carl B. Lorch, pp. 65–114.

Konstantinov, Y. 1997. 'Patterns of reinterpretation: trader-tourism in the Balkans (Bulgaria) as a picaresque metaphorical enactment of post-totalitarianism' in *American Ethnologist* 23(4): 762–82.

Korkmaz, Y. 1991. 'Rize ve Çevresinde Dil Eğitimi Meselesi' in *Yeşil Cennet Rize'nin Sesi* 1 (2).

Kriss, R. und H. Kriss-Heinrich 1962. *Volksglaube im Bereich des Islam*. I-II. Wiesbaden: Otto Harrassowitz.

Kuper, A. [1973] 1996. *Anthropology and Anthropologists: the Modern British School*. London: Routledge (3rd revised edition).

—— 1999. *Culture. The Anthropologist's Account*. Cambridge, Mass.: Harvard University Press.

Küper-Başgöl, S. 1992. *Frauen in der Türkei zwischen Feminismus und Reislamisierung* (Demokratie und Entwicklung 4): Münster: Lit.

Kurt, C. 1989. *Die Türkei auf dem Weg in die Moderne. Bildung, Politik und Wirtschaft vom osmanischen Reich bis Heute*. Frankfurt am Main: Peter Lang. (Europäische Hochschulschriften XI. Bd. 355.)

Kurtz, D.V. 1973. 'The rotating credit association: an adaptation to poverty' in *Human Organization* 32(1): 49–58.

Kushner, D. 1977. *The Rise of Turkish Nationalism, 1876–1908*. London: Cass.

Kutscher, S., J. Mattissen and A. Wodarg (eds) 1995. *Das Mutafi-Lazische*. Köln: Institut für Sprachwissenschaft Univ. zu Köln (Arbeitspapier Nr. 24, Neue Folge).

Kymlicka, W. 1995. *Multicultural Citizenship*. Oxford: Oxford University Press.

Landau, J. 1995. *Pan-Turkism. From Irredentism to Cooperation*. London: Hurst.

Lash, S. and J. Friedman (eds) 1992. *Modernity and Identity*. Oxford: Blackwell.

Leach, E. R. 1954. *Political Systems of Highland Burma*. London: Athlone.

Lerner, D. 1958. *The Passing of Traditional Society*. Glencoe: The Free Press.

Levine, N. 1982. 'Social change and family crisis – the nature of Turkish divorce' in Ç. Kağıtçıbaşı (ed.) *Sex Roles, Family, and Community in Turkey*. Bloomington: Indiana University (Turkish Studies 3), pp. 323–47.

Lewis, B. 1961. *The Emergence of Modern Turkey*. London: Oxford University Press.

Lomouri, N. 1996. 'Lazika Krallığı'nın Tarihi', in *Tarih ve Toplum* 147: 13–17.

Luzbetak, L.J. 1951. *Marriage and the Family in Caucasia. A Contribution to the Study of North Caucasian Ethnology and Customary Law* (Studia Instituti Anthropos 3), Vienna-Mödling: St Gabriel's Mission Press.

Mackridge, P. 1987. 'Greek-Speaking Moslems of North-East Turkey: Prolegomena to a Study of the Ophitic Sub-Dialect of Pontic' in *Byzantine and Modern Greek Studies* 11: 115–37.

Magnarella, P. 1974. *Tradition and Change in a Turkish Town*. New York: John Wiley.

—— 1979. *The Peasant Venture. Tradition, Migration and Change among Georgian Peasants in Turkey*. Cambridge, MA.: Schenkman Publishing Company.

—— 1998. *Anatolia's Loom: Studies in Turkish Culture, Society, Politics and Law*. Istanbul: ISIS.

Malinowski, B. 1922. *Argonauts of the Western Pacific*. London: Routledge and Kegan Paul.

—— 1935 *Coral Gardens and their Magic*, Vol.1. London: Allen and Unwin.

—— 1937. (1930) 'Culture' in *International Encyclopedia of the Social Sciences*, Vol. 4. New York: Macmillan, pp. 621–46.

Mansur Coşar, F. 1978. 'Women in Turkish Society' in L. Beck and N. Keddie (eds) *Women in the Muslim World*. Cambridge (Mass.), London: Harvard University Press, pp. 124–40.

March, K. and R. Taqqu 1982. *Women's Informal Associations in Developing Countries. Catalysts for Change? Women in Cross-Cultural Perspective*. Boulder: Westview Press.

Marcus, J. 1992. *A World of Difference. Islam and Gender Hierarchy in Turkey*. London and New Jersey: Zed.

Mardin, Ş. 1969. 'Power, Civil Society and Culture in the Ottoman Empire' in *Comparative Studies in Society and History* 11: 258–81.

—— 1973. 'Centre–periphery relations: a key to Turkish politics?' in *Daedalus* 102: 169–90.

—— 1982. 'Turkey: Islam and westernization' in C. Caldarola (ed.) *Religions and Societies: Asia and the Middle East*, Berlin: Mouton Publishers (Religion and Society 22), pp. 171–198.

—— 1989. *Religion and Social Change in Modern Turkey. The Case of Bediüzzaman Said Nursi*. Albany: SUNY Press.

—— 1991. 'The Nakşibendi Order in Turkish history' in R. Tapper (ed.) *Islam in Modern Turkey. Religion, Politics and Literature in a Secular State*. London: I.B. Tauris, pp. 121–42.

—— 1995. 'Civil Society and Islam' in J. Hall (ed.) *Civil Society: Theory, History, Comparison*. Cambridge: Polity, pp. 278–300.

—— 1996. 'Some Notes on Normative Conflicts in Turkey', in P. Berger (ed.) *The Limits of Social Cohesion: Conflict and Mediation in Plural Societies*. Boulder: Westview Press.

—— 1997. 'Projects as Methodology: Thoughts on Modern Turkish Social Science' in Bozdoğan, S. and R. Kasaba (eds) *Rethinking Modernity and National Identity in Turkey*. Seattle: Washington University Press, pp. 64–80.

Marr, N. 1910. 'Iz poezdki v turetskii Lazistan' [Travels in Turkish Lazistan] in *Bulletin de l'Académie Impériale des Sciences de St. Pétersbourg* 6 (4): 547–632.

McCarthy, J. 1979. 'Age, family, and migration in nineteenth-century Black Sea provinces of the Ottoman Empire' in *International Journal of Middle Eastern Studies* 10: 309–23.

Meeker, M. 1970. 'The Black Sea Turks: a study of honour, descent and marriage'. PhD dissertation, University of Chicago.

—— 1971. 'The Black Sea Turks: some aspects of their ethnic and cultural background' in

International Journal of Middle Eastern Studies 2 (4.1): 318–45.

—— 1972. 'The great family aghas of Turkey: a study of a changing political culture' in R. Antoun and I. Harik (eds) *Rural Politics and Social Change in the Middle East*. Bloomington: Indiana University Press, pp. 237–66.

—— 1976. 'Meaning and society in the Near East: examples from the Black Sea Turks and the Levantine Arabs': in *International Journal of Middle Eastern Studies* 7: 243–70 (Part I); 383–422 (Part II).

—— 1991. 'The new Muslim intellectuals in the Republic of Turkey' in R. Tapper (ed.) *Islam in Modern Turkey: Religion, Politics and Literature in a Secular State*. London: I.B. Tauris, pp. 189–219.

—— 1996. 'Concepts of person, family, and state in the district of Of' in G. Rasuly-Paleczek (ed.) *Turkish Families in Transition*. Frankfurt am Main: Peter Lang, pp. 45–60.

—— 1997. 'Once there was, once there wasn't; national monuments and interpersonal exchange' in S. Bozdoğan and R. Kasaba (eds) 1997. *Rethinking Modernity and National Identity in Turkey*. Seattle: Washington University Press, pp. 159–91.

—— forthcoming. *Nations of Empire: The Question of Modernity in a Turkish Province*. Berkeley: University of California Press.

Moors, A. 1991. 'Gender, property and power: mahr and marriage in a Palestinian village', in K. Davis, M. Leijenaar and J. Oldersma (eds) *The Gender of Power*. London: Sage, pp. 111–28.

Mumtaz, K. and F. Shaheed 1987. *Women in Pakistan: Two Steps Forward, One Step Back?* Lahore: Vanguard.

N.N. 1999. 'Ümitler söndü – moraller bozuldu. Rize'lilere göre açıklanan çay parası değil tuz parası sayılır' in *Rizem'in Sesi* 1 (1): 29.

Nugent, S. and C. Shore (eds) 1997. *Anthropology and Cultural Studies*. London: Pluto.

Olson, E. 1985 'Muslim identity and secularism in contemporary Turkey' in *Anthropological Quarterly* 58(4): 161–71.

Onaran-Incirlioğlu, E. 1991. 'Gender relations in rural transformation: two central Anatolian villages', unpublished PhD dissertation, University of Florida.

Özbek, N. 1997. 'Arabesk culture: a case of modernization and popular identity' in S. Bozdoğan and R. Kasaba (eds) *Rethinking Modernity and National Identity in Turkey*. Seattle: Washington University Press, pp. 211–32.

Özbudun, E. 1987. 'Constitutional Law' in T. Ansay, and D. Wallace Jr (eds) *Introduction to Turkish Law*. Dewenter: Kluwer Law and Taxation Publishers (3rd edition), pp. 23–60.

Özbudun, E. and A. Ulusan (eds) 1980. *The Political Economy of Income Distribution in Turkey*. New York: Holmes and Meier.

Özbudun, E. and A. Kazancigil (eds) 1981. *Atatürk: Founder of a Modern State*. London: Hurst.

Özdalga, E. 1998. *The Veiling Issue: Official Secularism and Popular Islam in Turkey*. London: Curzon.

Özgün, M. 1996. *Lazlar*. Istanbul: Çiviyazıları.

Öztan, B. 1974. 'Evlilikte Mal Rejimi' in Güriz, A. and P. Benedict (eds) *Türk Hukuku ve Toplumu Üzerine Incelemeler*. Ankara: Türkiye Kalkınma Vakfı Yayınları, pp. 41–91.

Özyılmaz, Ö. 1998. '8-jährige schulpflicht: erwartungen probleme und folgen' in H. Coşkun and S. Ağdemir (eds) *Bildungsdiskussion in der Türkei und in Deutschland. 8 Jahre Schulpflicht Religionsunterricht*. Ankara: Hacettepe-Taş, pp. 85–95.

Özyurt, H. 1997. 'Rize Ilinde Çay Tariminin Yaptığı Sosyo-ekonomik Etkiler' in *Rize*. (T.C. Kültür Bakanlığı Yayınları 1898, Tanıtma Eserleri Dizisi 72). Ankara: Kültür Bakanlığı, pp. 162–82.

Paleczek, G. 1987. *Der Wandel der traditionellen Wirtschaft in einem Anatolischen Dorf* (Wiener Beitrage zur Ethnologie und Anthropologie Band 4). Wien: Verlag Ferdinand Berger & Söhne.

—— 1990. 'Einige Bemerkungen zur problematik der parallelcousinheirat' in *Mitteilungen der Anthropologischen Gesellschaft in Wien* 120: 199–216.

Papanek, H. 1989. 'Family status-production work: women's contribution to social mobility and class differentiation', in M. Krishnaraj and K. Chanana (eds) *Gender and the Household Domain. Social and Cultural Dimensions*. New Delhi/London: Sage, pp. 97–116.

Peel, J. D. Y. 1989. 'The cultural work of Yoruba ethnogenesis', in E. Tonkin *et al.* (eds) *History and Ethnicity* (ASA Monographs 27). London: Routledge, pp. 198–215.

Pelkmans, M. 1999. 'The wounded body: reflections on the demise of the "iron curtain" between

Georgia and Turkey' in *The Anthropology of Eastern Europe Review* 17 (1): 38–48.

Pereira, M. 1971. *East of Trebizond*. London: Geoffrey Bles.

Peristiany, J. 1965. *Honour and Shame: the Values of Mediterranean Society*. London: Weidenfeld and Nicolson.

Peristiany, J. (ed.) 1976. *Mediterranean Family Structures*. Cambridge: Cambridge University Press.

Picken, L. 1975. *Folk Musical Instruments of Turkey*. Oxford: Oxford University Press.

Polanyi, K. 1944. *The Great Transformation*. New York: Rinehart.

—— 1957. 'The Economy as Instituted Process' in K. Polanyi, C. Arensberg and H. Pearson (eds) *Trade and Markets in the Early Empires. Economies in History and Theory*. New York: The Free Press, pp. 243–70.

Poutouridou, M. 1999. 'The Of Valley and the coming of Islam: the case of the Greek-speaking Muslims', in *Deltio Kentrou Mikrasiatikon Spoudon* (Athens) 12: 47–70.

Rabo, A. 1996. 'Gender, state and civil society in Jordan and Syria' in C. Hann and E. Dunn (eds) *Civil Society: Challenging Western Models*. London: Routledge, pp. 155–77.

Rasuly-Paleczek, G. 1996a. 'Some remarks on the study of household composition and intra-family relations in rural and urban Turkey', in G. Rasuly-Paleczek (ed.) *Turkish Families in Transition*. Frankfurt am Main: Peter Lang. pp. 1–44.

—— (ed.) 1996b *Turkish Families in Transition*. Frankfurt am Main: Peter Lang.

Ritter, C. 1843. 'H. Koeler's geographisch-statistische notizen über die districte von Batum und Tchoruksu, nebst bemerkungen über die küste im östlichen theile des paschaliks von Trebizond', in *Monatsberichte über die Verhandlungen der Gesellschaft für Erdkunde zu Berlin*, Mai 1842–3. pp. 218–32.

Ritter, C. 1845. 'H. Koeler's geographisch-statistische notizen über die districte von Batum und Tchoruksu, nebst bemerkungen über die küste im östlichen theile des paschaliks von Trebizond' in *Monatsberichte über die Verhandlungen der Gesellschaft für Erdkunde zu Berlin*, Neue Folge: Zweiter Band, pp. 22–54.

Rize Il Yıllığı 1973. Rize.

'Rize'de el sanatları' 1991. Rize (typescript).

Rize. 1997. T.C. Kültür Bakanlığı Yayınları 1898, Tanıtma Eserleri Dizisi 72. Ankara: Kültür Bakanlığı.

Robertson, R. 1987. 'Globalization theory and civilizational analysis' in *Comparative Civilizations Review* 17: 20–30.

Rosen, G. 1845. 'Über die sprache der Lazen' in *Abhandlungen der Königlichen Akademie der Wissenschaften zu Berlin. Phil.-hist. Abhandlungen*.

Salt, J. 1995. 'Nationalism and the rise of Muslim sentiment in Turkey' in *Middle Eastern Studies*, 31(1): 13–27.

Sampson, S. 1984. 'Muddling through in Romania: why the mamaliga doesn't explode' in *International Journal of Romanian Studies* 3 (1–2): 165–85.

Sauner-Nebioglu, M.H. 1995. *Evolution des pratiques alimentaires en Turquie: analyse comparative* (Islamkundliche Untersuchungen 193). Berlin: Klaus Schwarz.

Saxokia, T. 1995. 'Megrel-Laz kültüründe akrabalık, evlenme ve cenaze' (translated by A.I. Aksamaz) in *Tarih ve Toplum* 140: 35–42.

Schiffauer, W. 1983. *Die Gewalt der Ehre*. Frankfurt: Suhrkamp.

—— 1987. *Die Bauern von Subay. Das Leben in einem Türkischen Dorf*. Stuttgart: Klett-Cotta.

—— 1991. *Die Migranten aus Subay*. Stuttgart: Klett-Cotta.

Seufert, G. 1997a. *Cafe Istanbul. Alltag, Religion und Politik in der Modernen Türkei*. München: Beck.

—— 1997b. *Politischer Islam in der Türkei. Islamismus als Symbolische Repräsentation einer sich Modernisierenden Muslimischen Gesellschaft*. Istanbul: in Kommission bei Franz Steiner Verlag, Stuttgart.

Scott, J. 1998. *Seeing like a State: How Certain Schemes to Improve the Human Condition Have Failed*. New Haven: Yale University Press.

Shankland, D. 1994. 'Social change and culture: responses to modernization in an Alevi village in Anatolia' in C. Hann (ed.) *When History Accelerates. Essays on Rapid Social Change, Complexity and Creativity*. London: Athlone, pp. 238–54.

—— 1996. 'The demise of republican Turkey's social contract', in *Government and Opposition* 31 (3): 304–21.

—— 1999a. *Islam and Society in Turkey.* Huntingdon: Eothen Press.

—— 1999b 'An interview with Paul Stirling' in *Turkish Studies Association Bulletin* 23 (1): 1–23.

Sirman, N. 1990. 'State, village and gender in western Turkey' in A. Finkel and N. Sirman (eds) *Turkish State, Turkish Society.* London: Routledge: 21–51.

Smith, A.D. 1986. *The Ethnic Origins of Nations.* Oxford: Blackwell.

Solak, A. (n.d.). *Gelenek Görenekleriyle Pazar.* Pazar.

Starr, J. 1978a. *Dispute and Settlement in Rural Turkey. An Ethnography of Law.* Leiden: E.J. Brill.

—— 1978b. 'Turkish village disputing behaviour' in L. Nader and H. Toold Jr (eds) *The Disputing Process – Law in Ten Societies.* New York: Columbia University Press, pp. 122–51.

—— 1992. *Law as Metaphor. From Islamic Courts to the Palace of Justice.* New York: SUNY Press.

Stirling, P. 1965. *Turkish Village.* London: Weidenfeld and Nicolson.

—— 1974. 'Cause, knowledge and change: Turkish village revisited' in J. Davis (ed.) *Choice and Change.* London: Athlone, pp. 191–229.

—— 1981. 'Social change and social control in republican Turkey' in *International Symposium on Atatürk.* Ankara: Türkiye İş Bankası, pp. 565–601.

—— 1993a. 'Introduction. Growth and changes; speed, scale, complexity' in P. Stirling (ed.) *Culture and Economy: Changes in Turkish Villages.* Huntingdon: Eothen Press, pp. 1–16.

—— (ed.) 1993b. *Culture and Economy: Changes in Turkish Villages.* Huntingdon: Eothen Press.

Stirling, P. and E. Onaran-Incirlioğlu 1996. 'Choosing spouses: villagers, migrants, kinship and time' in G. Rasuly-Paleczek (ed.) *Turkish Families in Transition.* Frankfurt am Main: Peter Lang. pp. 61–82.

Stocking, G. Jr 1993. *The Ethnographer's Magic and Other Essays in the History of Anthropology.* Madison: University of Wisconsin Press.

Stokes, M. 1992. *The Arabesk Debate: Music and Musicians in Modern Turkey.* Oxford: Oxford University Press.

—— 1993. 'Hazelnuts and lutes. Perceptions of change in a Black Sea valley' in P. Stirling (ed.) *Culture and Economy. Changes in Turkish Villages.* Huntingdon: Eothen Press, pp. 27–45.

—— 1998. 'Imagining "the South": hybridity, heterotopias and Arabesk on the Turkish-Syrian border' in T. Wilson and H. Donnan (eds) *Border Identities: Nation and State at International Frontiers.* Cambridge: Cambridge University Press, pp. 263–88.

Strasser, S. 1995. *Die Unreinheit Ist Fruchtbar. Grenzüberschreitungen in Einem Türkischen Dorf am Schwarzen Meer.* Wien: Wiener Frauenverlag.

Tandoğan, A. 1977. 'Çayeli ve Pazar Ilçelerinde Yerleşme-mesken tipleri ve nüfus' in *Ankara Üniversitesi Dil ve Tarih-Coğrafya Fakültesi Dergisi* 28 (3–4): 99–154.

Tapper, N. 1983. 'Gender and religion in a Turkish town: a comparison of two types of formal women's gatherings' in P. Holden (ed.) *Women's Religious Experience. Cross-cultural Perspectives.* London: Croom Helm, pp. 71–88.

—— 1985. 'Changing wedding rituals in a Turkish town' in *Journal of Turkish Studies* 9: 305–13.

—— 1990 'Ziyaret: gender, movement and exchange in a Turkish community' in D. Eickelman and J. Piscatori (eds) *Muslim Travellers. Pilgrimage, Migration, and the Religious Imagination.* London: Routledge, pp. 236–55.

—— 1992. '"Traditional" and "modern" wedding rituals in a Turkish town' in *International Journal of Turkish Studies* 5: 137–54.

Tapper, R. 1991a 'Introduction' in R. Tapper (ed.) *Islam in Modern Turkey. Religion, Politics and Literature in a Secular State.* London: I.B. Tauris. pp. 1–27.

—— (ed.) 1991b. *Islam in Modern Turkey. Religion, Politics and Literature in a Secular State.* London: I.B. Tauris.

Tapper, R. and N. Tapper 1987a. 'The birth of the Prophet: ritual and gender in Turkish Islam' in *Man* (N.S.) 22: 69–92.

—— 1987b. ' "Thank God we're secular." Aspects of fundamentalism in a Turkish town' in L. Caplan (ed.) *Aspects of Religious Fundamentalism.* London: Macmillan, pp. 51–78.

—— 1991. 'Religion, education and continuity in a provincial town' in R. Tapper (ed.) *Islam in Modern Turkey. Religion, Politics and Literature in a Secular State.* London: I.B. Tauris, pp. 56–83.

Taylor, C. 1992. *Multiculturalism and the 'Politics of Recognition'.* Princeton: Princeton University Press.

Tekeli, S. (ed.) 1995. *Women in Modern Turkish Society.* London: Zed Books.

Tezcan, S. 1981. 'Health problems of Turkish women' in N. Abadan-Unat with D. Kandiyoti and M. Kıray (eds) *Women in Turkish Society*. Leiden: E.J. Brill, pp. 96–106.

Therborn, G. 1995. *European Modernity and Beyond*. London: Sage.

Timur, S. 1972. *Türkiyede Aile Yapısı [Family Structure in Turkey]*. Ankara: Hacettepe Üniversitesi Nüfus Etüdleri Enstitüsü Yayınları No. 15.

—— 1981. 'Determinants of family structure in Turkey' in N. Abadan-Unat with D. Kandiyoti and M. Kıray (eds) *Women in Turkish Society*. Leiden: E.J. Brill, pp. 59–73.

Tonkin, E., M. McDonald and M. Chapman (eds) 1989. *History and Ethnicity* (ASA Monographs 27), London: Routledge.

Toprak, B. 1981a. *Islam and Political Development in Turkey*. Leiden: E.J. Brill.

—— 1981b. 'Religion and Turkish Women', in N. Abadan-Unat, with D. Kandiyoti and M. Kıray (eds) *Women in Turkish Society*. Leiden: E.J. Brill, pp. 281–92.

—— 1990. 'Religion as state ideology in a secular setting: the Turkish-Islamic synthesis' in M. Wagstaff (ed.) *Aspects of Religion in Secular Turkey*. Durham: University of Durham (Centre for Middle Eastern and Islamic Studies Occasional Papers Series No. 40), pp. 10–15.

—— 1995. 'Islam and the secular state in Turkey' in Ç. Balım *et al.* (eds) *Turkey: Political, Social and Economic Challenges in the 1990s*. Leiden: E.J. Brill, pp. 90–6.

Toroslu, N. 1974. 'Kadın Kaçırma' in A. Güriz and P. Benedict (eds) *Türk Hukuku ve Toplumu Üzerine Incelemeler*. Ankara: Türkiye Kalkınma Vakfı Yayınları, pp. 413–67.

Toumarkine, A. 1995. *Les Lazes en Turquie (XIXe–XXe siècles)*. Istanbul: Isis.

Tylor, E. 1871. *Primitive Culture*. London: Murray.

Vanilişi, M. and A. Tandilava 1992. *Lazların Tarihi*. Istanbul: ANT Yayınları.

Ward, R. and D. Rustow (eds) 1964. *Political Modernization of Japan and Turkey*. Princeton: Princeton University Press.

Watson, H. 1994. 'Women and the veil: personal responses to global processes' in A. Ahmed and H. Donnan (eds) *Islam, Globalization and Postmodernity*. London: Routledge, pp. 141–59.

Webster, D. 1939. *The Turkey of Atatürk: Social Process in the Turkish Reformation*. Philadelphia: The American Academy of Political and Social Science.

Weiker, W. 1981. *The Modernization of Turkey. From Atatürk to the Present Day*. New York: Holmes and Meier.

Weinstein, B. (ed.) 1990. *Language Policy and Political Development*. Norwood, NJ: Ablex.

Weintraub, J. and K. Kumar (eds) 1997. *The Public/Private Distinction*. Chicago: Chicago University Press.

White, J. B. 1994. *Money Makes Us Relatives. Women's Labor in Urban Turkey*. Austin: University of Texas Press.

—— 1996. 'Civic culture and Islam in urban Turkey', in C. Hann and E. Dunn (eds) *Civil Society: Challenging Western Models*. London: Routledge, pp. 143–54.

Wolbert, B. 1996. 'The reception day – a key to migrants' reintegration' in G. Rasuly-Paleczek (ed.) *Turkish Families in Transition*. Frankfurt am Main: Peter Lang. pp. 186–215.

Wolf, E. 1998. *Envisioning Power: Ideologies of Dominance and Crisis*. Berkeley: University of California Press.

Yalçın-Heckmann, L. 1991. *Tribe and Kinship among the Kurds*. Frankfurt am Main: Peter Lang.

—— 1998. 'Some notes on the religious life of Kurdish rural women', in *Islam des Kurdes. Les Annales de l'Autre Islam No.5*. Paris: INALCO-ERISM, pp. 141–60.

Yazıcı, H. 1984. *Fındıklı*. Fındıklı: the author.

Zelizer, V. 1989. 'The social meaning of money: "special monies"' in *American Journal of Sociology* 95 (2): 342–77.

Zelizer, V. 1994. 'The creation of domestic currencies' in *The American Economic Review* 84 (2): 138–42.

Zhordaniya, E. 1996. 'Ethnicheskii sostav naseleniya Ponta v XIII–XV.vv. I: Lazy' in *Byzantinoslavica* 57 (1): 125–39.

Zitaşi, I. (1935) 1994. *Gürcüstan Sovyet Sosyalist Cumhuriyeti'nde Okutulan Lazca Alfabe. Alboni*. Istanbul: Gürkan.

Zürcher, E. J. [1993] 1998. *Turkey. A Modern History*. London: I.B. Tauris.

Index

240 Index